W9-AXJ-569

Latin American Studies Series

Sexuality and Marriage in Colonial Latin America

Edited by Asunción Lavrin

University of Nebraska Press
Lincoln and London

"Divorce in Colonial Brazil: The Case of São Paulo" has previously been published, in different form, as chapter 8 in *Sistema de casamento no Brasil colonial*, by María Beatriz Nizza da Silva (São Paulo: T. A. Queiroz/EDUSP, 1984): 210–43, and is used by permission of T. A. Queiroz.

Manufactured in the United States of America

The paper in this book meets the minimum requirements of American National Standard for Information Sciences—Permanence of Paper for Printed Library Materials, ANSI Z39.48–1984.

Library of Congress Cataloging in Publication Data
Sexuality and marriage in colonial Latin America.
Includes bibliographical references and index.
1. Marriage—Latin America—History. 2. Sex customs—Latin America—History.
3. Latin America—History—To 1830. I. Lavrin, Asunción.
HQ560.5.S48 1989
306.8'1'098 88-33980
ISBN 0-8032-2885-6 (alk. paper)

Contents

Preface

In June 1984 Dick Boyer, Ann Twinam, and I decided to gather the three papers we had just delivered at the Berkshire Conference on Women's History and attempt to put a book together on the subject of sexuality and marriage in colonial Latin America. I took over the steering role. Searching for contributions took almost two more years; despite its intrinsic interest, the topic had not been studied in depth by many historians. I believe that the efforts spent in locating the contributors to this book have been amply rewarded. We have now a set of carefully researched and thought-provoking studies on the interaction of the genders in the colonial period. The process that bound men and women in personal relationships before the formation of the family, and the social and religious mechanisms that attempted to regulate them, are examined here from a variety of angles, revealing the intensely human nature of the subject. This is a book about men and women, their loves and hatreds, their inhibitions, their prejudices, their fears and their joys in the process of relating to each other. I hope that the reader will find much here that is new but also much that strikes a cord of familiarity with our own contemporary world. I also trust that the publication of this collection will serve as an incentive to other historians to explore the many nuances and challenging complexities of the subject.

All of us are indebted to many people and institutions for their support and encouragement, and they have been remembered in the acknowledgments for each paper. Here I wish to express my special gratitude to William L. Sherman and Silvia Arrom for their critical comments. The staff of The Hispanic Division of the Library of Congress and the *Handbook of Latin American Studies* deserve a very special mention. They have gone beyond being cooperative and patient with my requests, offering me their generous and warm friendship throughout many years, So, my thanks go to Georgette Dorn, Dolores Martin, Everett Larsen, John Hebert, Kim Black, Anita Ross, Monserat Alayón, Zaida Alcalde, Reinaldo Aguirre, Andrea Mark and Guadalupe Jiménez. Armando González, of the Hispanic Law Division, has always been at hand to guide me through the legal materials. I should also mention the support received from Edith Couturier and Enrique Pupo-Walker, who have always been willing to discuss with me any issue on colonial history. The patience, understanding, and encouragement of my husband David have been proverbial and continue to be one of my greatest assets.

Abbreviations

AC	Arquivo de Curia, São Paulo
AE	Arquivo de Estado, São Paulo
AGI	Archivo General de Indias, Seville
AGN	Archivo General de la Nación, Mexico City
AGNA	Archivo de la Nación Argentina, Buenos Aires
AHAG	Archivo Histórico del Arzobispado de Guadalajara
AHAOM	Archivo Histórico del Antiguo Obispado de Michoacán
AHP	Archivo Histórico de Parral
AHPC	Archivo Histórico de la Provincia de Córdoba
AIPG	Archivo de Instrumentos Públicos de Guadalajara
APBA	Archivo de la Provincia de Buenos Aires
ASMG	Archivo de la Sagrada Mitra, Guadalajara
BPEJ	Biblioteca Pública del Estado de Jalisco
GSU	Genealogical Society of Utah

Asunción Lavrin

Introduction: The Scenario, the Actors, and the Issues

Few decisions in life should be more personal than the choice of a spouse or a lover. Yet, throughout history, this intimate experience has been subjected to painstaking social and religious regulation in the form of outright legislation or restraining social mores, indicating that more than physiological functions enter into personal bonding and family formation. While the reproduction of the species and the foundation of a home to raise the young have been regarded as the immediate objectives of the union of the sexes, the state and the church have also seen the family as the locus of moral and political socialization. The relationships that begin at a personal level mature into the basic social nucleus that preserves customs, order, and the continuation of specific traditions. Hence, the identification and choice of a partner and the recognition of the commitment within a couple have more than a personal meaning. These two decisions establish ties and beget interests between families, and as such, they inevitably stretch the radius of participatory concern. Irregularities in the process of engagement and marriage activate all the safeguarding mechanisms established by church, state, and families to preserve both the regularities of orderly behavior and the legitimation of inheritance, without which patrimonial preservation cannot survive. Thus, the norms ruling male-female relationships, and the tensions and conflicts resulting from departures from the social rules of personal bonding have always been of paramount importance. They have also become an important subject of study in recent historical research.[1]

In colonial Latin American history we have few studies of the private and/or social aspects of the relations between the sexes, whether within or without marriage. Marriage has been treated as a social and economic mechanism binding the interests of families and expressing class or group objectives rather than personal emotions. Demographic historians have focused on the rhythms of marriage as a social phenomenon, or on the patterns of marriage formed by the several ethnic groups that populated Latin America.[2] While such research pursuits are extremely useful they leave many questions begging for an answer, some of which will be addressed by the essays in this volume. Among them are the religious definitions of the socially acceptable relations between the sexes and the actual response to social and religious constraints within the colonial period; the variety of expressions of sexuality as the source of personal relationships in different periods and among persons of different levels of affluence, social status, and ethnic background; the politics of marriage as understood by the couple and by the families involved; the mechanisms of bonding within the family, the tensions created by social and personal dissent with the norms established by church and state, and the dissolution of marriage.

Marriage was neither the only outcome of courtship nor the only channel for the expression of sexuality in colonial Latin America. Premarital sexual relations, consensuality, homosexuality, bigamy and polygamy, out-of-wedlock births, and clandestine affairs between religious and lay persons have been a common daily occurrence since the sixteenth century. It is only recently, however, that historians have begun to examine the circumstances, nature, legislation, and social consequences of sexuality in colonial Latin America.[3] The few works on those subjects are mostly the result of research carried out in archival or primary printed sources by historians often working in groups or seminars. Like the essays in this volume, those works are based on the assumption that personal and domestic relations are the point of departure for understanding more complex forms of social behavior and the institutional role of church and state as mechanisms of control. The Mexican Mentalité Seminar, at the Department of Historical Research, National Institute of Anthropology and History, identifies the interrelation of community and domestic relations as its main research theme. Its goal is to study the more commonly accepted model of domestic relations, the daily behavior of people as they accepted or rejected the behavioral models, and the manner in which models and behavior interacted.[4] Accordingly, it has explored subjects such as "deviant" forms of behavior and the manipulation and reinterpretation of

church-imposed sexuality models by nonelite individuals. A similar line of investigation has been followed by Brazilian historians.

All current research indicates that in dealing with sexuality and marriage in colonial Latin America, we must explore both church and state sources since both had overlapping interests in their regulation. An understanding of the need for concerted control for the sake of social order bound church and state to maintain a delicate balance between their respective spheres of influence. The state was primarily interested in the worldly bonds, and it focused on the legal issues surrounding sexual behavior and the institution of marriage. Among them, the establishment of the legitimacy of the marital union to secure the allocation of inheritance and the division of benefits among spouses and offspring was of cardinal importance.[5] The church established a sacramental bonding connecting the material with the spiritual. Its goals were to place all actions expressing sexuality within a teleological objective: the salvation of the soul. Ecclesiastical scrutiny, therefore, was more comprehensive than that of the state and more intrusive of individual privacy, as it defined the proper engagement rituals and religious taboos of affinity and kinship.

The conquest and settlement of the New World posed special problems for the Iberian church and state insofar as European traditions had to interact with those of other cultures, creating a unique experiment in cultural adaptation of sexual behavior and the personal and social aspects of marriage. The conquistadors found a variety of indigenous sexual mores comprising strict definitions of sexual morality, as in the Aztec and Inca societies, and looser definitions in many groups of Central and South America.[6] Throughout the initial period of violence and lawlessness few legal or moral proprieties were observed. Men cohabited with indigenous women who were either given by the conquered people or taken from them.[7] The small numbers of female Iberian migrants to the New World affected the patterns of sexual selection in the colonial period, inasmuch as it encouraged unions of Spaniards with Indian or black women and put a high social price in the relatively few white immigrant women and their descendants.[8] After crown and church strengthened their physical and political control over the new settlements from the 1530s onwards, the urgency of enforcing correct Christian behavior on the indigenous and settler population prompted a thorough scrutiny of the nature of human bonding in the new societies.

Although the chronology of adaptation of sexual and social mores from European molds to colonial realities is different in Spanish and Portuguese America, the substance was similar. Early in the process of their respective territorial expansions, both crowns became aware of the need to develop population policies to foster stable settlements. Their objective was to encourage the formation of families patterned after Iberian models and following Iberian legal processes. Having the family as the basic social unit, they could hope to replicate their own cultural, legal, social, and economic societies in the newly discovered world. Spain took more decisive steps than Portugal in its attempts to regulate this process. Throughout much of the colonial period, however, both the Spanish and the Portuguese crowns solved problems as they arose, following largely ad hoc policies.[9]

For their part, the main preoccupation of canon lawyers and theologians of the sixteenth century was the acceptance of Christian marriage by the indigenous society.[10] The practice of polygamy among many indigenous groups was a problem difficult to uproot, and much ink was spilled in the effort to understand the meaning of marriage among different societies. But while theologians discussed the validity of Indian marriage, consensual unions among the three main ethnic groups flourished and began producing a mestizo population that became the demographic majority by the seventeenth century. The Iberian church did not focus systematically on this problem until after the Council of Trent (1545–63). The unbounded sexuality of the expanding heterogeneous population became one of the main concerns of the Inquisition after its transfer to the New World.[11] The secular church undertook the definition of marriage during its important pastoral councilar meetings (*concilios*) and through regional synods.

The regularization of sexual relations had to begin with the enforcement of the new legislation on bethrothal and marriage issued by the Council of Trent. The essays gathered in this volume point to the imposition of "colonial" or European patterns of sexuality on the New World. Since the rites of engagement and marriage practiced in the Iberian kingdoms and Catholic Europe were the only ones officially accepted by church and state in colonial Latin America, they must be reviewed to achieve an understanding of the manner in which the social and ethical goals of church and state influenced the individual as a member of society.[12]

Verbal promise of marriage (*palabra de casamiento*) was the key to initiating regular and irregular relations between colonial men and women. The medieval Iberian ritual of palabra de casamiento as a binding personal contract is best summarized in the Spanish *Siete Partidas,* which attempted to conciliate the different interpretations of the promise of marriage expounded by twelfth-century canonists Gratian and Peter Lombard. In his *Decretum* (1140) Gratian regarded the promise of marriage as an act of binding one person to another for a future union, and as such, an irrevocable commitment. Although the words of this promise were spoken in the future tense (*verba de futuro*) they initiated the process of marriage, which was finished when carnal union of the couple took place. Lombard assigned less weight to the promise spoken in the future in his *Sententiae* (1152). Only the promise stated in the present (*verba de praesenti*) as the couple received each other as man and wife, constituted matrimonial vows. Thus, promises to be carried out in the future (betrothal) were revocable.

The church, which for some time had been struggling to regularize the marriage canon, struck a compromise between Lombard's and Gratian's positions in 1179, when Pope Alexander III (1159–81) accepted the promise to marry in the future as an unconsummated marriage (*matrimonium initiatum*). If carnal union took place after the future promise, whether with or without the intervention of the church, the marriage was consummated and binding (*matrimonium consummatum*). A verbal promise was revocable, provided no sexual intercourse had taken place. The centrality of the physical union was paramount.[13]

The *Siete Partidas* explained betrothal (*palabra de futuro*) in detail.[14] Gratian's interpretation of betrothal was always the most popular in Castile, and the *Partidas* placed great weight on betrothal (*desposorios*) and accepted the right of bishops to compel those who had been betrothed to fulfill their words if they had been given with mutual consent, even if they had been exchanged without witnesses.[15] The emphasis given to bethrothal and the move towards making it a public, not a personal, contract were based on the assumption that secrecy could prevent the exertion of social pressure to formalize the marriage. Secrecy could allow a man to deceive several women under pretense of marriage, or to sustain an undesirable union carried against the wishes of the parents or the interests of the family.[16]

The final step in the regulation of marriage was taken by the

Council of Trent. By virtue of the *Tametsi* decree given on November 11, 1563, the Roman Catholic church established a definitive ritual of marriage, requiring witnesses to the ceremony and celebration by a clergyman.[17] *Tametsi* marked a watershed in canon law. Clandestinity was redefined as a valid canonical impediment, giving the church a theoretical tool to curb covert attempts to escape its surveillance.

This explains the usage and strength of palabra de casamiento in colonial Latin America. Popular usage preserved some features of the peninsular ceremonial and, above all, its ultimate intention: validating betrothal as the initiation of marriage. Although the wording of historical records makes it difficult to ascertain whether the couples made any distinction between future consent or present consent, the majority of the cases aired in ecclesiastical and civil courts were based on the breach of promise given before the initiation of sexual relations.[18]

Another important issue in the process of marriage was that of consent. Whether a marriage should be the expression of the will of the couple or whether it should respond to the will and interests of parents and family was also a much debated topic since the Middle Ages and remained a key issue in colonial Latin America. Gratian established the principle of consent or free will for marriage, positing that coercion of any kind invalidated the union. The couple was free to concert and carry out a marriage by mutual promise and/or by subsequent carnal union. The Council of Trent did not alter the concept of the need of mutual consent, which remained as one of the pillars of Christian marriage in the Roman Catholic Church. In practice, however, civil legislation continued to recognize the interests of the family and the state. The *Siete Partidas* followed mixed elements of personal and familial interest. It clearly stated that parents could not marry a daughter in the latter's absence or without her will. Nonetheless, the *Partidas* gave parents the right to disinherit daughters who chose to disobey their parents' advice on an appropriate marriage. The *Leyes de Toro* reiterated this principle, while the Portuguese *Ordenaçoes do Rey D. Manuel* also endorsed disinheritance in similar situations.[19] Disinheritance was voluntary, not mandatory, and there is no evidence that it was widely practiced. Civil legislation retained considerable leverage on marriage for reinforcing inheritance and property rights, and for strengthening the family as the social basic unit.[20]

The full impact of the Tridentine marriage reforms in Spanish America and Brazil was probably not felt until the turn of the sixteenth century. In Spanish America the rulings on betrothal, marriage rituals, and mutual consent began to be expounded in the provincial councils taking place in Lima in 1582 and New Spain in 1585. In Brazil marriage regulations were finally gathered in 1707, in the *Constitutções primeiras do Arcebispado da Bahia*.[21]

The rituals and canons of bethrothal and marriage were conveyed and reinforced through preaching and confession and through confessionals and treatises on moral theology printed throughout the seventeenth and eighteenth centuries. In this way the church handed down to its flock a set of behavioral norms that became moral in nature, insofar as breaching them was believed to lead to spiritual condemnation. By tying the transgression of canon law on gender relations to the concept of sin, the church maintained its mechanism of personal and social control in addition to its prerogatives on the spiritual. Thus, confessionals and moral theologies became guides for the exploration of the terrain of the soul, addressing all the potential weaknesses of humanity, prodding into all corners of the psyche, and exposing all the obscure sources of human shame. They established an intimate dialogue between the priest and his pupil, making the discourse on sin accessible and intimately familiar.

Asunción Lavrin and Serge Gruzinski use the confessionals as gates to open the discussion of sexuality and sin as they affected Indians and non-Indians. The definitions of sin in its sexual context, as understood and preached after the Council of Trent, were universal and applicable to the neophyte as well as to the seasoned Christian. The ecclesiastical explanations of sexual sins are more than a theological catalogue of repression. They indicate the deep knowledge of the church on the physiology and psychology of carnal desires, acquired after hundreds of years of scrutiny and dissection. Little was left to assumption. Shades and nuances in behavior and thought were thoroughly covered to leave as small a margin as possible for deviation by omission. These conceptual superstructures are the indispensable guideposts in the study of the mental contours of sexuality because they represent more than the intellectual construct of an institution. They were a reality for those who were brought up to believe in their validity, and such belief lies behind self-accusations and the denunciations of others. The dialogue between norm and the often contradictory fact of personal behavior was established because the acceptance of the concept of sin did not stop people from either committing or attempting to cover it.

In her essay Lavrin also explores several manifestations of sexual behavior among average men and women of central New Spain to learn how common people perceived and lived their own sexuality, and how they attempted to reconcile their own weaknesses to the rigors of prescribed morality. A survey of the most discussed forms of sexual relationships in colonial ecclesiastical sources serves as a point of departure for the examination of popular attitudes and responses and as an introduction for the discussion of topics that other essays in the volume probe in different circumstances and manners. Betrothal as an incentive to premarital sex, consensuality as a social reality, honor as a measure of social status, and sin as an internal burden for the people of central New Spain find parallels in the experience of people elsewhere in the continent, as portrayed by Ann Twinam, Kathy Waldron, Susan Socolow, and Thomas Calvo. The ecclesiastical definition and surveillance of conjugal relations discussed by Lavrin also lays a basis for understanding the constructive and destructive elements in the politics of married life presented by Richard Boyer and Maria Beatriz Nizza da Silva. Contrasting the severity of the ecclesiastical discourse on sin and sexuality with the permissive reality of daily life, Lavrin shows that the tension generated by these sometimes antagonistic elements seldom reached a breaking point. This tension represents a confrontation of power between the sociosexual dicta of the church and the state and the individual who made a choice in disregard of the institutional and spiritual constraints, or manipulated them to his or her advantage.

This essay suggests that the key for understanding the nature of the relationship between institutions in charge of social control, such as the church, and the community at large is to decode the terms of their dialogue. In this dialogue the meaning of all terms was known by all parties; few or no changes were allowed. The language of the church was stern in the prescription, but capable of accommodations and not lacking in understanding of the stark realities learned in the confessionals. The language of the community, symbolized by the actions of the individuals who at one point or another in their lives disobeyed the church, was acquiescent on the surface. The expressions of dutiful obedience, however, masked conscious choices dictated by other motives. To some extent, the church was a prisoner of the contradictory character of its own prescriptions. It favored free will and free choice, but condemned departures from its theological canons. It had the power to impose stern spiritual condemnation but was also bound to pardon the sinners. In practical terms, it was often forced to forgive and forget.

In the larger historical picture of the conquest of the indigenous world, that of the conquest of the mind remains the least explored.[22] Gruzinski uses confession as a vehicle for understanding how the rites and message of Christianity were conveyed to the Nahuas (Aztecs) of New Spain. His main concern is to follow the mental route of the transfer of Christian concepts such as sin and free will into the Indian mind. Confession is a psychological technique of persuasion, a subtle means of subverting cultural values, of eliciting acceptance, and achieving acculturation. Gruzinski stands on the assumption that confession is a tool both for acquiring knowledge and for imposing it. The confessor and the confessant learned about each other in a complex process in which those seeking conversion used inquiry as a device for eroding and eventually destroying existing mental and social structures. For their part, the converted used acceptance, adaptation, and subversion in a multiplicity of counteroffensive strategies.

Gruzinski places the concept of sin within a broad cultural context of "westernization." Christianity stressed the individual experience and attempted to supplant community-oriented indigenous values with the more personal orientation of the European religion. This was not an easy process, as Gruzinski posits. The prism of confession elicited many refractions in the indigenous mentality. Both Indians and confessors engaged in a process of mutual manipulation that became the more ironic for its persistence into the eighteenth century. Ultimately, we are facing a "popular" understanding of religious values, in which the converted played a double role of object and subject, altering the original meanings and adapting them to their spiritual needs. In this sense, the Nahuas were simply part of a larger colonial reality described by the rest of the essays in this volume, which highlight the many strategies used by different elements of the population to alternately break and restore moral commands and rules of personal and social behavior in sometimes gripping and very personal ways.

The fact that the higher as well as the lower social strata were affected by the ambiguities of written and unwritten assumptions on sexual behavior is amply documented by Ann Twinam's essay on honor, sexuality, and illegitimacy in colonial Spanish America. The concept of personal honor in colonial times eludes a precise definition since it was a mental construct expressed through a complex set of behavioral codes regulating personal and social conduct. The actions of any given individual had to match the mental codes of his peers to meet their approval and to be regarded as having honor or being honorable. At the same time, the feeling of possessing honor was central for personal self-assurance and for reinforcing familial and social values. The pressures to attain and retain the condition of "honorability" were numerous because honor distinguished people from each other, and such distinctions served to reinforce distance in a society stratified by ethnic, cultural, and economic factors.[23]

Of all the elements of personal behavior the one regarded as closest to being the touchstone of honor was sexual conduct. The restraint and control of male and female sexuality was partly defined in terms of honor because of its many social consequences. Throughout centuries Christianity succeeded in imposing an elaborate body of regulations on sexual behavior to ensure the preservation of the social and political interests that were best served by the patriarchal family and the control of children by parents. These male-defined restrictions assigned women the heaviest burdens of honor keeping: protecting their own as well as their family's honor. The main objective of the familial honor was to guarantee the legitimacy of the children, essential to sustaining the socioeconomic position of the family.[24]

One important ingredient in the concept of honor, as it applied to women, was the preservation of their virginity. Virginity had a dual physical and spiritual meaning in Christian tradition, but it also had important social connotations. Denoting a physical condition, it was also emblematic of a chaste life and respect for the moral canons of the church.[25] The state of virginity was significant in the politics of marriage and familial interest, insofar as a virgin bride ensured a trusted line of succession free of undesirable "stains" or intrusions. In colonial Latin America, a *doncella* was different from a *soltera*. The former was a virgin; the latter was not. Carefully stated in most civil and ecclesiastical records in which women were active subjects, the physical condition of virginity was used as an indicator of moral superiority, inferentially upgrading their social status.

The observance of sexual restraint was a credit to any woman and to her family and it could be astutely maneuvered for many different purposes. *Arras,* the groom's wedding donation to the bride, customarily referred to the bride's virginity and purity (*virginidad y pureza*) when such conditions were met. Wills of women who died unmarried and virgins, clearly stated the *doncellez* of the testator, their last expression of personal pride and social status.[26] In a milieu in which easy sexual relationships among women of lower socioethnic strata were frequent, virginity denoted a social quality worth keeping, although as most essays in this volume indicate, it was not a sine qua non condition to marriage or honor. However important, virginity was not the only condition of honor. Married men and women had to observe rules of conduct within that state to preserve their honor and that of their family. Faithfulness and a life of modest withdrawal at home (*recogimiento* or *modestia*) were the virtues that safeguarded a wife's honor.[27]

The tension between honor and sexuality affected women of all social strata. No less than others, élite women confronted with the temptations of the flesh made choices that threatened their own and their family's honor. How did they and their families cope with such situations? Elite women who challenged the established codes of honor on female sexuality found themselves in what Twinam describes as an "in-between" situation between sexual control and lack of control. Marriage was the only path out of the penumbra of dishonor. When this was not possible, several social strategies permitted bending the apparently inflexible sociomoral canons. The manipulation of social and personal situations was largely a bid for time to restore honor and respectability. The strategy of legitimation through *gracias al sacar,* available to a restricted number of applicants, was an astute use of time and circumstances; its chances of success depended on the conditions of the transgression. Nonetheless, for élite females transgression was not a "paying" game, as Twinam's analysis of the ultimate fate of unwed mothers makes clear.

The top social élite did not have a monopoly on honor. They simply had the financial resources to appeal to the Council of the Indies for legitimation to serve important personal, familial, and economic purposes. Others who considered themselves honorable but were unable to avail themselves of marriage or legitimization used other forms of redress, such as education or endowment for their out-of-wedlock children.[28] Further down in the social scale were those who simply ignored social taboos and acknowledged their out-of-wedlock offspring. Did they and their children pay for the violation of canon laws and social mores? Illegitimacy was pervasive in colonial cities in the seventeenth and eighteenth centuries. Thomas Calvo's essay in this volume documents high rates of illegitimacy in Guadalajara. The extent of this social problem is still in need of further definition, but the few recent works addressing this social problem suggest that, given its frequency, illegitimacy could not have constituted a very powerful stigma.[29] Notable colonial men and women such as the Inca Garcilaso de la Vega and Sor Juana Inés de la Cruz enjoyed personal success despite their out-of-wedlock births. However, institutional access, educational opportunities, and inheritance possibilities were hard to achieve for those born illegitimately and without the protection of a wealthy father, as Twinam and Calvo suggest.[30]

Twinam notes that the majority of those members of the social élite who aspired to legitimize themselves or members of their family offered "honor" as the most frequent reason. Women who sued men after the loss of virginity all throughout colonial Latin America were searching, in part, for a restitution of honor, whether through marriage or economic compensation. The ultimate reason for making public the loss of sexual honor was to regain it by the same mechanisms of publicity that a civil or ecclesiastical adjudication entailed. The personal and social quality of possessing honor remained a powerful force to contend with, a motivation strong enough to entice many to acquire status by adopting the canons of honorable behavior. In sexual terms, that meant to follow the route of holy matrimony.

The complex role played by the church in these conflictive situations illustrates again the ambiguity of its position as an institution of social control. While its baptismal and matrimonial records put a permanent mark on people's lives, it used euphemisms to protect those affected by such records and, through canon law, it offered the outlet of legitimation to some of those who had engaged in sinful behavior. Colonial honor, thus, was a flexible concept, capable of bending under stress and yet strong enough to remain a moral dictum. The discussion of the mechanisms of honor protection and honor flaunting at the highest social levels of colonial society should encourage further surveys of the response to the concept of honor among the lesser-endowed members of society. The high rates of illegitimacy, out-of-wedlock births, and foundlings in many cities and rural areas of Latin America beg for further inquiry. Urban demographics and the high occupational mobility among men in mining or cattle areas are factors to be discussed. Of equal significance are the mechanisms of sexual domination in slavery, the possible persistence of African attitudes about marriage, the high cost of marriage fees, and the lack of episcopal supervision due to lack of clergy or great distances between the parishes.[31]

Both Twinam and Calvo implicitly suggest the need to study the fate of the children born out of wedlock. The social origins of foundlings and orphans pose intriguing social questions. While they could not all have been the result of pregnancies of women whose social position precluded a public disclosure of out-of-wedlock motherhood, we know that some abandoned children received special consideration from colonial society because of their ambiguous origins. Most of the orphans abandoned in São Paulo were white. Claude Mazet points out that abandoned children could ascend socially by being either adopted by a white family or registered as "whites" since the very uncertainty of their origins worked on their favor. Socolow alludes to similar assumptions in Buenos Aires. Significantly, most of the charitable institutions accepting orphans during the colonial period placed restrictions on the admissions of nonwhites.[32] These correlations deserve further consideration.

The many contradictions and ambiguities of personal and sexual behavior in the colonial world were witnessed and recorded by the very institution that was assumed to oversee and control some of its key expressions. Inquisitorial and judicial activities are not the only sources to survey the attitude and reaction of the church to the expressions of sexuality. Another path to follow to ascertain church reactions to the problems raised by muddled social mores is the pastoral visits. The visit of Bishop Mariano Martí to his Venezuelan dioceses in the last quarter of the eighteenth century is a powerful testimony of the constant tension between social and religious controls and the daily personal challenges of the population.

Such pastoral visits were undertaken at least once by all colonial bishops to review the spiritual and material situation of their parishioners.[33] Bishop Martí's report of the social mores of the province of Venezuela provides an unusual account of the activities of a stern and resolute minister engaged in a "moralizing" campaign with his motley flock. Martí represented an attempt to revitalize the episcopal *moral imperium,* and his visit notes stand today as an important testimonial of the man himself, of the contours of male-female relationships in a slave society, and of the uses and limits of ecclesiastical controls. In her essay on the bishop's visit, Waldron highlights the sexist and racist nature of gender relations in Venezuelan society, and her work also confirms the findings of other essays on the prevalence of loose sexual relationships among men and women of all social extractions. But Waldron allows us to see society through the eyes of the judge, rather than the "sinners," and this change of perspective is important, particularly on account of the period it took place. In the process of rectifying problems, Bishop Martí represented both the Iberian upper echelons of the church and the spirit of reform of the late-eighteenth-century church. His reaction to the sexual disorder of Venezuela is emblematic of the attitudes adopted by a regalist Spain engaged in an attempt to reform the social order without changing its structure.[34]

Was Martí's visit a typical or an effective reaction of clerical supervision? Hindered by the scarcity of studies on episcopal government, we can only point out that the bishop was unable to change the substance of the problem. He attempted to impose propriety because the projection of images was very important in the maintenance of social, familial, and personal order in colonial society. The ecclesiastical hierarchy was fully engaged in the preservation of an image of order and morality in the community to reinforce the work it carried out at a personal level. Martí's visit was a grandiose mise-en-scène, the view from the top and the valiant, if possibly futile, effort to correct social problems that had stubbornly resisted the ministries of the church for several centuries.

How would a more intimate view of sexually related incidents allow us to perceive the motivations of those "sinners" denounced and chastised by bishops such as Martí? Could we get a different view from the bottom up to assess the interplay of religious acculturation, race, and gender on sexual behavior? Ruth Behar's study of sexual witchcraft in late colonial Mexico offers an unusual but significant possibility of examining not only "popular" beliefs and practices for the manipulation of sexual behavior, but also how women coped with institutional forms of sexual subordination.

Unlike northern Europe, colonial Latin America did not experience a "witch craze."[35] This was partly due to the limited spread of witch mania in the Iberian Peninsula itself and in part to the need of solving more critical issues of religious conversion. Nonetheless, wizardry and witchcraft formed part of the peninsular mental cosmology, and the vocabulary used by ecclesiastical authorities engaged in religious conversion betrays their concerns with the devil, the occult, and the supernatural. Pre-Columbian gods became idols or demons; local religious leaders are described as wizards (*brujos*); women who practiced ancient ceremonial rites are called sorcerers (*hechiceras*).[36] Before the establishment of the Inquisition in the Spanish dependencies (1570–71), purges of indigenous religions and their practitioners raised the accusations of sorcery against the men and women in charge of the rites (*nigromantes*).[37] In Brazil the 1591 inquisitorial visit uncovered examples of "sorcery" in Grão Pará and Maranhão, but here and elsewhere such popular practices were difficult to uproot.[38]

Cultural provenance and gender relations are central to the discussion of witchcraft. Peninsular, indigenous, and African traditions contributed to the creation of a rich popular lore of sexual witchcraft.[39] Almost everywhere such practices reveal interest in medical cures and sexual control.[40] The many issues raised by the study of sexual witchcraft as an expression of popular syncretic adaptation of diverse beliefs is important enough, but in her study Ruth Behar stresses three other cardinal themes: the challenge to the accepted pattern of female subordination; the subjugation of men's will to women's amorous objectives; and the role of the church as mediator between the sexes. Underlying those themes is the need to define alternative forms of female power in a patriarchal society. The discourse on feminine power in colonial Latin America is qualified by factors such as class and ethnicity. The women under the examination of inquisitorial authorities were largely *casta* or mixed blood; some of them were not even free. Witchcraft was largely a poor woman's means to seek sexual, class, and ethnic control, an effective tool to create a mystique of power by those less likely to have it in colonial society. The presence of white women in the inquisitorial examinations, however, suggests that gender was a powerful binding element among women. The commonality of motivations and objectives involved them in a dialogue of shared experiences. Revenge, jealousy, and desire for love and companionship brought women together to exchange knowledge on strategies aimed at subjugating the targeted members of the male sex. The desire to achieve the sexual freedom enjoyed by men was much less common. Even in the exploration of means to reverse the hierarchy of power, women showed an implicit acquiescence to female roles. They wished to be loved by a chosen one, rather than to have the opportunity of loving many men.

The dialogue between the church and those engaged in magical practices is important. Behar suggests that the eighteenth-century church aimed at undermining and devaluing female attempts to define power through unorthodox practices, and in this she shares the views expressed by Bartolomé Benassar for Spain.[41] To what extent this was a successful strategy remains a subject for discussion. Since sexual witchcraft endured through the end of the colonial period—and beyond—the effectiveness of the religious policies against sorcery and the women who practiced unorthodox rites remain questionable.

Thus far we have seen issues of sexual behavior under a personal or a social light, tied in one form or another to the evasion or debasement of marriage. Yet, home and family life were aspirations of all colonial peoples, whether attained by marriage or not. The social and personal politics of marriage are examined by the next group of essays. They scrutinize the manner in which the more personal aspects of marriage—such as the choice of a husband or a wife, or the type or relationships established between husband and wife—were connected to the larger interests of church and state, such as the strengthening of social order by marriage regulation or the protection of the stability of the Christian marriage. Sexuality remains a powerful historical element in these essays. The affective bases in the formation of a marriage or a sexual partnership are a critical element in the discussion of the social issues.

The supervision and control of marriage in the New World was tied to the demographic interests of Spanish and Portuguese crowns, but in their endeavors to establish a basic familial order in the new settlements they acknowledged the fact that marriage had a sacramental aspect that lay beyond civil legislation. The state's support of the ecclesiastical bases of marriage was assumed to be unconditional, but there were some tensions between the two spheres. To the extent that marriage had important economic and even sociopolitical consequences, it never ceased to be of paramount importance for the state. The state's strategy was to obtain the most favorable terms for familial interests without challenging the canons of the church.[42]

Freedom of choice and parental consent remained intimately bound in both civil and canon law, making marriage a kaleidoscopic process in which sexual, familial, state, and canonical issues converged and reflected a variety of sometimes conflicting interests.[43] A study of parental dissent in bethrothal and marriage cases in New Spain in the middle and late colonial years posits that the church was able to support freedom of choice through the seventeenth century although its power began to wane in the eighteenth century and was severely restricted after the enforcement of the royal *Pragmática* on marriages was extended to the New World in 1778.[44] The fact that the church supported the free will of couples does not mean, however, that it denied the rights of parents and the family to have a voice in the marriage of its members. The interests of family and society stressed the convenience of marriage between "equals." While no civil or ecclesiastical legislation endorsed forced marriages, the preservation of social status and the general social order through marriage between equals was preached through the literature of advice and education.[45] Freedom of choice to elect a partner and to marry was always tempered by the expected payment of filial respect. Parents and offspring were to balance their duties and rights in a harmonious agreement of wills. Both church and state agreed on these premises.

The eighteenth century saw a hardening of that position within the church, which began to tip in favor of greater parental say in the marriage of their children. Beginning with a 1741 encyclical by Benedict XIV that forbade skipping through parts of the matrimonial ritual in instances of parental opposition, the tide swelled as time passed. In the 1770s, the Synod of La Plata and the Mexican IV Provincial Council took provisions to ensure that ecclesiastical assessments of marital oppositions took parental opposition into consideration in cases of obvious social inequality. Whether or not these statements had a strong social influence is difficult to prove since the historical literature on marriage patterns is so scarce. In practice, however, endogamy had always been the rule among the white elite, as well as among the indigenous population.[46] While these two groups did not have the same socioeconomic objectives, they preserved traditional attitudes about the observance of filial and communal respect that may account for the similarity in outcome.

It may be argued, however, that marriage itself was not the main issue in the discussion of social mores. Sexual freedom was. To all indications a clear distinction between the two was made by élite and nonélite colonial peoples. Ann Twinam's work indicates that although the élite stressed marriage to restrict socioeconomic privilege, they did succumb to accidents and challenges. Among the nonélite the opportunities to make sexual choices were more frequent all along, as the works of Waldron, Lavrin, Calvo and Behar indicate. Casual liaisons with women of lower social and economic strata allowed men to marry their "equals" while maintaining sexual relations outside marriage.[47]

The 1776 *Pragmática* was an expression of sociopolitical patriarchalism from the Spanish Crown.[48] This law was first conceived and enacted in Spain in 1776 and extended to the American colonies in 1778 as part of a larger scheme of imperial reform. Neither the Spanish nor the Portuguese crowns had ever entertained the idea of establishing a society of equals in the colonies. The Spanish *Pragmática* on marriages was the best expression of the will to maintain a social élite. This attempt to regulate marriages through legislation presumed the power to change the sexual practices of the colonies, and it was bound to be ignored by the majority of the population to whom it could and would not apply. The *Pragmática* established the need for parental consent for bethrothal and marriage before a certain age, but this regulation applied only to whites (*españoles*) and, in an advisory manner, to Indians. Its goal was to reassert the desirability of equality, or at least symmetry, in the choice of a marriage partner and in the process of family formation.

Despite refinements and amendments, the evidence of compliance in the form of written permissions granted by español parents is not impressive. Only a small number of those statements have been found, certainly not enough to warrant any assumption that a significant number of couples followed the tenets of the law. The strength of prejudice and the incentive of preserving economic and social prestige—not legislation—determined the success of endogamy. Susan Socolow's essay on the choice of marriage partners in the Viceroyalty of La Plata supports this inference by studying the cases of legal dissent to marriages emanating either from parents wishing to stop their children's planned nuptials or from couples seeking to reaffirm their individual love preferences. Social mobility and the self-interest of urban élites were important factors in the suits and in the legal decisions taken by the judicial bodies of that viceroyalty.

As in most studies of applied legislation, this work underscores the observation that colonial interpretation of the law could change or modify its original objectives. The *disenso* (dissent) suits represented cases of exacerbated personal feelings and disclosed attitudes and perceptions that may have otherwise remained hidden under social euphemisms. Particularly important are the various patterns of perceived marriage inequalities among people of several socioeconomic strata. The differences Socolow observes between a traditional society, such as Córdoba, and the more fluid milieu of the port of Buenos Aires suggest that legal recourses reflected local or regional economic conditions as well as personal factors. That the Buenos Aires merchants' economic perception of equality strongly motivated their decisions in cases of marital dissent is not surprising, given the important consequences of marriage choices on their own social standing. A self-conscious late colonial society had as much to say on the definition of equality as the Crown itself.[49]

Are these exclusively late colonial attitudes? The analysis of the cases in which the marriage legislation had an opportunity to be legally tested suggests that the indicators used by colonial peoples to measure social equality had deep roots in the past and responded to the geographical and historical socioeconomic circumstances. The emphasis given to those indicators probably changed throughout time and should be studied more closely. At this point, however, it seems that despite the changing character of elite composition, attitudes about marriage as a means to preserve social status were well defined much earlier in the colonial period.[50] It is also significant that opposition to the *Pragmática* was voiced by some bureaucrats who considered the *Pragmática* an unsuitable piece of legislation for its times, arguing that demographic growth called for a policy of no restrictions on marriages. Some members of the church continued to support freedom of choice in marriage. Their dissent certainly contributed to erode the effectiveness of marriage control despite the increased severity of royal legislation after 1780.[51] An intriguing question is, To what extent did such attitudes persist into the nineteenth century? The text of the *Pragmática* was adopted in the Chilean post-independence legislation as a desirable protection for the institution of marriage, indicating that as a state policy, the regulation of marriages was still appealing to traditional élites.[52] It is obvious that the last word on the issue of the correlation between marriage legislation and social response has not been said, but these initial steps towards a clarification of its complexity are very promising.

If the choice of a marriage partner posed so many personal and social problems, understanding the nature, rights, and duties of marriage presented similar difficulties for couples, legislators, and ecclesiastical authorities. The sum and substance of the rights and duties that form the foundation of marriage and bind the husband and wife are elusive and vary in time. Transformations in the general fabric of society and its socioeconomic structures determine changes in the understanding of personal relationships. Apprehending the inner contours of marriage, as opposed to describing its demographic characteristics, is the purpose of the last three essays in this volume.

The essays by Boyer and Nizza da Silva reveal much about the nature of marriage by studying them in periods of stress or through the process of disintegration. Boyer unveils the private tensions leading to marital difficulties and the strategies used by women to cope with the misfortunes of abuse; Silva focuses on situations that had reached a breaking point and had led to the official mechanisms of separation accepted by the Church. In essence, however, the situations and grievances are similar despite the fact that Boyer focuses on men and women who attempted to solve their problems by circumventing the social controls imposed on marriage through abandonment and bigamy.

Both authors establish that *mala vida* was common, although not necessarily the norm in most marriages. *Mala vida* meant the abuse of power by one spouse, but its definition, more often than not, was feminine because women were the subordinate element in marriage and society. Precisely for this reason Boyer sees that we must resort to women to learn about the strategies to correct marital disfunction. Boyer and Nizza da Silva note that while the legal and physical control that the husband had over his wife lent him extraordinary power, misuse of such power opened avenues of redress for the wife. The husband was answerable for abusing the balance of order and justice that he was supposed to maintain within the marriage. The boundaries of his responsibility were clearly delineated in four distinct areas of personal behavior: 1. Assumption of the obligation of material support of the family. Abandonment and neglect of the material well-being of wife and children were morally and legally unacceptable, a breach of responsibility; 2. Respect for the per-

son of the wife, as the subject in the marital relationship. While the husband's prerogative for mild punishment as a means of teaching was regarded both as his duty and right, physical violence was not appropriate in a just ruler; 3. Propriety in the conduct of sexual relations. Abuse of the marital rights through unacceptable sexual practices became another breach of confidence and justice; 4. Respect for the fidelity he owed his wife. While church and state gave men a broader margin for defaulting on the canonical obligation of mutual faith, continuous and public disregard was an unacceptable defilement of the sacrament of matrimony and unworthy of the head of the family.

When men broke the ethical responsibilities of restraint set upon them, they destroyed the balance of hierarchies between husband and wife and the symmetry of mutuality and reciprocity existing under that order, and women had the right to challenge their power. The message in Boyer's work is that the definition of male power and authority also contained that which belonged to the female. The weakness of the system, however, lay in the fact that women had to wait until the abuse of just behavior from the *pater familias* reached extremes and triggered the protective mechanisms applicable to them.

The sexual inequalities involved in marriage were stressed by the church, insofar as sexual disharmony or dissatisfaction were not perceived as acceptable causes for divorce or annulment. At the personal level the church would sacrifice enjoyment or happiness to maintain the social respectability and the principle of indissolubility, despite the fact that the former was more a goal than a reality, as the frequency of consensual relations and the toleration of double standards of morality indicate.

The choices open to women faced with a bad marriage reflect not only the personal assumptions about how married couples should relate to each other, but also how others expected them to behave. Patriarchalism established a conjugal relationship of power that in the best instances was acknowledged and contributed to maintain personal harmony; at worst, spouses would establish a contest to establish control over each other. The predicament of crisis could make women more susceptible to abuse but, ultimately, the "ethical content of patriarchalism," as Boyer posits, allowed them to seek help against unjust enforcement of the power conceded to the male.[53]

1. Pictograph showing the concubines of Martin Xuchimitl in a legal process for polygamy. Source: Archivo General de la Nación, Mexico City, Inquisición, vol. 36 (1579).

2. The sacrament of matrimony. Marriage of Sayri Topa Inca and Cusi Huarcay, after dispensation of first-degree consanguinity (brother and sister) by Bishop Juan Solano. Source: Felipe Guamán Poma de Ayala, *Nueva corónica y buen gobierno* (Paris: Musée d'Ethnologie, 1936), p. 442.

BVEN GOBIERNO
DÕ IV.o SOLANO ARZO
enel cuzco

3. Spanish royal officials (*corregidores*) in their rounds engage in illicit sex with Indian woman. Source: Felipe Guamán Poma de Ayala, *Nueva corónica y buen gobierno* (Paris: Musée d'Ethnologie, 1936), p. 503.

4. Indian parents defend their daughter from "arrogant and lascivious" Spanish officials who take Indian women to make them their servants and concubines. Source: Felipe Guamán Poma de Ayala, *Nueva corónica y buen gobierno* (Paris: Musée d'Ethnologie, 1936), p. 868.

5. Properly married Christian Indians. Source: Felipe Guamán Poma de Ayala, *Nueva corónica y buen gobierno* (Paris: Musée d'Ethnologie, 1936), p. 821.

The study of divorce in colonial São Paulo also allows us to understand the personal circumstances of marital hostility. Although Nizza da Silva's work focuses on one Brazilian city, it reveals much of what is common to the institution of marriage elsewhere. A study of divorce in seventeenth-century Lima by Bernard Lavallé permits us to establish some key linkages between the Brazilian and the Spanish American examples and to assess to what degree individuals assimilated the ecclesiastical and legal canons defining the marital relationship.[54]

Although the church had struggled throughout the Middle Ages to establish the principle of indissolubility of marriage, it had left room for the separation of married couples and even for the dissolution of marriage and remarriage.[55] The Council of Trent made no changes on separation and nullification. At this stage in our research, it is difficult to establish the rate of divorce or annulment in Latin America with any accuracy, but we must assume that those resorting to it were a minority.[56] In the small town environment of southern Brazil free white women of several socioeconomic levels were the main plaintiffs. In Lima the ethnic spectrum was more varied, involving women of mixed ancestry as well as criollas. The occupational range of women is, of course limited, and the fact that *paulista* plaintiffs' occupations were rarely noted indicates that social recognition of women's roles was practically nonexistent. The *limeñas'* occupations, when noted, follow the expected path of "womanly occupations" even though they might be those ascribed to women of the lower strata, such as street vendors or seamstresses. Men involved in divorce suits came from a varied occupational spectrum, especially in Lima: artisans, merchants, professionals, and bureaucrats mingled with laborers and even the odd knight in the path of marital discord.

Two striking features of divorce and annulment in colonial Latin America are the decidedly female nature of decision taking in divorce proceedings and the persistent commonplace of physical mistreatment of the wife as its grounds. Both these features are intimately correlated, given the nature of gender relations. If education, love, or mutual understanding failed to establish psychological bonds between the spouses, power was defined and established in a physical manner. The intensity of the violence committed on women, however, is shocking to the modern reader. Public display of affection was not especially favored by the church or educators and, apparently, was not frequent. On the other hand, since the obedience of husband by wife was commonly accepted as a "divine" mandate, female submission was more acceptable for public demonstration.

An important difference between São Paulo and Lima is that in the latter the arguments offered for pursuing divorce were more varied. While women in São Paulo used the more traditional reasons of mistreatment or adultery, in Lima forced or ecclesiastically invalid marriages, inequality of condition, and deceit were common enough. São Paulo society preferred to use social euphemisms, as Nizza da Silva suggests, and hide behind the decorum of reasons acceptable as part of the prerogatives of the socially weaker sex. An important concession in the process of separation is highlighted by Nizza da Silva: the divorce by mutual consent allowed in São Paulo. Whether or not there was a counterpart in Spanish America remains to be corroborated, as well as whether this significant concession may be the result of local mores or an expression of ecclesiastical flexibility in the Brazilian church.

The analysis of the many layers of human interaction involved in the initiation of a family nucleus is probed by Thomas Calvo. His essay touches on many of the elements present in the rest of the essays in this volume and relates them to the urban experience of Guadalajara in the seventeenth century. He departs from the premises that the family is hardly a uniform institution, that there are no typical families despite the strong cultural elements underlying the institution, and that we must begin uncovering the variety of personal experiences hidden under statistical realities to understand the variety of familial experiences in Latin America.

Probably the most striking social feature of male-female relationships in the urban setting of seventeenth-century Guadalajara was the high incidence of illegitimacy and the pervasive nature of this phenomenon, which gradually permeated all layers of society throughout the century. Though not legally sanctioned, polygamy was sustained by an abundance of women and a movable male population. The ineffective and sometimes even condoning attitude of the church blunted the sharp edges of its own discipline and softened the phenomenon of illegitimacy. But while the commonality of the experience of being born out of wedlock united people across economic and ethnic lines, the individual results of shady liaisons could be harsh and unpredictable. Ultimately, Calvo questions the stability of family life in the seventeenth century. Under the stress created by a social and economic milieu in the process of self-definition, the internal cohesion of many Guadalajaran families was weakened by the fissures created by consensuality. While the contours of Guadalajaran society are representative of the period under study, the correlation of social, intellectual, and demographic elements presented in this work could serve to raise similar questions about the circumstances of family life elsewhere and at different periods in colonial Latin America.[57]

These essays have attempted to establish a foundation to construct a more personal history of colonial people by establishing a bridge between the individual and the institutional aspects of sexual behavior and marriage. In doing so we have assumed that social values and social behavior are complementary and that the explanation of many historical "facts" is to be found among the intricate paths of legislation, the religious forms of social and spiritual control, the conventions dictated by didactic materials, and the muted tones of personal information contained in legal phrases and judiciary renditions. Ideally, these elements will be intertwined with the realities of statistical configurations of social behavior. The outcome should yield, as the studies herein demonstrate, a richer and more human view of the past, a view the more absorbing for the more nuances it will discover in the experience of daily life. I am speaking for a future that is still to come. Patterns of marriage and divorce, consensuality and illegitimacy, regularities and irregularities in births, marriages and deaths are still as scarce in our historical literature as are the analyses of personal relationships between men and women engaged in the perennial rituals of love and family formation. We trust that we have achieved an *aproximación* or a step forward to bring that future closer.

Notes

1. See, for example, Peter Laslett, ed., *Family Life and Illicit Love in Earlier Generations* (Cambridge: Cambridge University Press, 1977); Lawrence Stone, *The Family, Sex and Marriage in England, 1500–1800* (New York: Harper and Row, 1977); Paul-Gabriel Boucé, ed., *Sexuality in Eighteenth-Century Britain* (Manchester: Manchester University Press, 1982); R. B. Outhwaite, ed., *Marriage and Society: Studies in the Social History of Mar-*

riage (New York: St. Martin Press, 1981); Alan MacFarlane, *Marriage and Love in England, 1300–1840* (London: Basil Blackwell, 1986); Belinda Meteyard, "Illegitimacy and Marriage in Eighteenth-Century England," *Journal of Interdisciplinary History* 10, no.3 (Winter 1980): 479–89. See also Philippe Ariés and André Béjin, eds., *Western Sexuality: Practice and Precept in Past and Present Times* (London: Basil Blackwell, 1985). For the United States see, Roger Thompson, *Sex in Middlesex* (Amherst: The University of Massachusetts Press, 1986).

2. See Marcelo Carmagnani, "Demografía y sociedad: La estructura social de los centros mineros del norte de México, 1600–1720," *Historia Mexicana* 21 (January–March 1972): 419–59; David A. Brading, "Grupos étnicos, clases y estructura ocupacional en Guanajuato (1792)," *Historia Mexicana* 21 (January–March 1972): 460–80; David J. Robinson, "Population Patterns in a Northern Mexican Region: Parral in the Late Eighteenth Century," in *Papers in Honor of Robert C. West,* ed. William V. Davidson and James J. Parsons, *Geoscience and Man* 21 (Baton Rouge: Louisiana State University, 1980): 83–96; Silvia M. Arrom, "Marriage Patterns in Mexico City, 1811," *Journal of Family History* 3, no.4 (Winter 1978): 376–91; Michael M. Swan, "The Spatial Dimensions of a Social Process: Marriage and Mobility in Late Colonial Northern Mexico," in *Social Fabric and Spatial Structure in Colonial Latin America,* ed. David J. Robinson (Syracuse, N.Y.: Syracuse Department of Geography and University Microfilms International, 1979); Susan M. Socolow, "Marriage, Birth, and Inheritance: The Merchants of Eighteenth-Century Buenos Aires," *Hispanic American Historical Review* 60, no.3 (August 1980): 387–406; Linda L. Greenow, "Marriage Patterns and Regional Interaction in Late Colonial Nueva Galicia," in *Studies in Spanish American Population History,* ed. David J. Robinson, (Boulder, Colo.: Westview Press, 1981), pp. 119–47; Eduardo Cavieres, "Formas de vida y estructuras demográficas de una sociedad colonial: San Felipe en la segunda mitad del siglo XVIII," *Cuadernos de Historia* (Santiago de Chile) 3 (July 1983): 79–98; Robert McCaa, "*Calidad, Clase* and Marriage in Colonial Mexico: The Case of Parral, 1788–90," *Hispanic American Historical Review* 64, no.3 (August 1984): 477–502. Note the lopsided character of the recent historiography in favor of New Spain in the late colonial period.

3. Solange Alberro, ed., *La actividad del Santo Oficio de la Inquisición en Nueva España* (Mexico City: Instituto Nacional de Antropología e Historia, 1981); *Familia y sexualidad en Nueva España* (Mexico City: Fondo de Cultura Económica, 1982); Sergio Ortega, ed., *De la santidad a la perversión* (Mexico City: Editorial Grijalbo, 1985); Ronaldo Vainfas, comp. *História e sexualidade no Brasil* (Rio de Janeiro: Edições Graal, 1986). In all instances

the influence of European historians—especially French—such as Jean-Louis Flandrin, Michel Foucalt, Georges Duby, and Philippe Ariès has been decisive.

4. Sergio Ortega Noriega, "Seminario de historia de las mentalidades y religión en México colonial," in *Familia y Sexualidad en Nueva España* (Mexico City: Fondo de Cultura Económica, 1982), pp.100–118.

5. The civil legislation affecting male-female relations, before, within, and outside marriage is contained largely in *Las Siete Partidas* and the *Leyes de Toro,* in *Los códigos españoles, concordados y anotados,* 12 vols. (Madrid: Imprenta de M. Rivadeneira, 1847–51). See vol. 3 for the *Partidas* and vol. 6, pp. 557–67, for the *Leyes de Toro.* See also, *Novísima recopilación de las leyes de España,* 6 vols. (Madrid: Boletín Oficial del Estado, 1805), vol. 5; *Recopilación de leyes de los reinos de las Indias,* 2 vols., 5th ed. (Madrid: Boix Ed., 1841); *Ordenações e leis do reino de Portugal, recopiladas per mandado del rei D. Filippe O Primeiro,* 3 vols. (Coimbra: Real Imprensa da Universidade, 1824), vol. 3; "Ordenações do Senhor Rey D. Manuel," in *Colecção do legislação Antiga e Moderna do Reino de Portugal,* part 1; *Constituções primeiras do arcebispado da Bahia, feitas e ordenadas pelo . . . D. Sebastião Monteiro da Vide . . .* (Coimbra, 1720); Alexandro Herculano, *Estudos sobre o casamiento civil* (Lisboa: Typografía Universal, 1866). For an overview of the laws of colonial Spanish American legislation see, José María Ots Capdequi, *El estado español en las Indias* (Mexico City: Fondo de Cultura Económica, 1946), pp. 83–115; Richard Konetzke, *Colección de documentos para la historia de la formación social de Hispanoamérica, 1493–1810,* 3 vols. (Madrid: Consejo Superior de Investigaciones Científicas, 1962), 2:229, 232; 3: 214, 394, 396.

6. The discourse of sexuality and marriage among indigenous societies remains a little-studied subject, despite the fact that it deeply preoccupied colonial ecclesiastical authorities. See Alfredo López Austin, "La sexualidad entre los antiguos nahuas," in *Familia y sexualidad en Nueva España* pp. 177–206; Serge Gruzinski, "Matrimonio y sexualidad en México y Texcoco en los albores de la conquista o la pluralidad de los discursos," in *La actividad del Santo Oficio de la Inquisición en Nueva España, 1571–1990,* ed. Alberro, pp. 19–74; see also his "La Mère Dévorante: Alcoolisme, sexualité et deculturation chez les Mexicas (1500–1550)," *Cahiers des Amériques Latines* 20 (1979): 7–35, and "Indios reales y fantásticos en documentos de la Inquisición," *Boletín del Archivo General de la Nación* 2, no.4 (October–December 1978): 18–39. Inga Clendinnen deals briefly with Maya women's sexuality in "Yucatec Maya Women and the Spanish Conquest: Role and Ritual in Historical Reconstruction," *Journal of Social History* (Summer 1982), pp. 427–42.

"Sirvinacuy" or "tincunacuspa," was a pre-Incaic trial-marriage practice which neither civil nor religious authorities were able to uproot and which survived through the twentieth century. See Roberto Mac-Lean y Estenós, *Sociología Peruana* (Lima: n.p., 1942), 249–59. The late William E. Carter in a revisionist interpretation of sirvinacuy redefined it as part of "consecutive states of marital development." See W. E. Carter, "Trial Marriage in the Andes?" in *Andean Kinship and Marriage*, ed. Ralph Bolton and Enrique Mayer (Washington: American Anthropological Association, 1972), 177–216. Revisions notwithstanding, such practice meant "consensual living" for the Roman Catholic Church.

7. Sexual mores of pre-Columbian societies varied greatly, but in large areas of the continent virginity in women was not particularly important for marriage purposes although adultery was not sanctioned. Most early travelers and early historians have sections on marriage rituals. Since a comprehensive bibliography on this topic is not relevant here, only a few titles are given as references. See, for example, Fernão Cardim, *Tratados da terra e gente do Brasil* (São Paulo: Companhia Editora Nacional, 1978), p. 103; Jean de Léry, *Viagem a terra do Brasil* (São Paulo: Livraria Martins Editora, 1967), pp. 105–6, 189–94. Nizza da Silva surveys Brazilian rites as perceived by various religious and lay sources in *Sistema de casamento no Brasil colonial* (São Paulo: Editorial da Universidade de São Paulo, 1984), pp. 31–36. See also Bernardino de Sahagún, *Historia de las cosas de Nueva España*, 3 vols. (Mexico City: Editorial Porrúa, 1956), vol. 3; Alvar Núñez Cabeza de Vaca, *Naufragios y comentarios* (Mexico City: Espasa-Calpe, 1985), pp. 48, 73, 140, 158–59, 234; Pedro Simón, *Tercera noticia histórica de la conquista de tierra firme en las Indias Occidentales* (Madrid: Publicaciones Españolas, 1961), pp. 39–47. Simón noted that most young women in Tierra Firme enjoyed sexual freedom. He recorded how conqueror Don Pedro de Heredia and his soldiers received a gift of one hundred young women from the cacique of Cipacuá, "all so good-looking, charming, beautiful and smiling, that we called the town *Las Hermosas*." See also Felipe Guamán Poma de Ayala, *Nueva córonica [sic] y buen gobierno* (Paris: Institut d'Ethnologie, 1936), p. 395. "Después de haber conquistado y de haber robado comenzaron [los españoles] a quitar las mujeres doncellas y desvirgar por fuerza y no queriendo le mataban como perros." References to sexual relationships between female Indians and Spaniards in the sixteenth century abound throughout his text. See also Inga Clendinnen, "Yucatec Maya Women," pp. 431, 433; Robert Padden, *The Hummingbird and the Hawk: Conquest and Sovereignty in the Valley of Mexico, 1503–1541* (New York: Harper and Row, 1967), pp. 230–32.

8. Peter Boyd-Bowman, "Patterns of Spanish Emigration to the Indies until 1600," *Hispanic American Historical Review* 56, no.4 (November 1976): 580–604.

9. Susan Soeiro briefly surveys the Portuguese crown's reasons for supporting marriage for demographic purposes. See Susan Soeiro, "The Feminine Orders in Colonial Bahia, Brazil: Economic, Social, and Demographic Implications, 1677–1800," in *Latin American Women: Historical Perspectives,* ed. Asunción Lavrin (Westport, Conn.: Greenwood Press, 1978), pp. 173–97; *Repertorio geral ou indice alphabetico das Leis Extravagantes do reino do Portugal* (Coimbra: Imprensa da Universidade, 1843); Magnus Mörner, *Estado, razas y cambio social en la Hispanoamérica colonial* (Mexico City: SepSetentas, 1974), pp. 24–33.

10. For a general history of the evolution of marriage in Spanish America, see Daisy Rípodas Ardanaz, *El matrimonio en Indias: Realidad social y regulación jurídica* (Buenos Aires: Conicet, 1977). Carlos Seco Caro, "Derecho canónico particular referente al matrimonio en Indias," *Anuario de Estudios Americanos* 15 (1958): 1–112. For Portuguese America, see María Beatriz Nizza da Silva, *Sistema de casamento no Brasil colonial.* The theological concern with marriage matters began immediately after the conquest of Mexico as a result of the high intellectual caliber of the missionaries involved in the evangelization of New Spain. See Sergio Ortega Noriega, "Teología novohispana sobre el matrimonio y comportamientos sexuales, 1519–1570, " in *De la santidad a la perversión,* ed. Sergio Ortega, pp. 19–48; Ernest J. Burrus, "Alonso de la Vera Cruz: Pioneer Defender of the American Indians," *Catholic Historical Review* 70, no.4 (October 1984): 531–46. An example of recent research into the problem of polygamy among the indigenous elite is Waldemar Espinosa Soriano, "La poliginia señorial en el Reino de Cajamarca: Siglos XV y XVI, " *Revista del Museo Nacional* (Peru) 43 (1979): 399–466.

11. The growing concern with bigamy and consensuality among non-Indians is patent in the activities of the Inquisition. See Richard E. Greenleaf, *The Mexican Inquisition of the Sixteenth Century* (Albuquerque: University of New Mexico Press, 1969). Any of the works of José Toribio Medina on the Inquisition in Spanish America offers abundant materials on the trials of irregular sexual unions. See, for example, his *Historia del Tribunal de la Inquisición en Lima (1569–1820),* 2 vols. (Santiago de Chile: Imprenta Ercilla, 1890); Ernesto Chinchilla Aguilar, *La Inquisición en Guatemala* (Guatemala City: Editorial del Ministerio de Educación Pública, 1953); Ronaldo Vainfas, "A teia da intriga: Delação e moralidade na sociedade colonial," *História e*

sexualidade, ed. Ronaldo Vainfas, pp. 67–88; E.D.O. Franca and S. Siqueira, "Segunda visitação do Santo Oficio as partes do Brasil: Confissões e ratificações da Bahia, 1618–1620," *Anais de Museo Paulista* 17 (São Paulo: Universidade de São Paulo, 1963). Inquisitors made several visits to Brazil but never established a permanent seat in Portuguese America.

12. European historians have focused sharply on canonical prescriptions and popular practices in marriage rituals. See the following early works: André Burguière, "The Marriage Ritual in France: Ecclesiastical Practices and Popular Practices (Sixteenth to Eighteenth Centuries)," in *Ritual, Religion, and the Sacred: Selections from the Annales,* ed. Robert Forster and Orest Ranum (Baltimore: Johns Hopkins University, 1982), pp. 8–23. In the same volume see Christiane Klapisch-Zuber, "Zacharias: Or the Ousting of the Father: The Rites of Marriage in Tuscany from Giotto to the Council of Trent," pp. 24–56; and Nicole Belmont, "The Symbolic Function of the Wedding Procession in the Popular Rituals of Marriage," pp. 1–7.

13. Domingo Cavalario, *Instituciones del derecho canónico,* 3 vols. (Paris: Librería de Don Vicente Salvá, 1846), 2:158–77; August Knecht, *Derecho matrimonial católico* (Madrid: Editorial Revista de Derecho Privado, 1932), pp. 419–83; Bishop Justo Donoso, *Instituciones de derecho canónico americano,* 2 vols. (Valparaíso: Imprenta y Librería del Mercurio, 1849), 2:148–52; Heath Dillard, *Daughters of the Reconquest: Women in Castilian Town Society, 1100–1300* (Cambridge: University of Cambridge Press, 1984), pp. 36–47; Georges Duby, *Medieval Marriage: Two Models from Twelfth-Century France* (Baltimore: Johns Hopkins University Press, 1978). Duby discusses the position of the church before the Gratian-Lombard controversy. See also Charles Donahue, "The Canon Law on the Formation of Marriage and Social Practice in the Later Middle Ages," *Journal of Family History* (Summer 1983), pp. 144–58. Innocent III, Gregory IX, Thomas Aquinas, and Spanish seventeenth-century canonist Thomas Sánchez accepted the theory that marriage takes place once mutual consent has been declared. Nevertheless, well-defined canonical impediments could invalidate a marriage even after consummation.

14. *Quarta Partida,* pp. 404–5. There were five different manners of betrothal: three by verbal expression, including one based on oath on the Bible; the fourth expressed by a gift and verbal promise; and the fifth by receipt of a ring as a sign of commitment. Marriage vows without carnal union established a valid marriage, known as *matrimonio rato.*

15. Dillard, *Daughters of the Reconquest,* p. 40.

16. To protect women and their families the Fourth Lateran Council (1215) prescribed a marriage ritual that would publicize the betrothal and allow

time for the community to learn about it and to investigate possible impediments. Clandestine marriages continued to take place not only in Spain, but elsewhere in Europe. In Spain the church did not nullify such unions. After a reprimand the marriages were legalized. See Dillard, *Daughters of the Reconquest*, p. 39.

17. Knecht, *Derecho*, p. 82. The goal of the church was to eliminate all possibilities of being forced to validate "clandestine" marriages, but in this task it had an uphill battle.

18. Unlike the cases studied by Donahue in seventeenth-century France in which the broken promise of marriage entailed relatively few cases of sexual consummation, in Latin America the consummation of the marriage was the most important issue, since in the vast majority of the cases the couple had carried out sexual relations.

19. *Quarta Partida*, Ley x, p. 410. See also Ley xi, which deals with other potential complications of engagements in which fathers had a considerable degree of legal power; *Leyes de Toro*, Ley xlix; *Ordenações del Senhor Rey D. Manuel*, 5 vols. (Coimbra: Real Imprensa da Universidade, 1797), Quarto Libro, Tit. xxxii, p. 91.

20. See Rípodaz, *El matrimonio*, and Nizza da Silva, *Sistema de casamento*, for a full review of the legislation. Konetzke's, *Colección de documentos*, should be consulted for ad hoc legislation on marriage issued by the Spanish crown in response to personal petitions.

21. María Beatriz Nizza da Silva, *Sistema de Casamento*, pp. 39, 45, 75, 84. In 1564 King Sebastián recommended the observance of the rulings of Trent, and in 1569 he authorized prelates and ecclesiastical justices to enforce them. See *Código filipino ou ordenações e leis do Reino de Portugal*, 2 vols. (Rio de Janeiro: Typografiado Instituto Philomathico, 1870), I:503–7.

22. Robert Ricard's work on the spiritual conversion of Mexico still stands as a piercing analysis of the many facets of the process. He was well aware of the importance of the sacramental, linguistic, and intellectual aspects of the conversion. Robert Ricard, *La conquista espiritual de México* (Mexico City: Editorial Jus, 1947).

23. Such religious prohibitions as the seven commandments established the basis for honorable social and personal conduct, although they were not regarded as the essence of honor. By establishing what was "sinful" and condemned the soul, however, they set strong connections between honor and morality.

24. For further discussion of the concept of honor in Spanish America, see Ramón A. Gutiérrez, "From Honor to Love: Transformations of the Meaning of Sexuality in Colonial Mexico," in *Kinship, Ideology and Practice in Latin*

America, ed. Raymond T. Smith (Chapel Hill: University of North Carolina Press, 1984), pp. 237–63. The discourse of honor, virginity, and chastity in colonial religious and advice literature remains to be fully explored. See Nizza da Silva, *Sistema de casamento,* pp.70–74. For further discussion of the topic in another Latin society, see Sandra Cavallo and Simona Cerutti, "Onore femminile e controllo sociale della riproduzione in Piemonte tra Sei e Settecento," *Quaderni Storici* 18,no.2 (August 1983): 346–83.

25. For a discussion of the concept of virginity in Christian theology, see John M. Bugge, *Virginitas: An Essay in the History of a Medieval Idea* (The Hague: Martinus Nijhoff, 1975); Juan de la Torre y Balcárcel, *Espejo de la filosofía y compendio de toda la medicina theorica y práctica* (Amberes: Imp. Plantiniana de Balthasar Moreto, 1668), pp. 57–58. This author defined honor as "the entailed daughter of virginity." As a physician and a priest, de la Torre bemoaned the loss of virginity before marriage but proceeded to give medical advice on how to narrow the entrance of the vagina to fake virginity, while praying for success "for the greater glory of God." For further discussion see, Clarissa W. Atkinson, "Precious Balsam in a Fragile Glass: The Ideology of Virginity in the Later Middle Ages," *Journal of Family History* (Summer 1983), pp. 131–43.

26. This discussion is based on my own research.

27. Fr. Alonso de Herrera, *Espejo de la perfecta casada* (Granada: Blas Martínez, 1636), pp. 131, 155, 143, 426; Fray Antonio de Guevara, *Libro primero de las epístolas familiares* (Madrid: Real Academia Española, 1950), pp. 370–74; *Reloj de príncipes y Libro de Marco Aurelio* (Madrid: Signo, 1936), pp. 48–66. Guevara was a preacher and chronicler during the reign of Charles V and his writings were translated into six languages in the sixteenth century.

28. Archivo de Notarías de México, Notary Martín del Río, 1695; Will of Captain Dámaso de Saldívar, merchant and *prior* of the Consulado; Will of José de Retes, Knight of Calatrava. These men, like many others of the local élite, had "natural" (out-of-wedlock) children. Zaldívar had a son and a daughter. The son had been endowed with a good education and was an Audiencia lawyer; the daughter was endowed with five thousand pesos. Retes, who died unmarried, endowed his natural daughter with eight thousand pesos.

29. Renato Pinto Venancio, "Nos limites da sagrada familia: Ilegitimidade e casamento no Brasil colonial," in *História e sexualidade,* ed. Ronaldo Vainfaz, pp. 107–23. Pinto Venancio registered illegitimacy rates between 11 and 40 percent in four Brazilian communities during several decades between 1760 and 1800. Maria-Luiza Marcilio, *La Ville de São Paulo: Peuplement et population, 1750–1850* (Paris: Presses Universitaires de France, 1973), pp.

183–85, 215. For colonial Sé, São Paulo (1741–1815), Marcilio recorded 39 out of every hundred children baptized were "foundlings" (*expostos*) or illegitimate; Alzira Lobo de A. Campos, "A configuração dos agregados como grupo social: Marginalidade e paneiramento (o exemplo da cidade de São Paulo no século XVIII," *Revista de História* (Nova Serie) 117 (July–December 1984): 71–86. In the parish of Se, between 1775 and 1822, 67 percent of the slave children were registered as "of unknown father." Among the free population 24 percent were registered in the same category, and 17.8 percent lacked the identity of both parents. For Lima, Mazet found that among españoles and mestizos out-of-wedlock births represented 37.5 percent of the baptisms registered in the parish of San Sebastián between 1562 and 1689. Between 1590 and 1599 the percentage of "natural" children was at least 40 percent; in the seventeenth century it ranged between 25 and 40 percent. The frequency was much higher among mixed-bloods. See Claude Mazet, "Lima aux XVI è et XVIII è siècles," *Cahiers des Amériques Latines* 13–14 (1976): 51–102. In the northern Mexican mining town of Charcas, Marcelo Carmagnani found a 30.8 percent illegitimate birth rate between 1635 and 1639, and 51 percent between 1650 and 1654 among all ethnic groups. Españoles varied between 26.2 and 47.7 percent in the two periods, while for mulattos the incidence rose from 65.1 to 75 percent of all births. Illegitimacy was in ascent among all ethnic groups. See Carmagnani, "Demografía y sociedad," pp. 456–57. Among the indigenous population of New Spain the rate of illegitimacy was lower. See Claude Morin, "Los libros parroquiales como fuente para la historia demográfica y social novohispana," *Historia Mexicana* 21, no.3 (January–March 1972): 389–418.

30. María Beatriz Nizza da Silva has found that in Brazil claiming a share of the family inheritance was a difficult process for "natural" or illegitimate children. See her "Família e herença no Brasil colonial," *Anais da* VI *Reunião da Sociedade Brasileira de Pesquisa Histórica* (São Paulo: Sociedade Brasileira de Pesquisa Histórica, 1987), pp. 19–25. In theory, Spanish legislation curtailed the rights of illegitimate children. See, for example, *Siete Partidas,* trans. Samuel Parson Scott (Chicago: American Bar Association, 1931), *Quarta Partida,* Title XV, pp. 952–55.

31. See Donald Ramos, "Marriage and Family in Colonial Vila Rica," *Hispanic American Historical Review* 55, no.2 (May 1975): 200–225; María Luisa Laviana Cuetos, "La descripción de Guayaquil por Francisco Requena, 1774," *Historiografía y Bibliografía Americanista* 26 (1982): 3–134. Requena, a military engineer well acquainted with the Audiencia de Quito, commented on the pastoral abandonment of the Indians and the high fees demanded for marriage licenses, which obliged them to live in concubinage for many years (p. 49).

32. The abandonment of children for economic reasons is not ruled out, of course. See the interpretation of Elsa Malvido in, "El abandono de los hijos: Una forma de control del tamaño de la familia y el trabajo indígena, Tula, 1683–1830," *Historia Mexicana* 34, no.4 (April–June 1980): 521–61.

33. Enrique D. Dussel, *El episcopado hispanoamericano,* 4 vols. (Cuernavaca: CIDOC, 1969), 3:217–48. One of the most notable episcopal visits was that of the Bishop of Trujillo (Peru), Baltasar Jaime Martínez Compañón, between 1779 and 1789. See, Jesús Domínguez Bordona, *Trujillo del Perú a fines del siglo* XVIII (Madrid, 1936). As an example of a Brazilian visit (*devassa*) see, Francisco Vidal Luna and Iraci del Nero da Costa, "Devassa nas Minas Gerais: Observações sobre casos de concubinato," *Anais do Museu Paulista* 31 (São Paulo, 1982): 221–33; Donald Ramos, "Marriage and the Family," pp. 224–25; Fernando Torres Londoño, *El concubinato y la Iglesia en el Brasil Colonial* (São Paulo: Centro de Estudos de Demografia Histórica de América Latina, 1988). Londoño offers further bibliographical references on episcopal visits to Brazil.

34. The civil legislation affecting betrothal and marriages is one example of this attempt at social reform by the Bourbons. For a survey of the reform issue between church and state see, Adrian C. van Oss, *Catholic Colonialism: A Parish History of Guatemala, 1524–1821* (Cambridge: Cambridge University Press, 1986), pp. 142–52; Nancy Farriss, *Crown and Clergy in Colonial Mexico, 1759–1821: The Crisis of Ecclesiastical Privilege* (London: Athlone Press, 1968); Asunción Lavrin, "Ecclesiastical Reform of Nunneries in New Spain in the Eighteenth Century," *The Americas* 22, no.2 (October 1965): 182–203. There were important moral fissures within the clergy itself. The lower clergy was involved in scandals of sexual nature, of which the "solicitation," or wooing of women in the confessional, was the most common. See Jorge René González N., "Clérigos solicitantes, perversos de la confesión," in *De la santidad a la perversión,* ed. Sergio Ortega, pp. 239–52, and "Pecados virtuosos: El delito de solicitación en la Nueva España (siglo XVIII)," *Historias* 11 (October–December 1985): 73–84; Laura de Mello e Souza, "O padre e as feticeiras," in *História e sexualidade,* ed. Ronaldo Vainfas, pp. 9–18.

35. For a general survey of witch hunts in Europe see Joseph Klaits, *Servants of Satan: The Age of Witch Hunts* (Bloomington: Indiana University Press, 1985). H. R. Trevor-Roper's "The European Witch-Craze of the Sixteenth and Seventeenth Centuries," in his *The European Witch-Craze of the Sixteenth and Seventeenth Centuries and Other Essays* (New York: Harper Torchbooks, 1969), pp. 90–192, remains a readable brief survey. For Spain see, Gustav Hennigsen, *The Witches' Advocate: Basque Witchcraft and the*

Spanish Inquisition (Reno: University of Nevada Press, 1980); Angel Alcalá, ed., *Inquisición española y mentalidad inquisitorial* (Barcelona: Editorial Ariel, 1984).

36. European witchcraft involved the cult of Satan, carnal commerce with the Prince of Darkness, witches' orgies, and other elements that did not appear frequently in the Americas. The Inquisition searched for traces of European witchcraft conceptualization and possibly injected them into the inquiries. For examples of the use of European language and concepts see Joseph de Acosta, *Historia natural y moral de las Indias (1590)* (Mexico City: Fondo de Cultura Económica, 1985), pp. 217–79; and Carmelo Sáenz de Santa María, "Revisión etnoreligiosa de la Guatemala de 1704," *Revista de Indias* 41 (July–December 1981): 445–98.

37. Greenleaf, *The Mexican Inquisition in the Sixteenth Century*, pp. 80–81, 104, 217, 223, 224. Processes began to be carried out in the mid-1530s; Greenleaf, "The Inquisition in Eighteenth-Century New Mexico," *New Mexico Historical Review* 60, no.1 (Spring 1985): 29–60; Irene Silverblatt, *Moon, Sun, And Witches: Gender Ideologies and Class in Inca and Colonial Peru* (Princeton: Princeton University Press, 1987), pp. 159–96.

38. *Anais do Museu Paulista* 17 (São Paulo, 1963): 128, 449, 452, 453. These early-seventeenth-century Brazilian sorcery cases have more to do with health, resolution of theft, and daily life preoccupations than with sexual issues. See, Laura de Mello e Souza, "Os padres e as feticeiras." One of the 1591 inquiry cases reported in this work involved a black slave who had learned her sexual lore in Lisbon.

39. Luiz Mott, "Etnodemonologia: Aspectos da vida sexual do Diabo no mundo Ibero-americano (séculos XVI aõ XVIII)," *Religião e Sociedade* 12:265–90; Bartolomé Bennassar, *L'Inquisition Espagnole.* XVè-XIXè siècle (Paris: Hachette, 1979), pp. 229–39; Noemí Quezada, *Amor y magia amorosa entre los aztecas* (Mexico City: UNAM, 1975). For Peru, see Federico Kauffman Doig, *Comportamiento sexual en el antiguo Perú* (Lima: Kompaktos G.S. Editores, 1978) and María Emma Mannarelli, "Inquisición y mujeres: Las hechiceras en el Perú durante el siglo XVII," *Revista Andina* 3, no. 1 (ler Semestre 1985): 141–54.

40. Silverblatt's data for Peru sustain this interpretation, although she is inclined to see a much stronger European input into the accusations raised before the Inquisition. In their depositions Indian women used the Spanish vocabulary, but their statements make clear that their practices had no resemblance to contemporaneous European lore. Everywhere in Latin America confessionals and inquisitorial records attest to the vigor of multiple

forms of "popular" religions. Magic words, spells of sleep, and divinations with corn, water, cotton, mushrooms, various plants, and birds were used to attract the favors of persons of the other sex.

41. Bartolomé Bennassar, ed., *Inquisición española: Poder político y control social* (Barcelona: Editorial Crítica, 1981), pp. 171–207.

42. Rafael Gibert, "El consentimiento familiar en el matrimonio según el derecho medieval español," *Anuario de Historia del Derecho Español* 18 (1947): 706–61. The text of Law IX, Title 2 of the *Novísima Recopilación de las Leyes de España,* which reformed the legislation on parental consent, stated the king had asked his ministers to propose reforms in the "civil contract and temporal effects" of marriage while "safeguarding the ecclesiastical authority and canonical dispositions on the sacrament of matrimony in its spiritual effects."

43. France contested the council's source of authority and proceeded to enact its own laws on the regulation of marriage, giving parents a good measure of control over the process. See James F. Traer, *Marriage and the Family in Eighteenth-Century France* (Ithaca: Cornell University Press, 1980), pp. 22–47; Jean-Louis Flandrin, *Families in Former Times: Kinship, Household and Sexuality in Early Modern France* (Cambridge: Cambridge University Press, 1979), pp. 130–34. In Spain, the respected canonist Thomás Sánchez asserted that, in principle, the election of a marriage partner belonged to the couple, not the parents. His criterion was followed by several canonists popular in the New World.

44. See Patricia Seed, "Parents vs. Children: Marriage Oppositions in Colonial Mexico, 1610–1779" (Ph.D dissertation, University of Wisconsin, 1980); *To Love, Honor, and Obey in Colonial Mexico: Conflicts over Marriage Choice, 1574–1821* (Stanford: Stanford University Press, 1988).

45. Juan Luis Vives, *Instrucción de la mujer cristiana* (Buenos Aires: Espasa Calpe, 1940); Fr. Luis de León, *La perfecta casada* (Mexico City: Editorial Porrúa, 1970); Josefa Amar y Borbón, *Discurso sobre la educación física y moral de las mujeres* (Madrid: Imprenta de D. Benito Cano, 1790); Francisco Manuel de Mello, *Carta de guía de casados* (Porto: Edição da "Renascenca Portuguesa," 1916), pp. 49–50. Mello Franco stated that "one of the factors contributing most to the future happiness of couples is balance *(proporção)* in marriage. Disparity in blood, ages, and properties beget antagonism; antagonism begets discord. . . . Peace is lost and life becomes hell. For the satisfaction of parents equality of blood is highly convenient; for the benefit of the offspring, equality of properties, and for the pleasure of the couple, equality of ages. . . . The greatest happiness in marriage stems from the greatest equality." One of the most popular moral theologies of the seventeenth cen-

tury allowed the rescission of betrothal—even after loss of virginity—if the inequality between the couple was too sharp. See Rípodaz, *El matrimonio*, p. 65. The theologian was Enrique de Villalobos, author of *Suma de teología moral y canónica*, first published in Madrid in 1622 and reissued thirteen times between 1622 and 1682. I follow Rípodaz in the historical discussion of free choice and parental consent; see pp. 259–310.

46. Stuart B. Schwartz, *Sugar Plantations in the Formation of Brazilian Society, 1550–1835* (Cambridge: Cambridge University Press, 1985), pp. 264–75. A recent study on the marriage of slaves and free persons in Brazil probes into the problems posed by "unequal" marriages at a lower social stratum. See Eliana Goldschmidt, "A motivação matrimonial nos casamentos mistos de escravos," *Revista da Sociedade Brasileira de Pesquisa Histórica* 3 (1986/87): 1–16.

47. See comments of Jorge Juan and Antonio de Ulloa on consensual unions in Peru. Characteristically, the authors blamed women for the "licentiousness" they criticized (Jorge Juan and Antonio de Ulloa, *Discourse and Political Reflections on the Kingdoms of Peru*, trans. John J. TePaske and Besse A. Clement [Norman: University of Oklahoma Press, 1978], p. 291); Rípodaz, *El matrimonio*, p. 265. For a brief historical survey of "unequal" sexual unions in Brazil see Eliana Maria Réa Goldschmidt, "O senhor e suas escravas: Um aspecto das unios mistas no século XVIII na capitania de São Paulo," *Anais da* V *Reunião da Sociedade Brasileira de Pesquisa Histórica* (São Paulo: Sociedade Brasileira de Pesquisa Histórica, 1986), pp. 191–95.

48. The original wording of the *Pragmática* stressed the "indispensable and natural obligation of children to respect their parents" and the intention of the law "to preserve for the *pater familias* their due authority" (*Novísima recopilación de las leyes de España*), vol. 5, Tit. 2, Ley IX. Portuguese legislation of 1775 stated that no marriage should take place without the consent of parents or tutors, and established mechanisms for dissenting cases. In 1784 the crown issued other laws establishing the proper procedure to grant consent and requiring the notarization of betrothals. We do not have any studies on the enforcement of this legislation. See *Repertorio geral*, pp. 105, 549. In England, the Marriage Act of 1753 ended centuries of freedom in marriage choice, establishing that those under twenty-one had to secure parental consent before marriage. See Alan MacFarlane, *Marriage and Love in England, 1300–1840* (Oxford: Basil Blackwell Ltd., 1986), p. 127.

49. The casuistic interpretation of the *Pragmática* to serve local situations is underlined by Rípodaz. See *El matrimonio*, p. 274.

50. Magnus Mörner, "Economic Factors and Stratification in Colonial Spanish America with Special Regard to Elites," *Hispanic American Histori-*

cal Review 63, no.2 (May 1983): 335–69; Fred Bronner, "Peruvian Encomenderos in 1630: Elite Circulation and Consolidation," *Hispanic American Historical Review* 57, no.4 (November 1977): 633–59. See also John E. Kicza, *Colonial Entrepeneurs: Families and Business in Bourbon Mexico* (Albuquerque: University of New Mexico Press, 1983), pp. 13–42; and Susan Socolow, *The Merchants of Viceregal Buenos Aires: Family and Commerce, 1778–1810* (Cambridge: Cambridge University Press, 1978).

51. Rípodaz, *El matrimonio,* pp. 279–89, 292–315. The use of the *Pragmática* by the élites for their own purposes is illustrated by the family of a wealthy Cuban family, who obtained an injunction against a 50-year-old male member of the family who wished to legitimize his long concubinage with a *parda* (light-skinned mulatto). This and two other cases of male adults wishing to marry with ethnically and socially lesser women prompted a royal *cédula* (decree) dated October 15, 1805, addressed to the Audiencia of Puerto Príncipe, stating the crown's desire that all persons of nobility and/or known blood cleanliness be subject to the tenets of the 1803 cédula. The majority of the *oidores* of the Audiencia of Puerto Príncipe had been of the opinion that such marriages might cause "ill sentiments" in the families concerned, but the benefit of the state demanded the protection of marriages because the foremost policy of the state was the increase of the population. A demographic need, they suggested, overruled the personal interests of families. The crown did not support this view. Archivo General de la Nación, Mexico City, Secretaría de Cámara, Serie Historia, Colección Hernández Dávalos, vol. 2, doc. 167, Bando of 18 December 1810 signed by Francisco Xavier Venegas.

52. Ramón Briones Luco, *Origen y desarrollo del matrimonio y el divorcio en la familia humana,* 2 vols. (Santiago de Chile: Imprenta de "La Ilustración," 1909–10), 2:261; Juan Carlos Rébora, *La familia chilena y la familia argentina,* 2 vols. (La Plata: Talleres Gráficos Tomás Palumbo, 1938), 1:37. In 1856 Bishop José Hipólito Salas issued a decree to bolster the new Civil Code, which upheld the principle of parental consent before marriage up to age twenty-five. Pedro Felipe de Azúa e Iturgoyen, *Sínodo de Concepción (Chile), 1744* (Madrid and Salamanca: Consejo Superior de Investigaciones Científicas and Universidad Pontificia de Salamanca, 1984), pp. 203–7. It is significant that parental authority was upheld in some legal codes, while *esponsales,* or betrothal, lost its binding legal effect in republican legislation.

53. The definition of patriarchalism used by Boyer excludes a rigid interpretation of this concept as one in which men had absolute control over women within the family and throughout society. For further comments, see

Silvia Marina Arrom, *The Women of Mexico City, 1790–1857* (Stanford: Stanford University Press, 1985), pp. 59–61.

54. Comments on divorce are based on the work of Maria Beatriz Nizza da Silva, in this volume, and on Bernard Lavallé, *Divorcio y nulidad de matrimonio en Lima (1651–1700)* (Bordeaux: Groupe Interdisciplinaire de Recherche et de Documentation sur l'Amérique Latine, 1986), Document de Travail no. 2. Examples drawn from Mexican archives have served to corroborate the main features of the Peruvian and the Brazilian models. The demographic patterns of divorce and their sociological and cultural features are a neglected aspect of colonial social history.

55. See Georges Duby, *Medieval Marriage.* Annulment allowed remarriage, while "divorce" meant physical separation of the couple. Remarriage after "divorce" could take place only after the death of one of the spouses.

56. For *Partidas* legislation on divorce, see *Quarta Partida,* Title x, pp. 929–45 in Scott's translation. In his study of divorce in Lima in the second half of the seventeenth century, Bernard Lavallé found 1,533 suits. Of these 928 (60.5 percent) were for divorce and 603 (39.4 percent) for annulment. Figures for the number of rulings are not available. Suits were not often brought to completion, and in many instances the outcome is not recorded. Lavallé, *Divorcio y nulidad,* p. 7. For divorce in nineteenth-century Mexico see Silvia Arrom, *Women of Mexico City.* The continuity of the spirit and practice of divorce throughout the first decades of postcolonial Spanish America is to be noted.

57. One important social feature of colonial family formation is the frequency of female-headed households. This phenomenon is correlated to the social instability of certain geographical areas, but must also be tied to the sexual mores of colonial society, in which many women began extramarital relationships, begetting "natural" or illegitimate children and forming families of unconventional nature. See Donald Ramos, "Marriage and the Family in Colonial Vila Rica," pp. 200–225; Elizabeth Kuznesof, "The Role of the Female-Headed Household in Brazilian Modernization: São Paulo, 1765 to 1836," *Journal of Social History* 13 (1980): 589–613; Rodney D. Anderson, "Race and Social Stratification: A Comparison of Working-Class Spaniards, Indians, and Castas in Guadalajara, Mexico, in 1821," *Hispanic American Historical Review* 68, no.2 (May 1988): 209–44. He states that one-fourth of Guadalajara households in 1821 were headed by women.

Part I: Sexuality

Asunción Lavrin

Sexuality in Colonial Mexico: A Church Dilemma

On the eleventh of November 1734, in the small city of Tescoco, close to the capital of Mexico, Juan de Baños, *castizo*—son of a mestizo and a white person—and single, appeared before Joseph de Güemes, a member of the Holy Office and ecclesiastical judge, to state that "better to serve God, Our Lord, that He may save his soul, he declares to be in illicit friendship with Gertrudis Fernández, from Xolalpa, [legitimate daughter of Antonio Fernández, mestizo, and Gregoria Sánchez, española] of the same parish of Tepetlaostoc, whose honesty he took under the word of marriage that both had exchanged, but being willing to make that promise good . . . and incapable of abandoning their long illicit friendship, he requests an investigation of the degree of relatedness between them, to be able to redeem through marriage the bad state in which they are." This request was eventually granted on November 27 by Bishop Juan Antonio Vizarrón Eguieta, archbishop of Mexico City, who, after finding that they were second cousins and had lived in "incestuous concubinage," imposed a general penitence of confession of all their sins, communion on all the festivities of the Virgin Mary for one whole year, and saying the Holy Rosary nightly on their knees for the same period.[1]

The story of Joseph and Gertrudis was not unusual. In mid-colonial New Spain problems of a sexual nature were routinely dealt with by the religious authorities of the several bishoprics of the colony. Among young couples, premarital sexual relations after a betrothal vow seemed to have been a common occurrence; cases of consensual unions were brought frequently to the attention of the ecclesiastical judges; illegitimacy and bigamy were not uncommon. Such instances of religiously unorthodox sexuality raise questions on the degree of acceptance by the common folk of the behavioral models set by the church as a codifier of sexual behavior, and on its role as witness and judge of the many irregularities committed by the faithful. The manner in which the church interacted with those who either challenged or broke its moral norms is a key element in understanding its effectiveness as a mechanism of social control.[2]

The late Michel Foucault posited that in Europe the seventeenth century was critical in the process of narrowing the definition of morality and imposing restrictive behavioral codes, especially in the area of sexual relations. This was partly the result of the work of the Council of Trent, which closed its sessions in 1563 after twenty years of work to reorganize the Roman Catholic Church, strengthen its traditional values, and answer the many challenges posed by humanists, freethinkers, and Protestants. To educate the faithful in the revised canons of the church and to foster spiritual conformity, theologians developed catechisms and confessionals, which laid out orthodoxy from the cradle to the grave. Such broad agenda, however, did not meet all its goals. There was always a gap between religious canons and the actual behavior of the people. Adaptation, confrontation, enforcement, and elusion in matters of personal behavior, especially in its sexual aspect, became important elements in the daily lives of many people, and this is an important if neglected chapter in the social history of the seventeenth and eighteenth centuries.

Here I propose to begin the examination of the effect of Counter-Reformation rules of social and personal mores in the Viceroyalty of New Spain. For a better understanding of the moral norms of sexual behavior stressed by the church and the degree of acceptance or resistance found among the general population, we should consider two levels of analysis. One is that of the sexual behavior prescribed in the treatises of moral theology and in the confessionals—books to help confessors in their tasks of inquiry and moral guidance of the confessants.[3] The second is that of the actual behavior of the population, as reflected in the cases brought before the ecclesiastical judges of the bishoprics of colonial Mexico. These cases were either self-confessions or denunciations of breaches of the ecclesiastical norms, and they represent the reality of daily life for those who failed to practice fully the teachings of the church.[4]

At the beginning of the seventeenth century the church had a solid basis for the canonical interpretation of sexual behavior. After the Council of Trent solved once and for all the format of the marriage ritual, the church made a concerted effort to make its teachings on the nature and objective of male-female relationships better known to the laity. The thrust of this task was pastoral and lay on the shoulders of bishops and parish priests, who through their daily contacts with their flocks learned about their personal habits and influenced their behavior. Confession and penitence, two essential elements in Roman Catholic spirituality, were the tools to correct errors and mold consciences into proper doctrinal observance.[5] In Spain some of the most distinguished theologians of the late sixteenth and seventeenth centuries paid special attention to the sacrament of marriage and the moral issues raised by the sixth commandment.[6] For practical purposes, the confessionals translated much of the abstruse scholarly discussion of moral theology into language more easily understandable by the parish priest and the laity. They furnished the general parameters of sexual morality handed down to the population at large by its religious guardians.

Sex and Sin: The Confessionals and the Definitions of Sexuality

Human sexuality as a constant challenge to the spiritual side of humankind was a source of constant preoccupation for the church. The confessionals analyzed the nature of human weakness and established the boundaries between the permissible and the nonpermissible, between actions blessed by the church and actions condemned by it.[7] Under the confessionals' meticulous examination of sin and transgressions, the contours of human behavior were indeed distorted by virtue of the undue emphasis put on all its negative aspects. The models proposed by moral theology as paradigms of piety were largely unattainable to most mortals but were assumed to be beacons for their guidance on this earth. Regardless of their feasibility, the norms set by the church are essential to our understanding of the cultural constrictions imposed on the daily lives of the laity.

The post-Tridentine concept of sexual behavior retained much of the patristic and medieval dialectic of flesh and spirit as two antagonistic forces engaged in a constant battle. The prevalence of the flesh could mean eternal condemnation for the soul. To avoid this, men and women should constantly control the demands of their bodies. The church defined rules to guide humanity in this struggle between the spirit and the flesh, but the final choice of behavior always rested in the hands of the individual, on whose own personal free will rested the decision to follow the path of salvation. This stress on the freedom to choose between good and bad was central to the definition of sin. Sin is the voluntary—thus knowledgeable—breach of the rules of behavior set by the church, leading to the loss of divine grace by the soul.[8] Sin could be absolved, however, and the soul restored to its communication with God through confession and penitence. The individual acknowledged error in confession and repented through contrition or penance. Absolution, granted by the minister of God, restored the ties between the soul and its maker.

Because of the cardinal importance of free will, one of the most important tasks of confessions was to establish whether the actions that led to transgression were voluntary or involuntary. The confessant assumed full responsibility for a voluntary infringement. In contrast, an involuntary action, even though it was recognized as a bad one, did not necessarily lead to sin.

The sixth and the ninth commandments dealt with the sins resulting from adultery and lust.[9] In most confessionals, however, it is under the study of the sixth commandment that "sinful" sexual behavior receives its most thorough review. The explanations of the sixth commandment hold the key to the discourse on sexuality and its manifold forms of expression and repression as they surveyed the nature of "turpitude" and all attempts against chastity and sexual restraint.

One of the most orderly explanations of lust and its consequences in seventeenth-century confessionals is that of Fr.Gabino Carta, S.J. As he reviewed the sixth commandment, Fr. Gabino explained how lust could manifest itself in seven forms, all conducive to mortal sin and comprising all manners of sexually forbidden behavior. These forms were: 1. simple fornication, 2. adultery, 3. incest, 4. rape, 5. abduction, 6.sins against nature, and 7. sacrilege.

Simple fornication ocurred when two single persons, unrelated to each other, engaged in sexual acts outside marriage. Adultery was committed when at least one of the two partners in an unsanctioned sexual relationship was married. Incest occurred when the couple was related by blood ties in the first or second degree. Other degrees of relatedness by blood were also subject to ecclesiastical supervision, but the degree of incestuousness lessened as ties weakened, i.e., for persons related in the third or fourth degree. Spiritual kinship also created incestuous bonds, and sexual relations between persons thus related were also considered sinful without ecclesiastical dispensation. Rape (*estupro*) was the sexual act forced on a female. Abduction (*rapto*) was commonly defined as a forced seizure of a woman. It was an ambiguous situation, since confessors and moral theologians understood that, in many instances, the abducted woman voluntarily cooperated with the abductor and engaged in willful sexual relations after the abduction. However, whether such relations were willful or coerced, the church did not condone the abduction. Whether the woman was or was not a virgin before the rape or the abduction, or whether her reputation was bad or good, was in theory irrelevant to the church. The forced nature of the action made abduction and rape mortal sins.

According to the moral theologians, sins against nature could be committed in three manners: 1. by voluntary pollution (masturbation), 2. by sodomy, and 3. by bestiality. Masturbation contravened the church's view that seminal emission must be carried into the female vagina (*intra vas naturale*) for the purpose of procreation. Sodomy or sin *contra naturam* was the copulation of two persons of the same sex. It also applied, however, to any form of sex between man and woman, married or not, contravening the physical position accepted by the church as "natural." Bestiality consisted in engaging in sex with an animal. In the seventeenth century it was still believed that the devil could assume the shape of an animal or even a person to tempt humans. Sacrilege was incurred when one of the two partners in a sexual act broke a vow of chastity, regardless of whether it was a simple or a formal vow. Hairsplitting theological distinctions and nuances led to important casuistic considerations. Thus, a person could incur several sins in one single act. This would be the case, for example, of a married man who in raping a woman committed adultery as well. If the woman happened to be a first-degree relative, incest would be added to the count. Sinning could be a complex issue.[10]

Masturbation, always described as an exclusively masculine problem, deeply concerned the church. Aware of the narrow restraints put on male sexuality by its own moral theologians, the church targeted the only channel left for the release of masculine sexual urges. Since engaging in sex with a prostitute was defined as a sinful act, masturbation seemed to have been the only choice open to single men. Religious authorities closed this option and proscribed situations that could lead to it, such as "dishonest" body contacts (*tactos deshonestos*) or any form of voyeurism. Furthermore, if during masturbation the person carnally desired another person, a second sin was committed. The sin became graver when another man or a woman was involved in the masturbation act, and it was at its most heinous if the helper incurred pollution himself. On the other hand, actions causing involuntary emissions, such as horse riding, eating in excess, or becoming drunk, did not per se lead to sin, as they were not originally intended to produce emission or pleasure.

Thoughts as well as actions counted in the definition of sin; confessants had to examine their innermost thoughts before, during, or after sinful behavior to be sure that the confession was complete and that full absolution would eventually be achieved.[11] By such standards, desiring another man's wife in thought was as much a sin as lying with her, and sacrilege was incurred if a man desired a nun or a beata. The complexities of the human mind were further explored and acknowledged in the definition of a state of mind halfway between dreams and voluntary thoughts. There lay another layer of mental activity described as "morose delight" (*delectación morosa*). This form of sensual pleasure took place in a dim state of the mind, in which the will not to entertain dishonest thoughts was lost and the person ended by enjoying sexual dreams. Loss of control was the qualification for sin. When the mind was in a state of rest, such as in sleep, involuntary acts or dreams could be conducive to sin if they were remembered and enjoyed by the individual. By that token, the involuntary character of seminal emissions during sleep had to be proved in order to avoid mortal sin. If a man took pleasure from this form of pollution because he procured it before falling asleep, or enjoyed the memory of it after waking up, mortal sin was incurred. Ultimately, the will to gain pleasure from sexual activities was the key to defining any situation as sinful.

Given the narrow confines established for sexual activities, the possibilities of sin were numerous while the opportunities for the legitimate (*honesto*) enjoyment of sex were indeed limited. The general tone of the confessionals and the attitude of the church toward sexual union were repressive, stressing restraint and control over release and fulfillment. How did sexuality become acceptable? In actions as well as in thoughts, sex was acceptable only when it was satisfied within marriage. Most theologians knew that it was unrealistic to expect single persons to deny consent of the will in experiencing sexual pleasure. The solution handed down to the single person was abstention and self-restraint. In that vein, Father Juan Antonio de Oviedo was of the opinion that one sinned every time that one fully consented in sensual pleasure outside marriage, even if such pleasure was triggered by small acts such as talking, listening, or holding hands. As he put it, failure to exert the mechanism of self-control over the weaker part of ourselves, and giving in to the desires of the flesh, was the source of human misery: it lost divine grace for men and women and endangered the salvation of their souls; it attached them to worldly pursuits; it made them hate each other and alienated them from God.[12]

Physical love was only legitimate as an expression of conjugal love, achieved through the sacrament of matrimony. In fact, within marriage both spouses were not only entitled to it, but obliged to perform it. Married couples had the duty of satisfying the sexual desire of the other whenever it was requested. Denying sexual satisfaction to the other was, by definition, a mortal sin. The sexual act became a "debt" (*débito*) to be paid, with very limited options available for evasion of such payment. Thus, the sexuality of both men and women was defined in a contractual manner. Under such strict regulations sexual activity was the opposite of the sin of "fornication," which consisted in engaging in any of the sexual practices forbidden by the church. The recognition of the existence of physical needs in matters of sexuality did not mean that the church approved more than what was necessary to stay away from sin. The Council of Trent did not alter the patristic vision of marriage as a preventive of or a cure for concupiscence.[13] Ultimately, all sexual activity approved by the church had one avowed and legitimate purpose: the perpetuation of the human species. Confined to the safe territory of marriage and legitimized by the need to procreate, sex in marriage was not totally unregulated, however. Couples should avoid "disorder" in their relations, a reference to the lust that was supposed to characterize adulterous relations. Those who married to satisfy their appetites, not to serve God, did not receive His grace. The pastoral effort to "spiritualize" conjugal love was still very much a reality in the late eighteenth century. An anonymous instruction for married couples written by a Franciscan priest ca. 1790 insisted on the possibility of a purified relationship between spouses that would elevate conjugal love to the higher levels of spirituality and reconcile the sacrament with its unavoidable physical reality. He advised a spiritual retreat of ten days before marriage, to achieve the understanding that a marriage based on the satisfaction of "brutal appetites" was bound to unhappiness since it was not approached in the best spirit to serve God in that state. Those to be married should reject the sensuality that could be "smelled" and the lust in need of "quenching."[14]

The confessionals stated that thoughts of sexual pleasure permissible between spouses had to be directed toward each other. Widows and widowers could legitimately remember past sexual acts, and engaged couples could licitly enjoy thoughts of future intercourse, as long as such thoughts would not result in obvious physical arousal (*si empero no se deleita, ni se expone a peligro de deleitarse de algún movimiento de sensualidad carnal, que entonces siente*). Any "commotion of the flesh," according to some confessionals, was the physical result of dishonest thoughts and a sign of having enjoyed sensual thoughts beyond acceptable boundaries, since they had not taken place in the only scenario where they could be fulfilled: the conjugal bed. Oviedo warned of the difficulty of making certain physical demonstrations of love such as kissing and embracing, or thinking about the sexual act, without experiencing physical stimulation. He advised against such activities until marriage had taken place.[15]

The Realities of Transgression

That the teachings of the church were not heeded by a good number of people is a historical commonplace. The preoccupation of the church with sexuality was not born of idle theological abstraction. The "discourse" of regulation and repression had a human side, both the source and target of moral theologians. In the particular context of colonial Mexico, a fluid and complex pattern of personal relationships had developed by the late sixteenth century. Consensual unions, bigamy, sexual witchcraft, and solicitation of sexual favors in confessionals were but a few expressions of sexual transgressions recorded by the ecclesiastical authorities. Here I will focus on several manifestations of sexuality leading to some of the most common transgressions: courtship as the initiation of male-female relationships, premarital sex, concubinage, rape, elopement, and incest. I will also review breaches of moral and spiritual propriety in conjugal relations.[16]

In attempting to retrieve the historical traces of sexual behavior, historians must acknowledge that any number of cases recorded represent a small part of a larger reality. The privacy of the confessional could be broken only when the cases coming before the priest clearly infringed the behavioral and spiritual canons of the church. Denunciations to ecclesiastical authorities for similar reasons provide the other main source of information. We should also remain aware of the fact that although transgressions reflect the social mores, they do not define them in toto, and while they are part of the main patterns of behavior not all people indulge in them.

One of the main means to identify "sinners" and the facts about their relationships was the requirement that couples intending to get married declare their free mutual consent to the union and that they state clearly if any blood or kin impediment stood in the way of their marriage; these affirmations were witnessed by several persons. This process was not concerned with sin itself, but it led to the revelation of hidden transgressions because bride and groom had also to confess premarital sex with the intended or with any blood or spiritual kin. Such relations were sinful and required canonical dispensation. Marriages contracted without such dispensation would be voided by the ecclesiastical authorities. Investigation of the couple's proposed marriage could also be brought about by the denunciation of a third party alleging previous betrothal to either bride or groom, revealing sexual relations with any of the two, or disclosing a previously secret or unknown degree of affinity. In yet another variation, the groom would present himself to the priest and confess an "illicit" relationship, asking the priest to regularize it.

Any form of canonical impediment demanded an investigation of its nature and the circumstances in which it took place. The couple and several witnesses were questioned and, after establishing all the facts pertaining to the case, the priest sent the information to the seat of the bishopric, where the ecclesiastical judges studied it and made a final recommendation to the bishop. Only the latter had the power to grant or deny dispensations in matrimonial matters. The process of review and judgment could take several weeks or several months, and the couple was supposed to abstain from further contact until a decision was reached.[17]

Impediments to marriage were of two kinds: *diriment* and *impendient*. The first invalidated a marriage; the latter did not. Among the diriment impediments were legal and spiritual kinship; age, for those too young to marry; bigamy; and male impotence. The last was widely discussed, and its circumstances were thoroughly scrutinized before a final decision was made. It became a diriment impediment if it verifiably existed before marriage, or if it persisted for over three years after marriage. Impendient impediments were caused by disparity of cult, by the taking of religious vows by one of the betrothed, by the forceful abduction of the woman, by a heinous crime committed by either bride or groom, by a previous promise of marriage, or by a promise of marriage given by a married person before his or her spouse died.

Blood and spiritual kinship were frequent impediments, and the church had a carefully designed system to judge the degrees of proximity and rule on dispensation requests. Several circumstances were considered when examining the problem of kinship. The ecclesiastical authorities had to judge if the small size of the town of residence could deny the bride the opportunity to marry somebody of her own social status who was not related to her. Just as important was her lack of a dowry, which could force her to marry a relative rather than an outsider. Excessive familiarity due to familial or spiritual ties could lead to a dishonest situation, and pregnancy resulting from this circumstance was an important consideration in granting dispensation, to insure a legitimate birth. An incorrectly performed marriage might have to be annulled and performed again. The potential stain of the family's reputation if the marriage did not take place was also an important consideration.[18] Of these, the most common reason for canonical impediment in New Spain was premarital sexual communication between persons related in several degrees of blood or spiritual kinship.

Those who formed the motley crowd of self-confessed or accused sinners in New Spain were a veritable cross-section of the population. People from all the walks of life appear in the ecclesiastical records. My sources seem to tip in favor of a greater number of smaller rural communities rather than the larger urban centers. Thomas Calvo's research in Guadalajara, however, suggests that similar sexual behavior flourished in the urban milieu as well.[19] The occupational spectrum of those involved was broad. In the northern town of Parral, white (*español*) miners, merchants, and muleteers (*arrieros*) joined mulatto cobblers and tailors in the ranks of sexual transgressors. One of the Indians involved was a rustler. In Michoacán and Mexico City the ethnic and occupational characteristics are not carefully or thoroughly recorded. Among twenty-seven cases of matrimonial irregularities, largely involving premarital sex and aired in the archbishopric of Mexico in 1732, there were *labradores* (rural workers), rancho leasers (*arrendatarios*), one government official, and one (high-ranking) *principal* Indian. Ironically, while the occupations of the grooms were scarcely described, those of the witnesses were better defined. Among them we have carpenters (*maestros carpinteros*), painters, surgeons (*maestros de cirugía*), tailors, candlemakers, cattle raisers, bakers, and a silversmith. This particular group in the Archbishopric was largely español.[20] In general, the Michoacán records do not state the occupation of the petitioner. Occasionally, the fact that either the man or the woman lived in an hacienda identifies them as rural people. Tailors, weavers, and *obrajeros* (textile-mill workers) are a few of the occupations mentioned for people living in smaller rural communities. Aided by notarial records for the purpose of identifying occupation and social status, we may safely state that small merchants, artisans, minor public officials, and small landowners or landleasers form the bulk of the social group represented in sexual transgressions.[21]

That people of various ethnic and socioeconomic backgrounds were involved in unorthodox sexual relationships is no surprise, since this is the essence of the process of *mestizaje* (racial mixing), which began with the Conquest in the sixteenth century. That a considerable number of the cases aired in the seventeenth and eighteenth centuries involve whites is significant. New Spain's demographic patterns had become increasingly complex by the beginning of the seventeenth century with the growing mixtures of white, Indian, and black. Confronting the church at the beginning of the seventeenth century was a situation of lax personal relationships and sexual interethnic encounters among the so-called lesser social elements. The noteworthy increase in the number of consensual unions and out-of-wedlock children involved *españoles* as well. Thomás Calvo has documented a considerable increase in the number of children born out of wedlock among the white population in seventeenth-century Guadalajara, suggesting a concomitant increase in premarital or extramarital affairs.[22] In other areas the ethnic affiliation of those involved in marital litigation is not always available. In 167 cases of premarital sex in Michoacán, Guadalajara, and Mexico City from mid seventeenth to late eighteenth century in which race was identified, I have found that 36 percent were concerned with white couples, 22 percent with couples in which one member was white, 26 percent with couples of other ethnic groups, and 16 percent with partners of undisclosed ethnicity. Although not all extramarital affairs came to the attention of the courts, these results suggest that whites were full participants in the sexual practices of the period. It is questionable, however, that they committed the greatest number of transgressions. What the figures indicate is that they were under stronger social pressure to regularize their situations and reconcile themselves with the church. That nearly a quarter of the recorded cases involve interracial relationships attests to the vigor of mestizaje, with a significant participation of the ethnic élite in that process.

Sex and the Sins of Fornication

The apparent frequency of premarital sex among the rural and urban population of colonial Mexico appears to have been based in popular assumptions about sexual practice and the legal and religious implications of the promise of marriage. A number of urban and rural poor seem to have believed that sex among single persons was not a sin.[23] Whether or not this was a widespread assumption will be difficult to test, but it was probably part of the folk reinterpretation of contemporary canonical dogma.

An examination of the process of courtship provides important clues for understanding prevailing attitudes about the initiation of sexual relations. Although data on courtship are sporadic, references to the initial contacts among partners—largely provided by women—are supplied in enough cases to permit a recreation of the process. *Requerir y tratar de amores,* a phrase appearing in suits and self-accusations indicates the existence of a courtship period in which the subject of love was raised by the man. Since dispensation for some degree of relatedness was a common request in matrimonial records (especially in those acknowledging premarital sex), we may safely infer that many young couples met socially because blood or affinal kinship permitted their encounter and subsequent visitations. Such was the course of the amorous relationship that developed between Gerónima Alcaraz, a mulatto, and español widower José Proquinto Acevedo, related in second and fourth degrees of affinity. Their love unfolded (*se fueron tomando amor*) during the visits their kinship allowed.[24]

Pasion y amor are very much part of the vocabulary of petitions and confessions. Such expressions as *engendró amores, el mucho amor que le profesa,* or *ciega inclinación* are common enough to suggest that lust was not the only emotion that joined men and women in premarital relations.[25] The existence of strong affective ties between partners should not be surprising. Love was an essential element of the religious discourse on sexuality and marriage, even though the ecclesiastical authorities took a dim view of its consequences if it remained unbridled. Moral theologians and confessors constantly referred to love as the force that should bind husband and wife.[26] The few examples of love letters preserved for posterity unveil the world of small concerns, endearing terms, and chatty communications that have always been exchanged by lovers of all ages.[27]

Courtship could take several months of *requiebro,* or persuasion. Part of the wooing must have been addressed to the topic of the eventual sexual consummation of love. "Obstinate and importune requests" were cited by María Francisca Santiago in 1798, who later stated that pleasing words and promises were used by the male sex to weaken the female will.[28] Such comments echoed the warning that seventeenth-century Franciscan author Fr. Alonso de Herrera gave to women about the dangerous flames of profane love.[29]

Sexual relations could and did begin during courtship in more cases than we have suspected until now. José Núñez had access to the home of María Manuela de Vargas for several years as a friend, when their relationship suddenly turned into courtship one evening after he took her and her sister to a private theatrical performance. Even though that was the first time he spoke of love to her they agreed to meet secretly the same night. After climbing through a balcony into her room, he spent the night with her. When she later sued him for marriage he declared that she had given herself to him without any resistance, as a "woman of the world."[30] Ideally, women were expected to stand firm against any male advance throughout courtship if they wished to preserve their reputation for honor and virginity. Easy submission or acquiescence to the man's desire could be interpreted as a sign of lack of moral fiber (*virtud*). While persuading a woman to grant him sexual favors did not tarnish a man's reputation, courtship could also prove to be an occasion for him to prove his honor by not requesting sexual relations, making it clear that marriage was his objective. For this purpose he could use the good offices of several persons to convince the woman of the seriousness of his intent. Herein lay the essence of wooing as a test of character for men and women.

Communication between lovers of certain social status was through letters or oral messages (*recaudos*) carried by servants or consenting relatives. Such mediators were necessary given the usual surveillance by members of the family, and they could become accomplices if inhibitions were broken down and premarital relations were established. The courtship of don Juan de Cárdenas and doña Josefa Monasterios, member of a well-to-do family in San Luis Potosí, had all the elements of passion, guilt, and social pressure for the restitution of honor to become a textbook case of colonial sexual mores.[31] Don Juan, a *peninsular* in the service of the alcalde of the town, did not hesitate to court Josefa after they made acquaintance while he walked on her street. He used letters to communicate with her until he succeeded in obtaining a midnight date in her own home. Other encounters took place in the house of an accomplice. They were later recalled in the greatest detail by the man himself and by the two female companions of doña Josefa, who stayed close to the couple even during the attempts at intercourse. The stories tell of kissing, embracing, and exchanging of love words in a brief courtship. Within a short time the man attempted to engage in sex with the willing but frightened woman, who feared the physical and moral pain of losing her virginity, she later confessed. Several other meetings took place during which don Juan apparently failed to consummate his desire and was only able to have seminal emissions *extra vas*, prohibited by the church. Josefa was willing and able to continue seeing the suitor under pretense of visiting a relative, and their meetings continued until, as he claimed, don Juan became tired of failing to have sex with doña Josefa. It is unclear whether or not he deflowered her, but she felt she had lost her honor and confessed to a priest. Soon enough her powerful brother-in-law established a legal suit against don Juan, demanding the repair of the family's honor.

The explicitness of the descriptions of the meetings between don Juan and doña Josefa reveal the lack of privacy in which many personal relationships were carried out. The suitor gave ample testimony of his actions, and the two women witnesses corroborated every detail. While his right to seek satisfaction for his sexual drive remained unchallenged and unquestioned, hers was never acknowledged by the authorities, who were interested only in the legal and social consequences that their sexual relations could have for her and her family.

Initiating a sexual relationship in the course of courtship seems to have depended very much on the exchange of verbal promises of marriage (*palabra de casamiento*), a binding agreement that carried legal and religious obligations even if it took place without witnesses.[32] The most astute women tried to have a witness who might be of use later on, should the man attempt to break his promise. A promise of marriage could involve a symbolic exchange of gifts, a ritual followed by many couples to seal their engagement and give it the solemnity of a betrothal. The gifts were often of small value, but expensive jewelry could be exchanged by wealthier persons. The ritual exchange of gifts assured the woman of the marriage intentions of the man, although the verbal promise was all that was required and what most women seem to have received. If the betrothal was not voiced secretly by the couple, it was celebrated by the whole family to make the engagement public to the community.[33]

The verbal promise of marriage apparently gave many women either sufficient assurance of the intentions of the man or enough confidence in its legal and religious implications to engage in sexual relations. As in late medieval Europe, it seems that couples in New Spain acted on the belief that once the verbal promise of marriage was given the marriage process had been initiated. If the word was not carried out, a question of honor was raised, and the woman was portrayed as having lost her public "credit," stained her family's name, and lost her chances to marry someone else. The fulfillment of the marriage promise was the key to regaining a measure of personal honor, to retaining social status and, just as important, to returning to the community of the religiously blessed.[34]

Men and women entering into illicit premarital sexual relationships acknowledged the pull of the flesh. The body was weak and it was difficult to resist its temptations; the frailty of the human condition underlined all confessions (*llevado de mi fragilidad; mi fragilidad me arrastro como miserable*). The messages of the confessionals and the preachers are echoed in the formalized official depositions of contrite sinners, who emphasized what was ugly and reprehensible in their relationships as part of the ritual of penitence. Women confessed to having acceded to the "gross desires" of men (*torpes deseos*); men and women alike referred to *torpe comunicación, torpe comercio, mala versación, desliz vergonzoso, ilícita amistad,* and *amor deshonesto* to describe their illicit relationships. Only exceptionally, men confessed to having enjoyed the relationship or declared that it was a challenge to their manhood that they expected to meet. Thus, a man at the end of the seventeenth century reported that after a friendship with a woman "he succeeded in enjoying her" (*consiguió gozarla*), while another stated that as a man he had done the right thing in courting a woman (*como hombre se había puesto a la obra*).[35] If women ever regarded sexual intercourse as a pleasurable act or a source of enjoyment, no records attested to such feelings.

Despite the fact that by force of circumstance love and lust were described as shameful and embarrassing, behind such declarations lay other motivations that call for further exploration. Premarital sex in a society so encumbered by religious and social controls may be regarded as a form of escaping such controls. The ease with which women acceded or "condescended"—as some of them put it—to having relations with a man after an exchange of gifts or a promise of marriage points to a desire to transcend or even defy the constraints imposed on them by family, religion, and law. And yet, since rarely did women acknowledge having entered into relationship without promise of marriage, the demands for redress nullified the spirit of the initial defiance and became the means to ensure the very goals that their behavior had apparently challenged.[36] Whether or not this internal contradiction was appreciated by those couples engaging in premarital relations, they did so willingly, as part of the process of courtship. Once the union was consummated, they had a card in their favor, as the situation forced an ecclesiastical review of their cases and removed the final decision from parental, familial, or communal nfluence.[37]

Relationships based on premarital sex amounted to consensual marriages, inasmuch as many couples lived together for several years and had several children before they either willingly requested or were forced to resort to the ecclesiastic authorities for the regularization of their union. The argument most frequently used by the man to request such regularization, and dispensation of consanguineous ties when it was required, reflects not only the rationalization of sin most akin to colonial mentalities, but also the arguments most likely to yield a positive ecclesiastical response. The most frequent reasons given to formalize a relationship were the man's desire to repay the woman for her favors, the need to protect the woman from poverty or even prostitution, the restitution of her honor, and the legitimization of the fruits of the union. Women suing men for default of marriage word stressed primarily the loss of their reputation. Some of the other arguments were more contrived than real, especially in instances when the couple had been living together for many years without benefit of public or religious approval.[38] However, public shunning or social pressure were not factors to be dismissed lightly. In rural areas or in small towns, a couple living together almost always received some form of public notoriety, and it was a question of time before some pious neighbor, better to serve God, would denounce them to the ecclesiastical authorities if they did not seek dispensation and penitence.

Most legal suits commenced by women for breach of promise initially demanded marriage, but some women and parents were willing to settle for a dowry, which was assumed to allow the woman to find a husband, not to mention the fact that it was a "price" for the loss of virginity.[39] In those instances where the final settlement for a dowry is available, it is clear that the social position of the woman determined the amount of the dowry. Doña Josefa Monasterios, the San Luis Potosí woman mentioned above, was awarded one thousand pesos, while a more humble mulatto woman was awarded one hundred pesos as damage payment for the relationship she had carried with a white man.[40]

The tensions created by suits over loss of virginity and palabra de casamiento revealed yet another significant nuance in the male-female relationships of the period. Marriage could not be forced on an unwilling party, and this traditional assumption protected many men. It was not a factor which could be taken for granted by any man before the final ecclesiastical settlement, however, since the church resolved all issues in a casuistic manner. To avoid the threat of being forced to marry or endow a woman, a man involved in a suit would question her morals, and cast doubts upon her behavior and the general tone of her life. Thus, he put her as much on trial as she had put him. Legal suits were lengthened for months while the parties argued and counterargued over the validity of their witnesses' words. When Rosa de Piedra, finding herself pregnant, sued Antonio de Zárate for loss of virginity, he argued that before he met her she had had relations with other men. She had also left her Guadalajara home for several weeks before the initiation of their relationship. The inquiry carried out as part of the investigation of charges contained questions to verify stories about Rosa and, put together with pieces of information provided by other witnesses, reveals the public character of personal relationships in small rural towns. Rosa had been seen closeting herself with a man on certain holidays and was supposed to having been caught in bed with yet another one from Aguascalientes. Her reputation as a *doncella* (a virgin) was questionable and questioned. Whether or not a woman was publicly held as honorable and virginal had a great deal to do with her social status and with her credibility, in case of a loss-of-virginity suit. In this instance Rosa was held a *mujer inquieta,* a term that signified a woman of loose morality with several known lovers. Although the outcome of the suit is unknown, the chances of her establishing her virginity and thus her lover's liability for its loss, were very small after the details of her private life had been aired.[41]

Contrary to conventional wisdom, violence as a form of revenge does not seem to have been part of the rituals of redress of female honor. Ecclesiastical or civil authorities acted as social and legal mediators, following procedures that seemed to have satisfied most parties: imprisonment for the man and *depósito* for the woman, until the end of the inquiry and final judgment of the case.[42] Only exceptionally are cases of personal or familial violence recorded. In such cases the male relatives of the dishonored woman made public displays of anger, either in words or in actions, such as walking around town with arms in search of the responsible man. Such behavior warned him of potential physical harm if he did not proceed to regularize the relationship before any further violence was required.[43] It also publicized the fact that the woman had effective male protection, which was very important in a situation of female dishonor. A "protected" woman had better chances of obtaining redress than one without male backing.

One of the most unusual cases of violence recorded was that of a free mulatto seeking marriage with a white woman in Zamora in 1732. Reversing the usual legal process but proving that canon law could be equally applied to either party, he was suing the woman to fulfill her marriage word to him. He claimed that they had lived in an illicit union for six years, defying family opposition to marriage. That opposition reached a peak one evening when several of the woman's male relatives entered her lover's room and attempted to castrate him. During the inquiry the woman denied having had relations with the man, while he denied having been made incompetent for marriage and insisted on having her fulfill her promise to him. The final ruling upheld the family's argument. It was decided that the man was impotent and that the proposed marriage was "unequal." The woman was relieved from her marriage promise.[44] In this case the socioethnic prejudice against a man who was considered inferior in race and class was stronger than the desire to restore the woman's or the family's honor through marriage. The publicity given to the castration attempt precluded it and was also a powerful message to others who may defy the social prejudices of the ethnic élite.

The assumption that women needed protection was based on the notion that a woman's will and her honor were fragile possessions. Defending a white woman who had carried out an adulterous relationship with an Indian official in the town of San Sebastián, San Luis Potosí, the lawyer developed the argument that women were weak and malleable (*deleznable*), especially if persuaded by a good talker. He recalled the example of Eve and requested a pardon for his client, who shared in the general fragility of her sex. This example illustrates how deeply rooted was the concept of the female proclivity for breaking the law of God. "Sinfulness" was almost a natural female characteristic, part of her nature. She was not accountable for it, however, and the law should be lenient about her inconsistencies and intrinsic feebleness.[45] Under such circumstances, those women who initiated suits without male representation showed remarkable strength. An important factor in their decision, however, was their knowledge that they were appealing to the institution that, despite its traditional misogynist stand, still provided them a significant modicum of protection as long as they obeyed its rules of behavior or repented from their lack of observance of the religious canons. Weakness had its strengths. Women saw a "paternal" symbol in the church and felt confident that, even in a patriarchal society, the men of the cloth had many mechanisms at their disposal to make lay men answerable for their actions.

Distortion of the normal course of courtship could also take the form of abduction and elopement. Forcing a relationship on either a family or on an individual, such as in the cases of abduction or elopement, violated the trust, mutuality, and consent that the church regarded as indispensable conditions of acceptable sexuality. Furthermore, by sidestepping the regular canonical sequence in the rituals of marriage, abduction and elopement challenged the church itself.

The most frequent reasons for couples to elope were to overcome socioreligious opposition to the marriage or known consanguineous impediments that would require an ecclesiastical investigation. After living together for several weeks the man would request the blessing of the church to repair the woman's loss of virginity.[46] Both family and church were forced to accept a de facto marriage. Although elopement was often prompted by some perceived inequality in the man by the family of the woman, this was not always the reason, as corroborated by a case in which an alcalde eloped with the Indian maid of a priest, or other cases in which the couple belonged to comparable socioethnic groups.

The reaction against elopement was initially social. The aggrieved parties, for the most part family members, sought public revindication of their honor through the imprisonment of the man. Civil and ecclesiastical law strongly condemned elopement or abduction, and while the judgment of the spiritual transgression belonged to the church, the accused was physically under the jurisdiction of the state throughout the investigation and during his punishment. The fact that a suit against the eloping couple or the alleged abductor meant the "exposure" of the woman and the public acknowledgment of her loss of virginity did not seem to bother the relatives since the woman was depicted as a victim, deluded by the man's intrigues. The words used to describe the physical removal of a woman in elopement—*sustraer, extraer*—conveyed the idea of theft. The woman had been stolen from her family, whether or not she left willingly, and this backhanded manner of revealing the family's inability to defend its females and protect its own honor caused the greatest ire among the offended relatives. Despite all familial efforts, in practice eloped couples seem to have been not only willing partners in the escape but also able to evade the authorities. Some lived together for several years in another town before civil and ecclesiastical justice reached them. When that happened, the penalty was surprisingly mild. The customary "punishment" they would receive was to legalize their marriage, a solution that was easily adopted most of the time.

As a challenge to public morality and a defiance to norms of Christian behavior, elopement had its nuances and degrees of criminality. When a Tarascan Indian was accused of repeated elopements with a number of women of the Parral area, the attorney argued that in no case had the elopements been carried out with force. He stated that among the Tarascans, women easily left with any man who propositioned them, since they lacked "much understanding" of the implications of their actions. This diminished the degree of the offense. The sentence imposed on the accused man was temporary imprisonment in an hacienda.[47] On the other hand, the elopement of two religious men with young women of good families created a public stir leading to long criminal suits. In the case of Fr. Juan de Salazar, a lay Franciscan brother who lived with several women in the Querétaro–San Luis Potosí area, both civil and ecclesiastical justices pursued the case vigorously, because the "scandalous and atrocious" actions of the priest against religion had "filled the public with horror and fear of their reiteration for lack of punishment."[48] The socioethnic élite assumed that certain ethnic groups and the lower elements of society were more inclined to loose sexual behavior than they. An offense emanating from a member of the church and involving sacrilegious relationships, however, was a different matter and demanded a strong public censure.

Although consensual unions, whether of short or long duration, seem to have been frequent, adulterous concubinage formed a category by itself and was less defensible than relationships between single parties. Moral Theology was especially stern about adultery. It violated one of the two sexual bases of marriage, the prohibition of sharing the consort's flesh with that of another person.[49] Adultery was associated with insatiable and sinful lust that did not find enough satisfaction with one's spouse. Adulterers became like demented people and walked a road of long thorns that pierced the soul, according to an anonymous late-eighteenth-century Franciscan priest. His condemnation of men who abandoned their wives and children for another woman stressed the economic penalty paid by the family. For adulterous women he had stronger words. He quoted Saint John the Evangelist, who compared them to animals in heat, "lascivious unbridled beasts." Such women were as deadly as poison, the epitome of evil.[50]

In the daily experience of colonial life, it was the misappropriation of forms of behavior belonging canonically to married couples that raised personal and communal disapproval. Most cases of adultery came to the knowledge of ecclesiastical authorities via denunciations of "God-fearing" persons who saw themselves representing the community and its moral and social interests. Given the difficulties of proving actual adultery, witnesses would resort to circumstantial evidence, such as the prolonged time spent by the man in the home of his presumed mistress (*de puertas adentro*) or his open display of courtship forms (like riding behind her coach, or talking to her through a window). Whenever possible, ecclesiastical authorities admonished the guilty, trying to avert a public confrontation with the other consort and prompting the end of the relationship.[51]

Adultery investigations involved thorough and entailed depositions by several witnesses and the involved parties. In addition to jail sentences, the authorities could fine the male culprit with a heavy monetary fee. Ecclesiastical authorities imposed a strong religious penitence to recover the state of grace. In colonial society adultery by a man was viewed as a more excusable failing, one that would only bring him strong censure if it was carried out without discretion and in a manner offensive to the wife and the family. Women accepted this situation and were less likely to sue for separation or divorce on grounds of male adultery. They did have rights, however. Exercising those rights, wives could request their preferred form of punishment for an erring husband and his mistress. Most, however, were more interested in having the husband return to maintain the family.[52]

In the small towns and rural areas of central Mexico, when royal officials engaged in concubinage the ecclesiastical concern doubled, because public men were expected to be the role models for the nonelites. If, after receiving the benefit of ecclesiastical and civil advice, they persisted in their sinful behavior the ecclesiastical authorities moved against them and their mistresses. The official could be sent elsewhere or left in town but deprived of his mistress. The "erring" woman would be exiled from town, interned in a *casa de recogidas* or in depósito in a private home.[53] Such ecclesiastical intrusion was more difficult with powerful men in the social hierarchy.

Instances of concubinage among Indians suggest that a certain degree of community action was taken before calling in the ecclesiastical authorities. Before the Conquest, indigenous societies exerted strong communal pressures in sexual matters, and this cultural trait does not seem to have changed significantly.[54] Agustín Gabriel, of Charo in Michoacán, having found his wife in an illicit relationship with his cousin, sent her to their "own" Indian community judge to be punished. In San Luis Potosí, Indian and ecclesiastical authorities agreed to act against a couple living in adulterous concubinage by entering the house at night and finding the couple in bed. Having undeniable evidence of the adultery, the man was temporarily exiled from town and the woman sent to a *depósito*, as she did not have a home of her own.[55] The "governor" of the Indian towns or neighborhoods was often involved, acting in conjunction with the Spanish authorities. Although the men involved spent part of the time in the public jail, the aim of the authorities was to end the relationship and remove the bad example from the community.[56]

As in the case of premarital sex, violent revenge for adultery does not appear to have been common. One murder in Parral illustrates how the feeling of stained honor moved men to kill.[57] This case took place in an hacienda, where a mulatto blacksmith, married to an Indian woman, claimed that he had found her and her lover in bed. Without much warning or argument he shot the presumed lover to death. In his own declaration he expressed no sorrow and expected to be declared innocent (*porque me hallo inocente de culpa por el mal caso en que cayó el dicho en ofensa mia*). A milder response was found among other husbands. A small-town hatmaker claimed to have born his cuckoldry with fortitude, even though the open relationships of his wife led people in his town of Apaseo to place cattle horns in front of his house. After eight years of separation he finally requested that she return to him or be sent to a convent. She refused to return to him, and possibly got her way. Other men seem to have been satisfied with a public denunciation of the lover, while yet others preferred to weather the situation or to settle it privately to avoid having "their dishonor" made public.[58] In some instances the husbands tried to avoid a public disclosure, but the gossip about their honor obliged them to take action against the offender. As in other cases involving sexual transgressions, what became public knowledge (*de voz pública*) required some form of social redress. For men who were unable or unwilling to resort to violence, the exposure and shunning of the wife and the imprisonment of the lover were satisfactory solutions. In a case in Parral the adulterous wife was condemned to stay secluded in a home for eight months, at the end of which time she would return to her home if her husband so wished. Another aggrieved husband asked the ecclesiastical authorities to repair his honor by sending his wife to a convent and punishing the lover according to their own judgment.[59]

Among the sexual transgressions reported to ecclesiastical authorities, many had incestuous overtones. Canon law defined "incestuous" as not only relationships within the forbidden degrees of relatedness, direct or transversal, such as between parents and children and brothers and sisters, but also those among relatives such as aunts and nephews or first cousins, and among affinal relatives.[60] Relations of a woman with two male cousins, or between an aunt of the bride and the potential groom, or between the groom and a sister-in-law were canonically incestuous, yet not at all rare in colonial records. Dispensation for such relations was never assured, although an inclination towards leniency—whenever canonically permissible—is patent in the cases in which the final judgment is available.

When dispensation was denied it seems that the authorities wished to mark the limits of public impropriety. Raymundo Velázquez, a white man from Huehuetoca, wished to marry a widow who had had adulterous relations with his own uncle while her husband was still alive. The religious authorities denied the dispensation on grounds of incestuous relations in the first and second degree due to illicit sexual relations, adding that an adulterous woman could hardly be expected to remain faithful in her second marriage.[61] Ignacio Ramírez, a mulatto hacienda resident, was condemned to exile in Havana after both having relations with two sisters and their mother and marrying one of the girls without confessing the impediments. The ecclesiastical authorities refused his petition to revalidate his marriage to "save" the honor of the girl and legitimate their child.[62]

Other instances of incestuous relationships found in the records were created by the close family ties existing in rural areas and the limited range of choice of partners for proper marriage among certain groups. In areas such as Saltillo and Monterrey many of the white families were related by marriages, and some of their members argued that it was difficult to find partners who were not connected by some degree of blood affinity. The fact that unchecked extramarital sexual relations commonly produced offspring complicated "proper" marriage for some couples who, on wishing to regularize their consensual unions, found out that they were related to some degree, either as children of out-of-wedlock unions or due to known illicit relationships among their ancestors.[63]

Rape posed the most severe moral challenge to ecclesiastical and civil authorities. Despite the strong religious and social condemnation of this crime, however, the weight of the punishment meted out did not always measure up to the assumed abhorrent nature of the crime. The usual punishment for rape was public shunning, imprisonment for a period of time, and corporal punishment (two hundred lashes in the sternest case). The man was then ordered to return to his legal wife and to carry out marital life without any further cause of public scandal. In cases of husbands who had forced sexual relations with their wive's niece and daughter, the repentance and penitence of the culprits was deemed sufficient punishment. In one instance the priest acting in the case ordered the removal of the young victim from the house, while in another she was sent to a depósito to learn Christian doctrine and to be held in honest seclusion at the discretion of the ecclesiastical authorities.[64]

Two recent studies of rape in the eighteenth century help delineate some of its main contours. Rape knew no racial barriers, but it most often committed against young rural and poor girls under nineteen who were not carefully guarded by their families. They were the victims of men who seem to have known their habits well and assaulted them when left alone or sent alone for work or errands. Indian girls were more exposed and the most frequent victims of reported cases. Itinerant men of dubious reputation and between the ages of twenty and thirty were the most frequent aggressors. As with other sexual crimes, rape became a community concern and public knowledge through the investigation process. A midwife was usually called to establish the damage suffered by the victim, and the girls were questioned in an effort to determine the degree of malice and force used by the rapist. The sum of evidence gathered in terms of the physical examination of the girl and the identification and questioning of the culprit was deemed sufficient to issue a verdict. As the authorities in a 1642 Parral case stated, rape was difficult to prove for lack of witnesses and "it was enough to have sufficient indications of its occurrence."[65]

Despite the readiness to punish the crime of rape with haste, the mechanisms of justice had little to offer to the women involved. The only redress available to the victims of rape was a financial recompense. In the Parral case one hundred pesos endowment was determined to be an adequate sum. When parents prosecuted for repair of rape damage, they were interested in monetary compensation, but suing the rapists seemed to have been the exception rather than the rule. Although the forcible rape of small girls and young women was a crime distinct enough not to be confused with other forms of behavior, the terms *violación* and *estupro* carried a certain ambiguity, and they were also used in circumstances that did not involve forced sexual relations. Here, the assimilation of socioreligious values is betrayed by the vernacular forms of speech. Thus, in the confessions of illicit relationships or in the legal suits about loss of virginity, the expression *violó mi virginidad* is very common, and yet the relationships described were voluntary. The loss of the state of virginity—regardless of whether the woman had consented—if taking place outside the state of matrimony implied an inflicted violence, one for which the man was assumed to be responsible because a degree of seduction had been used.[66] However, both parties bore the brunt of penitence because both had participated. In the forcible rape of nonconsenting females, their innocence exempted them from sharing the burden of sin, while the man not only sinned but committed a crime.

Débito Matrimonial and the Control of Conjugal Sexuality

Conjugal relations, the only outlet to human sexuality bearing the endorsement of the church, were too important to escape definition, scrutiny, and regulation. Marriage consisted in the physical union of the bodies. The essence of the sacrament was carried out by the actors themselves, and the priest performing the ceremony was regarded as a witness in the name of God and the church. Nonetheless, the church was entitled to define not only the purpose but the manner of sexual relations as part of its pastoral duties.

Unquestionably, the church did not neglect to assume that responsibility and did not recoil from emphasizing the sexual base of marriage in all its implications. In 1587, over twenty years after the Council of Trent, the Pope sought to amplify the physiological meaning of the sexual act by stating that it had to be open to, and capable of, procreation (*generationi aptum*). This capability was defined in masculine terms. For a marriage to be considered complete and valid, seminal emission had to occur during intercourse. This definition used the only possible active physical evidence of sexuality at the time: that of the man, but in a sense it confused potency with fertility.[67]

The papal statement revealed a key concern of the Counter-Reformation church: that the procreative purpose of marital relations be clearly understood by all. Pursuing such understanding, the confessional of Fr. Clemente Ledesma examined six potential objectives in the conjugal union: 1. the propagation of the species, 2. the satisfaction of the *débito* (debt, duty) to preserve the faith upon which marriage was built, 3. the respect of the sacrament, which meant the indissoluble union of human nature with the church, 4. the preservation of the body's health, 5. the prevention of concupiscence, 6. the sole pleasure of the sexual act.[68]

He affirmed that procreation for the preservation of the human species was to remain the main purpose of marriage and that any action taken to impede it was sinful.[69] While four of the remaining objectives were acceptable, the sixth was not. This denial posed a most important moral dilemma to all couples: that of assessing the importance of procreation vs. pleasure. Since the church prescribed that licit enjoyment of sex could take place only within marriage, how much pleasure could a couple take in the sexual act? Confessors explained that physical expressions of love such as kissing, touching, and embracing were permissible to the extent that they stimulated mutual love. However, certain boundaries did exist. Pleasure for pleasure's sake, excessive enjoyment of the "delectations" of the flesh, and situations leading to "pollution" outside the sexual act were condemned as indecent and alien to Christian modesty and leading to mortal sin.[70] These dicta applied to both sexes.

At the very foundation of conjugal relationship lay a concept of "justice" in the sexual exchange, which served to ascertain the practical ways of fulfilling the marital duty (*débito matrimonial*). Since sexual relations were described in contractual terms, confessors and moral theologians sought to establish what was "just" in the sexual act. Justice was achieved by balancing the request and the payment between the sexual partners. Ecclesiastical knowledge was the result of a long exposure to problems of marital sexuality, and most of the advice contained in confessionals are efforts to maintain peace within married couples. Amicably requested and denied débito was just and acceptable if both partners agreed. Unreasonably frequent requests were unjust on the partner who had to pay, but if discords or sexual "incontinence" outside the home ensued, the requested spouse should accede for "charity's sake." Temperance in the use of the débito was the recommended rule. Spouses who indulged excessively in sexual relations could exhaust their sexual abilities—a medical assumption of the period—and thus become unable to pay the débito, which was an act of injustice to the partner. Equally unjust was the situation in which one spouse used too much corporal penitence on him/herself and exercised sexual abstention that could ultimately lead to the impairment of the sexual faculties.[71]

A number of "just" causes permitted denial of payment of the débito. Fear of endangering either one's own life due to infectious illness in the consort or that of the offspring conceived in the act was cause for abstinence. If a pregnant woman had reason to believe the fetus could die as a result of sexual relations she could deny it. Débito requests that would lead to mortal or venial sin, such as those from a legally or spiritually consanguineous person or in any of the physical positions prohibited by the church, could also be denied.

Although the confessionals tried to be gender-unspecific, it is obvious that some of this advice was intended either for the wife or for the husband. Excessive frequency of request was most likely addressed to men; charity and forbearance in the toleration of undesired relations, to the women. In practice, women had few possibilities of escaping the obligation to pay the débito when requested. Husbands were more likely to raise complaints about their wives' noncompliance to a Christian duty. In all cases, a dialogue of power was established through sexual relations. Due to the rigid privacy in which sexual relations were maintained, verification of such exchange will remain difficult. That such a dialogue was, nonetheless, real is indicated by the evidence disclosed in several available cases.

Under normal circumstances only occasional references were made in legal suits or ecclesiastical records to the intimate details of débito matrimonial, *uso del matrimonio,* or *vida maridable.* When an abandoned wife requested the ecclesiastical authorities that her husband be returned home to carry on their married life (*para hacer vida maridable*), she was undoubtedly referring to marital cohabitation, as was the judge issuing such return order. Under the stress of marital quarrels, abandonment, or emotionally charged relationships, husbands and wives became sometimes more explicit about the sexual basis of their disagreement. Joseph de Ibarra, suing his wife to obtain her forced return to their home, complained to the authorities that her family had instigated her to deny him the débito, as she had indeed done.[72] Juana Ortiz, married by force by her mother, confessed to have refused the débito to her husband for fifteen days but finally gave in under the physical abuse of her husband and mother.[73]

More specific was the suit of María Francisca Velarde, who abandoned her husband Vincente Alvarez after three years of marriage. As he complained of being rebuffed (*desaires* and *repugnacias*) by his wife and of the denial of marital rights, "as God orders," she declared that her husband had made "excessive and vicious demands" on her (*por serlo en sumo grado [excesivo y visioso] su esposo*). Marital obligations were "notoriously against her health." During her marriage, she claimed, she had not experienced an hour of pleasure, and had been plagued by constant ailing, thus offering reasons for the imbalance in the marital correspondence. In response, Alvarez argued that his wife's capricious arguments could deprive him neither of the right he had over her person as her legitimate husband nor of her company and her marital gifts (*obsequios*). His claim was based on the "reciprocal exchange of services," a passage of the suit underlined by a legal hand. Alvarez suggested that his wife be punished on account of the scarcity and repugnance he had tolerated from her in the payment of the marital debt.[74] In this unusual disclosure the débito appears as the symbol of the wife's submission, since she could only deny her husband his sexual requests under fear of physical damage. This explains why the woman's attorney tried to make a case against the importunate request of the marital obligation on grounds of health. The ecclesiastic attorney showed discomfort with the public disclosure of "defectos ocultos" in the marriage but, avoiding the issue of the husband's sexual demands, stated that his alleged mistreatment had not reached the degree of abuse to merit a divorce. But, while canon law dictated female compliance, in practice some women succeeded in avoiding it. In this case the wife appears to have claimed the last victory. In 1766 the husband was still claiming her from Puebla, where he had moved.

The divorce suit of Andrea de España was also largely based on conjugal disagreement over what was a reasonable sexual life. She claimed that her husband, Mateo de Velasco, made unusual and frequent demands of débito. Apparently obsessed by unfounded jealousies, Mateo requested conjugal relations during the day and at a frequency that his wife found unreasonable. When she refused to pay the débito they had loud and heated arguments, overheard by all the neighbors, and he often ended beating her. She claimed that débito should be paid "proportionately," and at night. During the ensuing inquiry the ecclesiastical judges requested several witnesses to express their opinions on the subject. A friend of the husband acknowledged that he had advised him that a husband "could have [his wife] whenever he wished." On the other hand, a married woman friend of the couple stated that she had told Mateo that sexual relations had to be "as God ordered, without lust, and not too often" (*"como Dios mandaba, no con lujurias, a cada ratito"*). However, a sixty-year-old spinster (*doncella*) advised the wife never to deny the débito to her husband. Andrea confessed that her anger and her husband's crazed behavior drove her to deny him sexual relations (*por sus incontinencias se lo negaba de enfadada*).[75] No common agreement was found among the witnesses on the "normal" frequency of intercourse, but the old spinster's submissive advise matched the men's view that women should make themselves available on their husbands' terms. Between the anger of the young woman and the advice of the married matron ran a common thread: the feminine hope and desire for consensus on the frequency of débito and a modicum of self-regulation in the man. Their opinion, not surprisingly, coincided with the advice of the church on the subject. However, ecclesiastical rules for the regulation of conjugal relations were weakened by the repudiation of the possibility of the denial of sex and by a heavy reliance on mutual understanding to maintain matrimonial harmony. The few available records speak of difficulties in communication between couples and of sexual relationships fraught by opposite interpretations of domination and submissiveness.

Canonical regulation of marriage gave the church other rights over the sexual lives of colonial couples. It was possible for a priest to ban relations between a husband and wife when either party had engaged in an incestuous or adulterous relationship until the guilty party repented and returned to the fold of the church through penitence. Thus, if a couple was involved in the investigation of concubinage, the right to reinitiate intercourse had to be approved by the priest. This was called *habilitación de matrimonio*. In 1687, Lorenzo de Roelos, of Valladolid, appealed to his spiritual adviser for permission to request and pay the marital débito after ending a relationship with his wife's cousin.[76] In the case of an Indian woman who had carried on illicit relations with her husband's brother before her marriage, the priest determined that the union was illegal and requested a dispensation to legalize the marriage from Bishop Elizacochea of Michoacán. In the meantime he advised the woman "not to ask or pay the débito because if she did, she sinned mortally." Should she be requested by her consort, she should feign herself sick to avoid "an offense against God."[77]

Another form of sexual regulation was the dispensation of the mortal sin incurred by *pacto nubendi*. This referred to adulterous relationships carried out by a married person who made a pact to marry his or her lover after the death of the spouse. The Archbishop of Mexico, Antonio Núñez de Haro, granted dispensation to at least eight of these cases in 1789.[78] Indians, whites, and mestizos were all represented in these adulterous relationships, which took place during the sickness of a spouse. In one case the request for dispensation commented on the inability of the church to control the sexuality of the couple.[79] Marriage, in these cases, was adopted as the Pauline solution for sin. The experience of many a parish priest left him with little hope of instilling self-control among the majority of the people. Acting on the recommendation of the priest of Sultepec, the religious attorney of the Archbishopric of Mexico recommended the blessing of the marriage of a couple who had been living consensually because "these working people are of a licentiousness that Your Excellence does not ignore, and the priest is afraid that he will elope with her and their souls will be left without remedy."[80] The parish priest's first-hand knowledge of the personal difficulties encountered by his flock in regulating their sexual relations was considerable. It should not be surprising that the anonymous author of a book of advice for married couples instructed them on how to behave when crowded living quarters made difficult or impossible the payment of the conjugal debt in intimacy. Married couples should deprive themselves of what otherwise would be licit, if children or servants could see or hear them. Children should sleep separate from their parents, so as not to encourage them to do what they saw their parents do.[81] Although he chose not to go beyond this allusion, counting on the understanding of his readers, this veiled comment points to the lack of privacy in which many people carried out sexual relations and to the church's concern about the possible shocking impression on children caused by the discovery and witnessing of their parents' sexuality. It was also assumed that promiscuity was a learned behavior.

In addition to the regulation of sexual life in the stated cases, the clergy had the right to bring together couples who lived separate for a number of reasons. Repeatedly, bishops and vicars gave orders, under pain of excommunication, to husbands and wives to return to their homes and live with their consorts. Neither sex was favored over the other; both consorts had the same duties, and rarely did the ecclesiastic authorities allow any appeal of their decisions.[82] Several situations leading to such separations became possible in daily life, although none could receive the approval of the church. Men could leave their homes to engage in trading or mining or because they developed total distaste for their partners. While the abandonment of wives was more common, the abandonment of husbands was by no means a rarity. In most of the cases in which the husband demanded the return of his wife home to carry out marital life, the wife had left him due to bad treatment.[83] The descriptions of physical abuse suggest a strain of sexual sadism in some husbands but also the prevalent assumption that husbands had the right to administer some physical "discipline" to their wives. Women suffered beatings with sticks, straps, firearms, and stones. They were threatened or hurt with knives and firearms, thrown out of their homes, and humiliated publicly by husbands before they decided that they could stand no more such mistreatment.[84] The majority, however, opted to suffer and remain silent rather than rebel against their husbands. Only a small number of battered or mistreated wives refused further *ayuntamiento carnal* (carnal union) with their husbands, choosing to return to their families or to appeal to ecclesiastical authorities to obtain better treatment from their spouses.[85] The exacerbation of marital tensions was the result of the inflexible rule of the church in regard to the obligation of carrying out vida maridable. In the sexual dialogue of power within marriage, the woman's position was weakened by the circumstances of her economic dependence, lesser physical strength, legal and social subordination to her husband and, not the least, by her "obligation" to fulfill the physical demands of matrimony.

A survey of normative sources and the activities of ecclesiastical courts in midcolonial Mexico confirms a tight theological interpretation of sexual relations. The actual behavior of people in the same period suggests, however, that the response to religious dictates was far from a uniform acceptance or conformity.[86] Men and women had subtle manners to avoid compliance, to challenge them, or to use them to their advantage.

Unquestionably, as a codifier of social behavior the church attempted to enforce its norms as strongly and broadly as it could. The detailed attention given to the classification of all possible forms of sexual behavior became a form of behavioral taxonomy in which only a narrow and precisely delimited territory was allocated for the expression of one of the strongest human drives. That such carefully defined norms had a powerful effect on social behavior is beyond doubt. The Inquisitorial and matrimonial records offer testimony to the pervasiveness of the religious message. Those who transgressed could be caught and punished. Men under trial were sent to the public jail. Women under scrutiny were separated from their families, either to be deposited somewhere else or to be sent to public institutions in case of stubborn recurrence. The curtailment of the personal freedom of the "sinners" was a somber reminder to all members of society of the power of the church. The fact that the transgressors of ecclesiastical norms resorted to self-denunciation or to confession of their own accord to ease their own feelings of guilt speaks of their ultimate acceptance. By the same token, those who followed the letter of ecclesiastical rules made sure to leave testimonies of their acquiescence and conformity "for the greater glory of God" (*para mayor honra de Dios*).

And yet, despite such carefully worded and exhaustively catalogued thesauruses of human weaknesses and the many institutional mechanisms available to the church, the same records testify of the uncontrollable nature of sexual behavior. Despite the language of regret and the formulae of penitence men and women acted their sentiments without undue regard to the consequences. Thus, some questions arise. How strong were those ecclesiastical pressures? What was the degree of institutional and collective intolerance? The ambivalence of the social situation in Mexico is obvious. Since the missionary friars confronted a process of conquest in which the sexual mores of the victors underwent significant relaxation, in practice the church had to bend and accommodate its theoretical norms to the social reality. By the seventeenth century certain cultural and behavioral patterns had already been set. A high degree of social tolerance lay behind the high incidence of consensual unions, the numerous illegitimate children, and the variety of ethnic mixtures. Recent demographic studies underline the magnitude of the problems created by what was basically an issue of sexual behavior. At the basis of these population trends are patterns of sexuality, personal choices of partners, and family formation that merit further consideration and show that a strong tension between norm and practice characterized the sexuality of the colonial population. Also important is the dilemma of the church, which in its role of guardian of sexual mores was caught between its own rigid standards and the inevitable acquiescence to the unruliness of human nature.

Acknowledgments

I would like to thank the Department of History of Howard University for a summer grant that supported part of this research. I am also in debt to Dauril Alden, Steve Stern, Edith Couturier, and Richard Boyer for reading earlier versions of this work and offering critical comments.

Notes

1. Archivo General de la Nación, Mexico City (hereafter AGN), Bienes Nacionales, leg. 742, exp. 44.

2. See Sergio Ortega, ed., *De la santidad a la perversión* (Mexico City: Editorial Grijalbo, 1985); *Familia y sexualidad en Nueva España* (Mexico City: Fondo de Cultura Económica, 1982); Solange Alberro, ed., *La actividad del Santo Oficio de la Inquisición en Nueva España, 1571–1700* (Mexico City: Instituto Nacional de Antropología e Historia, 1982); Noemí Quezada, *Amor y magia amorosa entre los aztecas* (Mexico City: Universidad Nacional Autónoma, 1975); William L. Sherman, "Manners and Morals in Sixteenth-Century Central America," paper given at the 1983 meeting of the American Historical Association in San Francisco; Ramón A. Gutiérrez, "From Honor to Love: Transformations of the Meaning of Sexuality on Colonial New Mexico," in *Kinship Ideology and Practice in Latin America* (Chapel Hill: University of North Carolina Press, 1984), ed. Raymond T. Smith, pp. 237–63. For the restraining effects of ecclesiastical control after Trent, see Joseph Klaits, *Servants of Satan: The Age of Witch Hunts* (Bloomington: University of Indiana Press, 1985), pp. 76–83.

3. Michel Foucault, *The History of Sexuality* (New York: Random House, 1978). John Van Engen argues the need to assess the value of religious source books in the shaping of "popular" Christian beliefs and practices. See John Van Engen, "The Christian Middle Ages as an Historiographical Problem," *American Historical Review* 91, no.3 (June 1986): 549.

4. In this essay I have used the cases known as *matrimoniales* under the jurisdiction of the ecclesiastical judges and the bishops. The majority of the

cases studied come from the records of matrimoniales of the Bishopric of Michoacán, between the years 1664 and 1800. They cover a broad geographical area within the bishopric, embracing rural and urban zones and a representative cross-cut of the various ethnic groups of colonial society. I have also examined the records of Parral, a mining town in northern Mexico, from 1642 through 1790 and matrimonial records from the core areas of New Spain and Guadalajara throughout the same period. The Criminal section of the Archivo General de la Nación in Mexico City holds many cases of sexual and moral transgressions among Indians. The notarial records of Mexico City, Guadalajara, and Puebla have also helped identify further individual examples of people coping with some of the problematic results of colonial sexual mores, such as the children born out of wedlock. They are also rich sources to study the subtleties in the use of social labels and practices to identify transgressions or compliance with social norms. I did not use Inquisitorial records because the Holy Office dealt only with cases of bigamy. Other forms of irregular sexual behavior were under the jurisdiction of the secular church.

5. See Stafford Poole, "The *Directorio para confesores:* Finishing the Counter-Reformation," paper presented at the 100th annual meeting of the American Historical Association, New York, 1985. Poole underscores the significance of the Fourth Provincial Council in New Spain in the task of implementing the directives emanating from Trent, stating that "the confessional, together with the parish mission, became one of the key means for securing a general improvement of morals and religious life." Church synods were also important in keeping an eye on the orthodoxy of behavior of both clergy and parishers. See, for example, Manuel Gutiérrez de Arce, *El Sínodo Diocesano de Santiago de León de Caracas de 1687* (Caracas: Academia Nacional de la Historia, 1975); Pedro Felipe de Azúa e Iturgoyen, *Sínodo de Concepción (Chile) 1744* (Madrid and Salamanca: Consejo Superior de Investigaciones Científicas and Universidad Pontificia de Salamanca, 1984).

6. The most important sixteenth-century inquiry into marriage and its meaning was that of Alonso de la Vera Cruz, who wrote a classic treatise on the matrimonial customs of the indigenous population and the theological problems they posed to Christianity (*Speculum coniugiorum*). In the seventeenth century the most distinguished canonist of marriage was Thomás Sánchez, who wrote *Disputationes de sacro matrimonium sacramentum*, 3 vols. (Madrid, 1602, 1605). Another theological treatise was that of Basilio Ponce de León, author of *Tractatus de sacramentum matrimonium* (Salamanca, 1624). See also Ernest J. Burrus, "Alonso de la Vera Cruz: Pioneer Defender of the American Indians," *Catholic Historical Review* 70, no.4 (Octo-

ber 1984): 531–46; Sergio Ortega Noriega, "Teología novohispana sobre el matrimonio y comportamientos sexuales, 1519–1570," in *De la santidad*, ed. Sergio Ortega, pp. 19–48.

7. The following confessionals and works on moral theology have been consulted: Anon., *Ave María Purísima: Breve instrucción a los cristianos casados y utiles advertencias a los que pretenden serlo*, 4th ed. (Mexico City: Imprenta de los Herederos del Lic. Don Joseph de Jauregui, 1791); Joan Baptista, *Advertencia para los confesores de los naturales* (Mexico City: M. Ocharte, 1600); Gabino Carta, *Práctica de confessores: Práctica de administrar los sacramentos, en especial él de la penitencia* (Mexico City: Viuda de Bernardo Calderón, 1653); *Cinco circunstancias de una buena confesión y método de examinar para ella la conciencia. Por un religioso de la regular observancia de N.P.S. Francisco* (Mexico City: Felipe Zúñiga y Ontiveros, 1788); Jaime de Corella, *Práctica del confesionario y explicación de las 65 proposiciones condenadas por la Santidad de N.S.P. Inocencio XI* (Valencia: Imprenta de Iaume de Bordazar, 1689); *Doctrina christiana y catecismo para instrucción de los indios y de las demás personas que han de ser enseñadas en nuestra Santa Fe. Con un confesionario y otras cosas necesarias para los que doctrinan* (Ciudad de los Reyes: Antonio Ricardo, 1584); Vicente Ferrer, *Suma moral para examen de curas y confesores* (Mexico City: Imprenta Nueva Madrileña de D. Felipe de Zúñiga y Ontiveros, 1778); Clemente de Ledesma, *Confesionario del despertador de noticias de los Santos Sacramentos* (Mexico City: María de Benavides, Viuda de Juan de Ribera, 1695); Juan Machado de Chávez, *Perfeto [sic] confesor y cura de almas* (Madrid:Viuda de Francisco Martínez, 1646); Juan Antonio de Oviedo, *Destierro de ignorancias: En orden al más acertado y fácil uso de los santos sacramentos* (Mexico City: Imprenta de D. Francisco Xavier Sánchez, 1738); Pablo Señero, *El penitente instruído para confesarse* (Mexico City: Juan José Guillena Carrascoso, 1696); Juan de la Torre, *Espejo de la filosofia y compendio de toda la medicina theórica y práctica* (Amberes: Imp. Plantiniana de Baltasar Moreto, 1668); Diego de Torres, *Vida natural y católica* (Madrid: Imprenta del Convento de La Merced, 1734). For an analysis of confessionals in Portuguese and used in Brazil, see Lana Lage da Gama Lima, "Aprisionando o desejo: Confissao e sexualidade," in *História e sexualidade no Brasil*, comp. Ronaldo Vainfas (Rio de Janeiro: Graal, 1986), pp. 67–88.

8. A mortal sin leads to the condemnation of the soul; it "excludes from the kingdom of God." It needs to be confessed in the sacrament of penance. A venial sin "does not make it impossible for one to be intent upon God as the ultimate end" (*New Catholic Encyclopedia* [New York: McGraw Hill, 1967], 17

vols. See 13:241–45). For the Fathers of the church on sexuality, see Joyce E. Salisbury, "The Latin Doctors of the Church on Sexuality, "*Journal of Medieval History* 12, no.4 (December 1986): 279–90.

9. The Sixth Commandment forbade adultery. Seventeenth-century confessionals extended its purview to all sins generated by lust. The Ninth Commandment forbade desiring somebody else's wife. Moral theologians explained it as "ill wishes of the will against chastity." See Gabino Carta, *Práctica de confessores*, pp. 62v, 80.

10. A simple vow was that taken by *beatas* and lesser members of the male ecclesiastical hierarchy; a formal vow was that taken by ordained priests, monks, and nuns. Having sexual relations in a sacred place, such as the church or a cemetery, was also sacrilegious, even if the act was carried out between husband and wife. For further analysis of sin and its distinctions, see Bonaventure A. Brown, *The Numerical Distinction of Sins According to the Franciscan School of the Seventeenth and Eighteenth Centuries* (Washington, D.C.: Catholic University of America, 1948).

11. In determining the many nuances and degrees of sin, the ecclesiastical authorities did not always agree among themselves. Thus, a complicated casuistic examination of circumstances was undertaken by doctors in moral theology and confessors to determine the degree of sin and the qualifying circumstances surrounding it. Confessionals and moral theology writings often cite the opinions of several sources, some of whom may contradict the interpretation of the author.

12. Oviedo, *Destierro*, p. 39.

13. For a review of the ideas on the sexual nature of men and women and the meaning of sexuality in marriage prevailing in Europe in the sixteenth century, see Steven Ozment, *When Fathers Ruled: Family Life in Reformation Europe* (Cambridge, Mass.: Harvard University Press, 1983), pp. 10–12. See also Ana María Atondo, "De la perversión de la práctica a la perversión del discurso: La fornicación, " in *De la santidad*, ed. Sergio Ortega Noriega, pp. 129–64.

14. *Ave María Purísima*, pp. 8, 14–15, 17. As a counselor for the education of married women, Fr. Alonso de Herrera also advised against lust in marriage. See his *Espejo de la perfecta casada* (Granada: Blas Martínez, 1636), pp. 139–40. A man approaching his wife with unreasonable lust was compared to an adulterer: "*será muy grande [el pecado] el llegarse a la propia mujer como bestias, encendidos en fuego libidinoso.*" The Synod of Concepción (Chile) urged those who were to contract marriage to confess all their sins several days before the wedding. See Azúa e Iturgoyen, *Sínodo*, p. 90. The Synod of

Santiago de Cuba (1684) gave similar advice. See Juan García Palacios, *Sínodo Diocesana* (sic) (Havana: Imprenta del Gobierno y Capitanía General, 1844), p. 145.

15. Oviedo, *Destierro,* p. 39. In a recent work, Jean-Louis Flandrin points out that among the early Christian theologians the mention of love in the discussions of sexual practices between spouses is sorely missing. Only Thomás Sánchez and Francisco de Vitoria, in the sixteenth century, make concessions to that sentiment. It is perhaps due to this peninsular tradition that we have acknowledgment of passions and affection in the moral guides used in Spain and Spanish America during the seventeenth and eighteenth centuries. See Jean-Louis Flandrin, "Sex in Married Life in the Early Middle Ages," in *Western Sexuality: Practice and Precept in Past and Present Times,* ed. Philippe Ariès and André Béjin (Oxford: Basil Blackwell, 1985), pp. 114–29.

16. See Solange Alberro, "El discurso inquisitorial sobre los delitos de bigamia, poligamia y solicitación," in *La actividad del Santo Oficio de la Inquisición en Nueva España,* ed. Solange Alberro (Mexico City: Instituto Nacional de Antropología e Historia, 1981), pp. 215–26; Dolores Enciso, "Bígamos en el siglo XVIII," in *Familia y sexualidad,* pp. 267–74, and "Un caso de perversión de las normas matrimoniales: El bígamo José de la Peña," in Sergio Ortega, *De la santidad,* pp. 179–96. See also José Toribio Medina, *Historia del Tribunal del Santo Oficio de la Inquisición en México* (Santiago de Chile: Imprenta Elzeveriana, 1905), for citations of bigamy cases coming before the Inquisition.

17. The Council of Trent (1545–63) determined that impediments of consanguinity, incurred to the fourth degree of relatedness by previous councils, were to be reduced to the second degree, but the church stressed that such impediments applied both to legitimate and consensual unions. No changes were made on the impediments incurred by spiritual kinship. Stronger strictures were placed on the marriage between eloped couples and transient members of any parish. Concubinage was excoriated. The council also reiterated the need to respect the free will of the contracting partners. See Ignacio López de Ayala, tr., *El sacrosanto y ecuménico Concilio de Trento,* 5th ed. (Madrid: Imprenta Repulloa, 1817), pp. 293–309.

18. See August Knecht, *Derecho matrimonial católico* (Madrid: Editorial Revista de Derecho Privado, 1932). This source discusses the historical origins and development of all legislation on marriage. See also Justo Donoso, *Instituciones de derecho canónico americano,* 2 vols. (Valparaíso: Imprenta y Librería del Mercurio, 1849). Donoso was an expert Chilean canonist who wrote shortly after the closing of the colonial period and had a first-hand

knowledge of canonical law during that period. See also Carta, *Práctica,* p. 92; Machado de Chávez, *Perfeto Confesor,* pp. 463–65.

19. See Thomas Calvo's essay in this volume.

20. AGN, Bienes Nacionales, leg. 742. Among the localities registered were Texcoco, Metepec, Huehutla, Temoyan, Tesontepec, Tepoztlan, Itapalapa, and Tepetlastoc. Those living in ranchos or haciendas, either in Mexico City or in Michoacán, should be considered strictly rural people. On the other hand, the smaller communities partake of both rural and urban characteristics. The cases recorded in Criminales, involving mostly Indians, are sparse in occupational descriptions. Among those noted are small merchants, miners, and muleteers. Sixteenth-century cases do not state occupations. Women's occupations are missing.

21. The notarial records provide wills in which people acknowledged offspring born out of wedlock and some of the circumstances surrounding the upbringing of those children. The testators had also to declare their own birth status. These clues help identify the socioeconomic circumstances of many people. High-ranking members of society are less frequently represented in records of moral transgression, but by no means absent. See Ann Twinam's essay in this volume.

22. See figures of out-of-wedlock births provided by Thomas Calvo for seventeenth-century Guadalajara in his essay in this book.

23. Richard Greenleaf, "The Inquisition in Eighteenth-Century New Mexico," *New Mexico Historical Review* 60, no.1 (Spring 1985): 29–60; AGN, Criminales, vol. 57, exp. 4.

24. Genealogical Society of Utah, Archivo Histórico del Antiguo Obispado de Michoacán. (Hereafter referred to as GSU AHAOM.) Section 5, leg. 734, reel 763602, José Proquinto Acevedo, 1798. They probably were second cousins with related great-grandparents; in the same source see expedientes on Eusebio V. Zabala and María Eugenia Gaitán and on Vicente Valencia, Section 2, leg. 75. reel 751242; Isidro Pérez de Vargas, 1686, section 5, leg. 256, reel 733975; Juan Rueda, 1759, AGN, Bienes Nacionales, leg. 93, exp. 36; Salvador de Avila, 1789, leg. 742, exp. 39.

25. GSU, AHAOM, section 5, leg. 734, reel 763202, José Torres, español, 1798; section 5, leg. 770, reel 763247, Rosa de Espino, española, 1705; section 2, leg. 88, reel 757264, Cristóbal de la Cerda, mestizo, 1691; section 5, leg. 734, reel 763202, José Leandro de Chávez, *mulato,* 1798.

26. "*El amor hace suaves y dulces los trabajos, y como en la vida conyugal se ofrecen tantos y tan grandes, si falta el amor entre los casados, se vuelven intolerables—pero el amor los hace más fáciles,*" Anon., *Ave María Purísima: Breve Instrucción,* p. 13; Fr. Antonio de Guevara, *Libro primero de las*

epístolas familiares (Madrid: Real Academia Española, 1950), pp. 286–91, 369.

27. AGN, Bienes Nacionales, leg. 292, exp. 2. A love letter of the late 1790s is addressed to "*Amado: Dueño de mi vida*" (My love: lord of my life) and confesses these feelings: "Every day I wake up very happy thinking that you will be my lord and I yours. All my dreams, my thoughts, and my senses belong to you; I wish to speak of nothing else but you . . ." In a letter addressed to her husband in the late 1720s, a wife calls him "dear owner of my eyes" and "darling of my heart," although later on she temporarily left him on grounds of marital quarrels. See GSU, AHAOM, section 5, leg. 770, reel 763239, Doña Manuela Maldonado. Other eighteenth-century love letters contain expressions such as "*mi vidita,*" "*te adoro,*" "*corazón herido,*" and other endearments (Criminales, 215, fols. 109–39; 8, exp. 10; Bienes Nacionales, Leg. 1056, exp. 1).

28. GSU, AHAOM, section 18, leg. 2, reel 793805, María Francisca, mestiza, 1798; section 5, leg. 770, reel 763238, Francisca Méndez de Torre, española, 1720; María Teresa, española, 1721. The last used the term "*ruegos importunos*" to describe her lover's persuasive words. See also section 1, leg. 20, reel 778785, Josefa Sánchez de Aldana, 1700; section 5, leg. 734, reel 763202, Eusebio V. Zabala, español; AGN, Bienes Nacionales, leg. 742, no. 17, 39. "When I met the aforesaid Mariana I instigated and chased her to have her yield to the relationship," confessed Andrés de la Cruz, mestizo from Tesontepec, Mexico.

29. Alonso de Herrera, *Espejo de la perfecta casada*, pp. 145, 171. Wisely, he compared love to drunkenness.

30. GSU, AHAOM, section 5, leg. 770, reel 763238, María Manuela de Vargas, española, 1717.

31. GSU, AHAOM, section 5, leg. 770, reel 763238, José Dávila Morales a nombre de Josefa Monasterios, 1723.

32. For a full explanation of the meaning of betrothal in canon law, see Knecht, *Derecho matrimonial*, pp. 111–51; Daisy Rípodas Ardanaz, *El matrimonio en Indias* (Buenos Aires: Conicet, 1977), pp. 63–67. See my comments on betrothal in the introduction.

33. GSU, AHAOM, section 5, leg. 770, reel 763238, María Manuela de Vargas, 1717; section 1, leg. 20, reel 778785, Doña Josefa Sánchez de Aldana, 1700. A well-to-do white woman who tried to prove the double dealings of her lover pointed out that he had celebrated *esponsales* with another woman at night and with concealment, whereas everybody knew that such occasions were celebrated with joy and the attendance of relatives (*con regocijo y concurrencia de deudos*). Women of several ethnic groups declared having received ob-

jects such as rings, rosaries, medals, and pieces of cloth. Some had reciprocated by giving the men a handkerchief and several medals. References to this custom are found for both the seventeenth and eighteenth centuries. See AGN, Bienes Nacionales, leg. 742: 33; Criminales, 29, exp. 10. These cases refer to Indians in 1732 and 1799, indicating that they had assimilated this practice. See also section 5, leg. 770, reel 763239, Matilde de la Encarnación Cerrato, *mulata*, 1727; section 5, leg. 174, reel 768731, Isidoro Baquedano y Francisca Nicolasa Serdaneta, españoles, 1744. Ritual exchange of gifts was a custom also practiced in Brazil and some European countries. See André Burguière, "The Marriage Ritual in France: Ecclesiastical Practices and Popular Practices (Sixteenth to Eighteenth Centuries)," in *Ritual, Religion and the Sacred. Selection from the Annales. Economies, Sociétés et Civilisations*, ed. Robert Forster and Orest Ranum, vol. 7 (Baltimore: Johns Hopkins University, 1982); Maria Beatriz Nizza da Silva, *Sistema do Casamento*, pp. 84–89. For a discussion of betrothal and Canon Law in medieval France and England, see Charles Donahue, Jr., "The Canon Law on the Formation of Marriage and Social Practice in the Latter Middle Ages," *Journal of Family History* (Summer 1983), pp. 144–58.

34. For a discussion of honor, see Ann Twinam's essay in this volume. Records of suits for loss of virginity and attempt to enforce marriage promises are not preserved in any particular order in most ecclesiastical archives, making quantitative analysis difficult and time consuming, although potentially possible for future investigators. Researchers could compare the numbers of marriage permits in which premarital sex is confessed, against those in which no irregularities existed. This is the method used by Robert McCaa in a demographic study of a community in northern Chile. See Robert McCaa, *Marriage and Fertility in Chile: Demographic Turning Points in the Petorca Valley, 1840–1976* (Boulder: Westview Press, 1983).

35. GSU, AHAOM, section 2, leg. 101, reel 755456, Alonso Gómez de Esparza, español, 1698; section 2, leg. 35, reel 764998, Josefa de los Reyes, 1664.

36. GSU, AHAOM, section 2, leg. 101, reel 755456, Gregorio Pérez de Vargas, 1698; section 5, leg. 772, reel 763247, Luisa Lazcano, 1704, and María de Torres, 1706; section 5, leg. 770, reel 763239, María Teresa, española, 1721; section 5, leg. 36, reel 762781, María Sotelo, española, 1726.

37. GSU, AHAOM, section 2, leg. 101, reel 755456, Antonio Alonso, español, 1698; section 5, leg. 770, reel 763238, Antonio de Cárdenas, 1723; Salvador Romero, mestizo, 1720; Matías Corral, mulato, 1720; section 5, leg. 772, reel 763247, Luisa Lazcano, 1704; Antonio Zamudio, 1701. See Susan Socolow's work in this volume.

38. GSU, AHAOM, section 5, leg. 254, reel 753973, Juan de Chavarra, mu-

lato, 1756; section 5, leg. 174, reel 768731, Manuel Julian Vidal, español, 1744. See also Genealogical Society of Utah, Archivo de la Sagrada Mitra de Guadalajara. (Hereafter referred to as GSU, ASMG.) Matrimoniales, reel 167980, Matías Núñez, español, 1697. This man, for example, stated that he wished to marry the woman to save her from falling, as she was poor (*que no quede perdida, siendo como es pobre*). See also Cristóbal Torres, mulato, 1695, in the same source.

39. GSU, AHAOM, section 5, leg. 36, reel 768731, Antonia Méndez, 1732; GSU, ASMG, Matrimoniales, reel 167980, Domingo de Padilla, 1709; GSU, AHAOM, section 5, leg. 36, reel 762781, María de Sotelo, española, 1728; leg. 772, reel 763247, Francisca Torre, española, 1701. Torres sued a well-to-do man in San Miguel el Grande who had fathered her two children. He won the suit but gave her one thousand pesos for her upkeep and that of their natural children; section 2, leg. 35, reel 764998, Josefa de los Reyes.

40. GSU, AHAOM, section 5, leg. 772, reel 763247, Margarita Gutiérrez, mulata, 1703; section 5, leg. 770, reel 763238, José Dávila Morales, 1723.

41. GSU, AHAOM, section 2, leg. 102, reel 755458, Rosa de Piedra, 1699. When Catalina del Castillo sued Nicolás Morales for loss of virginity, he offered a settlement of clothes. She demanded money instead, later raising the amount she first claimed. He lost patience and, changing his mind about a settlement, demanded that she prove her loss of virginity, thus turning the challenge of proof on her. See section 2, leg. 86 bis, reel 757261, Josefa de los Reyes, 1693; section 2, leg. 102, reel 755458, Catalina del Castillo, 1699. The term *inquieta* was also used in a 1757 case in Huehuetoca to describe an adulterous woman who was presumed to have had many lovers. See Rosenbach Collection, Philadelphia, 462/25 pt. 11, no. 8, 175761.

42. *Depósito* was the term used for the internment of the woman under inquiry in a safe and moral home throughout the period of inquiry and until the final judgment in her case was rendered. Depósito could last for months. During this time, women were not supposed to leave the house in which they were "deposited." In the late eighteenth century the property of the man involved would be placed in escrow until the end of the suit. AGN, Criminales, 223, exp. 1; AGN, Criminales, 184, exp. 6.

43. GSU, ASMG, Matrimoniales, reel 167980, José Manuel Marín, *castizo*, 1692; GSU, AHAOM, section 5, leg. 770, reel, 762781, Francisco de Garibay, 1732.

44. GSU, AHAOM, section 5, leg. 36, reel 762781, Francisco de Garibay.

45. GSU, AHAOM, section 5, leg. 235, reel 772320, Sebastián de Jesús y María Isabel Navarro, española, 1759.

46. GSU, AHAOM, section 1, leg. 18, reel 778780, Antonio Díaz Comparán, 1674; section 2, leg. 89, reel 766499, Fr. Antonio Sánchez Caballero; section 11, leg. 1, reel 793803, Fr. Juan de Salazar, 1800; Archivo Histórico de Parral, Criminales, 1642 (Hereafter referred to as AHP). Cases of husbands eloping with another woman, or ecclesiastics abducting women, took place but do not appear to have been very frequent. Such cases added complications of adultery and sacrilege.

47. AHP, Criminales, 1720.

48. GSU, AHAOM, section 1, leg. 20, reel 778785, Antonio Samudio, 1701; section 1, leg. 1, reel 793803, Fr. Juan de Salazar.

49. Herrera, *Espejo*, pp. 131, 135, 137; Ferrer, *Suma Moral*, pp. 375–76; Machado de Chávez, *Perfeto confesor*, pp. 312–13. For a legal discussion of adultery see *Quarta partida*, Laws 7–8, 920–22 in Scott's translation.

50. *Ave Maria Purísima*, pp. 32–38.

51. GSU, AHAOM, section 2, leg. 76, reel 757243, Juan de Abrego, 1687; section 2, leg. 88, reel 757264, Alonso de Aviles, 1691; AGN, Criminales, 223, exp. 1; 142, exp. 18. For an Indian community in 1749 it was decreed that no adultery case should be considered unless the husband initiated it.

52. GSU, AHAOM, section 5, leg. 253, reel 753973. AGN, Criminales, 29, exp. 9. See also the essays by Boyer and Nizza da Silva in this volume, and Bernard Lavallé, *Divorcio y nulidad de matrimonio en Lima (1651–1700): La desavenencia conyugal como revelador social* (Bordeaux: Université de Bordeaux, 1986).

53. GSU, AHAOM, section 5, leg. 254, reel 753975, Pedro Alvarez, 1756; ibid., Joaquín Velázquez Duque de Estrada, 1756; section 1, leg. 18, reel 778780, Antonia Díaz, 1674.

54. Serge Gruzinski, "Matrimonio y sexualidad en México y Texcoco en los albores de la conquista o la pluralidad de los discursos," in *La actividad del Santo Oficio*, ed. Solange Alberro, pp. 19–74; Alfredo López Austin, "La sexualidad entre los antiguos nahuas," in *Familia y Sexualidad*, pp. 141–76.

55. GSU, AHAOM, section 2, leg. 81, reel 757248, Agustín Gabriel, 1688; section 5, leg. 235, reel 772320, 1759, Sebastián de Jesús.

56. AGN, Criminales, 40, exp. 21; 41, exp. 5; 57, exps. 2, 4; 138, exp. 24; 142, exp. 18; 190, exps. 6, 18, 19; 184, exp. 223, exp. 1.

57. AHP, Criminales, 1729.

58. GSU, AHAOM, section 2, leg. 76, reel 757243, Joseph de Abrego, 1687; section 5, leg. 253, reel 753973, Manuela Josepha Arreguín; AGN, Bienes Nacionales, leg. 292, exp. 1. Francisco Pía requested a divorce on grounds of adultery. Having been advised by friends to "return the offense" he chose against

it because "he did not wish his dishonor to become public." Cases found in Criminales involving adultery among Indians show similar calm responses from the husbands. See expedientes quoted in note 55.

59. AHP, Criminales, 1727, 1790; GSU, AHAOM, section 5, leg. 773, M.A. Torres, 1705; section 2, leg. 81, reel 757248, Agustín Gabriel, 1688. Ferrer stated that after two years of punishment an adulterous woman could return to her husband if he was willing to receive her. See *Suma moral*, pp. 353–72.

60. *Instituciones*, 2:157–58.

61. Rosenbach Collection, 462/25 pt. 11, no. 8, Juana G. Villareal, 1757–61.

62. AGN, Bienes Nacionales, 1056, exp. 1 (1777). Civil and ecclesiastical authorities demanded the full rigor of justice.

63. Knecht, *Derecho matrimonial*, p. 189. *Angustia loci* was the canonical dispensation applied in cases in which the birthplace and domicile town of the bride was too small for her to have a good opportunity to marry.

64. GSU, ASMG, reel 167980. See cases of Mateo García, Juan Sánchez Valdés, Francisco de la Garza and other members of his family, Juan de las Casas, etc.; GSU, AHAOM, section 5, leg. 734, reel 763202, Vicente de Valencia, 1798; leg. 254, reel 753975, Juan A. Gutiérrez and Francisco Ramírez, 1756.

65. Carmen Castañeda, "La memoria de las niñas violadas," *Encuentro* 2, no.1 (October–December 1984); 41–56; François Giraud, "Viol et société coloniale: Le cas de la Nouvelle-Espagne au XVIIIe siècle," *Annales: Economies, Sociétés, Civilisations* 41, no.3 (May–June 1986): 625–37; AHP, Criminales, 1642.

66. French canonists after Trent, and up to the early eighteenth century, supported the concept of seduction in cases of rape of minors. Other canonists argued that such interpretation was not in the spirit of the statements of the Council of Trent. See Donoso, *Instituciones*, 2:170.

67. This amplification of the concept of *per copulam aptam ad generationem* (capability to generate life) was issued at the request of the Spanish Nuncio, who asked for a dictate on whether or not eunuchs could be validly married. Since the finality of marriage was procreation, and eunuchs could not impregnate, the Pope invalidated their marriages. On the other hand, the marriage of old people was still acceptable even though procreation was not probable, because the male organs had not been mutilated. See Knecht, *Derecho matrimonial*, pp. 257–63. The *Partidas* dealt in detail with impotency, reflecting medieval concerns about spells and sustaining the ecclesiastical concept of the centrality of procreation in sexual relations. See *Quarta Partida*, Title VIII, pp. 913–16 in Scott's translation.

68. Ledesma, *Confesionario*, p. 336.

69. Some theologians were of the opinion that couples could agree "not to

have sexual intercourse to prevent a multitude of children." Common accord on this subject was essential, however, since the denial of payment of débito to prevent offspring was not acceptable to the church. See Ferrer, *Suma moral*, pp. 377–80.

70. Ibid., p. 382; Oviedo, *Destierro de ignorancias*, p. 49; Diego de Torres, *Vida natural*, p. 74; Ledesma, *Confesionario*, p. 336.

71. Ferrer, *Suma moral*, p. 379. Ferrer stated that there was no obligation to pay the débito when it was "requested much too frequently, which is repugnant to decency and health" (Ibid., p. 370). The *Partidas* endorsed the ecclesiastical duty of the débito even on days when the ecclesiastical calendar suggested avoidance of "carnal intercourse." "If one of them should make a request of the other for this purpose on any of these days, the latter should manifest no opposition, but is bound to comply." See *Quarta Partida*, Law VIII, p. 889 in Scott's translation.

72. GSU, AHAOM, section 1, leg. 20, reel 778785, María Ruiz, 1701; section 5, leg. 770, reel 763239, Angela Gómez y Juan Francisco de los Reyes, españoles, 1724. Angela had rejected her husband, "not wanting to sleep with him one night." She had had an adulterous relation with another man, bearing him three daughters with the knowledge of the husband. Her priest confessed having given up on her spiritual salvation, due to her obstinate refusal to return to her husband. As a punishment for refusing to carry out *vida maridable* with her spouse, he had held her in deposit, far from the town of San Pedro Petatlan, where the couple resided.

73. GSU, AHAOM, section 2, leg.75, reel 757242, Da. Juana Hortiz, 1686. The use of force in marriage was a cause for invalidation. In these cases, however, it is obvious that neither the woman was aware of Canon Law nor did the priest care to enforce it. See section 5, leg. 773, reel 763247, Catarina del Castillo, 1711.

74. GSU, AHAOM, section 5, leg. 235, reel 772320, Vicente Alvarez, 1759.

75. AGN, Bienes Nacionales, leg. 911, Mexico, 1715. Separated for some time from her husband, Andrea returned to him when she found herself pregnant.

76. GSU, AHAOM, section 2, leg.76, reel 757243, Lorenzo de Roelos, 1687.

77. GSU, AHAOM, section 5, leg. 254, reel 753975, Ber. Joseph de Pereda, 1756. See also section 5, leg. 254, reel 753975, Juana María Briceño, 1757. These cases were based on the concept of diriment impediment of consanguinity in the first degree, on the transversal line.

78. AGN, Bienes Nacionales, leg. 93, unnumbered expedientes. See Donoso, *Instituciones*, 2:160.

79. AGN, Bienes Nacionales, leg. 93. The priest referred to *"el peligro de*

incontinencia que resulta de una amistad tan inveterada, y de una reincidencia tan contumaz es difícil de evitar por otro medio que el del matrimonio. . . ."

80. Ibid., leg. 93. Simple vows of chastity made by the laity were impendient impediments. They had to be rescinded by the bishop. A Chalco man who had made a rash vote of chastity at eighteen requested to be released because he was "gravely agitated by the stimulus of concupiscence." His petition was granted. Ibid.

81. *Ave María Purísima,* p. 45.

82. GSU, AHAOM, section 2, leg. 56, reel 765260, Juan de Arias, 1675; section 2, leg. 192, reel 755458, Nicolás Patiño, 1699, section 3, leg. 772, reel 763247, María de Silva, 1705; Da.Catarina Martínez de Borja, 1706. There are many other cases for the 1710s; section 5, leg. 254, reel 753975, Francisco Téllez Carvajal, 1756; GSU, ASMG, Matrimoniales, hojas sueltas, reel 167971. See investigations of Juan de Dios Rivera, Vicente López, and Juan de Salvada, 1691, 1692.

83. See Richard Boyer's paper in this volume.

84. AGN, Criminales, 29, exp. 9, 1800; 138, exp. 24, 1785; 140, exp. 18, 1749; 190, exp. 6, 1802; 176, exp. 5, 1753. GSU, AHAOM, section 1, leg. 10, reel 778780, Antonia de la Cruz, *india*, 1687; section 2, leg. 56, reel 765260, 1675; section 2, leg. 60 bis, reel 765269, Joseph de las Heras, 1678; section 1, leg. 20, reel 778785, María Ruiz, 1701; section 5, leg. 770, reel 763238, José Manuel Méndez, 1723. These forms of physical abuse were experienced by women of all ethnic groups, and they could be just cause for divorce if the wife decided to request it. See work by Maria Beatriz Nizza da Silva in this volume. For a study of divorce proceedings in nineteenth-century Mexico, see Silvia Arrom, *La mujer mexicana ante el divorcio eclesiástico* (Mexico City: SepSetentas, 1976).

85. GSU, AHAOM, section 5, leg. 770, reel 763239, Manuela Maldonado, 1728. She entered a convent after leaving her husband for bad treatment.

86. All the essays in this book corroborate the existence of a dialectic of power and defiance between socioreligious norms dictated by the church and the people who challenged them.

6. Sexually explicit drawing. Cartoon-like "bubbles" refer to "powers" given to choose husbands in metaphorical obscure language. Source: Archivo General de la Nación, Mexico City, Inquisición, vol. 1505, exp. 3 (1789).

(*on page 94*)

7. Sexually explicit drawing showing couples. Garbled messages refer to the loss of virginity by a woman and a condemnatory allusion to anal sex. Source: Archivo General de la Nación, Mexico City, Inquisición, vol. 1505, exp. 3 (1789).

8. Drawing with human and animal couples alluding to marriage, and fountain scene with sexual symbols. Source: Archivo General de la Nación, Mexico City, Inquisición, vol. 1505, exp. 3 (1789).

simiento

Casamiento

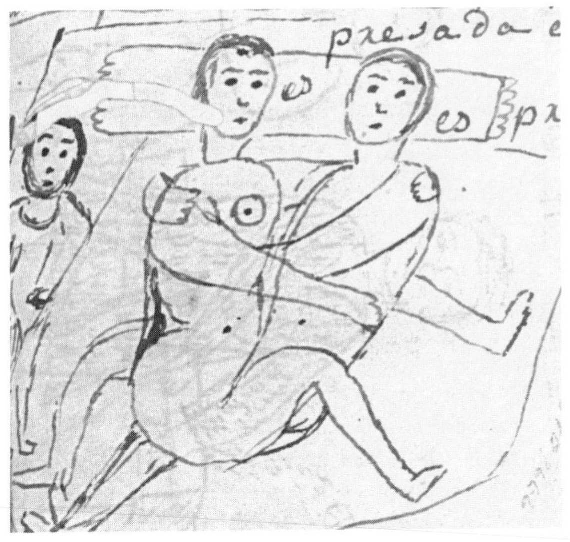

9. Drawing showing a couple engaged in sexual intercourse. Source: Archivo General de la Nación, Mexico City, Inquisición, vol. 1505, exp. 3 (1789).

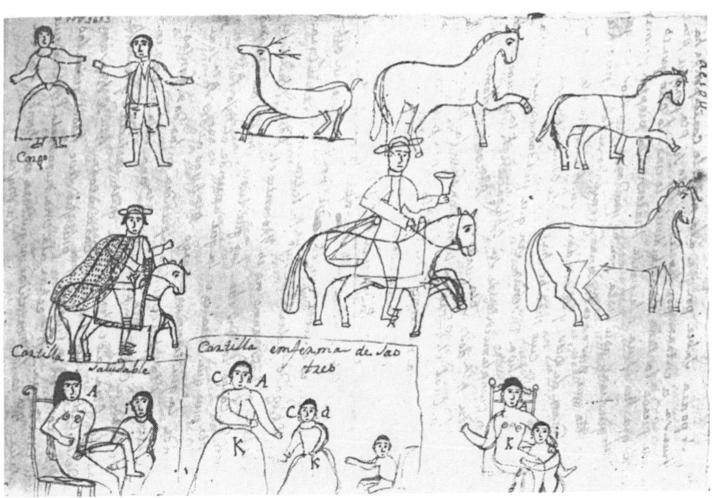

10. Drawing showing figures in sexually suggestive positions. Source: Archivo General de la Nación, Mexico City, Inquisición, vol. 1505, exp. 3 (1789).

Serge Gruzinski

Individualization and Acculturation: Confession among the Nahuas of Mexico from the Sixteenth to the Eighteenth Century

Beginning with the concept of confession within the Roman Catholic Church, the focus of my analysis will follow that of Michel Foucault in his *History of Sexuality,* in which he discusses the scope and the Western heritage of the sacrament of penitence. Foucault convincingly demonstrates that, beginning with the sixteenth century and the Counter-Reformation, confession became a more pressing and invasive practice, an anchor of power in which "forms of subjection and schemes of knowledge develop in constant fluctuation." An example of the new strategy is that established by the church in New Spain within the framework of colonial domination. As a result, we have the development of a discourse centered on sex and the flesh; upon it revolved both power and knowledge.[1]

Confession can go beyond the church's spiritual goals, its objectives of dominion, and its systems of categories and interventions that would lead to the notion of "sexuality." Confession can also become an instrument for expressing church-approved forms of individualization and guilt, eroding the traditional ties and interpersonal relations of colonized societies. This has already been suggested by ethnographers studying the changes of confession in western Africa and inquiring into the dissolving and contradictory effects of certain forms of confession among ethnic groups in the process of acculturation.[2]

In the light of these different but complementary studies, the reading of manuals written to facilitate the confession of the Indians in New Spain, especially the Nahuas (or Aztecs), reveals facts that might have otherwise been inadvertently overlooked or regarded as obvious and trivial. Thus, for example, confession imposes on the indigenous penitent a series of fixed categories to evaluate his own acts and thoughts. These categories form a system of values that claims to be universal and leaves no margin for the most minimal improvisation, since they are supported by written texts and thus protected from the hazards of oral transmission.

Confessors impose upon the indigenous penitent an order of enunciation: "Put your sins in order," "Tell your sins in order."[3] This indisputable order, a "natural" one for the Catholic priests, leads to hierarchical series: the Ten Commandments, the five commandments of the church, the seven capital sins, the five senses, etc. These series are partially balanced by a dualistic principle that counterposes the seven virtues to the seven sins; in turn, it subdivides the sin category into mortal and venial sins and aligns the three potencies of the soul against its three enemies. In other words, the Indians were forced to pass from systems of multiple references, varying according to their ethnic group, location, social group, and ritual context, to a single conceptual framework, lacking geographical roots and incapable of apprehending "the other" in his cultural and intellectual specificity.

As an example, let us examine the concept of the soul. The Indians saw their own pre-Hispanic concept of three vital entities, whose harmonious interrelation determined the physical, mental, and moral equilibrium of the person, replaced by the Christian notion of the soul.[4] This transposition presented untold difficulties, not only because of the inextricable character of the concepts and the systems supporting them, but also because of the radically different manner of apprehending them. On the one hand, we have a uniform system (the Christian) with a strictly defined content that demands the unqualified adhesion to faith. On the other hand, we have among the indigenous societies a network of notions expressing themselves in their rites and influencing their behavior, but without being the object of systematic elaborations such as those achieved by the Western researcher.[5] Furthermore, Christianity is inseparable from writing, which permits it to assign a definite place to all beings and things. The midsixteenth-century "equivalences and oppositions of propositions" of Alonso de la Vera Cruz illustrate the systematic character that writing confers upon Western thought.[6] The indigenous cultures seem to handle a more flexible and mobile form of thought, open to alternative solutions and constructed upon a broad range of oppositions, distinctions, and parallelisms.

We assume that a concept such as free will must have perplexed the Indians as much as that of the soul. Confessionals are particularly insistent on this point. "You will not say that the devil forced or provoked you to sin; neither will you say that my friend or my relative made me sin. . . . Inasmuch as I did what he ordered me, I am guilty for what I did and for my own folly."[7] Such are the words of Fr. Alonso de Molina in 1565; ten years later the Augustinian Juan de la Anunciación put the following words on the lips of his penitent: "I deprived myself of my Father God on my own will."[8] These are formal texts based on a fundamental assumption of sixteenth-century catholicism: the Indian should act on his own will, and thus he is responsible for his own behavior. He has to put aside his surroundings, his social group, the weight of his tradition, and the external forces that used to influence his behavior, such as the power of a god's ire, the incantations of a witch, the envy of a neighbor or a relative, the ill-omened emanations of a sexual deviant or a transgressor of prohibitions. In other words, by centering on the "subject"—in the Western meaning of the word—the interrogation of the confession breaks down the ancient solidarity and social networks, as well as the physical and supernatural ties. Thus, the belief in a family force, related to the *tonalli* (fate) and vital to the cohesion of the group and the well-being of the family components, all but disappears.[9] It is obvious that this interruption (discontinuity or suspension) of the past, the customs, and the environment is related to the appearance of the omniscient and all-powerful figure of the Catholic priest.

This process of "desterritorialization," or brusque break with the traditional context, was supported by a system of psychological mechanisms designed to explore the penitent's conscience. The first one was introspection. "It is very necessary first to learn what is inside your soul, which is not what it seems outwardly; know thyself . . . the right knowledge is the knowledge of yourself."[10] The ancient Greek dictum was thus transfered to the newly converted Nahuas through the pen of Alonso de Molina. The process began with a questioning of the self that led the penitent of Juan de la Anunciación to state, "I am not the one I used to be."[11] This questioning, perhaps banal to us, establishes the relationship of the subject to himself within the Western humanist perspective and even Erasmian thought. As we know, Bishop Juan de Zumárraga, and Molina in his translations, were both inspired by the writings of Erasmus of Rotterdam.[12] There could be no wider gap between the autochthonous, largely peasant cultures and the discourse of the confessor.

Introspection cannot take place without previous memorization. Thus, it is indispensable to "know and remember all the sins," "bring into memory all the sins."[13] This memorization does not suffer mere approximation; it has to be exact, exhaustive, copied from an arithmetic model, "as a lord taking account from his mayordomo." This exercise comprehends the entire course of life, concerning itself with actions as well as "thoughts, desires, intentions." It is an attempt to master the new categories, to read into the past actions through the individualistic filter of the Christian ethic. That is to say, to organize such material according to a concept of "Western" time, perceived as a concatenation of causes and personalized consequences that shape the singular and irreducible trajectory of the biographical self.[14]

This reading and deciphering lead to the selection of the appropriate formulation of the sins, the manner "in which you will tell them."[15] Certain limits must be respected, however: "you will think about them fast, and survey them briefly." Under no circumstances should this dangerous mental gymnastics give way to pleasant but perverse deviations to avoid exerting the required self-censorship. These mental operations had to give the subject a feeling of guilt, a profound internalization of that feeling. "It is very necessary to know thyself as a sinner, to cry for your sins." "Tell your sins with feelings and crying; declare them with an abundance of tears and deep sighs." The penitent takes charge of the drama of guilt, not only by assimilating the concept of evil (sin) but also by modifying his own consciousness of evil and misfortune. This process is not specific to New Spain in the sixteenth century. It takes place, in one way or other, in the acculturation and transitional processes of traditional cultures facing modern Western cultures.

As a final step in the process of accepting guilt the Indian is invited to disclose his transgressions: "I wish to cast out all my sins before the priest." This disclosure precedes the eventual resolution of the anguish created by the "guilty" conscience and exacerbated by the questioning during confession. Two rites, absolution and penitence, allow the penitent to reach his "medicine" and his "consolation."[16] Such is the intellectual and psychic base upon which rests the practice of Catholic confession. It requires two fundamental prerequisites: the assimilation of an exotic conceptual apparatus, and the acceptance by the Indians of their position as western *subjects* in a double sense: as vectors of an embryonic individualism and as ideologically and psychologically dominated subjects of the Catholic confessor.

Thus conceived, the device for domination has several fields of application: the body, sex, the world of dreams, personal fantasies, and even work. Let us begin with the body or, rather, the new image of the body introduced by the confessor. Affected by broadly negative connotations, the body is a form of anti-soul. "The third enemy of the soul is our body; the soul seeks its heavenly salvation, and the body, earth and mire, is always wishing for dirty carnal things."[17] This concept is placed within a binary frame that assigns the dyad "soul-heaven" an antithetic place to that of "body-hell." The intellect—or reason—is the exact counterpoise of the body.[18] It is obvious that Christianity imposed a narrow game of synthetic categories and an abstract dichotomy, where as the Nahuas conceived a series of multiple components that broke down at the time of death to lead to different destinations (mansions).[19] Nevertheless, both cultures agreed on the need to impose the concept of mastery over the body to reinforce, among other goals, their control over society. Whether the weakness of the bureaucratic and political controls—in the pre-Hispanic world—or the cultural distance—in the case of the church—encouraged the choice of the body in preference to other objectives will remain an unanswered question. It is significant, however, that slightly over fifteen percent of Molina's *Confesionario mayor* is devoted to the body and sexuality, while only one percent deals with the more urgent and threatening subject of idolatry.[20]

To remedy the "lewdness" of the flesh, the church imposed the sacrament of Christian marriage, which represents a uniform institutional tie, both personal and public. Its celebration altered a traditional allocation of roles by implicating only the church and the engaged couple. The church reserved for itself the definition of the forbidden degrees of relatedness (*parentesco*), and the impediments or negative elements of the ceremony, while the contracting parties enjoyed complete freedom in the election of their partners. Thus, the concept of the marital union as part of a cosmic vision dominated by the play of fate (*tonalli*) disappeared.[21] The intervention of the authorities of the community was forbidden; the relatives, the lineage, and the matchmakers lost the essential role that Nahua tradition had assigned them. Similarly, the consorts were all by themselves within the conceptual space of indissoluble monogamy. "We advise fathers and mothers that once they have married their children, not to be concerned with them and therefore stop meddling with them or talking to them about each other, because they may break the marriage with hatred and ill-will."[22] Christianity promoted conjugal intimacy, intensified spiritual and affective communication among the spouses, established a complete parity and reciprocity on the subject of sexual relations within marriage, and assigned the confessor the task of watching over the functioning of the conjugal pair.

The confessor's inquiry also delineated the narrow space of the nuclear family: the duties of the parents towards their offspring and the obligations of the children towards their parents. The family circle, thus restricted, substituted for polygamy and lineages and transformed the nature of the relationships, which ceased being interchangeable. The affinal relations were better defined, although excluded from any possible sexual or matrimonial relationship, while the ties between father, mother, and child were more firmly fixed. Confessionals consider only the "modern" family model in which the classic oedipal triangle may develop.

It would be a mistake to reduce confession to a critical examination of the subject's behavior. Its intention is to penetrate into thoughts and into the most intimate and subjective experiences, with special predilection for sexual fantasies. Let's listen to Molina: "How many times do you think dirty lust thoughts? Do you try to forget and discard them? Do you return quickly to yourself or do you wish to carry them out?" In other words, the penitents, men or women, were entreated to express the particulars of their fantasies, their attempts to repress them, or their fickleness in trying to carry them out. Thus the explicit apology of self-repression: "It is an abominable sin that you committed . . . because you did not wish to restrain yourself or return to yourself when your vicious flesh coveted without shame the filthy pleasure."[23] Mental pleasure, "the filthy pleasure inside your heart," is also reviled.[24]

Even more subtly, the inquiry attempted to induce the penitents to establish correspondences among desires, thoughts, illicit relationships, condemned forms of seeking sexual pleasure (whether or not the relationship was licit or not), pleasurable dreams, and the mental images of couples in their legitimate union.[25] Undoubtedly the confessors in New Spain attempted to subject their penitents to a veritable "technology of the flesh" and pleasure. It is also true that this "sexuality device"—to use Foucault's term—combines the imperatives of salvation with an unlimited will to maintain vigilance over the individual.[26] I wish to focus here on the process of individualization and will use the case of masturbation to illustrate it.

The first sources tell little about the solitary pleasure, which seems to escape the systematic and violent repressions applied to sexual deviations and perversions. It makes a timid appearance in Molina's *Confesionario mayor* (1569) as an insignificant two percent of the text devoted to the Sixth Commandment. In 1575 Juan de la Anunciación devoted five percent of the questions on this commandment to masturbation, alluding to rather than describing it. Almost a quarter of century later, in 1599, the Franciscan Juan Baptista uses a tenth of that same part of the confessional's questionnaire to deal with the topic, addressing both men and women. Finally, in 1611, one-fourth of the questions of the Dominican Martín de León are concerned with masturbation, carefully avoiding a separation of the act from the thought accompanying it: "When you did that, did you have as an object of thought a married, a single, or a virgin woman?"[27] Later in the seventeenth century (1673) the Franciscan Agustín de Vetancurt was similarly preoccupied with the subject, devoting twenty-seven percent of his questions on the Sixth Commandment to the subject of autoerotism.[28]

It may be argued that these percentages are either the result of prurient arithmetic or the reflection of the obsessions of the confessionals' authors. Nevertheless, we must not forget that in western Europe late marriage and an increasing repression of illicit heterosexual relations seem to have heightened the practice of the solitary pleasure among the youth of the period under review.[29] Nine years after the publication of Vetancurt's work, in 1682, a French manual did not hesitate in placing this "deviation" among the most frequent capital sins.[30] The intensification and internalization of desire and guilt in onanism propitiated an exacerbation of the individual sensitivity and encouraged psychological withdrawal and further individualization. Paradoxically, in his efforts to uproot that "vice," the Mexican confessor continued to impose a conception of the self deeply Western and individualistic.

For the confessor, fantasy and dream were very close. As an involuntary activity, dreams escaped the sphere of sins, as long as the Indian denied any meaning to them and did not use them to foster erotic fantasies. It sufficed that he stopped believing in dreams.

Diego Durán, however, was more demanding: "It is necessary that in dealing with dreams, they be examined on what was that they dreamed . . . and thus, it is necessary that on this subject we ask: What did you dream?"[31] In the same vein, the doors to the consumption of pulque or halucinogens such as mushrooms, *ololiuhqui,* and *peyotl* were tightly shut. What were before sources of revelations, of knowledge, of communication with the gods are rejected as folly or madness, confining the individual to the narrow circle of Western reality and its boundaries, which may be trespassed only exceptionally.

We should not assume that the model imposed by the church in sixteenth-century New Spain limited itself to familial, sexual, or mental patterns. We should not forget the interest shown in regulating economic activities through numerous advisory remarks delineating, in individualistic terms defined by the medieval church, the relation of the indigenous to property, wealth, and temporal goods.

The penitential discourse developed through time, evolving toward more diversified and sophisticated definitions, as if trying to enmesh the penitent in the increasingly tighter nets of confession. Thus, for example, in the eighteenth-century confessional of Gerónimo Thomás de Aquino Cortés y Zedeño, there is a pronounced intensification of guilt about the sexual act. The questionnaire adds, and describes in detail, new zones of pleasure and perversions such as exhibitionism, voyeurism, sadism, and fetishism.[32] New objects took an unusual profile, such as male virginity, child sexuality, other conflicts within the family circle, and the incestuous desire for the mother, which is openly quoted in the confessional of Carlos Celedonio Velázquez de Cárdenas.[33] In successive and continued steps confessionals brought together more intimately family and sexuality in a century in which, according to Foucault, the family became "the obligated center of affection, sentiments and love" and "the most active focus of sexuality."[34]

Altogether, the rite of confession went beyond the spiritual sphere to become a complex enterprise of dominion and control over bodies and minds, an enterprise of "desterritorialization" that alienated the individual from his culture and his environment and imposed upon him an explanation of sorrow and sin expressed in a single form of speech with universalist pretensions. It is obvious that the diffusion of confession was contemporary to the fall of the Indian societies and the installation of the colonial order. It would be difficult to deny that confession contributed in an indirectly and intellectual manner to the erosion of mental, social, and familial structures and to the crumbling of ancestral codes and ancient forms of solidarity that regulated the functioning of pre-Hispanic societies.[35]

Indian Reaction

Given the constrictions of space, I will stress only some of the responses to the exigencies of confession, without aspiring to draw a total picture. After a bright beginning—according to the Franciscan chroniclers—the number of confessants in the second half of the sixteenth century offered an unflattering picture. Towards 1566, over eighty percent of the adult population died without confession in the Archbishopric of Mexico. In Tlaxcala, only twenty percent of the faithful confessed annually. In other parishes the frequency of the sacrament varied between six and forty percent of the Indian population. In the city of Mexico, the number was less than ten percent in 1556.[36]

The attitudes of the minority who practiced confession allow us to assess the mental and conceptual obstacles faced by the penitents. According to the works of the Franciscan Juan Baptista and the Dominican Martín de León, published in 1600 and 1611 respectively, the concepts of classification and categorization of sins were badly assimilated. The Indians failed to distinguish between venial and mortal sin; they even failed to recognize the difference between a meritorious deed and guilt.[37] They used to answer in an "incoherent" fashion to the confessors. For example, they "easily say something now and something else later in the confession; an Ave María within another."[38] They could not provide an accurate assessment of the number of their transgressions. "Sometimes they say they have sinned twice, and they add everything else in the confession."[39]

Without the comprehension and assimilation of the conceptual frame of Christianity, any attempt to keep account of the number of sins became foolish and senseless. The Indians stuck to numbers arbitrarily chosen. The effort made to fulfill the rite and please the confessor seems to alter completely the content of the answers; it was almost impossible to them "to order their remembrances in succession." Faced with this report we should not discard the possibility that such behavior was part of a deliberate attitude. Under a superficial conformity lie alienation and indifference, similar perhaps to those described by Richard Hoggart in contemporary popular situations.[40]

In fact, the vicissitudes of acculturation determined the capacity for assimilation and produced the most bizarre reactions. Some Indians ignored the rules of confession. Others, in an excess of scruples, lost themselves in irrelevant details.[41] Yet others never succeeded in overcoming the psychologically anguishing conditioning required for confession. Mentioning the "confusion" of the penitent, Martín de León comments: "He goes to confession so confused that he does not know what he says."[42] Thus, "a thousand absurdities," contradictions, and misunderstandings were added to the mental confusion of the subject. Incapable of attributing their failures to the cultural distance between themselves and the Indians, confessors conceived the difference as inferiority, lamenting the small capacity, the dullness and rusticity, and the ignorance and lack of understanding of the indigenous penitents. Nonetheless, at least in the work of Juan Baptista, an underlying optimism softens the contempt of the colonial discourse: "Their dullness is not natural, but due to lack of instruction by able and discreet persons."[43] Martín de León, more disillusioned, proposed to limit the exigencies of confession: "It is necessary that we adjust ourselves, more in this matter than in others, to their lowly and narrow understanding."[44]

It would be a mistake to confine the dialogue created by the confession to the alternatives of domination or incomprehension, making the Indian penitents mere passive, confused, and ignorant receptors. By the end of the sixteenth century we find knowledgeable Indians—possibly principals—"well versed and Hispanized," in the words of Juan Baptista.[45] They succeeded in deflecting, and even distorting, the discourse of the confessor, facing him with astute answers. "They tell stories. To confess a sin they first give a thousand excuses to lessen and mask it to make it look less bad, and for that purpose they use fastidious words so as not to be understood."[46] Although the tactics used varied, all gave evidence of the Indians understanding and their assimilation of the Christian categories. They were also a form of sabotage of the dominant discourse, drowning it "in a multitude of words and unnecessary stories."[47] They manipulated the rules of confession, toying with the attenuating circumstances of sin. Their astuteness takes surprising forms. When facing confessors insisting on formulating their questions in an intelligible and accessible manner, the penitents use a language of their own, wilfully unusual and disconcerting.[48] The verbal exuberance, the making up of guilt, the terminological hermetism, or the plain lie intended to confuse the priests in the very same field they chose and imposed: the religious discourse.[49]

At the beginning of the eighteenth century the situation had changed very little. The author of *El farol indiano*—published in 1713—echoed the complaints of Juan Baptista and Martín de León: "the majority of them ignore the manner of a good confession."[50] Fifty years later, another confessor wondered, "with the exception of a few, all Indians confess themselves badly."[51]

Although these critiques denounced not the limited practice of the rite but its deficient quality, for part of the population the Christian set of values continued as confused as it was at the end of the sixteenth century. "They take what is bad for good, and vice versa," stated Manuel Pérez. "For confession, the Indians examine their conscience very superficially or not at all." He cited obstacles similar to those cited in the sixteenth century by others: the difficulty in remembering their actions and thoughts, of offering an account of their transgressions, or of distinguishing between venial and mortal sin.[52] There is also a repetition of the adjectives used by the confessors: pejorative, not to say racist, expressions, not tempered by the hope of any betterment. "The Indian at the knee of the confessor is quite unfit."[53] Even more severe is the author of *Ayudante de cura,* who in 1766 does not spare a single disparaging adjective, citing "their ignorance, dullness, lack of capacity, fickleness, and great infidelity."[54] Elsewhere he states: "We cannot give them understanding." It is inconceivable and, worse, hazardous, to attempt reasoning with them, since "to attempt showing them their inconsistencies . . . is to confuse them."[55] This amounted to arguing that the Indian penitents had remained impervious to Western logic as it is developed in the confessional interrogatory.

Along with these judgments, however, we find other different and even contradictory observations. At the beginning of his *Farol indiano,* Manuel Pérez expresses his own perplexity: "These are rustic but otherwise able people." He does not know whether to lament "the inconveniences of their rusticity or their ability."[56] Both Manuel Pérez and Andrés Pérez de Velasco agree in differentiating two kinds of Indians, following a city/countryside dichotomy instead of the social classification adopted by Juan Bautista. Urban Indians (Mexico City, Puebla, and their vicinities) were more able than those "who should be held as purely Indian on account of their rusticity and ignorance." The former, more *ladino,* seemed to be more familiarized with the sacrament of confession. "They have discretion enough to examine their own conscience, to explain their guilt, to assume its gravity . . . they know well what sin is."[57] The responses of the Indians were, nevertheless, varied. Some handled the notion of sin according to a logic of their own that differed sensibly from the criteria of the church. This corroborates the indigenous assimilation of the process of conscience examination. These people seem to have elaborated a specific casuistry of their own by combining the Catholic rituals, such as the obligation to fast on Saturdays, to attend mass, and to abstain from eating meat while sick, with prohibitions against drinking pulque, lying with their wives during the Holy Week, or spitting after taking communion, etc.[58] While the church explained these practices as the mistakes of "erring minds," we may ask whether they were not the efforts of the Indian penitents to interpret and assimilate the dogma, since they are important and "ordinary" enough to take fifteen titles and over twenty pages of *Farol indiano.*

Paradoxically, far from softening or depleting the meaning of the ecclesiastical prescriptions, the practices that the Indians accused themselves of neglecting extended those obligations and strengthened the prohibitions of Roman Catholicism. Thus, from the sin of believing in dreams, one passed to the sin of dreaming; from the sin of drunkenness, to that of drinking pulque. They erroneously chastised themselves for eating eggs and drinking milk before paying for the Bull of *Santa Cruzada*; they assumed as sin eating meat on Wednesday, "while carrying the scapulary of the Virgin," excessively valorizing the cult of Mary. They also denounced nonexistent incests committed by presumed affinal relatives (*compadres*) who were not related, since "they call all relatives *compadres* and *comadres.*"[59] The inflation of the spiritual affinal relations and the exaggeration of the ritual prescriptions—whether they were respected or not—distorted the logic of Catholicism. Such practices reflect a rigorous perception of ecclesiastical law, which could mean both the need for stricter rituals or the obsessive fear of not complying with them. In some instances, however, the motivation raises some doubts. The Indians aspired to copy the religious usages of the Spaniards and the *gente de razón* in general, in an obvious attempt of cultural identification and social promotion. Thus, they assumed that not attending mass on Saturdays, or eating beef during Lent, was a form of evil requiring penitence.

In other instances, the Indian interpretation of the Christian norms may have led to new forms of sin hierarchization, such as when they assumed witchcraft to be a mortal sin.[60] They could also find new forms of expressing transgressions. To emphasize the gravity of drunkenness, the penitent confessed: "I committed the seven mortal sins."[61] Their interpretation of sin might also guide them to more misleading assumptions. According to Pérez de Velasco, "it seems that most Indians assume that sins are only those committed during Lent . . . such as eating meat, becoming drunk, skipping mass, or incurring sensuality, which are among them the most common faults."[62] Using the transgressions defined by the church and the Christian periodization, the penitents constructed a code that favored the observance of liturgical time, rather than addressing the act itself. This resulted in a displacement of prohibitions—such as those related to fasting and mass—and a complete misunderstanding of the sexual and alcoholic transgressions. Their reasoning was the effort of attempting to put some order and logic in the maze of ecclesiastical rules that, although based on a universal concept of sin, showed some notable variations according to the ethnic origin of the penitent.

The manipulation of the Christian norms produced subtle and Machiavellian arguments that would prove the knowledge and assimilation of the exigencies of the Catholic ethics and confession. For example, when the male Indian pretended to gain a woman's favor, "he tells her—and the woman believes it—that it is a greater sin not to give in to him, because such behavior raises his desire and makes him sin; should the woman give in, he would commit only one sin."[63] By using such apt casuistic argumentations, the Indians appropriated the Christian logic of guilt, twisting it for the satisfaction of personal ends and showing an astuteness comparable to that used by priests (*solicitantes*) urging the favors of their defenseless female penitents.[64] Using Foucault's reasoning, we could point to the use of the same discourse—that of confession—to fulfill opposite strategies, encouraging criminal behavior and escaping completely from the grip of the institution originating it.[65]

The free election of a marital partner was an important factor in the process of individualization, and on this point the treatises of the eighteenth century suggest the presence of an evolution. They remind applicants of "the freedom demanded by this sacrament" and expose cases of Indian women who married without or against their parents' will, or who obtained the dissolution of betrothal (*esponsales*). They point to the conflictive situations created between parents and children-in-law, suggesting that couples acquired a significant degree of autonomy after marriage. They probe into conjugal intimacy, pointing to women who gingerly denied sexual relations to their husbands.[66] However, we are far from being able to state that the family (the parents of the engaged couple) lost the role it had enjoyed in pre-Hispanic times. It was not uncommon for parents to oppose the union: "fathers and mothers are continuously putting obstacles to their children's marriages."[67] It was just as common for the family of the bride to arrange her marriage, fixing the conditions to their own benefit. Sometimes the future son-in-law had to agree to reside in the home or in the neighborhood of his fiancée—a form of uxorlocality—and sometimes he was obliged to serve "for a fixed period of time" in the house of his in-laws. This was a common practice in the rural areas.[68]

On the other hand, both in the rural and the urban areas, the practice of resorting to matchmakers, who had a very important role in pre-Hispanic societies, was still in use.[69] Their presence at this late period confirms the weight retained by the relatives in concerting a marital alliance. We have some indications of problems in the understanding of the Christian norms, however. One of them is the early age of the couple: "as soon as they are ten or eleven years old they think of nothing but marriage."[70] In remote areas such as the southern coast of Guerrero, the parents represented the groom.[71] Indians misunderstood the nuptial rites, assuming that "marriage was not the expression of consent and giving hands, but the reception of nuptial blessings."[72] In general, the key moment of marriage for the Indians was not the religious ceremony, but the betrothal. As soon as the matchmakers had performed their tasks, the groom began not only to serve in the bride's home but also to carry out sexual relations with her, a practice attributed to their promiscuity as much as to their desire to verify the bride's virginity. "They have in great dishonor to marry a woman who is not a virgin (*doncella*) . . . and this is why they communicate [carnally] with them before marriage, and if they find the woman nonvirginal (*corrupta*) it is difficult to proceed with the marriage."[73] These premarital relations were allowed by the parents, much to the scandal of the helpless confessors. Under these circumstances, only the groom enjoyed personal autonomy and power in the decision to marry, while women remained confined to an obscure and silent role. These observations should be broadened by taking into consideration Indians' "procedures of escaping" the strictures of ecclesiastical marriage, including bribing false witnesses, pretending to be married without the benefit of the ceremony, or using to their advantage the corruption of local officials (*alguaciles*) to continue to live in concubinage.[74] Such practices, introduced in the urban zones and among the more mobile indigenous sectors, undermined the sacrament of marriage and became modes of adaptation that suggest—as in the case of confession—the understanding of the Christian model.

It is riskier, if not impossible, to assess the impact of confession on the subconsciousness of the indigenous penitents. The insistent attempt to eradicate the belief in dreams—denounced in all confessionals throughout the colonial period—seems to have yielded some fruit, although not the expected one. It succeeded in lending a guilty character to most oneiric activities. As we have seen, the Indians confessed their dreams as if they had committed a grave sin. Pérez de Velasco, author of *Ayudante de cura,* gives us a significant piece of information: "To confess their lewd dreams they say that the dream deceived them."[75] The wording used by the Indians suggests that they knew the difference between a "lewd" dream and other dreams, but the preoccupation for the meaning—or false meaning—continued to dominate the indigenous mind, against the will of the confessors, who rejected what they judged irrelevant petty oneiric images.

In the same text, Pérez de Velasco points the ambiguity of the Nahuatl word *elehuia,* used by the penitents. It could express, at the same time, the heterosexual impulse, the thought, and the act.[76] Curiously, we do not find the same continuity in the practice of masturbation. While the Indians entertained sexual fantasies, they did not satisfy them by masturbating. At least, this is what both Pérez and Pérez de Velasco inform us, attributing the absence of masturbation among Indians "to the great easiness with which they can obtain women."[77] Masturbation is thus almost the only sin from which Indians escaped, despite all the bad traits they were accused of. Why then the increasing interest of confessionals, from Molina's to Vetancurt's, in solitary pleasure? If we consider the curiosity of the confessors on this subject as a mere projection of European anxieties, and the above-mentioned observations of two confessors as a reflection of an indigenous reality, then we could interpret the infrequency of onanism as a symptom of the failure of the individualization process, or as the absence of the privatization of pleasure due to the persistence of collective behavioral patterns.[78]

Doubtless, the practice of confession became a refined tool of ideological subjection and of dominion over the individual, although its scope remains to be more fully investigated. Confession may be regarded as a device to bring the Indian faithful within the boundaries of a process that remained spiritual in its goals. Without denying this dimension, I must underline the complementary purposes of confession as "consolation and medicine," as explained by Alonso de Molina. In this perspective, the rite of penitence appears more as a side effect of colonial domination than as one of its generating forces. Confession offered a structure of support and comfort amidst the disturbances of deculturation. In other words, confession became a defensive and therapeutic mechanism, capable of appeasing not only the anguish raised by its own practice but also the traumas generated by colonial rule. Furthermore, by conferring a meaning to the new order, to the new misfortunes, and to the multiplicity of new cultural references overtaking the indigenous reality, confession helped create a buffer between the traditional cultures and the naked violence of colonial exploitation. If we fail to take into account the ambiguity of this Catholic rite, we run the risk of remaining ignorant about the adaptive strategies conceived by certain sectors of the indigenous population, and of overlooking attitudes and activities that reflect the capacity of reception, assimilation, and recreation on the part of the indigenous cultures in colonial society.

Notes

1. Michel Foucault, *Historia de la sexualidad,* vol. 1: *La voluntad de saber* (Mexico City: Siglo XXI, 1977) (French edition Paris: Gallimard, 1976). See, especially, pp. 54 ff.

2. See, for example, Marc Augé, et al. *Prophétisme et thérapeutique: Albert Atcho et la commanauté de Bregho* (Paris: Hermann, 1975).

3. Fr. Juan de la Anunciación, *Doctrina christiana muy cumplida donde*

se contiene la exposición de todo lo necesario para doctrinar a los indios . . . (Mexico City: Pedro Balli, 1575), p. 142; Martín de León, *Camino al cielo en lengua mexicana . . .* (Mexico City: Diego López Dávalos, 1611), p. 109. The first volume of a project collecting all colonial catechisms for the instruction of the Indians is now available. See Juan Guillermo Durán, ed. *Monumenta catechetica hispanoamericana (siglos* XVI-XVIII) (Buenos Aires: Publicaciones de la Facultad de Teología de la Universidad Católica Argentina, 1984). On the general process of Westernization, acculturation, and evangelization, see Serge Gruzinski, *La colonisation de L'Imaginaire: Sociétés indigènes et occidentalisation dans le Mexique espagnol, xviè–xviiiè siècle* (Paris: Editions Gallimard, 1988); Serge Gruzinski, "Confesión, alianza y sexualidad entre los indios de Nueva España," in *El placer de pecar y el afán de normar,* by Seminario de Historia de las Mentalidades (Mexico City: Joaquín Mortiz, 1988), pp. 169–215.

4. Alfredo López Austin, *Cuerpo humano e ideología: Las concepciones de los antiguos nahuas,* 2 vols. (Mexico City: Universidad Nacional Autónoma de México, 1980), 1:285–318, and passim.

5. I have in mind the works of Alfredo López Austin, such as that cited in the preceding note, or that of Christian Duverger, *L'esprit du jeu chez les Azteques* (Paris-La Hague: Mouton, 1978).

6. See, for example, *Recognitio summularum* (Mexico City: Juan Pablos, 1554). See also Ernest J. Burrus, "Alonso de la Vera Cruz: Pioneer Defender of the American Indians," *Catholic Historical Review* 70, no.4 (October 1984): 531–46. This work provides a short biographical survey and analysis of the main writings of this sixteenth-century Augustinian theologian.

7. Alonso de Molina, *Confesionario mayor en lengua mexicana y castellana* (Mexico City: Antonio de Espinosa, 1569), pp. 12–13.

8. Juan de la Anunciación, *Doctrina christiana,* p. 141; Martín de León, *Camino,* p. 113.

9. López Austin, *Cuerpo humano* 1:281–961.

10. Molina, *Confesionario,* pp. 5, 6.

11. Juan de la Anunciación, *Doctrina,* p. 141.

12. Antonio Rubial García, "Evangelismo y evangelización: Los primitivos franciscanos en la Nueva España y el ideal del cristianismo primitivo," *Anuario de Historia* 10 (1978–79): 95–124. See also, Juan de Zumárraga, *Regla cristiana breve* (Mexico City: Editorial Jus, 1951), and also his *Doctrina christiana: Suma de lo que más conviene predicar y dar a entender a los indios* (Mexico City: Impressa por mandado del Ro. Señor Don Fray Juan Zumárraga, 1545–46). Molina translated this work into Nahuatl.

13. Molina, *Confesionario,* pp. 6v, 8v, 9.

14. I am using here the concepts developed by Marie-Cécile and Edmond Ortiguez in *Oedipe africain* (Paris: Plon, 1966).

15. See Molina, *Confesionario,* pp. 7, 11, 8v, 15, respectively for these citations.

16. Ibid., pp. 14, 17.

17. Juan de la Anunciación, *Doctrina,* p.215; Molina, *Confesionario,* p. 23.

18. Juan de la Anunciación, *Doctrina,* pp. 217–18. See also in Molina, *Confesionario,* p. 115, the opposition of the concepts of the weakness of the flesh and the fervent desires of the soul. Martín de León, in his *Camino del cielo,* mentions the sickness of the body deriving from the sickness of the soul (1:362).

19. López Austin, *Cuerpo humano* 1:362.

20. Molina, *Confesionario,* p. 20.

21. López Austin, *Cuerpo humano* 1:342.

22. Juan de la Anunciación, *Doctrina,* p. 67.

23. Molina, *Confesionario,* pp. 33v, 80v.

24. Juan de la Anunciación, *Doctrina,* p. 87.

25. Ibid., p. 88.

26. Foucault, *La voluntad de saber,* p. 153.

27. Martín de León, *Camino,* p. 115v.

28. Fray Agustín de Vetancurt, *Arte de la lengua mexicana* (Mexico City: Francisco Rodríguez Lupercio, 1673).

29. Jean-Louis Flandrin, *Le sexe et l'Occident: Evolution des attitudes et des comportments* (Paris: Seuil, 1981), pp. 297 ff.

30. *Instructions pour les confesseurs du diocese de Chalon-sur-Saone* (1682). Cited in Jean-Louis Flandrin, *Le sexe et l'Occident,* p. 297.

31. Diego Durán, *Historia de las Indias de Nueva España e Islas de la Tierra Firme,* 2 vols. (Mexico City: Editorial Porrúa, 1967), 1:132; Juan de la Anunciación, *Doctrina,* .114.

32. Gerónimo Thomás de Aquino Cortés y Zedeño, *Arte, vocabulario y confesionario en el idioma mexicano como se usa en el obispado de Guadalajara* (Puebla: Colegio Real de San Ignacio, 1765).

33. Carlos Celedonio Velásquez de Cárdenas y León, *Breve práctica y régimen del confesionario de indios . . .* (Mexico City: Bibliotheca Mexicana, 1761).

34. Foucault, *La voluntad de saber,* p. 143.

35. We could ask to what extent the immigrant (*naboría*) Indian, disjoined from his community and offering his labor in the mining communities, the homes, and haciendas of the Spaniards, resembles the imaginary interlocutor of the confessionals for Indians. The mobility and autarchy of the former is

close to the autonomy demanded from the latter. See, for example, *Provinces of Early Mexico,* ed. Ida Altman and James Lockhart (Los Angeles: University of California Press, 1976), pp. 18–19.

36. Francisco del Paso y Troncoso, *Epistolario de Nueva España,* 16 vols. (Mexico City: Editorial José Porrúa e Hijos, 1940), 10:132; 8:74.

37. Juan Baptista, *Advertencias para los confesores de los naturales* (Mexico City: M. Ocharte, 1600), pp. 3–3v.

38. Martín de León, *Camino,* p. 101.

39. Baptista, *Advertencias,* p. 2v.

40. Richard Hoggart, *The uses of Literacy* (London: Chatt and Windus, 1957).

41. Martín de León, *Camino,* p. 110.

42. Ibid., p. 102.

43. Baptista, *Advertencias,* pp. 4v, 5, 6, 59.

44. Martín de León, *Camino,* p. 104.

45. Baptista, *Advertencias,* p. 13v.

46. Martín de León, *Camino,* p. 110 v.

47. Ibid.

48. Or more simply, they lie. See, Agustín de Vetancurt, *Teatro americano* (Mexico City: Maria de Benavides, 1698), p. 91. It is also worthwhile to mention dilatory tactics consisting in blaming third persons. "They spend a lot of time without confessing a personal sin but, instead, talking about those of their husbands, neighbors." (Manuel Pérez, *Farol indiano y guia de curas de indios . . .* [Mexico City: Francisco de Rivera Calderón, 1713], p. 76).

49. Anthropologist Jack Goody has raised an important question about the impact of the written discourse on oral cultures; this remains to be answered in the Nahua case. See Jack Goody, *The Domestication of the Savage Mind* (Cambridge: Cambridge University Press, 1977), p. 153. We are thinking of the confessionals that, according to Fr. Diego Valdés, some Indians read and also of the learning techniques developed by the Indians, using paintings and stones. See Esteban J. Palomera, *Fr. Diego Valadés, O.F.M.: Su obra* (Mexico City: Editorial Jus, 1962), pp. 256, 308.

50. Manuel Pérez, *Farol indiano,* p. 16.

51. Andrés Pérez de Velasco, *El ayudante de cura . . .* (Puebla: Colegio Real de San Ignacio, 1766), p. 45.

52. Manuel Pérez, *Farol indiano,* pp. 16, 27.

53. Ibid., p. 19.

54. Pérez de Velasco, *El ayudante,* p. 66.

55. Ibid., pp. 63, 67.

56. Pérez, *Farol indiano,* p. 1.

57. Pérez de Velasco, *El ayudante,* p. 67.

58. Ibid., pp. 26ff.

59. Ibid., p. 77.

60. Ibid., p. 61.

61. Ibid., p. 50.

62. Ibid., p. 75.

63. Ibid., p. 44.

64. See Jorge René González Marmolejo, "Clérigos solicitantes, perversos de la confesión," in *De la santidad a la perversión,* ed. Sergio Ortega (Mexico City: Editorial Grijalbo, 1986), pp. 239–52.

65. Foucault, *La voluntad de saber,* p. 133. See also Pierre Bourdie, *Sens pratique* (Paris: Editions de Minuit, 1980), for the concept of "the logic of practice."

66. Manuel Pérez, *Farol indiano,* p. 186.

67. Ibid., p. 168.

68. Ibid., p. 158; Pérez de Velasco, *El ayudante,* p.87.

69. Serge Gruzinski, "Matrimonio y sexualidad en México y Texcoco en los albores de la conquista," in *Seis ensayos sobre el discurso colonial relativo a la comunidad doméstica* (Mexico City: Instituto Nacional de Antropología e Historia, 1980), pp. 17–59.

70. Manuel Pérez, *Farol indiano,* p. 129.

71. Ibid., 149.

72. Pérez de Velasco, *El ayudante,* p. 89.

73. Manuel Pérez, *Farol indiano,* p. 160.

74. Ibid., pp. 134, 154.

75. Pérez de Velasco, *Ayudante,* p. 53.

76. Ibid., p. 51.

77. Manuel Pérez, *Farol indiano,* p. 85; Pérez de Velasco, *Ayudante,* p. 51.

78. On the importance of the role of the community among the Indians, see William B. Taylor, *Drinking, Homicide and Rebellion in Colonial Mexican Villages* (Stanford: Stanford University Press, 1979), pp. 154, passim: "the Indian concept of the individual . . . in contrast to Hispanic concepts, stressed the responsibility to the community over self-realization." See also Margarita Loera, *Calimaya y Tepemaxalco: Tenencia y transmisón hereditaria de la tierra en dos comunidades indígenas en la época colonial* (Mexico City: Instituto Nacional de Antropología e Historia, 1977). This work underlines the persistence of the communitarian concept of territorial property.

11. The sacrament of confession: the examination of soul by the penitent. Source: Felipe Guamán Poma de Ayala, *Nueva corónica y buen gobierno* (Paris: Musée d'Ethnologie, 1936), p. 616.

12. Indian couple in bed. Source: Felipe Guamán Poma de Ayala, *Nueva corónica y buen gobierno* (Paris: Musée d'Ethnologie, 1936), p. 871.

Ann Twinam

Honor, Sexuality, and Illegitimacy in Colonial Spanish America

In 1754, doña Margarita Martines Orejón of Tasco, Mexico, discovered that she was pregnant. She was eighteen, she was single, she belonged to one of the town's most distinguished families. Her brothers were priests, her ancestors had been conquistadores.[1] Although her lover, Tasco miner don Antonio Villanueva, never married her, he did plot with doña Margarita and her family to hide her pregnancy and to protect her from public scandal. Decades later, don Antonio remembered their affair and

> the union from which she became pregnant. In order to guard this fact, which was totally hidden and so without discredit for him or for her, it was not made public knowledge, but their indiscretion remained totally hidden, for the contacts they had in her house were not suspicious nor scandalous, given the high standing of both of them and the luster and reputation of her family.

After doña Margarita had given birth secretly, don Antonio took their son to be baptized. He eventually introduced him as an "orphan" into his own bachelor establishment, which he shared with *alcalde mayor* Miguel de Rivera, his mining partner. For the next two decades these men carefully and lovingly supervised the upbringing and education of the young Josef Antonio.[2]

Doña Margarita remained a spinster in her family home. Another eighteen years would pass before she would publicly come forth and acknowledge her illegitimate son. It was only then that her testimony revealed the high price exacted by her youthful love affair. Remembering those days doña Margarita confessed that "she never had anything to do with any other man, neither before nor after she conceived the said Josef Antonio, nor even after this incident has she ever had relations with don Antonio, but she has lived with honor and sense, and with no loss of her good reputation."

Why would a woman who had paid such a high personal price, who had forfeited her child for her reputation, and who had lived for eighteen years of honorable spinsterhood now publicly admit that she was an unwed mother? Doña Margarita herself supplies the answer: "I do not want to take away the good that could come to him if he knew who his parents were." And so, with the passage of years, the future welfare of her son began to outweigh any detriment to her own reputation.

The particular reason why doña Margarita emerged to confess her motherhood was that her son, Josef Antonio, had made formal application to the Council of the Indies to purchase his legitimation through a *gracias a sacar.* This royal dispensation literally gave petitioners "permission to take" themselves from the legal category of illegitimacy, to move to that of "legitimated" offspring. Such applicants belonged to an exclusive group, as there were few in the Spanish colonies who combined the necessary racial and social background with the resources to pay for such bureaucratic approval. In this case, the social position of Josef Antonio's parents proved more than sufficient, for, like the fathers and mothers of other successful petitioners, doña Margarita and don Antonio were members of their local élites. Fathers of cédula petitioners were typically men of power and wealth in their communities. Some held high rank in the army or the navy or served in prestigious positions in city councils or the imperial bureaucracy. They were judges, landowners, merchants, miners, and clerics who belonged to the peak of a self-consciously defined social pyramid. The mothers of these illegitimates were the daughters, sisters, nieces, cousins, and sometimes even the wives of males of similar preeminence. It is no accident that don Antonio stressed the "luster and reputation" of doña Margarita's family and emphasized his own "high standing."

To win approval from the Council of the Indies it was not sufficient that Josef Antonio confirm the identity of his parents and prove their social rank. He also had to document their marital state at the time of his own conception and birth. Applicants who could show that they were *hijos naturales*, the illegitimate children of single parents, were much more likely to be successful than those who were *adulterinos* (illegitimates with a married parent) or *espurios* (offspring of priests).[3] Given this demand for details, petitioners commonly sought depositions not only from surviving parents but also from relatives, neighbors, friends, or servants who might detail the extenuating circumstances surrounding their births. Decree requests such as Josef Antonio's thus provide rare, intimate, and frank accounts of the sexual and personal relationships between élite women and men and of the emotional ties that linked them with their illegitimate children, surrounding kin groups, and colonial society at large. In this case, since Josef Antonio's mother and father had been single at the time of his birth, and officially acknowledged their parentage, the Council of the Indies readily granted the desired decree in 1780.

Josef Antonio's plea for legitimation was but one of 244 such cases that arrived for consideration by the Council of the Indies during the seventeenth and eighteenth centuries (see graph).[4] Such requests originated from every jurisdiction of Spanish America. The empire-wide distribution of such petitions makes it possible to reconstruct shared colonial attitudes and practices relating to sexuality and illegitimacy[5] (see table 1). The number, chronological, and geographical scope of these detailed requests make them powerful tools with which to uncover some of the lost topics of Spanish America's colonial past.

The history of female sexuality emerges as one such theme. Lacking much research on the subject, we might begin with the assumption that the Roman Catholic cult of virginity importantly shaped popular attitudes concerning female sexual activity. The post-Trent church presented the Blessed Virgin as a role model as it enthusiastically sponsored the reform of feminine orders, founded nunneries in Spanish America, and elevated Therese of Avila and Rose of Lima to sainthood. Although the secular cult of virginity recognized that most women were not saints, it still emphasized the importance of sexual abstinence. A woman was to refrain permanently from intercourse if she remained single or was to maintain her virginity until she became a wife. Presumably, a woman was either "in" sexual control, or "out of" such control, and society did not recognize anything "in between." For that reason, single women who lost their virginity, or wives who strayed, lost any claim to respectability. They were "out of control" and approximated the moral, if not the actual, state of the prostitute.

Clearly this exclusive dichotomy, with its foreshadowing of more contemporary stereotypes of machismo and *marianismo*, omits critical analytical elements such as class, race, and epoch. It is here that the collected biographies of élite women who engaged in premarital or extramarital sexual relations and who bore illegitimate

Graph 1. Frequency of Petitions by Decade, 1730–1820

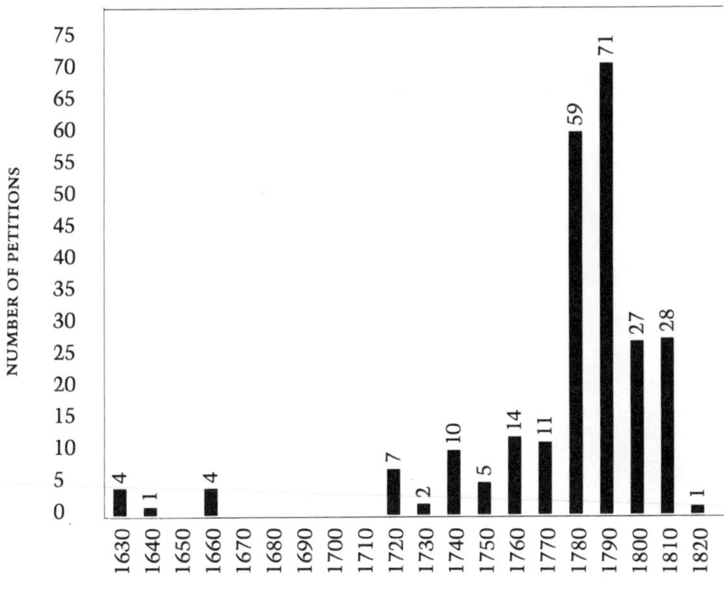

Source: AGI, Audiencias, "Cartas y Expedientes"; Indiferente General, exp. 16, 1535. Before 1720 the Spanish government had no widely publicized or established mechanism through which subjects might submit legitimation petitions. This makes petitions before 1720 difficult to locate. After 1720 the Council of the Indies and the Council of Castille established procedures for such requests. The peak decades of application (1780–90) may well coincide with increased publicity concerning the legitimation options. Probably more important was the movement of illegitimates into established élite ranks in regions such as Cuba, where economic prosperity produced social mobility. A broader issue is still unclear: increase in petitions might reflect a loosening of eighteen-century sexual mores, leading to a corresponding increase in out-of-wedlock liaisons and illegitimate births. Statistics may also reflect a contrary trend of tightening of élite attitudes toward illegitimacy which accelerated the purchase of cédulas to erase birth "stains." At the moment the former appears more plausible than the latter, although individual case histories suggest that both patterns were working simultaneously.

Table 1. Frequency of Petitions by Audiencia and Decade (*N* 244)

	Decade																			
Audiencia	1630	1640	1650	1660	1670	1680	1690	1700	1710	1720	1730	1740	1750	1760	1770	1780	1790	1800	1810	1820
Buenos Aires														1	3	3	9	2		
Caracas												1			1	5	1	1		
Charcas															1		6	4		
Chile																1	4			
Guadalajara														2	1	2				
Guatemala City	1													1		5	5	5	1	
Lima		1													1	10	9	6	2	
Mexico City	3									1	1	4	4	3	1	9	5	3	2	1
Panama														1		1	2			
Quito				2													3	3		
Santo Domingo										6	1	5	1	5	3	20	23	4	21	
Santa Fe				2									1		3	4	3	2		
Total	4	1	0	4	0	0	0	0	0	7	2	10	5	14	11	59	71	27	28	1

Source: AGI, Audiencias, "Cartas y Expedientes"; Indiferente General, exp. 16, 1535. The relative preponderance of petitions from the Audiencia of Santo Domingo (Cuba) is noteworthy. A possible explanation for this situation may be that the geographical and psychological proximity of Cuba to the Spanish mainland, given the frequent sailing between Havana and the mother country, generated widespread publicity and familiarity concerning the legitimation options. The increased economic and social mobility brought by the Cuban sugar boom and slave trade profits seemed to have created upwardly mobile people anxious to erase any legal obstacles hindering that ascent.

children can provide rare glimpses of the fate of those who crossed such forbidden boundaries.

Doña Margarita gives us her idea of the proper sexual conduct expected of the unmarried colonial female. She tells us that she has shown "sense" since the birth of her son, for she has abstained from sexual relations. This control of her sexuality has brought its own reward, for she has now "lived with honor . . . and with no loss of her good reputation."[6] She was not alone in linking the prescribed ideals of feminine behavior with the Latin American concept of honor, as other mothers of illegitimates—possibly because they had violated such standards—seem veritably obsessed with the topic. Their testimony makes clear that honor served as an overarching complex of ideas, attitudes, and values that set the ideal standards for élite behavior, including sexual behavior. We must meet Spanish American élites on their own ground and use their own concept of honor as the lens through which to view colonial sexual standards and practices. Since there were often significant gaps between the ideal and the real, let us first consider the linkage between theoretical norms of feminine sexuality and honor, before we can explore its expression in real life.

Honor

Although members of colonial Spanish society from the most exalted to the most lowly might feel that they possessed honor, it was only members of the colonial élite who defined it in exclusive terms. For them, honor was the ethos which rationalized the existence of the colonial hierarchy.[7] It included those self-conscious differences of birth and conduct that distinguished people who had it (*gente decente*) from those who did not (*gente baja*). Honor molded intra-élite relationships, as those who had honor recognized it in others and treated these peers with an attention and respect that they denied the rest of colonial society.[8]

Honor placed élite families not only in social space, but in family time. Part of honor was inherited, including the concept of *limpieza de sangre* (purity of blood), as those of the upper strata had to prove their ancestors had not been Moors, Jews, or heretics or, in the colonies, Indians or blacks.[9] Honor was not only a heritage of racial and religious purity, but a family history of proper action, as signified by generations of sanctified marriages and of legitimate births. The three most important documents in a colonist's life—the birth certificate, the marriage certificate, and the will—recorded the personal histories of preceding generations by noting whether a person was or was not legitimate. As such, they also provided the basis for elaborate family genealogies that colonial élites maintained and treasured as proof that a chain of religiously confirmed, racially pure marriages and legitimate births bound them to past generations. If there was a break in such continuity, they acted to close it, and a few families even purchased legitimation degrees for dead relatives.[10]

All family members had an immediate responsibility to maintain their own personal honor and thus pass on the collective chain of honor to future generations.

When the chain was broken by illegitimacy, it produced family members who were blood kin but lacked the perquisites of honor. Illegitimate males who did not possess honor could be excluded from public offices and from higher positions in the church, the military, and the civil service. Illegitimate women not only found their pool of potential marriage partners restricted, but their illegitimacy could adversely affect the occupational choices of their sons and the marriage potential of their daughters.[11] Absence of honor could thus limit the social mobility of both sexes, as well as the future of succeeding generations.

Questions of honor, female sexuality, and illegitimacy thus become inextricably linked. Women who engaged in premarital or extramarital sexual relations not only lost personal reputation and honor, but could beget additional family members whose illegitimacy excluded them from family honor. The double standard characteristic of a patriarchal colonial society meant that similar sexual activity did not as certainly threaten the personal honor of the élite male as that of the female. Nonetheless, men who engaged in sexual encounters with females of equal rank did have to consider that public knowledge of a sexual affair could bring certain dishonor to their female lover.

The colonial code of honor thus attempted to control female sexuality through either virginity or marital chastity. There were, however, gaps between how the honor code functioned in theory and how it operated in practice. Those who violated sexual norms need not always pay. The out-of-wedlock pregnancy of doña Margarita shows, for example, that it was possible to manipulate the system for years and avoid loss of honor. Colonial élites employed diverse strategies to achieve such ends. These included "immediate or post hoc matrimony" as well as forms of "private" and "public" (extended engagements, concubinage) pregnancies. The frequency with which élites throughout the colonies resorted to such tactics reveals that there were intermediate positions between the honorable states of unmarried virgin or chaste wife, on the one hand, and the dishonorable positions of single mother or promiscuous spouse on the other.

Immediate Marriage: The Post Hoc Option

The different strategies of élite women facing an illegitimate birth had the same ultimate personal goal: to minimize or to avoid public loss of their honor. The simplest and probably the most frequent solution, if it were possible, was for the pregnant woman and her lover to marry immediately and to have a "premature" but legitimate first child, thereby avoiding all scandal.[12] What may not be well known is that a pregnant woman need not marry before the birth of her child to legitimate it. A long European tradition, with roots in Roman and Canon law and codified in the Spanish medieval code, the *Fuero Real*, provided a fall-back position. If both lovers were single when they had a sexual relationship and were not related by prohibitive degrees of kinship, any subsequent marriage between them, even years after the birth of their illegitimate offspring, would automatically legitimate their children (*hijos naturales*).[13] This legal tradition still found popular expression in Latin America in the seventeenth and eighteenth centuries, and the presumption that such post hoc legitimation could occur significantly affected the immediate and long-term plans of pregnant spinsters.[14] The strategies of "private pregnancy" and "extended engagement" could not have totally or partially protected the honor of pregnant single women without the eventual potential of the legitimating effects of matrimony.[15]

Private Pregnancy

In societies where premarital chastity is the ideal, one simple expedient to mitigate consequences of violating it is to hide the resulting pregnancy so that it apparently never happened. In colonial Spanish America, such "private pregnancies" took a subtle form, for a single woman might be nine months pregnant (privately) but still maintain her public reputation as a virgin and woman of honor. This might be so, even though her condition was known to relatives, selected outsiders, or even a wider social circle, for all would conspire to maintain the distance between her private, pregnant reality and her public, virtuous reputation. Even the Catholic Church cooperated to protect her honor, as the mother's name would not be listed on her child's birth certificate. If a mother was to maintain her public reputation as a virgin, however, she could not openly acknowl-

Table 2: Classification of Pregnancies in Legitimation Petitions

Type of Pregnancy	Number of Cases	Percentage
Private	67	35.8
Public		
With *palabra de casamiento*	11	
Concubinage	13	
Other[1]	20	
Subtotal	44	23.5
Unknown status of pregnancy[2]	76	40.7
TOTALS	187	100.0

Source: AGI, Audiencias, "Cartas y Expedientes"; Indiferente General, exp. 16, 35.

1. These are cases in which the mother can be clearly identified as having had a public pregnancy, but her status (single, engaged, or married) cannot be determined.

2. These cases do not provide data permitting classification of the mother's status as to private or public pregnancy.

edge or raise her child. Of the 187 mothers of illegitimates who appear in cédula petitions, 67, or 35.8 percent, had identifiable private pregnancies. Their identity was protected on birth certificate, and the mother did not take the child (see table 2).

Private pregnancy could occur because colonial society was flexible and often permitted disparities between a person's private reality and his or her public reputation. Although it may be novel to discuss this dichotomy in terms of sexuality, it has long been customary for historians to recognize this phenomenon in Latin American race relations. A wealthy colonist of mulatto ancestry could be accorded the respectful honorific of "don"—which was not a traditional form of address for those of mixed blood—and could enjoy a public reputation as a "white" man. There could be gaps between a person's private reality—a mulatto mother that most of the town knew had existed—and a person's publicly acknowledged persona—in this case as a rich "white" man of honor. In such circumstances an acquired characteristic such as wealth could blur private reality and provide upward racial and social mobility in the public sphere.[16]

This potential for disparity between private reality and public reputation also benefited pregnant Latin American spinsters. They and their kin could use the ascriptive advantages of birth to prevent loss of élite status even when customary mores had been breached. In the case of élite white women, the public presumption—at least at the start—was toward female innocence and virtue. Just as wealthy mulattos could be white, so pregnant, élite spinsters could still be virgins.

The private pregnancy of doña María del Carmen López Nieto demonstrates the lengths to which an unwed mother might go to hide her pregnancy, and the degree to which family members would support her. Doña María and her family belonged to the highest levels of Spanish colonial bureaucracy: her father, don José López Lisperguer, was a judge on the Bolivian high court, or *audiencia*. Nor was doña María's fiancé and lover, don Ramón de Rivera, unequal to her in rank, as he too sat on the high bench. Doña María and don Ramón could not marry, as Spanish law forbade the marriage of high bureaucrats, such as judges, to colonists who lived in the jurisdictions where they served.[17] Technically, doña María and don Ramón had to receive dispensation from Madrid before they could consecrate their union. For this reason don José, doña María's father, prohibited an early marriage. He felt particularly vulnerable, he later admitted, because one of his relatives in Chile who had married without the necessary royal permission had found his later career at a standstill. "Fearful of losing my own post," don José later remembered, "I resisted the marriage, even though I could not stop the union of wills."

Doña María and don Ramón were not disposed to wait either to marry or, as time passed, to have a sexual relationship. Don Ramón finally engineered a transfer and a promotion to Lima, where, since he was no longer in the jurisdiction of his fiancée, he theoretically should have been able to marry without delay. By then, however, it was too late. Doña María discovered that she was pregnant while don Ramón was far away in Lima and unable to help her. Ashamed, and possibly afraid of confessing to her authoritarian father, doña María sought help from her sisters and brothers. They helped her fake an accident, and she received permission from her parents to visit her brother, Dr. José Ignacio, a priest with a parish in Puna. It was there that she gave birth to a baby girl, Gregoria, and there that she died of complications after the birth.

The secrecy surrounding doña María's pregnancy did not end with her death, for her brothers and sisters rallied to protect her reputation beyond the grave. In this case, it may have been as much to spare their father, and to protect family honor, as it was to guard the reputation of a sister presumably beyond such concerns. One of the sisters, doña Nicolasa, a member of the nouveau riche Bolivian silver aristocracy and countess of la Casa Real de Moneda, traveled to Puna to collect her illegitimate baby niece. She took the child back with her to La Plata and raised her in secret. While doña María's mother and father mourned the death of their daughter from complications of an "accident," her brothers and sisters maintained a conspiracy of silence concerning the true cause of her death.

It was only when her father, don José, was about to die that the countess confessed that Gregoria, who was now approaching nine years old, was his illegitimate grandchild. The remorse of don José for condemning his daughter to die away from home and family was enormous, but he died knowing that Gregoria was generously provided for, as he left her the portion of his estate that would have gone to her mother. His children, Gregoria's aunts and uncles, then pressed for her official legitimation, which was readily granted when Gregoria was twenty-two, in 1795, due both to her parents' single status when she was conceived and to her high social rank.

The elaborate obfuscations of doña María's case were not atypical, as confirmation of similar family concealment strategies comes from other parts of the empire. In Mexico City, for example, doña Magdalena de la Vega engaged in sexual relations with *regidor* (city councilman) don Vicente de Borboya. This couple, like their Bolivian counterparts, needed official permission to marry, since don Vicente was a major officeholder. Years later, doña Justa, the natural daughter of this couple, described how her parents' desire to save public face led to a private pregnancy.

> Seeing that doña Magdalena was pregnant and recognizing that marriage could not then take place . . . in order to ward off and guard against the danger to her honor and good reputation . . . and the blushes and the emotions to which she would be exposed, they adopted the expedient of moving her to the city of Puebla, under the excuse that she was sick, to the house of her sister, doña Teresa, where she remained hidden until she gave birth.[18]

Like doña María, doña Magdalena died soon after childbirth. A friend of the Mexican couple later remembered, "and this result was so hidden that [doña Magdalena] died with the reputation of a virgin." Death in childbirth claimed doña María and doña Magdalena, as it did 4.8 percent of those pregnant women who appeared in legitimation petitions.[19] In both these cases collusion with brothers and sisters and geographical removal from the scene had temporarily saved their reputations. But what would have happened if doña María and doña Magdalena—as did the majority of their counterparts—had survived this ordeal?

Personal correspondence and oral testimony make clear that both women would have married their fiancés and lovers. Don Ramón, in a letter written to the countess (doña María's sister) two decades after the event, affirmed that "I recognize [Gregoria] as my natural daughter born of your sister doña María del Carmen, who is in heaven and with whom I would have married, as you know, if the royal permission had arrived to do it, but as God chose to carry her away, I was not able to put into practice my desires after I obtained the necessary license and my transfer to Lima."[20]

Father Joaquín del Moral, a confidant of don Vicente de Borboya, confirmed the similar circumstances of the Mexican couple: "Because of the close friendship and confidence [I had] with the subject [don Vicente] he told me various times that when he was trying to contract marriage with doña Magdalena de la Vega, he had a daughter named doña Justa Rufina by her . . . and that he was not able to verify [the marriage] due to the death of doña Magdalena."[21]

The testimony of these witnesses provides evidence about some customary norms that governed sexual relations between colonial couples. Both doña María and doña Magdalena had lost their virginity. However, both women had done so only after they had presumably exchanged the *palabra de casamiento* or "promise to marry" with their fiancés. Their surrender of virginity under such circumstances was not unusual, as local society apparently tolerated (even if it did not condone) premarital intercourse between engaged couples. Nor did these women "lose the respect" of their fiancés because they had engaged in intercourse. Although an élite Latin male customarily demanded virginity of his intended wife, he apparently expected her to prove this aspect of her honor at the time of first intercourse, which might take place significantly before the marriage ceremony.

We see a conscious delineation of such sexual mores in an intimate and revealing letter written by Querétaro regidor don Joseph Martín de la Rocha to his spinster sister, doña Elvira, who lived in Veracruz. The subject was most delicate, as don Joseph confessed that he had fathered an illegitimate child, and he begged his sister to assume responsibility for her baby niece. Don Joseph confessed: "I tell you in all confidence, and confident in the love you have for me, that this baby is my daughter, and I recognize her as such, that her mother was a lady, that nothing takes away from my circumstances that I knew her as a virgin, and that she died in childbirth, and for that reason all my plans have been frustrated."[22]

The manner in which this eighteenth-century élite Mexican male chose to describe this affair to his spinster sister tells us much about customary élite attitudes toward honor and premarital intercourse. Don Joseph is clearly taking pains to inform his sister that he had conducted this affair in an "honorable" manner. What, then, does he consider to be the telling variables in his favor? He informs doña Elvira that his lover was a social peer, as she was a "lady." She was a woman of honor as she was a "virgin" at the time of first intercourse. Nor had don Joseph seduced her with underhanded motives ("nothing takes away from my circumstances that I knew her as a virgin") as the couple had exchanged the palabra de casamiento ("all my plans have been frustrated").

If a couple were social equals and were engaged, the man did not lose honor by claiming the virginity of his intended. Furthermore, even though don Joseph succeeded in shifting the child-care burden to his spinster sister, he acknowledged his responsibility to his daughter and promised to pay all expenses. It is notable that don Joseph insisted that his honor had not been diminished by his conduct of this affair. Perhaps one reason that he could boast of the probity of his actions was that he had rigorously guarded the honor of his fiancé as well, as he had protected her reputation with a private pregnancy. Even after her death, he omitted her name in the crucial letter to his sister, nor is she identified two decades later in the legitimation petition of her daughter, doña Josepha. If don Joseph's unknown fiancé had survived childbirth, she presumably would have suffered no public loss of her honor, and the couple would have married.

What would have been the next step for unwed mothers if, unlike doña María, doña Magdalena, and don Joseph's intended, they had survived childbirth and married their prospective husbands? As long as both lovers were single and not related by prohibitive degrees of kinship, a post hoc marriage ceremony would have automatically legitimated their children. These offspring would have inherited equally with any additional children the couples might have had, and would, in the eyes of the law, have been equal to future siblings in every way.

Immediately after their marriage, in order to save face, such couples might have hidden their indiscretion by introducing these recently legitimated children into their homes as "orphans" or as "adopted" children. As time passed, the couples might eventually allow the true circumstances surrounding their first child's birth to become public knowledge. Even if they did not, they could write "private wills," which were kept from public domain but which fully explained past circumstances and protected the legal rights of their firstborn.

There must have been many unwed mothers who, in conjunction with their lover-fiancés and close kin, engineered private pregnancies, survived childbirth, married, and automatically legitimated their children. Such a successful outcome would mean that these families need never have applied for gracias a sacar. Such records cannot tell us, therefore, about the frequency with which the colonial élites protected female honor by keeping pregnancies private as a preface to matrimony. What the cédulas reveal is the how such pregnancies were organized and the customary roles and responsibilities of the unwed mothers, fathers, and families who engineered them.

Colonists also used private pregnancy to protect a woman's reputation when marriage was not a chosen or a possible conclusion. Such cases occurred either when men refused to wed their pregnant lovers or were unable to do so because they were already married or were priests. Private pregnancies could also protect married women who bore children that were not their husbands'. In these instances the involved parties had to take extraordinary precautions to save the honor of the mother, as well as to care for her newborn.

Such secrecy was not maintained without personal sacrifice. The history of doña X illustrates such costs, as she had to endure not only rejection by her lover but loss of her baby as well.[23] Witnesses agree that doña X belonged to one of the most honored families in Buenos Aires society. It is unclear whether she had a firm promise of marriage from don Manuel Domecq, a merchant who had an extensive commerce in the Argentine interior, but her subsequent actions suggest that she hoped that a marriage would take place. Their relationship resulted in a pregnancy, and in early 1753 doña X gave birth to a baby boy. Apparently she had the child at home, which suggests that her family conspired to protect her and their good name. Immediately after the birth, don Manuel arrived to collect the boy and deposited him at the house of María Josepha de Abalos, a "respectable" married woman whom he paid to care for his natural son. As was common in such circumstances, don Manuel openly acknowledged the child as his—the double standard applied here, as paternity did not negatively affect the reputation of the élite male. He protected the name of the mother, for the birth certificate, issued in February 1753, listed baby Pedro simply as "the natural son of don Manuel Domecq, a Spaniard, and of a lady who is also Spanish."

Consistent with the goal of maintaining the privacy of doña X's pregnancy, don Pedro did not reveal her identity to baby Pedro's foster mother. However, doña X could not tolerate such a separation from her son. She arranged to be introduced to María Josepha, cultivated her friendship, and began to frequent her house. The marked attention she paid to baby Pedro, the many presents she brought him, and the kisses she lavished upon him soon aroused María Josepha's suspicion. Finally, doña X confessed that she was the mother. In testimony that still remains pitiful centuries after the event, María Josepha's daughter, recalled how doña X had begged that "when she would not be able to come and see him, in order not to arouse suspicion, that they send a servant with the baby to her house under some pretext." Doña X's obsession with secrecy—to hide from society her identity as an unwed mother—dictated that she deny her relationship with her child.

Doña X not only continued to visit her child, but she apparently still hoped that her private pregnancy was a temporary expedient until don Manuel would legitimize their union and their son. Don Manuel, however, announced his engagement to another woman. María Josepha's daughter, Juliana, explained doña X's response to this betrayal: "Doña X continued to visit as long as don Manuel Domecq remained single, but when she found out that he was engaged, she became furious, and *never returned to see her son again*" (italics mine).

With don Manuel now openly engaged, doña X had no alternative but to abandon her child if she wished to maintain her public honor.

This wrenching decision on her part illustrates the hard choices faced by unwed mothers whose identity had been protected. The story of doña X, unlike that of most of her peers, ends on a somewhat happy note. Although she relinquished her child, she eventually married, had other children, and held an honored place in Buenos Aires society.[24]

Although an unwed mother might have a public reputation as a virgin while she carried or even after she bore her child, any subsequent recognition of her offspring would stain her honor. Such was the fate of doña Gabriela Márquez, whose early profile—a youthful romance, first promise of marriage, a secret birth—repeats the private pregnancy pattern.[25] Even though her lover, don Antonio de Aguilar, was under twenty himself, he came from a prominent family of Chilean landowners. He recognized his illegitimate daughter, María, at her birth and insisted that he be named as the natural father on her baptismal certificate—which did not name the mother—and he arranged for his sister, doña Mercedes, to take and to raise the baby secretly. For two years doña Gabriela maintained her identity as a private unwed mother and waited for don Antonio to make good his promise to marry her and to legitimate their child. Like doña X, doña Gabriela was betrayed, for don Antonio announced his engagement to another woman. Unlike doña X, doña Gabriela chose her child over her honor. She arrived at doña Mercedes' house, took her two-year-old baby back with her, and spent the remainder of her life as a single mother.

Private pregnancies not only guarded the honor of spinsters who did not marry their lovers, such as doña X or doña Gabriela, but also that of already-married women who lacked this alternative. Married women engaged in extramarital affairs at great personal risk to themselves and to their lovers. Therefore, such cases are rare, and in all such instances it is not surprising to note that the husbands of these women had been long absent. After doña Y from Havana was abandoned by her husband, for example, she eventually had two daughters by don Juan Antonio Morejón. He protected her name during and after their affair, effectively "adopted" their two daughters, and, with great difficulty, given that their daughters were adulterine in the eyes of the law, eventually achieved their legitimation.[26] In Cumaná, Venezuela, don Josef Antonio Betancourt arranged such a private pregnancy for married doña Z. Witnesses expressed much sympathy for her sufferings under her husband, don Esteban Lizcano, who had abandoned her long before he ran off to the Llanos. They remembered "the horrible life (*mala vida*) that Lizcano gave her by his troublesome and ridiculous character, for he even refused to support her, and it was these events that no doubt led her to fall into her present situation."[27] In these two cases private pregnancy saved the honor of these élite women as their married state foreclosed any other options.

Public Pregnancy and Extended Engagements

Although private pregnancies could save honor, they entailed extraordinary precautions on the part of the woman, her lover, and their families. At least 44, or 23.5 percent, of legitimation petitions reflect an alternative strategy of "public pregnancy" where élite women carried, bore, and raised their illegitimate children under the full scrutiny of their social peers. Included in this category are "extended engagements" as well as certain forms of "concubinage." One-fourth of public pregnancies can be clearly identified as "extended engagements" (see table 3). In such cases unmarried women who had exchanged a promise of marriage lived openly for years and even decades in public, monogamous relationships with prospective husbands. Although the documents show that these women felt shame and experienced loss of reputation and honor, their situation was not totally irreparable. Subsequent marriage with their lover could, at any time, transform these unwed mothers into wives, and their hijos naturales into legitimate heirs. The situation of such unwed mothers challenges any stereotypical view of colonial sexuality that characterizes single women as either virgins who were "in control" or nonvirgins who were "out of control," and presumably beyond the pale. Instead, colonial reality was far more complex. "In-between" circumstances such as a palabra de casamiento could provide marginal legitimacy to the status of nonvirgin spinster or even to that of unwed mother. Even though a public pregnancy deprived an unmarried mother of honor, public knowledge that there had been a palabra de casamiento provided a mitigating circumstance.

We see such circumstances in the case of doña Juana Díaz de Estrada, the daughter of a former governor of Veracruz, who in the 1690s began a relationship with don Diego de Alarcón Ocaña, a naval ship's captain from Havana. The captain promised to marry her, and as his courtship proceeded, and their sexual intimacies as well, doña

Juana put more and more pressure on him to fulfill this pledge. The captain's secretary, don Agustín Henríquez, remembered those days with great clarity: "I was there on occasions in which the lady rightfully pleaded with him to fulfill his word, reminding him of the damage to her reputation and the discredit of her family."[28]

The captain "swore not to defer it." However he did not fulfill his promise, and the secretary noted that doña Juana's pleas became even "more forceful when she found out that she was pregnant." Finally a daughter, doña María Cathalina, was born. Don Diego still balked at tying the knot. Mother and father treated the birth of their baby in quite different ways. Don Diego showed great joy at her birth. His secretary remembered that "he took her in his arms . . . he recognized her as his natural daughter, and he publicly celebrated her as such in view of all the city."

Doña Juana, far from showing any elation, retreated and was reluctant to face public scrutiny. The secretary recalled that "doña Juana withdrew into great privacy." Her guilt and shame impressed others as well. One witness recalled that she had "visited her house often, and her modesty was such that before the dawn [she had dressed herself so that] not even her fingers could be seen." Now publicly marked as an unwed mother, doña Juana literally went into mourning for an honor that could only be restored by marriage. Unfortunately, she suffered an accident, and although don Diego sped to her side, she was unconscious and died before the couple could be wed. The captain knew he had not satisfied the requirements of honor, as he considered his later "reverses" as a "punishment of God" for "having delayed the fulfillment of his obligation."

The case of doña María Josepha Pérez de Balmaceda, from Havana, shows how a marriage promise could provide a "fallen" woman a measure of public honor, although the protagonist of this case may well have carried her obsession to neurotic extremes. During her courtship, doña María had taken the rare step of demanding, and receiving, a written promise of marriage from her fiancé before she agreed to have intercourse with him. The couple then lived together for years and produced three illegitimate children. Finally, witnesses agree, the marriage was imminent: "after the birth of Pedro Antonio, the said [don Pedro Diez de Florencia] tried very earnestly to fulfill the word that he had given to doña María Josepha, and [the couple] prepared clothes and finery, and fixed up the house."[29]

Just before the ceremony, don Pedro may have had second

thoughts, for he broke off the preparations, took off to Spain to look for a better job, and sailed to Mexico to assume his new position. For years he sent pleading letters, envoys, and money to doña María, begging her to join him and be wed. Doña María may well have had enough of his delays and broken promises, for she claimed fear of the sea and refused to follow him.

Nonetheless, she never let her relatives or local peers forget that she was an engaged woman. She kept her lover's written promise to marry her knotted in a ball that she tied to the rosary that she wore around her neck, and she constantly opened his note and read it aloud to relatives and town officials. As one witness somewhat wearily recounted,

> many times [doña María] read that paper in the presence of this witness and of all of her house and family, and many other persons. . . . and even many years after the absence and death of [her fiancé] doña María carried [the paper] hanging from the rosary she wore around her neck which proved her good faith and her well-founded hope that she would have married.

A palabra de casamiento, then, provided a certain legitimacy in that it separated unwed mothers who had surrendered their virginity with a firm promise of marriage from women who engaged in sexual intercourse with no guarantee or possibility of eventual matrimony. Since the gracias a sacar chronicled only those instances where marriage never occurred, it is impossible to calculate the frequency with which colonial élite couples became engaged, produced illegitimate offspring, and then eventually married. It is indicative, however, that colonists throughout the Indies familiarly spoke of this practice, and it was commonplace enough to produce its own patterns.

Couples who had exchanged palabra de casamiento customarily recorded the names of both mother and father on the baptismal certificates of their illegitimate children. Such a public acknowledgment not only indirectly informed society of the couple's marriage promise, but it presumably put pressure on the parties to execute it. This openness could later benefit their illegitimate offspring, who, by presenting their birth certificates identifying them as the natural children of X and Y, could more easily prove their legitimated status.

The baptismal certificate of the illegitimate daughter of doña Thoribia María Guerra Mier and her fiancé, military officer don Lorenzo de Parga, from Valledupar, New Granada, reflects this custom. Sometime before 1779 don Lorenzo arrived in Valledupar, where he met doña Thoribia, the daughter of don Juan Guerra, who belonged to one of the "first families" of the city. Years later don Lorenzo remembered how he had "proposed matrimony with . . . doña Thoribia . . . and under this belief and word had a daughter named doña María Josepha."[30] The couple was waiting for official permission from the military authorities to wed when war broke out, and don Lorenzo was transferred to Cartagena.

Doña Thoribia may well have postponed the baptism of her illegitimate daughter, born in 1779, in the hope that she might first be married and that her child might then be baptized as a legitimated offspring. By 1782, she and her family could apparently wait no longer, but they made sure that the circumstances of doña María's birth were public knowledge. Perhaps it was the family's exalted position that led the local cleric to take the rare option of omitting any reference to the circumstances of the birth of the three-year-old child in her certificate. He simply noted that she was "the baby, María Josefa," rather than that she was an illegitimate child.[31] Such delicacy did not, however, extend to her parents, who were clearly identified as "don Lorenzo de Parga, Lieutenant of Granaderos of the Fixed Regiment of the Plaza of Cartagena and . . . of doña Thoribia de la Guerra, legitimate daughter of don Juan de la Guerra of the Kingdom of Spain and of doña Ana Mestre." To clinch the case, doña Thoribia's family apparently routed out the town notables (who included her mother's kin) to swear on the baptismal certificate to the extenuating circumstances surrounding the birth: "also present in this act the Captain don Diego Facundo Mestre and the Señor Alcalde Ordinario don José Francisco Mestre to witness that this aforementioned baby was conceived under the promise of matrimony."

If doña Thoribia hoped that this certificate might spur the lieutenant to return for a wedding, she proved mistaken. He later cited the demands of war as a rationale for his continued postponements. Doña Thoribia died in 1787 before they could wed, and years later the guilt-stricken father, now a lieutenant colonel, petitioned for his daughter's legitimation.

It is noteworthy that one of the clearest statements concerning such extended "engagements" comes from a Spanish official who customarily reviewed colonist applications for the gracias a sacar. His official commentary appears in the legitimation petition of doña Antonia del Rey Blanco, of Havana, who was born under murky circumstances. Her unwed mother, doña Beatris Blanco de la Poza, had spent her young adult years in a Havana convent but was finally forced to leave due to ill health. Even while living at home she did not participate in local society, but remained a recluse in the family house.[32]

Perhaps this inexperience explains why she was particularly vulnerable to the advances of don Lázaro del Rey Bravo, a business associate of her brother. Although don Lázaro had been married in Spain, he had word that his wife had died in his absence, and so he proposed matrimony to doña Beatris, and the couple began a sexual relationship. It was only after the birth of her child that doña Beatris and her family learned, to their horror, that don Lázaro's first wife had been alive when the couple conceived their baby, although she had since passed away. Her family then refused to permit doña Beatris to marry don Lázaro, even though he remained willing to do so. Decades later, when the legitimation petition of doña Beatris' daughter, doña Antonia, appeared before the Council of the Indies, did the legal question surrounding her birth find an answer. Was she an hija natural—the much more acceptable product of a sexual union between single parents—or was she an adulterina, the despised result of an adulterous alliance? As was customary in Spanish law and culture, the royal official did not rule solely on the actual facts of the case, that is, when had doña Beatris and don Lázaro begun a sexual relationship, or when did don Lázaro's wife die. Instead, the official also took into account the couple's intent, that is, how their actions reflected their perception—even if it was an erroneous perception—of reality. The official gave the couple the benefit of the doubt as he ruled that

> doña Antonia is an hija natural for all the favorable civil benefits without any legal difficulty, given that it is fully proved by witnesses and by documents that she not only was conceived under this belief and the good faith of doña Beatris her mother, but that even don Lázaro her father thought he was a bachelor and able to carry out the promise of matrimony he seems to have given.

One of the deciding factors in this case was doña Antonia's birth certificate, which the official saw as compelling proof that the couple assumed that they were single and able to wed. The official concluded, and instead of putting on the baptismal certificate the expression that is customary of their class, that of "daughter of unknown parents," the couple used the much less common "hija natural of the aforementioned," which goes to corroborate the mutual understanding of all [concerned], for it is not customary to declare it this way except when the parents are commonly conceived to be single and with the disposition or the desire to legitimate their offspring by a subsequent marriage.

These remarks demonstrate that although the tendency of engaged couples to have illegitimate offspring first and to marry later may have been uncommon, it was apparently common enough to develop a body of generally understood practice.

What was life like for these unwed mothers who lived for years or even decades in the expectation of future matrimony? Their case histories show that their social position might remain, at best, ambiguous. As in the case of private pregnancy, élite women might customarily benefit from an initial presumption that they were innocent. Even when relatives and neighbors knew that a questionable liaison was occurring, they did not always choose to acknowledge it openly. As time passed, however, and particularly as extended engagements seemed less and less likely to end in matrimony, the situation of such unwed mothers became more and more difficult.

Public awareness that a single woman was having an affair with her fiancé, that the couple were living together, or that she had borne a child was not always immediate. Colonial architecture could cooperate to hide incriminating evidence, as the homes of the prosperous tended to be large, with many rooms for family, servants, and servants' children. In the beginning courting couples might find private spaces for amorous activities, and later even the addition of an extra baby might not make much a spatial impact.[33] Since a traditional charity of Latin American élite families was to care for orphans and homeless children, the presence of minors with vague antecedents was not that uncommon. The few cases I have detailed here of relatives or nurses who sheltered babies born out of wedlock illustrate the frequency of infant adoption. Since not all women who took in children were guilty of sexual transgressions, they provided the pattern through which unwed mothers might try to assimilate their sons and daughters into their own homes without scandalous notice.

The case of Chilean doña María Rosa de la Torre provides some details as to the variety of social interactions that took place as friends and neighbors discovered that a spinster was now an unwed mother.[34] Although doña María Rosa and her fiancé, don Felipe Briceño, belonged to the Santiago élite, their economic resources were not substantial. Doña María Rosa did not have the backing of powerful kin, as she lived alone with her mother—her father had died in Peru. Don Felipe's father had held the prestigious position of alcalde, but he was not himself prosperous.

Lacking the presence of a father, doña María Rosa's home must have provided a convenient locale for don Felipe's courtship and promise of matrimony. In 1775 a baby boy named José Félix was born. A next-door friend, who was also the baby's godfather, later testified that don Felipe had ordered that both his and doña María Rosa's names appear on the baptismal certificate because "he wanted to legitimate him." Although the promised marriage did not occur, there was no immediate public recognition that doña María Rosa had given birth to an illegitimate child. Fray Agustín, a brother of don Felipe and a priest, remembered that when Jóse Félix petitioned to be legitimated he had discovered that

> With the entry and communication that I had in the house of doña María Rosa de la Torre, I saw there a little boy whom she loved very much, but I was unclear who his parents were for some time until my brother don Felipe told me that he was his son and also the child of doña María Rosa, although they were hiding this, no doubt to protect her honor. But once I was knowledgeable of this, she no longer hesitated in my presence to kiss her son.

Another witness recalled that he had heard a rumor that the infant that doña María was raising was hers but that "because of her honor there was secrecy about this, even though the boy was raised at her side and in her own house." As time passed, doña María Rosa and don Felipe no longer hid their affair. In the meantime doña María Rosa's mother may have died, for, possibly still promising marriage, don Felipe moved into her house. Even then, some neighbors thought they might be married. The precariousness of doña María Rosa's situation became manifest when don Felipe, aiming to make his fortune, left her and their son and took off to the Andean mining districts. Unfortunately, he experienced "total ruin." Even though the signs were not propitious, doña María Rosa did not abandon hope that he would return and carry out his promise to marry her. A friend spoke of the "tears and pleas" that she directed to her erring lover. He never returned to Santiago, and when he died he left the little money he had, not to doña María Rosa, but to his mother.

Doña María Rosa's case illustrates the long-term ambiguities that might surround the lives of unwed mothers as society gradually discovered and acknowledged their situations. Even don Felipe's brother did not immediately know that doña María Rosa's child was his illegitimate nephew, nor did neighbors seem eager to clarify the marital status of the couple. The initial social assumption, perhaps because don Felipe and doña María Rosa belonged to the class that possessed honor, was toward innocence. Even after the passage of years, when the pretense could no longer be maintained, her neighbors seemed more inclined to sympathize, rather than to criticize her situation.

Women such as doña María Rosa might spend years in limbo waiting for their fiancés to marry them and only discover in middle or old age that their hopes would never be fulfilled. The legal securities of matrimony, such as inheritance from a spouse or reliable maintenance for children, could be denied them. As time passed, many such "engaged" women found that their positions moved beyond ambiguity as the men they had lived with for decades abandoned them to marry, or to take up affairs with, other women. Such abandonment naturally produced bitterness between the unwed mother and her lover, and often soured the relationship between the father and his illegitimate offspring.

Such sentiments clearly emerge in the case of widow doña Antonia Hernández of Havana.[35] She had lived for years with don Nicolás Joseph Rapun, who rose successfully in the bureaucracy and eventually attained the important post of intendent of the Royal Treasury in Havana. Doña Antonia had three children by her first husband and, almost annually, from 1747 to 1752 she presented don Nicolás with an illegitimate child, four of whom survived childbirth. Although don Nicolás did not share her home, all the town knew of their affair and of his daily visits. Don Nicolás promised to marry her, but "His not having married the mother of the petitioners is explained because he put her off with flattering hopes that he was going to do it when he reached the heights that were destined by fortune, and after he succeeded, he continued delaying from day to day. And now that he is the intendent it is impossible to compel him to satisfy that obligation."

Even though doña Antonia tried to sue and force him to marry her, don Nicolás never gave in. He not only broke off their long-term relationship but had a final illegitimate son with another woman.

Although doña María Rosa and doña Antonia were eventually abandoned by their fiancés, they never appear to have been ostracized by friends and neighbors. Social peers might initially be disposed to show tolerance toward women trapped in such "extended engagements" for several reasons. First of all, at any time, their status might change through subsequent matrimony. Although don Felipe may have failed in the mining districts, there must have been others who succeeded in their endeavors and returned in triumph to marry their fiancées and to legitimate their offspring. Even if society were disposed to criticize the relationship of doña Antonia and don Nicolás, he was a man of power in Havana, and doña Antonia would have shared his status if the couple had ever wed.

Testimony in such cases makes clear that, although the strict dictates of honor might demand that engaged women who bore illegitimate children be rejected by their social peers, in practical day-to-day living such was not the case. Instead, neighbors apparently moved with ease and familiarity in and out of such houses. The illegitimate children of these unions played and were educated with legitimate offspring of equal rank.[36] Here, the pervasive tolerance of a Latin Catholic society where sins could always be forgiven seems to have eased the daily exigencies of social discourse. There were limits to this tolerance, however, for unwed mothers generally remained spinsters all their lives, and their children could be subjected to the civil and social barriers imposed against those who lacked honor.[37]

Public Pregnancy and Concubinage

As time passed, women such as doña María Rosa and doña Antonia must have realized that they would pass the rest of their lives as aging "fiancées" and as mothers of illegitimate offspring. If they had any consolation, it must have been that they were honorable women who had followed local customs, as they had engaged in sexual relationships solely as a prelude to matrimony. The real fault lay with their lovers, who had failed to honor the marriage promise. Such rationalizations could not provide comfort to a last group of women, who had publicly entered into affairs without a promise of matrimony or who had become the acknowledged mistresses of clerics or of married men[38] (see table 3). Such women had openly borne their illegitimate, adulterine, or sacrilegious offspring. Their sexual indiscretions were not only public knowledge, but they were neither mitigated by extenuating circumstances such as a palabra de casamiento nor hidden by a private pregnancy. A world of difference separated the status of those single élite women who had lived as the mistresses of bachelors or widowers from those who had had affairs with priests or married men.

The case history of single mother doña Josepha María Valespino of Havana belongs to the first category, as she lived with a Canarian ship's captain, don Amaro Rodrigues Pargo, without a promise of matrimony and eventually bore an illegitimate son named Manuel. Doña Josepha was a woman of means as she owned two houses, some slaves, and valuable jewelry. The captain lived with her when he traded in Havana. He paid her bills, carried the infant Manuel with him on visits to neighbors and to visit his ship, and was generally acknowledged as his father. Significantly, however, he never promised to marry doña Josepha, and when local neighbors described their affair, they characterized it as "illicit."[39]

Eventually, the captain sailed back to his home port in the Canaries. Although he occasionally sent doña Josepha some wool and other items to sell to support Manuel, he never returned to Cuba. The final break between the couple occurred when the captain wrote and asked that doña Josepha send Manuel to live with him in the Canaries. When she refused, the captain broke off all contact and, at his death, failed to acknowledge his son. As the years passed, doña Josepha exhausted her resources in raising Manuel, and when he petitioned for legitimation at twenty-six, he described her as "blind . . . and in the most extreme poverty." The most telling characteristic of this affair is the absence of the palabra de casamiento. However, other more subtle characteristics—the temporal limitations of the relationship, the lack of much commitment to mother and son, as well as outsiders' description of the affair as "illicit"—may also serve to place it within the realm of public concubinage, rather than that of extended engagement.

Legitimation petitions additionally reveal some rarer cases where women publicly defied the civil and ecclesiastical codes of honor, to engage in sexual affairs with clerics or married men. Significantly, such documents do not provide much information as to how society treated those who trespassed such forbidden boundaries. No doubt petitioners wanted to make the strongest case possible for legitimation and would omit any information concerning any possible ostracism of their mother or father. Instead, more than others, such legitimation requests emphasize the discretion of the lovers or detail the exalted personal connections of the participants or confirm their willingness to pay exorbitant sums to achieve the desired legitimation. Especially here, only the most powerful and wealthy made such applications, as the Council of the Indies was less likely to approve them[40] (see table 3).

It is probably no accident that two of the most extraordinary of such cases originated in Bolivia, for the silver millionaires of La Plata and Potosí combined the wealth and connections that were the prerequisites for such pretensions. The petitions of don Melchor and don Agustín Varea y Lazcano of La Plata, for example, emphasized their notable parental backgrounds. Their mother, doña Gertrudis de Varea y Lazcano, belonged "to one of the principal, distinguished, and richest families" of Potosí.[41] Her lover, don Domingo Herboso y Figueroa, was a priest and dean of the cathedral of La Plata. He be-

Table 3. Parents' Marital State and Success of Legitimation Petitions (*N* 142)

	Father's Marital Status									
	Single		Priest		Widower		Married		Unknown	
	N	%	*N*	%	*N*	%	*N*	%	*N*	%
Yes	70	87.5	11	78.6	5	83.3	9	69.2	16	55.2
No	8	10.0	3	21.4	1	16.7	4	30.8	13	44.8
?	2	2.5	—	—	—	—	—	—	—	—
Total	80		14		6		13		29	
	Mother's Marital Status									
	Single				Widow		Married		Unknown	
	N	%			*N*	%	*N*	%	*N*	%
Yes	83	88.3			5	55.6	7	87.5	16	51.6
No	11	11.7			2	22.2	1	12.5	15	48.4
?	—	—			2	22.2	—	—	—	—
Total	94				9		8		31	

Source: AGI, Audiencias, "Cartas y Expedientes"; Indiferente General, Exp. 16, 1535.

longed to an extremely powerful political clan, as his father had been president of the Audiencia of Charcas, thus ranking among the top dozen executive officers in the Spanish Empire. Don Domingo's uncle was an archbishop, his brother was a high treasury official in Lima (contador mayor del Tribunal Real de Cuentas), and another brother was governor of the nearby province of Cochabamba.

Family rank and wealth, however, could not obscure the fact that doña Gertrudis was an unwed mother, while the father of her two sons, don Domingo, was a priest. Witnesses who testified in this case emphasized the care the couple had taken to avoid public scandal. Although don Domingo openly visited doña Gertrudis, the lovers maintained separate residences. The couple did not recognize their sons on their baptismal certificates, but listed them as *expósitos*, or "abandoned."[42] One witness, who lived near doña Gertrudis, remembered that don Domingo "in particular used a certain caution and reticence because of the dignity and nature of his position."

After don Domingo's death, his now-adult sons apparently found some acceptance in La Plata society. At least they found witnesses who could testify that they were looked upon "with reputation and honor in all their dealings . . . in the houses of . . . distinguished persons." Their still-surviving mother may well have lost most pretensions to honor. Although the petition contains much information on family pedigree and wealth, the sole comment on her immediate situation is the rather defensive note that her sons "looked on her with respect and veneration."[43] Family wealth and rank notwithstanding, the brothers never fully restored their honor through legitimation.

During those same years that doña Gertrudis and don Domingo carried on their affair in La Plata, a few blocks away, spinster doña Juana Risco y Agoretta lived openly with a married man. Although Dr. Francisco de Moya y Palacios was a regidor and alcalde in the rich silver town of Potosí, where he was married to the daughter of a royal official, his residence was with doña Juana in La Plata. The couple had five illegitimate children, all of whom reached high positions in local society. One daughter married a lawyer, another a high court judge and another a regidor, while one son became a priest and the other a lawyer. The money from silver seemed to smooth all paths, and when one of her widowed daughters, herself a silver magnate, petitioned for legitimation, she not only received it but later used her wealth to purchase a title of nobility.

We know little, however, of the fate of doña Juana. The few comments on her situation bear some resemblance to those made concerning her neighbor, doña Gertrudis. Witnesses noted that her lawyer son, don Agustín, still lived with her, even though he had the means to establish a separate residence, because of "the love and veneration that he feels for her."[44] It is difficult to know what the rest of society thought.

Epilogue

It is important to remember that the large majority of the women whose stories appear here did not benefit from the strategies designed to preserve or restore honor. Once a single woman engaged in premarital sex, the surest method to protect or to restore her honor was through matrimony. The most "successful" private pregnancies, extended engagements, and cases of concubinage were those in which the woman married her lover and automatically legitimated her offspring. The gracias a sacar cédula cases were, by definition, those where eventual marriage did not occur or did not lead to such automatic legitimation, but necessitated an official intervention.

What, then, was the final fate of the mothers? Although a detailed examination of their later lives is beyond the scope of this paper, some general trends can provide a final commentary. The cédula documents fail to provide follow-up stories on more than half (N 104) of them, but it should come as no surprise that nearly two-thirds of those whose fate we do know remained spinsters and widows (see table 4).

Table 4. Fate of Unwed Mothers (*N* 191)

Later Fate	Private Pregnancies		Other Pregnancies	
	N	%	*N*	%
Spinster, widow	13	19.4	38	30.7
Married lover	2	3.0	12	9.7
Married other	3	4.5	4	3.2
Died in childbirth	4	6.0	5	4.0
Religious	2	3.0	—	—
Unknown	43	64.1	65	52.4
TOTAL	67	100.0	124	100.0

Source: AGI, Audiencias, "Cartas y Expédientes"; Indiferente General, exp. 16, 35.

In this work I have considered the later lives of some of them. Included among them are spinster doña Margarita of Tasco, Mexico, whose story introduced this paper and who, after eighteen years, voluntarily ended the secrecy of her private pregnancy to recognize her son. Doña Gabriela of Chile also gave up the benefits of a private pregnancy, retrieved her daughter, and remained single after her lover became engaged to another. The extended engagement of doña Beatris of Havana ended in spinsterhood when her family forbade her to wed her fiancé. Doña María, of Chile, continued to raise her son alone after she could not pry her lover from the Andean mining districts. Doña Antonia, also of Havana, remained a widow and the mother of four illegitimate children after intendent don Nicolás Rapun broke his promise to marry her. The histories of these women, with their traumas of delayed marriage and ultimate betrayal, are typical of those of the rest.

The next most common fate of the women, marriage, has not been considered here. Fourteen, or 7.5 percent, eventually married their lovers. For various reasons, however, these marriages could not automatically legitimate children conceived before the ceremony, and the families made applications for the gracias a sacar. Affairs between first cousins, for example, fell under this classification, and such couples needed official church permission to wed. Any children conceived before such marriages were classified as incestuous, and could not be automatically legitimated by a post hoc ceremony. Subsequent marriage also failed to legitimate offspring born when one of the lovers had been married to someone else. Don Cayetano Yudice, of Guatemala, presented such a legal tangle to the Council of the Indies when he fathered four children with doña María Dominga de Astorga. Their first two children were adulterine, as they had been born while his wife was alive. Their third child was conceived when his wife was alive but was born after she died. Their fourth child was born when don Cayetano was a widower, but before he married doña María. After much debate the Council decided that the couple's eventual marriage had automatically legitimated only their fourth child and that their first three offspring could be legitimated only through gracias a sacar.[45]

There were a few instances—among them was doña X of Buenos Aires—where a woman had an illegitimate child and then married another man (*N* 7; 3.8 percent). The infrequency of this option shows that élite women who lost their virginity closed dramatically most options of marriage to anyone other than their lover. Equally noteworthy is the cédula mothers' avoidance of the religious life, as only two (1.0 percent) eventually entered convents. It may well be that the existence of other women whose status was equally ambivalent provided sufficient peer support, so that women who had lost honor did not consider their plight so dire as to necessitate rejection of secular society. Convents were not refuges for unwed mothers.

The last group of women (*N* 9; 4.8 percent) had the worst fate of all, as they died during or soon after the birth of their illegitimate babies. The stories of doña María of La Plata, doña Magdalena of Mexico City, and doña Juana of Veracruz are typical of those whose maneuverings to protect their honor paled in comparison to their ultimate tragedy.[46]

Conclusion

Colonial élites of the late seventeenth and eighteenth centuries structured their actions according to their understanding of the ethos of honor, either as they abided by its norms or as they tried to escape its consequences. The honor code emphasized control of female sexuality through virginity and marital faithfulness. However, Spanish American élite women could be not only "in control" and "out of control," but also somewhere "in between." The large majority of the women who appear in cédula petitions fit somewhere "in between." They were neither single virgins nor faithful wives who possessed honor because they were "in control." Nor were they promiscuous wantons devoid of honor who were "out of control." These élite women used ambiguities inherent in the honor code to maintain an intermediate position and sometimes regain an honorable state in spite of their violation of prevailing sexual codes.

Two distinct and, at times, complementary tactics permitted such flexibility. One was the socially recognized dichotomy between private reality and public reputation. Although not without cost or risk of eventual disclosure, a successful private pregnancy permitted a woman to preserve honor no matter what the severity of her sexual indiscretion. A second, and not mutually exclusive, option for some women was eventual marriage to their lovers. Critical here was the degree to which a sexual relationship had violated honor and the extent to which it approached dishonor. As in the case of race, where Latin society consciously distinguished a complex range of colors, so too in sexual relationships society recognized varying degrees of illicit activity. Just as colonists perceived mulattoes as neither white nor black, women who engaged in premarital or extramarital sex were neither virgins nor whores. Instead, just as society acknowledged indeterminate areas where racial mobility might occur, some sexual relationships permitted the preservation or recovery of honor. The closer the sexual violation was to what was permissible within the honor code, the easier the restoration of honor.

Prevailing canon and civil law, as well as popular custom, provided fine guides as to the measure of dishonor attached to illicit sexual relationships, as well as to the illegitimate products of such unions. Thus, single parents who had exchanged the promise of matrimony—and their resulting hijos naturales—were among the mildest offenders of prevailing codes, requiring only a post hoc ceremony to automatically restore all parties to honor. Although couples engaged in adulterous relationships might also eventually marry and obtain some social acceptance, marriage would not legitimize their offspring, who had to seek restoration of honor through the gracias a sacar. Women who engaged in sexual relationships with priests found themselves too far removed from the honor code. They not only lacked any marriage option, but they found that the Council of the Indies was most reluctant to legitimize their offspring. Even here, however, the council was at least willing to consider a legitimation plea, for the state bureaucracy complemented the creative ambiguity that was inherent in a colonial society with few absolutes. The Council of the Indies thus became a court of last resort when human frailty broke the chain of honor that linked Spanish American élites to their past, bound them to their present, and defined their responsibility to the future.

Acknowledgments

I would like to thank the American Philosophical Society, the Spanish Fulbright Commission, the Tinker Foundation, and the University of Cincinnati Research Council for funding various phases of this research.

Notes

1. The account of doña Margarita is taken from Archivo General de Indias, Seville, Spain (hereafter AGI), Mexico 1770, no. 35, 1780. Two of her brothers were priests. In 1596 one of doña Margarita's ancestors had participated in the "pacification and population of the Californias."

2. Ibid. His father spoke of the "love and affection" that his partner had shown toward Josef Antonio, who was left money in his will. Don Antonio himself mentioned that he "looked on him with the affection of a son." It was not uncommon after private pregnancies for fathers to raise their illegitimate children. Further discussion of such topics can be found in my "Honor, Paternity, and Illegitimacy: Unwed Fathers in Colonial Latin America," paper given at the 45th International Congress of Americanists, Bogotá, 1985.

3. The distinction among such categories can be found in the *Siete Partidas*, 6 vols. (Valencia: Thomas Lucas, 1757), *Quarta Partida*, Tit. 15; Sexta Partida, Tit. 13.

4. The full documentation concerning gracias a sacar derives from the petitions and testimony submitted to the Council of the Indies and the sub-Council of Gracias y Justicia and the resulting cédulas if the request was successful. The petitions can be found in the "Cartas y Expedientes" section of the Archivo General de Indias under each audiencia designation. Another rich source are *legajos* 16 and 1535, in Indiferente General, which contain copies of the actual cédulas issued when a petition was successful. These decrees contain a paragraph or so about the particulars of each case, but not the tens, and sometimes hundreds, of pages common in a petition. The 244 cases that I have collected include 101 cases with a full petition as well as resulting cédula, 41 with full petition (some of these include petitions that were denied), and 69 cases of cédula only; 5 came from other sources (Council testimony). The 28 remaining cases are a special category, as they derive from index references to cases from 1799 to 1820 that appear in nineteenth-century handwritten indexes to each section but that, with the exception of Santo Domingo, cannot be located in the archive. To make the coverage as complete as possible, these cases were included in the 244 totals when calculating factors such as total number of cases, time of petition, and geographic distribution of cédula requests. The 28 index cases were not used in calculations concerning other variables, which are based on data bases that vary according to the topic. For example, when calculating relative success rate of petitions, the data base used only those cases where there are petitions and either refusals or issuance of cédulas. When data concerning the mothers of illegitimates were examined, the computer data base considered each mother only

once, rather than counting her two or three times if she had more than one illegitimate child.

5. It also permits us to analyze regional variations, although such a detailed analysis is beyond the scope of this paper. It is notable, however, that the Caribbean is overrepresented in cédula requests, as 36.5 percent (*N* 89) of petitions originated from Santo Domingo, primarily Cuba. The South American audiencias accounted for 39 percent (*N* 95) of the remainder, with petitions from Panama north equaling 24.5 percent of the total (*N* 60). See table 2.

6. AGI, Mexico 1770, no. 35, 1780.

7. Given the importance of honor in understanding Spanish and Spanish American value systems, the topic needs further investigation. Relevant works include: Julian Pitt-Rivers, *People of the Sierra,* 2d ed. (Chicago: University of Chicago Press, 1971). By the same author, see *Mediterranean Countrymen: Essays in the Social Anthropology of the Mediterranean* (Paris: Mouton, 1963), and "Honor," *International Encyclopedia of the Social Sciences,* ed. David L. Sills, 2d ed. (New York: Macmillan and The Free Press, 1968), pp.503–11; J. G. Peristiany, *Honor and Shame: The Values of the Mediterranean* (Chicago: University of Chicago Press, 1966); Jane Schneider, "Of Vigilance and Virgins: Honor and Shame and Access to Resources in Mediterranean Societies," *Ethnology* 10, no. 1 (January 1971): 1–23; Ramón Gutiérrez, "Marriage, Sex, and the Family: Social Change in Colonial New Mexico, 1690–1846" (Ph.D. dissertation, University of Wisconsin, Madison, 1980). By the same author, see "From Honor to Love: Transformation in the Meaning of Sexuality in Colonial New Mexico," in *Interpreting Kinship Ideology and Practice in Latin America,* ed. Raymond T. Smith (Chapel Hill: University of North Carolina Press, 1984), and "Honor Ideology, Marriage Negotiation, and Class-Gender Domination in New Mexico, 1690–1846," *Latin American Perspectives* 12 (Winter, 1985): 81–104.

8. AGI, Guadalajara 368, no. 6, 1761. The petition of Pedro Minjares de Salazar contains just one of many classic testimonies as to the self-conscious way that élites distinguished who was "in" and who was "out." Witnesses noted that Minjares (who thought he was legitimate and found out in adulthood that he was not) had been treated as a man of honor, "for all have cooperated to honor him and to attend him publicly and privately, frequenting his house, dealing with him with particular confidence and intimacy, inviting him to their functions, being with him, and finally treating him with the same courtesy that is given to any other noble and distinguished person." Also notice here the conscious distinction made between private and public spheres.

9. AGI, Santo Domingo, 1474, no. 11, 1789. For that reason petitioners com-

monly included witnesses who could attest that they "have always been known, held, and commonly reputed to be white persons, Old Christians of the nobility, clean of all bad blood and without any mixture of commoner, Jew, Moor, mulatto, or *converso* (a Jew converted to Roman Catholicism) in any degree, no matter how remote."

10. AGI, Indiferente General 16, 10 October 1789. Havana widow doña Gabriela Rizo legitimated her dead husband and deceased father-in-law.

11. Not only illegitimates, but also those related to illegitimates might experience limited upward mobility in the Spanish colonial bureaucracy or in local officeholding. Doña Petronila Peralta, for example, asked to be legitimated because her son-in-law had applied for a public post in Buenos Aires. One of the ostensible reasons that he had been rejected was the unacceptable illegitimacy of his wife's mother (AGI, Buenos Aires 161, no. 2, 1762). The husband of doña María Rosa Aguilar y Márquez requested her legitimation as he feared it might otherwise damage the officeholding potential of their children (AGI, Chile 290, no. 9, 1792). The occupation of public notary, which often dealt with sensitive matters such as "closed wills," demanded that holders be not only discreet but also of legitimate birth (AGI, Charcas 562, no. 30, 1796). Illegitimacy could also hinder marital alliances. Doña Juana de Figueroa filed a petition of legitimation because the relatives of her fiancé opposed the match due to her birth (AGI, Caracas 299, no. 20, 1788). Doña Gregoria de Rivera y López was legitimated so that she might contract a marriage equal to her state (AGI, Charcas 560, no. 15, 1795). A number of petitions originated from parents who left only illegitimate children and wanted to provide legally for their inheritance. See the case of don Manuel de Escalada in AGI, Buenos Aires 183, no. 14, 1771. Others, such as don Josef Cañete de Antequera of Paraguay, applied for petitions because they felt illegitimacy deprived them of honor (AGI, Buenos Aires 228, no. 27, 1770). The data base breakdown of general reasons given by petitioners for legitimation requests shows that 45.4 percent (*N* 98) wanted it for "honor and inheritance"; 27.3 percent (*N* 59) for "honor"; 6.0 percent (*N* 13) for "inheritance"; 10.6 percent (*N* 23) for "occupational" reasons; and 10.6 percent (*N* 23) for "other" reasons.

12. For that reason the only sure method to measure the frequency with which Latin American élites customarily engaged in premarital sex would be to use parish records to compare marriage dates with baptismal records of firstborns. On the subject of premarital sex and illegitimacy, see essays by Lavrin in this volume.

13. See Barry Nichols, *An Introduction to Roman Law*, rev. ed. (Oxford: Oxford University Press, 1979), pp.84–85. Also, Domingo Cavalario, in *Insti-*

tuciones del derecho canónico, 3 vols. (Paris: Librería de don Vicente Salvat, 1846), 2:178–96, discusses the marriage prohibitions. I thank Professor Asunción Lavrin for this reference. The original Spanish civil law is cited in the "Fuero Real", book 3, title 6, law 2. "Si one sotero con muger soltera ficiera fijos e despues casar con ella, estos fijos sean herederos." (If any single man has children with a single woman and later marries her, then these children are heirs.) "Fuero Real", in *Opúsculos legales del Rey don Alfonso el Sabio,* 2 vols. (Madrid: Imprenta Real, 1836), 2:79. Most of the Spanish ordinances concerning illegitimacy, however, appear in the fourteenth-century *Siete Partidas.*

14. Numerous references in the cédula cases make it clear that post hoc legitimation was a popular option. Knowledge of such automatic legitimation figured in the strategy of the parents of doña Rafaela Espinosa de los Monteros, who was eighteen months old when they married. Her parents assumed that their marriage, per custom, automatically legitimated her, but they later found out that since they were first cousins, and thus related by prohibitive degrees of kinship, the post hoc legitimation did not apply. They, therefore, purchased a cédula for her, so that she might inherit equally with her siblings (AGI, Caracas 259, no. 4, 1779).

15. For an example of such a case see Ann Twinam, *Miners, Merchants and Farmers in Colonial Colombia* (Austin: University of Texas Press, 1982), pp.118–23.

16. C. H. Haring, *The Spanish Empire in America* (New York: Harcourt Brace, 1963), p.126.

17. The account of doña María del Carmen López Nieto is taken from AGI, Charcas 560, no. 15, 1795.

18. The account of doña Magdalena de la Vega is taken from AGI, Mexico 1771, no. 6, 1785.

19. See table 5.

20. AGI, Charcas 560, no. 15, 1795.

21. AGI, Mexico 1771, no. 6, 1785.

22. The account of don Joseph Martín de la Rocha is taken from AGI, Mexico 1778, no. 6, 1793.

23. The account of doña X is taken from AGI, Buenos Aires 250, no. 14, 1785.

24. It was rare for an unwed mother to wed another man. Although witnesses refused to identify her, they did testify to her situation.

25. AGI, Chile 290, no. 9, 1792.

26. AGI, Santo Domingo 1484, no. 14, 1793.

27. AGI, Caracas 200, no. 22, 1788

28. The account of doña Juana Díaz de Estrada is taken from AGI, Santo Domingo 421, no. 1, 1723.

29. The account of doña María Josepha Pérez de Balmaceda is taken from AGI, Santo Domingo 425, no. 2, 1741.

30. The account of doña Thoribia María Guerra Mier is taken from AGI, Santa Fe 720, no. 26, 1796.

31. In only four of the 216 cases are children referred to without any notice of illegitimacy, but simply called "*niño*" or "*niña*."

32. The account of the legitimation of doña Antonia del Rey is taken from AGI, Santo Domingo 1483, no. 38, 1792.

33. For example, note the opening quote by don Antonio Villanuena in which he refers to the "contacts . . . in her house."

34. The account of doña María Rosa de la Torre is taken from AGI, Chile 297, no. 21, 1796.

35. The account of doña Ántonia Hernández is taken from AGI, Santo Domingo 1467, no. 1, 1782.

36. It was not uncommon for prominent members of local society to testify in favor of an illegitimate's petition and to note that they had played together and gone to the same schools.

37. See table 5 and note 11.

38. There is a final group of 20 women (45.5 percent) who can be classified as having had public pregnancies, but the exact circumstances (i.e., extended engagement, concubinage) are unknown.

39. The account of doña Josepha María Valespino is taken from AGI, Santo Domingo 1456, no. 5, 1761.

40. The question of success or failure of the petition is a very complicated one, as the guidelines of the Council of the Indies changed according to circumstances such as time period, sex of petitioner, and amount they were willing to pay. See table 5. Cases were most likely to be turned down if the petitioners had not supplied data on the marital state of the mother and father. Presumably such petitioners were either ignorant of the details demanded by the Council, or they deliberately omitted facts that might prejudice their cases. The most successful petitions involved single parents. The Council discriminated less against the illegitimate children of married women than against those of married men. Perhaps because most of these women had been abandoned by their husbands, the Council was more sympathetic to their difficulties.

41. The account of the Varea y Lazcano is taken from AGI, Charcas 554, no. 25, 1791.

42. A knowledgeable observer, however, would have noted an additional comment on the certificates that the babies had been "exposed" at the house of doña Gertrudis, although she was not identified as their mother.

43. AGI, Charcas 554, no. 25, 1791. The Council of Gracia y Justicia of the Council of the Indies originally approved this petition if the brothers were willing to pay the extraordinary sum of 8,000 pesos apiece. When this decision went to the king, however, the council was overruled. This is the only case that I have discovered in two centuries' records where higher officers rejected a Council decision on legitimation.

44. AGI, Charcas 562, no. 22, 1796.

45. AGI, Guatemala 411, no. missing, 1784.

46. The fate of a woman was not much different if her honor had been protected by a private, as compared with a public pregnancy. Women with private pregnancies still tended to remain single. They were much less likely to marry their lovers than women with public pregnancies. This makes sense, however, when we consider that couples who went to the extreme of organizing a private pregnancy must have been either much more likely to marry when they could (and thereby avoid cédula applications) or much more likely to hide the pregnancy because they knew that they would not marry, because of personal aversion, current marriage of one party, or involvement of a cleric. The two women who went into convent had had private pregnancies.

Kathy Waldron

The Sinners and the Bishop in Colonial Venezuela: The *Visita* of Bishop Mariano Martí, 1771–1784

Mariano Martí landed in La Guaira in March of 1770 and proceeded along the winding mountain road into the city of Caracas, whence he would oversee his bishopric for the next twenty-two years. Martí, a Spaniard by birth, was at the height of his career, just having completed eight years as bishop of Puerto Rico before accepting the next assignment to Venezuela. At the age of forty-nine, Martí was the epitome of the late-eighteenth-century peninsular religious reformer, well educated, experienced, and determined to invigorate church authority, wealth, and clerical prestige.[1] He also intended to instill a new ethical climate in his diocese, undoubtedly believing, like many of his religious contemporaries, that the New World lacked a rigorous morality due to its vast numbers of marginally Christianized and Hispanicized peoples. This task, however, would not prove easy in Venezuela, a large, decentralized province with scattered clusters of inhabitants.

To help accomplish his goal, Martí decided to conduct a *visita* of the bishopric in 1771, a tour that would last thirteen years and take him across thousands of miles. The bishop began his journey in Caracas and traveled throughout the province, visiting the cacao-growing regions of the coast, the rugged Andes to the southwest, and the expansive *llanos* of the interior. He stopped in Indian *doctrinas* (ecclesiastical geographical units), plantations filled with African slaves, small Spanish villages, and the larger cities of Coro, Mérida, San Sebastián, and Trujillo.

What is exceptional about Martí's visita is the private journal he kept throughout the trip. Aside from a travelogue of eighteenth-century Venezuela, the journal includes two lengthy volumes of *Libros personales*, the primary source of the present study.[2] The *Li-*

bros personales are a detailed account of the peccadillos, petty quarrels, scandalous behavior, and more serious crimes committed by the inhabitants of the places he visited. Although the bishop ordered the books to be destroyed at his death, his aides disobeyed, preserving a rich manuscript, unique in its description of the sexual and social behavior of a broad spectrum of colonial people.

Through the visita, the bishop hoped to familiarize himself with his new diocese, review the physical condition of each parish, assess the worth of individual priests, and evaluate the spiritual and moral behavior of his subjects. To accomplish the last objective, Martí chose a unique tactic: that of inviting the populace of each town he visited to speak to him in confidence about the "sinful" activities of their own, as well as those of their neighbors. The unusual request was not a form of public confession, nor was it within the scope of the church's more traditional concept of private confession to a priest. Instead, adopting the traditional role of a parish priest, the bishop set himself up as the ultimate confessor and judge, to mete out punishment to those he considered guilty.[3] Martí clearly intended to make his power known and to establish his authority among the disparate factions of Venezuelan society. His efforts, while highly successful, often earned him the enmity of regional élites and of some local clerics who also came under his scrutiny.

The response to Martí's open-ended request was overwhelming: over fifteen hundred individuals stood accused, primarily of sexual misdeeds; nearly ten percent of the clerics in the province came under attack; and even the governor of Maracaibo was denounced. The accusations included adultery, fornication, concubinage, incest, rape, bigamy, prostitution, lust, homosexuality, bestiality, abortion, and infanticide. Also cited as problems were drunkenness, gambling, irreligiosity, witchcraft, murder, theft, and idolatry. The bishop added to this list by noting the cruelty of the hacendados toward their slaves, the harshness of certain village priests toward the mission Indians, and the usurious practices of merchants and shopowners.[4]

Martí not only recorded all the accusations; he also initiated investigations and forced the accused to present themselves. Where witnesses had obviously exaggerated or lied, he dismissed the charges as self-serving or motivated by jealousy. In one case, he stormed out of a village after listening to days of denunciations, concluding that the entire town was narrow-minded, malicious, and gossip-prone.[5] But in most situations, Martí entered all the details in his journal, dutifully noting the type of sin, the names of the accused and, in many instances, his judgment.

The *Libros personales* are filled with reports on the sexual behavior of eighteenth-century Venezuelans. Over eighty percent of all cases involved premarital sex, fornication, concubinage, and adultery. Among these, fornication and concubinage dominated. In describing fornicators, Martí usually recorded cases where men had more than one lover, often women from different ethnic groups or social classes. Of the 300 cases of fornication and concubinage mentioned in the diary, 174 involved sexual relations between white males and free Indians, mestizas, and mulatto women, or slave females. Implicit in Martí's record is the notion that these men took advantage of their power, wealth, and rank to seduce women who either could not defend themselves or could not resist the temptation of material gain.[6]

In Barquisimeto, for example, the bishop criticized several sons of the Alvarado and Anzola families, members of the local élite, for their notorious womanizing. The men had mulatto and slave lovers, had fathered a number of illegitimate children, and had not tried to conceal their activities. As a remedy to this situation, Martí ordered the young men to marry immediately, commenting that many young people of the Barquisimeto upper class did not appear anxious to marry. The bishop blamed the snobbery of their mothers, who, he said, disapproved of potential marriage partners for being unequal to their children's social rank. Whether this was true or not, Martí strongly disapproved of the young men of the Alvarado and Anzola families, an attitude shared by other community members whose respectable, virtuous daughters would not consent to marry members of the Alvarado family because of their scandalous behavior.[7]

Couples who had lived together for years but had never sanctioned their unions through the sacrament of marriage were reported as sinners indulging in concubinage. In most cases, the bishop ordered a search of the parish registers to determine whether a formal marriage had ever occurred. Where it had not, and in the absence of any legal impediments, Martí expected the couple to wed immediately and instructed the local priest to carry out the ceremony. Quite often, the couple voluntarily requested marriage before being called by the clergy. They admitted their wrongdoing, but rarely explained why they had neglected to legally sanction their unions for so many years. Quite likely, many couples took advantage of the bishop's visit to quietly and discreetly rectify their irregular union, rather than expose themselves to the wrath of the bishop and the subsequent gossip of their community.

Some of these couples, seeking to avoid a scandal, must have been quite surprised when Martí refused to perform a marriage because of canonical impediments, such as consanguinity or inability to prove the death of a former spouse. Such a denial undoubtedly created a crisis, since, having presented themselves to the religious authorities, the couple would no longer be allowed to remain together. This happened to Joseph Herrera, a *pardo* (light-skinned mulatto) bachelor, who had promised to marry his relative, María Aparicio, and had subsequently engaged in sexual relations and established a consensual union. Years later, the couple requested dispensation from the rules prohibiting marriage between close relatives, a plea Martí refused to grant on the grounds that he did not wish to encourage sinful conduct among kin. The local priest and civil official then recommended that Herrera be exiled from the township and that Aparicio be placed under supervision until another marriage could be arranged, despite her long involvement with Herrera.[8] Similar judgments fell on other blood-related men and women with cruel consequences. Don Herminio León and doña Ignacia César had lived together for many years as a couple and had had two children. As cousins, they had never wed because their close blood ties required a dispensation, which they had never obtained. Martí did not bend the rules for Léon and César and ordered the couple to separate.[9] Whether they did or not is unknown, but the bishop charged the parish priest with enforcing his decision. Martí did allow some couples to legitimize their unions. He particularly proved willing to do away with *ex copula illicitum,* an impediment prohibiting a legal union between a couple when one of the pair had participated in relations with a close relative of the betrothed. In one example, Martí recorded the story of don Joseph Marín, who had had an affair with a *zamba* (Indian and black admixture) woman whose sister he later married. The couple apparently did not obtain a dispensation before marrying. Having learned of their situation, the bishop nullified their union. However, he proceeded to grant them a dispensation to renew and validate their marriage vows. Marín and his wife knew nothing about the accusation or the bishop's decision until approached by the local village priest, who had been ordered to carry out the bishop's instructions to dissolve their union and then remarry them.[10]

In studying cases of fornication and premarital relations that came before Martí, one sees that many single women engaged in sexual activity, but only after they received specific promises of matrimony. Such a promise, often made public in the community, was a serious commitment that could not be broken without repercussions. An informal promise, however, could lead to disputes among families when a change of heart occurred. In the records of the visita, young women, often accompanied by their parents, appeared privately before the bishop to denounce a fiancé for breach of promise. Admitting to sexual intimacies and "deflowering," the women insisted on protection from public scandal. The church, anxious to settle such incidents, usually supported the injured party by insisting that the marriage be regularized. In the interim, the betrothed were placed under parental or local custody, especially to prevent the potential flight of the man.[11]

When doubt existed as to the true intent to marry, an individual could be released from an obligation. Manuel Oliva, for example, lived for several years with Isabel Linares; both were single and white. At the time they appeared before the bishop, they had two children and a third on the way. Manuel denied ever proposing marriage, but Isabel insisted she never would have consented to live with him had marriage not been promised. Isabel, as Martí noted, was poor and without the means or support to file a formal complaint, while Manuel was the brother of the parish priest and well connected in the small village's society. In the end, the couple parted on the condition that they each marry a partner of their choice within two months or risk incarceration. To induce a suitor to approach the by-then very pregnant Isabel, Martí ordered Manuel to endow her with a small hacienda and one hundred pesos. How the woman fared is unknown, but she did complain that the hacienda was half-flooded and not worth much.[12] That Martí expected her to be able to marry at this point is revealing and attests to the acceptability of nonvirgins for wives in the colonial society.

A man could buy his way out of a commitment; since the church believed in the willingness of both parties to freely undertake a marriage, it proved reluctant to force a union. Money was an acceptable restitution for some broken promises of marriage, especially where the couple were of different social and racial groups. Don Estevan

Díaz, the ecclesiastical notary of Guanare, was ordered to marry or endow a young woman he had promised at one point to marry. Since the woman was not his social equal, he chose to give her six hundred pesos, a rather large settlement that undoubtedly made "La Tunjana," as she was called, an affluent woman and, therefore, eminently marriageable. Díaz remained unremorseful about carrying on affairs despite the punishment. After escaping "La Tunjana," he rekindled an earlier affair with "Botada de Chaves," another female of humble birth. Although exploits of this type were frequent throughout the province, Díaz had political enemies who denounced him to the bishop and thus caused his exile from the community. Once removed from Guanare, Díaz lost his political power, permitting his opponents to take control of municipal and religious positions.[13]

Religious strictures against consanguineous marriages and the disdain of marrying a social or economic "inferior" interfered with the sacrament of marriage and contributed heavily to concubinage throughout the eighteenth century. Canonical legislation against marrying relatives was quite complicated and varied by race, since Indians had been granted special dispensation from rules by Pope Paul III in the sixteenth century.[14] Whites could not intermarry among relatives to the fourth degree of "licit" consanguinity or to the second degree, if consanguinity was due to "illicit" or out-of-wedlock relations. This rule was particularly troublesome for white families living in isolated small towns. With populations of only two thousand to three thousand and only a handful of whites, families quickly ran out of eligible marriage partners. Martí spent a great deal of time invalidating marriages among the white rural population and advising couples to obtain formal dispensation of consanguinity. This could be obtained directly from him during his visita or from the diocesan prelate. Since ecclesiastic authorities often lived in distant cities, many individuals did not undertake this expensive and time-consuming process despite the bishop's insistence. In one particular instance, Martí jailed a white soldier, Juan Pablo Muños, when the man claimed he was too poor to follow the prescribed procedure. This episcopal decision neither relieved his poverty nor enabled him to marry his lover, who already had a child by him.[15]

Inequality as defined by race and economic status prevented many marriages, or proved an acceptable excuse to avoid a legal union. The church, the civil authorities, and the white creole élite, however, did not share similar views on mixed marriages. While local creole priests fully understood and sympathized with the unwillingness of the upper class white families to form any legitimate ties to pardos, mulattos, or blacks, the Spanish clergy, represented by Martí, showed more concern about unsanctified unions than about racial mix. Racial distinctions, while an obvious and significant social reality, were less important to the Spanish clergy than religious orthodoxy and personal morality. In their opinion, unofficial unions damaged the moral fiber of the community, produced illegitimate children who did not receive proper religious training, and undermined the authority and influence of the church. The Venezuelan élite emphasized other factors. For them, political order based upon hierarchy, wealth, *limpieza de sangre* (purity of blood), racial distinctions, and the preservation of a slave labor force produced social and moral order. Throughout the second half of the eighteenth century, they were prepared to argue their case with the clergy and the crown whenever their world view was challenged.

In the mid-1770s the crown, however, assumed a marriage policy that was akin to the interests of the social élite, by acknowledging that marriage between unequals was a continuous social problem and by trying to curtail its further occurrence. In 1775, Charles III called for a Junta de Ministros to study the issue, and the following year the junta issued the Real Pragmática on marriage, which was extended to the colonies two years later. The Pragmática, directed at whites and Indians, stated that men under the age of 25 years and women under the age of 23 could not become engaged to marry without parental consent, nor could they contract marriage with individuals of different "quality."[16] Men and women over the stated ages also were required to ask for parental advice. Parents could not deny their consent or advice unless they had a "rational" reason. Although admitting that some parents could prevent their offspring from marrying for personal or selfish reasons, the junta believed parental involvement in the choice of a marriage partner would save many young people from "the serious harm that such unions will cause to themselves, their families, and their villages besides making the descendants incapable of obtaining municipal positions of honor."[17] The Pragmática excluded blacks, mulattos, and other *castas* (people of mixed blood) in the belief that so many of them were illegitimate that it would be impossible for them to obtain parental approval. In addition, neither the white élite nor the crown ever expressed much concern with the marriage patterns of people of color unless they tried to marry a white or an Indian.

Slaves' marriages presented special problems of their own, although the church tried to ameliorate the harshness of many slaveowners who actually intervened to prevent their slaves from marrying. Damaso Plasa's owner refused to allow his marriage to María Rodríguez, a free black woman, because any children born to the couple would also be free, thus denying the slaveowner access to what he considered his property. Don Xavier de Osorio was accused by his slave, Juana Sison, of lusting after her and preventing her marriage. While Juana struggled to put Osorio off, her fiancé found a new lover and withdrew his marriage offer. This case came to the attention of Martí, who intervened, unraveled the relationships, reprimanded Osorio, removed Juana from her owner's hacienda, and ordered the two slaves to marry.[18]

Despite his great concern about legalizing marriages, extramarital unions among slaves rarely caught Martí's attention, either because these unions were not reported as acts of sin by slaveowners or because the unions were so common and widespread that the bishop chose to ignore the subject. Repeatedly throughout his visita, Martí chastised slaveowners for neglecting the religious training of their slaves, rather than for not enforcing their marriages. It is quite possible that slaveowners who refused to allow their slaves to attend weekly religious services also discouraged formal marriages, seeing no advantage in officially sanctifying a union between two slaves who later might need to be separated or have their children removed. While marriage was perceived by the church as a means to help a slave lead a Christian life, the slaveowner undoubtedly was more concerned with the fecundity of female slaves and the ability to dispose of his property at his convenience than with the immortality of slaves' souls.

The Venezuelan experience clearly shows that marriages between whites, Indians, and castas were infrequent although liaisons among the groups were common. In Caracas, where one-third of the adults were listed as married in the 1792 census, fewer than 100 out of 3,500 married couples involved a white and a nonwhite. Social prejudice and widespread concubinage discouraged interracial marriages, a pattern that seemed to hold for the entire province. Speaking about the case of a potential marriage between a white man and a mulatto woman, Martí commented, "as he is white and she is mulatta, it is to be expected that the relatives oppose this marriage."[19] On the same topic, the eighteenth-century traveler Françoís Depons stated that union between free pardos and whites was frowned upon, even though it had not been "prohibited" until recently. He probably understood the Pragmática as a prohibition of such marriages, although it was not. He added, however, that such marriages did take place when the beauty of the woman carried the white man away, especially if she was not inclined to grant him her favors at another price.[20]

Fornication, concubinage, and broken promises of marriage—all behavioral transgressions under the spiritual purview of the church—were complemented in Martí's journal by over 250 cases of adultery. Not surprisingly, adultery between married men and unmarried women, often of different social or racial groups, was not uncommon. The white married male regularly stood accused of illicit relationships with his servant or poor village women. Hacendados, merchants, and soldiers stand out among the most commonly engaged in "sin," possibly because their occupations required them to spend time away from their families. Wealthier hacendados living in towns and cities absented themselves regularly and at length from their homes to supervise their estates, especially during harvest. There, they formed liaisons with local women, often resulting in the birth of children. Don Juan Manuel de Trejos, for example, traveled frequently from the city of San Sebastián to the village of San Francisco de Cara to visit his property. While there, he imposed upon a pardo family, forced them to give him lodging, and seduced their young daughter, who became pregnant and gave birth to a child. Trejos denied the charges, but several unnamed denouncers convinced Martí that the hacendado was indeed the seducer. Trejos's wife later came to his rescue by assuring the bishop that she and her husband were still on good terms and intended to remain together, whereupon the cleric dismissed the man with the warning that he should immediately resume marital life with his wife and that he would be imprisoned if he returned to visit the girl. In slave societies, such as eighteenth-century Venezuela, race lightened the moral burden of the seducer.[21]

Liaisons between black slave women and married slaveowners were quite frequent, as attested by the proliferations of mulatto children in the haciendas. In Venezuela, nearly one-third of the entire population was in bondage, and slave-master relationships not only were inevitable but could also offer the enslaved women a decided advantage: an easier path to freedom than paying for it. For an unskilled female slave, purchasing freedom was practically impossible, but more feasible either by marrying a free man, regardless of ethnic origin, who was hardworking and motivated enough to liberate her or by gaining the favors of someone with the power to emancipate her.[22] Martí's records indicate that many slaves selected the latter route. Not documented in his visita, of course, are the casual unions, the rapes and seductions of the female slave population. The frequent reference to mulatto children of unwed slave mothers in census material attests to miscegenation, but the historian can only speculate as to how much of that mixing was voluntary.

Martí recorded only a small number of slave-nonslave unions, probably those that became sorely public. In most cases, word never reached him, as few slaves dared or had an opportunity to complain. A female slave discovered with an upper-class male would receive the brunt of Martí's condemnation. For example, Sasimira, a domestic slave of don Francisco Hidalgo, had two children by her master before the bishop was informed of her liaison. While Hidalgo was chastised for his behavior, Sasimira was sold to another slaveowner. Her children remained the property of their father.[23]

For the female slave, it was a precarious existence, where clerics or jealous wives could force a separation at any time. This happened to a woman named Lucía, a domestic slave belonging to don Alexandro Delgado in the small town of Chavasquen. Delgado's brother-in-law moved into his house and began a relationship with Lucía, who bore him three children. A fourth one was on the way when someone reported their case to Martí. The frightened couple refused to appear before the bishop, who then ordered the slave to be sold in auction in another town. Neither her lover nor her owner dared to interfere after the bishop took his decision.[24] A more difficult situation ensued for María Regina, a slave of don Juan Antonio Briceño. She was married to a former slave who had the bad timing to walk in on his wife while she was in bed with her owner. Apparently, the slave was not there against her will, and she probably forfeited any chance that her husband would buy her freedom. The bishop ordered her transfered to another hacienda before being sold.[25] Another slave who confessed to an affair with her master complained that her lover had not kept his promise to emancipate her. The bishop, refusing to comment on the broken promise, ordered her sold too.[26] Numerous cases of this type appear in the records of Martí, with the punishment usually placed on the slave rather than the married man.

Casual liaisons represented only one form of adultery; also frequently cited were cases of men, living apart from their wives, who if not accused of adultery were almost expected to commit the "sin" given the absence of their legitimate sexual partners. Martí reported 150 examples and took strong measures to rectify the situations. Citing both royal and canon law, Martí pointed out that it was prohibited to live apart from a spouse, even for married *peninsulares* with business interests in the colonies.[27] Those men reported to the bishop as adulterers were exiled from the towns they lived in while those with wives in Spain were requested to have their partners join them. The bishop personally took responsibility for composing letters to the Spanish wives, and one can only imagine their reaction when told to leave Spain and move to Venezuela within a few months.

Despite the bishop's position, male adultery was generally tolerated if not expected. Long absences, the proximity of vulnerable female slaves and servants, crowded households, and few if any negative social consequences contributed to what appears to be a fairly common situation. Some men clung stubbornly to their lovers, much to the dismay of their wives and the bishop, returning to their mistresses even after banishment or imprisonment. Other men, forewarned of the approaching visita, temporarily returned to their wives and sent their mistresses to the countryside, out of Martí's reach. Others just absented themselves on business until the bishop moved on to another town, thereby escaping any disciplinary action. Although among men of the upper class adultery with slaves or servants was not uncommon, some married males of the local élite became involved with women of their own class, to the outrage of their families. Don Joseph Ignacio del Pumar, an official in the king's army and a wealthy and very much married hacendado, seduced the fourteen-year-old daughter of don Juan Montero. When the enraged father discovered the affair, he threw his daughter, Michaela, out of his house, whereupon she fled to her lover's hacienda. The girl was about to give birth when Martí convinced her father to remove her from the hacienda, by force if necessary, and place her under the care of a married sister. No doubt the father protested, but since the hacendado was already married, he could not wed Michaela and restore her good name.[28]

More of an affront to Venezuelan élite mores was the adulterous union between a married mestizo and the single daughter of don Domingo Briceño, a leading member of a notable Trujillo family. Adultery, seduction of a virgin, and crossing a racial barrier threatened to dishonor the entire family if the affair became public. To cover up the incident, Briceño bribed the mestizo and his wife, offering them a hacienda in a distant town for their own use if they promised never to return to Trujillo or reveal the white family's secret. The couple obliged, presumably preserving young Cathalina's reputation.[29] But not all young women escaped dishonor; at times Martí forced public penance upon the offender or required her to live under the supervision of a respected member of the community. Such treatment, however, was usually reserved for nonélite women.

Married women from the most renowned and wealthiest families in the province also entered into adulterous relationships. Of the two hundred fifty cases cited by Martí, forty-eight involved married women in unions with unmarried men, and another twenty-two were unions in which both men and women were married to someone else. Unlike white males, however, most white women accused of adultery were linked to males of the same race. Doña Bárbara Pérez regularly entertained a male visitor in her home at night while her husband traveled. Angela María Celis fled from her husband to be with her lover and still refused to return home after a jail sentence. But the most scandalous case of adultery was that of Doña Bárbara Villamil and her daughter, Isabel. While Isabel's husband traveled, Isabel started an affair with the unwed governor of Maracaibo, don Alfonso del Río, and conceived his child. After a time, the governor replaced Isabel with her mother, Bárbara, who remained Alfonso's lover for over eight years. The second affair became notorious when Bárbara's husband, don Francisco Carrasquero, complained to his neighbors about his wife's conduct. The informants claimed that Carrasquero's shame was so great that he died of a broken heart. The feud between mother and daughter endured for years and eventually involved the entire city. Finally, Isabel died under mysterious circumstances, and Martí and the civil authorities managed to have del Río removed from office, but not before every detail of the long affair was recorded in the bishop's diary.[30]

While adultery, fornication, and concubinage dominate the sexual offenses recorded by the bishop, cases of incest, prostitution, abortion, and homosexuality are also noted. By the latter part of the century, prostitution was a recognized problem, at least in Caracas. A casa de corrección (correctional home for women of ill-repute), established in the 1790s, was used to imprison nonwhite females, especially former slaves who, as one official complained, "without known profession live in the most luxurious style . . . without other means than the prostitution of their persons." These prostitutes, the audiencia noted, spread venereal disease and provided bad examples to the young people of their own class.[31] Many other women, while not professional prostitutes, agreed to sexual relationships for financial reward. Although the bishop did not deal with many prostitution cases, what is most noticeable in his diary is the sense of outrage expressed by the women when they did not receive their due after performing their services. María Rita Prieto, a married slave, personally appeared before the bishop in a vain attempt to collect twenty-five pesos owed to her by an ecclesiastic judge for thirty nights of sex. She claimed she performed her part of the bargain, only to discover that the judge did not intend to pay. The bishop only responded in amazement at her audacity, and dismissed her.[32]

The only time Martí demonstrated strong moral outrage at an offer of money in exchange for sex was when a corregidor de indios (official in charge of Indian affairs) tried to prostitute an impoverished young white woman by offering her a petticoat. When the woman refused, her would-be seducer increased his offer to three hundred pesos and solicited the assistance of his friends to gain the woman's acquiescence. Since she had no protector, she defended her honor and asked the bishop for his protection, thus challenging the cleric to chastise a member of the local élite. Martí, never one to shy away from confronting the Venezuelan provincial élite, did just that and embarrassed all the men involved.[33]

More common than prostitution, however, were the instances of incest. Social taboos against incest and strict religious definitions of prohibited relationships prevailed in Venezuela as they did in other Catholic countries. Yet, cases of incest were regularly reported with no apparent concentration among any racial group. Martí recorded thirty acts of incest, mostly between men and their daughters or nieces. Other cases involved sisters or sisters-in-law. One case involved a priest, don Pedro Sanojo, who carried out an irregular sexual union with his niece over an eight-year period and fathered her child.[34] When fathers seduced their daughters, the law was quite severe, usually requiring the men to be jailed and the daughters removed from home. In cases where husbands had sex with their wives' sisters, the guilty female left the parish while the man was required to reunite with his spouse. If the affair was not generally known, the penance could be private, but in public situations, public atonement became necessary. The punishment enforced in the eighteenth century, however, was less severe than that imposed a century earlier. In seventeenth-century Caracas, a famous case came before the Inquisition involving a brother and sister of a prominent family. They were accused of having sexual relations and producing three children. The couple were arrested and tortured repeatedly over a period of months, causing the woman to miscarry. When her brother escaped from jail, the authorities, led by Bishop Mauro de Tovar, imprisoned the couple's mother and some family slaves. All were tortured and excommunicated for their knowledge of the affair.[35] In the eighteenth century, the Inquisition did not engage in severe punishment of this kind.

Incest is frequently cited as grounds for divorce or as the reason why some women refused to live with their spouses. Often the wife had witnessed the sexual act, to her disgust and repugnance. In such situations, the bishop deviated from his normal insistence on reuniting couples and permitted women to leave their husbands. Other women sought to protect their husbands and denied accusations. Francisco Limas's wife swore that her husband was innocent of sleeping with his stepdaughter even after he had served a prison sentence for the same offense. The testimony of the stepdaughter's husband convinced the authorities of Limas's guilt despite his wife's insistence to the contrary. In yet another case, Magdalena Trujillo convinced Martí that her daughter had become deranged after accusing her father of seducing her. In most situations, wives simply kept quiet and the denunciations came from the husbands or brothers of the young women.[36]

Both civil and religious authorities expressed their desire to eliminate potential cases of incest before they occurred. Martí, in particular, tried to advise his parishioners of the dangers involved in too close contact among relatives. His strongest decree, enacted in Caracas, warned heads of households to prevent members of the opposite sex from sharing beds and sleeping quarters. Urban families customarily welcomed their country relatives on feast days, holidays, and trips. Since many relatives traveled great distances to attend town festivities and stayed for days at a time, crowding into the homes of relatives became quite common. Martí acknowledged this custom and pointed out that it was precisely during the holidays that parents let down their guard in supervising their offspring's behavior. Having to share beds, rooms, and small houses promoted sexual contact among relatives and encouraged fornication, incest, and indecent conduct. Possibly there was some truth in Martí's complaint. Households in colonial Venezuela contained numerous individuals: family members, servants, slaves, and related kin. In Caracas, the mean household had 7.6 people; over 40 percent of the dwellings contained extended families; about one-third of the households owned slaves; and the mean number of slaves per slave-owning household was 5.5 individuals. Very few dwellings were of ample size; families often shared living space with completely unrelated families; and households changed composition with alarming regularity.[37]

Poverty, overcrowding, racial discrimination, slavery, absent husbands, and stricter rules governing the age and suitability of marriage partners all contributed to the sexual patterns of Venezuelans. But Martí, true to his times and to his role, did not cite these factors as reasons for concubinage, illegitimacy, and adultery. Rather, he focused on the seductive nature of women and on lax parenting.

Martí blamed women for much of the sexual misconduct in his dioceses. Girls walked around unaccompanied throughout the town, day and night. They attended dances where they permitted men to hold their hands and embrace them. In the river towns, women boarded and disembarked from small boats in an indecent manner, hoisting their skirts too high. When washing clothes in the streams, women did not stay properly robed and were careless in front of passing men. On St. John's Day, they mounted horses with men, sharing the same saddle pressed tightly together. At night, they frequented *pulperías* and *guaraperías* where crowds of men gathered to drink and gamble. During the day, they deliberately went off to the rivers to fish. In one of the earliest complaints against unisex clothing, Martí criticized women for wearing capes that made them appear to be men. Wearing the garment permitted women to mingle among men without detection and to commit all types of "indecent and lewd" acts. Women were not even ashamed when their sins became public, complained Martí. In the small towns in the interior, unwed women walked around in public with their illegitimate children, brazenly displaying the fruits of their misconduct. Some even had the temerity to bring their children inside churches, a fact which particularly outraged the bishop.[38]

Martí's stern attitude toward women as culprits and seducers is also apparent in the punishments prescribed. Invariably, single women found guilty of violating the moral code were placed under the care of an *hombre formal*, nearly always a prominent married white male of the community. Forced to live in this man's house, subject to his will and authority, many single women were reduced to servile positions for having engaged in sexual activity. The offending male, in contrast, only had to promise to change his behavior and confess his sins, although in more scandalous cases he was exiled from the own.[39]

Martí faulted women for their wanton nature but he blamed men, as fathers and as priests, for their lack of responsibility. If fathers properly supervised their children, insisted upon chaperons for their daughters, taught virtuous behavior, discouraged vanity, separated the sexes, and corrected ignorance, they could safeguard the virtue of their offspring and the honor of their families. The bishop also believed the clergy had a primary role to play in improving moral conduct. Yet he undoubtedly was dismayed by many of the priests he encountered during his visita. Repeatedly, Martí states that he is the first bishop ever to visit certain remote villages left to the care of local clerics, who were often guilty of the same sins as their parishioners. Page after page of the diary points to the unethical behavior of local parish priests, their lack of education, their isolation from the church hierarchy and current ideas. While unwilling to criticize openly his clerics before their own constituency, Martí hoped by decree and instruction to educate the priests about what constituted acceptable Christian behavior. Thus, Martí would order the parish priests to preach sermons on canonical laws relating to proper social and sexual behavior and on subjects such as adultery; he issued proclamations prohibiting dancing; and he outlawed certain styles of dress for women. Martí believed that the integrity and maintenance of the marital bond was crucial for eliminating sin. Fornicators, therefore, should wed; adulterers should return to their mates; separated couples needed to reconcile; absent individuals were to reunite with their partners; and quarreling spouses needed to make peace.[40]

The bishop's view of how society should be and what he actually saw during his visita were obviously contradictory. For the majority of Venezuelans, particularly the nonélite, marriage was not a well-entrenched institution, the lack of virginity did not impede future unions, illegitimacy brought no great dishonor, and casual unions were acceptable. To most individuals without property to inherit, with no possibility of attending university or obtaining government position, and with little chance of acquiring wealth, practical motives for marriage and legitimate heirs did not necessarily exist. Even among the upper classes, which did value marriage and legitimacy for purposes of inheritance and public office, infidelity did not represent a serious threat to most marriages, nor was it held as a flagrant breach of acceptable conduct. That Martí appears shocked by what he observed indicates that his tenure in Puerto Rico and his service in Spain did not fully prepare him for Venezuela, and that he emerged from a Spanish society that followed more conservative sexual codes of behavior.[41] If consensual unions, adultery, and illegitimacy were as frequent as Martí indicates, then the moral code of the Roman Catholic Church and the values of European bourgeois society had not yet penetrated Venezuela. It may be argued that this transition never fully occurred, as attested to by the continued high Venezuelan levels of illegitimacy and consensual union throughout the nineteenth and twentieth centuries.

Notes

1. Mariano Martí received his doctorate in civil and canon law from the University of Cervera in Catalonia. For additional biographical information, see Pablo Vila, *El Obispo Martí: Interpretación humana y geográfica de la larga marcha pastoral del obispo Mariano Martí en la diócesis de Caracas* (Caracas: Universidad Central de Venezuela, 1980). There is no general history of the church in colonial Venezuela, and most studies focus on missionary activities. See *Colombia y Venezuela,* vol. 8 of *Historia general de la iglesia en la América Latina,* by Enriqúe D. Dussel, et al. (Salamanca: Cehila, Ediciones Sígueme, 1981). Volume 8 consists of a series of monographic studies by several authors and covers the most important issues of the history of the church in Venezuela. For the eighteenth century, the most comprehensive work focusing on a religious order is Lucas G. Castillo Lara, *Los Mercedarios y la vida política y social de Caracas en los siglos* XVII *y* XVIII (Caracas: Academia Nacional de la Historia, 1980), pp.143–44. An interesting

study of the moral education of many élite male Venezuelans is provided by José del Rey Fajardo in *La pedagogia jesuítica en la Venezuela hispánica* (Caracas, Academia Nacional de la Historia, 1979), p.138. See also John V. Lombardi, *Venezuela: The Search for Order, the Dream of Progress* (New York: Oxford University Press, 1982), and P. Michael McKinley, *Pre-Revolutionary Caracas: Politics, Economy and Society, 1777–1811* (Cambridge: Cambridge University Press, 1985).

2. The two volumes of *Libros personales* are the first of seven volumes published by the Academia Nacional de la Historia reproducing the bishop's record of his *visita*. The other five books contain church inventories, geographic descriptions, and census material for the province: Mariano Martí, *Documentos relativos a su visita pastoral de la diócesis de Caracas, 1771–1784*, 7 vols. (Caracas: Academia Nacional de la Historia 1980), vols. 95–101 of Fuentes para la Historia Colonial de Venezuela."

3. The methods of church confession with respect to Indian conversions are analyzed in Serge Gruzinski's article in this volume.

4. For an interesting comparison of other church reformers, consult Charles C. Noel, "Missionary Preachers in Spain: Teaching Social Virtue in the Eighteenth Century," *American Historical Review* 90, no. 4 (October 1985): 866–92. Martí's pronouncements, decrees, and some sermons are in volume 5, *Providencias*, of the 7-volume edition published by the Academy. Other material is located in the Archivo Arquidiocesano de Caracas, Section "Episcopales." Specific references to usury are in Martí, *Documentos*, 1:215–16, 225, 245, 247.

5. Martí, *Documentos*, 1:63, 66.

6. Martí, *Documentos*, 1, 2. The *Libros personales* are carefully indexed by name and locale but not by topic. For another opinion on female virtue, consult the memoir of the eighteenth-century French traveler, François Depons, who claimed that women from the *castas* (of mixed race) tended toward promiscuity (François Depons, *Viaje a la parte oriental de Tierra Firme en la América meridional* [Caracas, Banco Central de Venezuela, 1960], 1:122–23).

7. Martí, *Documentos*, 2:70–74.

8. Martí, *Documentos*, 2:229.

9. Martí, *Documentos*, 2:310. Martí did grant dispensation in one case because the woman was over forty years old and presumably would not find another partner. See doña Teresa León and don Pablo León in Martí, *Documentos*, 2:310.

10. Martí, *Documentos*, 2:49. For other cases, see 2:187. In another instance, Martí forgave the act of *ex copula illicita* but refused to revalidate the

marriage. The male, a slave accused of having relations with three sisters before marrying one of them, was arrested (Martí, *Documentos*, 2:321–22).

11. A public promise of marriage that was later broken could result in a judicial suit brought by the injured party. The "Libros de Matrimoniales" in the Archivo Arquidiocesano de Caracas contain numerous examples of formal procedures. For the Martí period, consult *carteras* 64–116. During the visita, the bishop tried to resolve the disputes personally. See Martí, *Documentos*, 1:23, 24, 45, 55, 58, 83, and 2:48.

12. Martí, *Documentos*, 2:354. For other examples, consult Ermila Troconis de Veracoechea, *Historia de El Tocuyo colonial* (Caracas: Universidad Central de Venezuela, 1977), pp.278–83.

13. Martí, *Documentos*, 1:533, 551. On the importance of kinship networks for an earlier period, see Stephanie Blank, "Patrons, Clients, and Kin in Seventeenth-Century Caracas: A Methodological Essay in Colonial Spanish American Social History," *Hispanic American Historical Review* 54, no.2 (May 1974): 260–83.

14. Daisy Rípodas Ardanaz, *El matrimonio en Indias: Realidad social y regulación jurídica* (Buenos Aires: Conicet, 1977), pp.103–44; Martí, *Documentos*, 5:203–4.

15. Martí, *Documentos*, 2:435. A list of all dispensations granted by Martí is available in the Archivo Arquidiocesano de Caracas, Section "Libros," 130, "Dispensas concedidas por el Obispo Martí desde 1776 hasta 1788."

16. The Pragmática is published in *Colección de documentos para la historia de la formación social de Hispanoamérica, 1493–1810*, ed. Richard Konetzke, 3 vols. (Madrid: Consejo Superior de Investigaciones Científicas, 1958–62), 3:401–13. This law demanded that young people ask and obtain parental permission to become betrothed. If the couple disobeyed the law, they would be liable to disinheritance if their parents chose to do so (*privados de la calidad de herederos forzosos*). Dissenting parents of couples under age could legally oppose their offspring's choices and sue to prevent the engagement/marriage. Children could also challenge parental opposition before the courts. Charles III wished to establish compulsory disinheritance in 1783, but Charles IV did not endorse such legislation.

17. In 1803 the Pragmática was redefined, giving parents the right to deny permission to marry to sons over 25 and daughters over 23. After that year, in the colonies, persons of well-known nobility or well-established "clean" lineage (*limpieza de sangre*) wishing to marry people below their state could be challenged by their families in court. See Daisy Rípodaz Ardanaz, *El matrimonio en Indias*, pp. 280–315; Magnus Morner, *Race Mixture in the History*

of Latin America (Boston: Little Brown, and Company, 1967), p. 39. An important contribution on marriage partner selection is by Robert McCaa, "Calidad, Clase, and Marriage in Colonial Mexico: The Case of Parral, 1788–90," *Hispanic American Historical Review* 64, no.3 (August 1984): 477–501. See also Susan Socolow's essay in this volume.

18. Martí, *Documentos*, 1:24–25. On Venezuelan slavery, consult Federico Brito Figueroa, *La estructura social y demográfica de Venezuela colonial* (Caracas: Ediciones Históricas, 1961); Miguel Acosta Saignes, *Vida de los esclavos negros en Venezuela* (Caracas, Ediciones Hespérides, 1967); Ermila Troconis de Veracoechea, *Documentos para el estudio de los esclavos negros en Venezuela* (Caracas: Academia Nacional de la Historia, 1969), p. 103.

19. Martí, *Documentos*, 2:410. The census material for the late eighteenth century in Venezuela is quite good thanks to Martí, who ordered every priest to conduct an annual household list of his parish. The censuses, or *matrículas*, for most of the provinces are available in the section "Parroquias" of the Archivo Arquidiocesano de Caracas. For a systematic study of the population of the Archbishopric of Caracas consult John V. Lombardi, *People and Places in Colonial Venezuela* (Bloomington: Indiana University Press, 1976). Lombardi reaches similar conclusions for the Venezuelan city of San Carlos. For comparative purposes, see Michael M. Swann, "The Spatial Dimensions of a Social Process: Marriage and Mobility in Late Colonial Northern Mexico," in *Social Fabric and Spatial Structure in Colonial Latin America*, ed. David J. Robinson (Syracuse and Ann Arbor, Syracuse University Press and University Microfilms International, 1977), pp. 117–80. Swann concludes that interracial marriages in Mexico were frequent.

20. Depons, *Viaje*, pp. 121–22.

21. Martí, *Documentos*, 2:527–28.

22. For comparative purposes, see Verena Martínez Alier, *Marriage, Class and Colour in Nineteenth-Century Cuba: A Study of Racial Attitudes and Sexual Values in a Slave Society* (Cambridge: Cambridge University Press, 1974).

23. Martí, *Documentos*, 2:408–9.

24. Martí, *Documentos*, 2:501.

25. Martí, *Documentos*, 2:422.

26. Martí, *Documentos*, 2:520.

27. *Recopilación de las leyes de los reinos de las Indias*, 2 vols. (Madrid: 1841), 2:490.

28. Martí, *Documentos*, 1:508.

29. Martí, *Documentos*, 1:438.

30. Martí, *Documentos,* 1:219, 230, 473, 510, and 2:369, 377, 520, 666. The writings of the sixteenth-century Agustinian, Fray Luis de León, were read as the ideal of wifely comportment. See Luis de León, *La perfecta casada* (Madrid: Espasa-Calpe, 1968); Juan Luis Vives, *Instrucción de la mujer cristiana* (Buenos Aires: Espasa-Calpe Argentina, 1944).

31. Martí, *Documentos,* 1:157–59, 188, 190–91, 216, 230–50, 289.

32. Information on prostitution is scant. The account books of the casa de corrección, located in the Archives of the Concejo Municipal del Distrito Federal, in Caracas, contain some general comments on the subject under the section "Libros de Cárceles 1790–1796."

33. Martí, *Documentos,* 1:483.

34. Sanojo and his niece were discovered by her husband, who sued for divorce, thereby making the crimes public. Sanojo fled while the niece was exiled to an isolated hacienda under her mother's supervision. Later, when Sanojo returned, he was reprimanded by Martí but allowed to continue with his priestly duties. Martí, *Documentos,* 2:153–55, 157.

35. Ermila Troconis de Veracoechea, "Cárceles coloniales," in *Memoria del tercer Congreso Venezolano de Historia del 26 de septiembre al 1 de octubre de 1977* (Caracas: Academia Nacional de la Historia, 1979), 3:480–515.

36. Martí, *Documentos,* 1:479, 510; Kathleen Waldron, "A Social History of a Private City: The Case of Caracas, 1750–1810," Ph.D. dissertation, Indiana University, 1977, chapter 3.

37. Ibid.

38. Martí, *Documentos,* 1:223, 225, 250, and 2:177, 183, 369, 409, 520, 667. Martí was no exception in his acid critique of female behavior and dress. Monsignor José Antonio de San Alberto, bishop of Tarija, began a campaign against the "provocative" dresses of females of all conditions in the mid-eighteenth century. He called for a theologians' meeting to discuss this issue, and sent a 73-page report to the crown, illustrated with drawings of the dresses. See Guillermo Furlong, *Historia social y cultural del Río de La Plata: El Transplante Cultural* (Buenos Aires: TEA, 1969), pp. 295–96.

39. Martí, *Documentos,* vols. 1, 2.

40. On the conduct of the clergy, see Martí, *Documentos,* 1:33, 59, 60, 61, 63, 67, 78, 124–25, 148–51, 220, 226, 240–42, and 5:136, 159. For the importance of the parish priest, see Timothy Tacket, *Priest and Parish in Eighteenth-Century France* (Princeton: Princeton University Press, 1977). While his information is not necessarily applicable to Spanish America, Tacket demonstrates the role of the local priest in developing political consciousness and social values.

41. European historians describe a transition to more proscribed modes of

sexual conduct and more defined rules for family life beginning in the seventeenth century. The transfer of such a value system to America would be slowed by distance, but it is also probable that the colonial class and racial structure impeded the absorption of European mores. See Lawrence Stone, *The Family, Sex and Marriage in England, 1500–1800* (New York: Harper and Row, 1977); and Michel Foucault, *The History of Sexuality: An Introduction* (New York: Vintage Books, 1980), vol. 1.

Ruth Behar

Sexual Witchcraft, Colonialism, and Women's Powers: Views from the Mexican Inquisition

In 1774 José de Ugalde, a white (*español*) muleteer from a town near Querétaro, appeared before the Mexican Inquisition to lodge an accusation against his mestiza wife, who he claimed had used witchcraft to make him "stupid" (*atontado*) throughout the seventeen years of their marriage.[1] He had recently threatened to kill her if she did not admit what she had done to put him in this state; his wife then told him about the yellow, green, and black herbs which her sister had given her, advising that she serve them to him in water, the corn drink of atole, or food, "so that he would never forget her, or watch over her, or get back too early from his trips." He had learned that she was having an affair, and she shocked him when she went to confess and took communion as though nothing had happened. This so angered him that he tied her to a mesquite tree in order to beat her, reproaching her for having confessed and taken communion sacrilegiously, but "she had gotten loose without his knowing how." When he bound her to the tree a second time, she "called for help to all the saints in the heaven's court and he was not even able to give her a single beating." When for a third time he took her out to the countryside with the intention of beating her, he had no sooner accused her than "they made up and returned home together."

For José de Ugalde, the fact that his wife was misbehaving and that he could not give her the beating she properly deserved was only explainable as the effect of witchcraft. That she, rather than he, was shamelessly having an extramarital affair and that he could do nothing about it showed the extent of her supernatural powers. In bringing his case to the Inquisition he did not worry about admitting his intentions to beat his wife, because it was considered perfectly legitimate for a husband to physically punish his wife when she infringed upon the norms of proper female behavior in marriage. What made him believe the Inquisition would take an interest in his case was his wife's use of food magic to stupefy him, and the larger threat to a patriarchal social structure that was implicit in this act: turning the world upside down by making husbands submissive to their wives.[2]

This brief but tantalizing narrative contains, in compact form, the major themes that animated women's magical power in colonial Mexico, a discourse that had roots in sixteenth-century Spain. This essay will focus on the different meanings given to this discourse by men and women, highlighting the particular characteristics of the Inquisition and of witchcraft in Spain and Mexico. I will concentrate on the specific genre of sexual witchcraft, epitomized in Spain by the literary image of the witch-procuress or Celestina; in Mexico it took on a further cultural elaboration, with uncanny power being ascribed to women of the marginal Indian and mixed castes. Three major themes from the example of José de Ugalde's bewitchment will orient this discussion of women's power. One theme is the image of the world in reverse; the aim of women in these cases, according both to the women themselves and to the men who accused them, was to reverse their subordination to men and gain some degree of control over their husbands or lovers. There was a local language in which this search for control was expressed: in Mexico, a man could be atontado or *asimplado* "stupefied" or "dummied," as happened to José de Ugalde; an especially abusive and violent husband might be subject to his wife's attempts to *amansar,* to "tame" or "domesticate," him; a man who dropped his mistress would perhaps find himself *ligado,* "tied" in such a way that he was rendered impotent; and finally, unnatural illnesses caused by *hechizo* or *maleficio,* sorcery or malefice could make a man waste away.

A second theme in these cases is the efficacy of women's witchcraft. As we see in José de Ugalde's reaction to his wife's use of herbs, the witchcraft powers of women were clearly not ones that women simply ascribed to themselves but were culturally viewed as inherent in their nature. These powers, however, usually needed to be awakened, and thus we find networks of women from all the castes and classes of colonial Mexico passing on stories about various "remedies" (*remedios*) that could be employed when a man was recalcitrant, violent, or unfaithful. José de Ugalde's wife, for example, claimed to have obtained the three magical herbs from her sister. Both in Mexico and in Spain, women who were professional healers and often midwives as well were also consulted for advice and cures.

Typically, women made men "eat" their witchcraft, using their power over the domain of food preparation for subversive ends, a practice that was common in pre-Hispanic times as well as in sixteenth and seventeenth-century Castile.[3] From the number of cases in which food was the medium for witchcraft, it appears that ingestion was thought to be one of the most effective ways of passing on the polluting substances of witchcraft; in eating, the pollution was introduced directly and effectively into the body. Women frequently used menstrual blood or the water that had cleansed their "intimate parts" to make up the ensorcelled food or drink that they served to their husbands. The logic behind this was clearly that of the "metaphorical extension," by which the ingestion of a woman's bodily essences worked, by means of analogy, to subdue, tame, or attract the man who consumed them.[4] The belief that food could be used to harm rather than to nurture gave women a very specific and real power that could serve as an important defense against abusive male dominance. And perhaps, too, women's serving of ensorcelled food to men was another kind of reversal, sexual rather than social: a way for women to penetrate men's bodies.

A last, and crucial, theme of all these Inquisition cases is the mediating role of the church in domestic and sexual matters. Whether the discourse of sexual magic and witchcraft took place among women passing on "remedies" or between bewitched and bewitcher, the church was there to listen in. The church solicited such discourses by requiring confession and by making public the Edicts of Faith in which superstition, witchcraft, and magic were denounced as sins.[5] The church had also insinuated itself into the domain of the family and sexuality, by controlling the rites of marriage and by defining sexual and domestic sins.[6] So, it was natural for men and women to bring their confessions and their denunciations about these matters to the church, and especially to the Inquisition, translating their domestic conflicts and sexual ambivalence into a religious discourse. Thus, José de Ugalde thought that the Inquisition would be interested in his marriage and the fact that it had, in his view, gotten mysteriously out of control.

Gender, Power, and Religion: From Spain to Mexico

What these three themes point to is an intersection of gender, power, and religion. I will consider this intersection from the various points of view of the actors involved in women's witchcraft: that of the religious élite, who in large part set the terms of the discourse; that of the men who felt themselves bewitched; and that of the women who attempted to gain power through witchcraft.

As Michelle Rosaldo and other feminist anthropologists have pointed out, in most societies women are denied culturally legitimate authority in the public sphere.[7] Thus, whatever power women do have is thought to be illegitimate, negative, and disruptive. Beliefs about women as pollutors are one widespread example of the negative powers attributed to women, as in parts of New Guinea, where men will carry out their wives' wishes for fear that if a woman is angered she may pollute her husband by serving him food while she is menstruating.[8] This analogy is significant given the frequent use of menstrual blood by colonial Mexican women in preparing ensorcelled food for their husbands, a practice that has persisted in various parts to this day.[9] Beliefs about the witchcraft powers of women likewise attribute to women a negative, polluting influence. In viewing women's power as illegitimate, we have to ask a key question: in whose eyes is this power illegitimate? Clearly, in a male-dominated society, it is from the male point of view that women's power becomes defined as negative, as an inversion of the social/sexual order. Even from the female point of view, this power appears illegitimate to the degree that women internalize the values of the male-dominated symbolic order.

In northern Europe the illegitimacy of women's power was dealt with, in the sixteenth and seventeenth centuries, by carrying out witch-hunts, in which women were the main targets of persecution and extermination.[10] Women's witchcraft was taken seriously by the religious élite of northern Europe, but in the process of the hunt their powers were magnified and transformed from a simple power to heal or to harm on a one-to-one basis into a demonic conspiracy that threatened both God and the state. As Christina Larner has pointed out in her study of witch-hunting in Scotland, an essential prerequisite for a witch-hunt was the existence of an élite with the zeal and the bureaucratic machinery to carry out the investigations, arrests, and punishments of those accused of witchcraft.[11] The presence of an élite convinced of the fact that witches did exist and did have dangerous powers is, in large part, what fueled witch-hunts, as opposed to witchcraft beliefs, in northern Europe.

Spain was different. Spain had true heretics to contend with: the *conversos* (converts) from Judaism and Islam, whose supposed insincere conversion threatened the purity of the faith. The Inquisition, after all, was instituted to deal with them.[12] Yet Spain was not completely devoid of small-scale witch panics; these involved only the local authorities and took place during the sixteenth and early seventeenth centuries in the northern regions of Galicia, Cataluña, and the Basque Country, with the most famous being the witch panic of Zagarramurdi in Navarra.[13] By the 1620s these panics were mostly over, however, because they were put down by the Suprema, the Supreme Council of the Inquisition in Madrid, which took a decidedly skeptical attitude towards witchcraft. Epitomizing this attitude was the work of the inquisitor Alonso de Salazar Frías, whose close, legalistic examination of the confessions concerning sabbats and intercourse with devils in the Zagarramurdi witch panic led him to conclude that "I have not found the slightest evidence from which to infer that a single act of witchcraft has really occurred . . . I deduce the importance of silence and reserve from the experience that there were neither witches nor bewitched until they were talked and written about."[14]

The general view of the Spanish religious élite was that witchcraft was a sign of ignorance rather than heresy and could be dealt with through such religious means as Christian instruction, confession, and absolution.[15] Witches flying through the air and meeting in sabbats were delusions and fantasies, beyond the legal province of cause and effect and the rules of evidence. It is significant that the word for the witches' sabbat used in Spain is *aquelarre,* a Basque word. The idea of the sabbat apparently never really took hold in Castile and southern Spain, either on the popular or élite level. Instead, the kind of witchcraft one finds in Castile and southern Spain involved love magic and sexual bewitchment. Julio Caro Baroja has suggested that the witchcraft which flourished in northern Spanish communities was of a distinctly rural order, concerned with community tensions—like, I would add, the witchcraft that existed in northern Europe. On the other hand, the love magic and sexual witchcraft common in Castile and southern Spain (as well as in much of Italy) was decidedly urban, and more concerned, in the tradition of the Celestina, with dyadic domestic and erotic relationships.[16] Unlike the northern European image of the witch as an old, ugly, and poor woman, the women involved with witchcraft in Castile were usually young unmarried women, widows, wives abandoned by their husbands, or women living in casual unions with men; they were maids and servants, sometimes prostitutes, and in southern Spain often *moriscas,* women of mixed Spanish and Moorish blood.[17]

To give a few examples of the discourse of sexual witchcraft employed by Spanish women, we can mention the sixteenth-century case of Catalina Gómez, who claimed to have used witchcraft to improve her relationship with her husband, who mistreated and beat her.[18] Leonor de Barzana, a conversa of Jewish descent from Toledo, claimed that many of her female neighbors had approached her for remedies to increase their husbands' love for them. Similarly, Juana Hernández, apparently a prostitute, claimed to have used techniques of divination "at the request of many women, who wanted to know the goings-on of their lovers and husbands, whether they took on other women." Significantly, she had learned about divination from a morisca. Isabel de la Higuera, from Daimiel, explained to a man that he had been rendered impotent by means of a magical ligature that had worked its way into his body through an orange, given to him by a woman, that was filled with "certain dirty things."[19] This Castilian tradition of sexual magic and witchcraft crossed the Atlantic and took hold in Mexico, flourishing in urban centers like Mexico City, as well as in the more open, racially mixed, and economically fluid mining, ranching, and hacienda areas farther orth.

The confessions and accusations of love magic and sexual witchcraft that people brought to the Inquisition, both in Spain and Mexico, were placed in the category of "superstition" and dealt with leniently, for the most part. The Spanish Inquisition and its colonial Mexican tribunal shared a common inquisitorial style, seeking to understand the motives of a person's beliefs or acts rather than being concerned with establishing legal responsibility for the deeds of witchcraft or magic, as were secular judges in northern Europe. Thus the outcome of a case hinged less on the question of whether a person was guilty or not guilty than on subtler distinctions between "repentant and unrepentant sinners, between accidental and deliberate sinners, between knaves and fools."[20] What mattered most to the inquisitors was that penitents have a sense of guilt and shame, and display a willingness to confess all and be reintegrated into the church. And if the confessions touched on sex, all the better, since the lusts of the body, both in thought and in deed, were especially singled out for close inspection and castigation.[21]

While men like José de Ugalde in central Mexico went to the Inquisition with sincere complaints about the magical powers women wielded, the inquisitors tended not to take these accusations seriously. Unlike the secular judges of northern Europe, who viewed women's power as illegitimate in the sense that it threatened the state and society through the conspiracy of the "coven," the inquisitors of Spain and Mexico viewed women's power as illegitimate in the sense that it was a delusion and therefore not really a form of power at all.[22] By thus devaluing the discourse of women's magical power, not taking it altogether seriously, the Hispanic religious élite trivialized and denied what on the local level was viewed as a source of power for women.

Sin, Guilt, and Confession: Women's Ambivalence

The attitude of the Inquisition had two contradictory effects on women in colonial Mexico. On the one hand, the leniency of the inquisitors made it possible for networks of women to pass the word on about magical alternatives to the church's mediation in domestic affairs; in some cases, women were even able to construct an alternative religious ideology, centering on devil pacts, that challenged the dominant religion. On the other hand, those women who internalized inquisitorial ideas about the delusion of believing in witchcraft found themselves devaluing their own efforts to gain magical power and becoming angry and disgusted with themselves for seeking to subvert the established order.

As an example from colonial Mexico of how women could internalize inquisitorial ideas, we have the case of Magdalena de la Mata, a woman over fifty years of age who appeared before the tribunal of San Juan del Rio in 1715.[23] She began her confession by recalling an incident of domestic violence: on one occasion, her husband, a mestizo like her and the owner of a drove of beasts of burden, had beaten her so badly that he had made her bleed. Seeing herself treated so wretchedly by her husband, upset and angry, Magdalena went to Beatris, an Indian woman, and asked her to give her an herb she could use on her husband so he would cease treating her so badly.

Beatris, admonishing her to keep the remedy a secret, explained to Magdalena how to go about producing a magical ligature or "tying" that would make her husband impotent. The remedy was to take an egg, pierce it with a straw, and in it place a few of her husband's hairs; then she was to bury the egg in the ground where her husband urinated. Following these steps, Beatris claimed, Magdalena's husband would be "tied."

Ligatures caused by witchcraft were the usual explanation for male impotence both in popular and learned European belief. Heinrich Kramer and James Sprenger, the German inquisitor-authors of the witch-hunting treatise known as "The Hammer of Witches," went so far as to suggest that witches collected the male organs of the men they made impotent, putting them in a "bird's nest, or shutting them up in a box, where they move themselves like living members, and eat oats and corn."[24] Or, at least, the devil made such illusions possible. From the Spanish Inquisition, a case is preserved from Puebla de Montalbán, stating that in 1758 the townspeople believed that Aunt Fruncida had a little pail in which she kept the members of men who had suffered magical ligatures; in Lillo, in 1780, rumor had it that La Gorrinera kept male members hung up on a clothesline.[25]

In Mexico, women both confessed to having attempted ligatures and were accused by men of having carried out ligatures—but this ultimate effort to strike at the central symbol and reality of male dominance by rendering the phallus powerless was for some women so radical that they often ended up censoring and repressing their own desires. Thus, Magdalena pierced the egg, filled it with her husband's hairs, and buried it, pouring some of his urine over the ground. But one day later, she confessed to the inquisitor and ran back to the site and unburied the egg, overcome with repentance for having carried out such a ludicrous act. Throwing the egg away, she exclaimed, "'To the devil with you!' And she had been crying ever since, begging God to have mercy on her, as she also begged of this Holy Tribunal."

Her local parish confessor, she said, had refused to absolve her until she confessed to the Inquisition. She admitted, she had been on the verge of keeping quiet about this sin altogether, but looking into her soul she had seen that she had to confess it. She cried as she spoke, and the inquisitor, "seeing her tears, and her repentance, and her demonstration of faith . . . told her to attend to the fact that she is

Christian, and that she should never be afraid to confess her sins to her confessor and that she should always confess what is most particular, and that which seemed the most shameful to her." So long as she confessed and truly repented, the inquisitor assured her, she would always be pardoned by the Holy Tribunal. With this, and a caution about not paying heed to superstitions and criticizing them whenever she came across them, she was absolved.

The notions propounded by the church about sin, guilt, and devotion, which women were taught to take especially seriously, often made it impossible for them to use the magical resources at their disposal for retaliating against husbands who exceeded the bounds of proper conjugal dominance.[26] What political and economic control lower-class women, especially married women, had was negligible, and they were frequently victims of a husband's aggression both in the countryside and in towns.[27]

Since women were left with few domains in which to assert themselves, they developed, in Mexico and elsewhere in Latin America, a rich symbolic language of beliefs and acts for resisting, punishing, and even controlling the men who dominated them. This was a language saturated with violence: just as men hit their wives, women retaliated with a more subtle form of violence. And because the Mexican Inquisition treated offenders in a lenient, paternal fashion, it participated in the dialogue about male/female conflict and sexual witchcraft. The details of that dialogue were of little interest to the inquisitors; what mattered most to them was that what was confessed be "that which seemed the most shameful" and that the confession be accompanied by the sinner's requisite "tears of contrition," so important to early modern Spanish religious devotion.[28]

The Inquisition did little to hinder the diffusion of sexual witchcraft among women of the various caste strata of colonial Mexico. Yet the position of women remained equivocal. Women, unable to reconcile the contradictions between the proper behavior expected of them as Catholics and the witchcraft they knew for taming and tying men, ended up by expressing disgust and self-hatred. They threw away the remedies they had used, became angry with themselves for the violent emotions they had given vent to, and ran tearfully to confess to the parish priest and the inquisitors, seeking absolution. It was as if an internalized Inquisition, an alternate discourse, sounded inside their heads, muting the discourse of women's magical power.

13. Representation of the devil in an inquisitorial investigation for heretical activities. Source: Archivo General de la Nación, Mexico City, Inquisición, vol. 1281, fol. 61 (1790).

14. Collage of dolls imitating religious images, found in a suit against a woman (Rosalia López) for witchcraft. Writing suggests favors received after intercession. Source: Archivo General de la Nación, Mexico City, Inquisición, vol. 1533, exp. 1 (1767).

Entertaining thoughts of cutting off their husband's sexual powers (a quite literal emasculation in the cases of "tying") was for many women a sinful fantasy, associated with the devil. When Magdalena de la Mata threw away the egg she had tried to use to tie her husband, she exclaimed, "To the devil with you!" Other cases like this abound. Marcelina Gertrudis, the 25-year-old wife of a free mulatto, confessed that, five years before, she had been upset and in tears because her husband was having an affair with another woman. She lamented her condition to her neighbor, María, a mulatta, and María responded, "Don't worry, sister, once when my husband was lost like yours is now, and I was suffering like you are now. An uncle of mine named Juan de Bargas, seeing my suffering, for pity of me made up a remedy with which my husband came to despise the other woman." This remedy, something her uncle gave her to place in her husband's food, had worked extremely well, María said, and she had begged her uncle to tell her of what it had consisted. When her uncle at last began to tell her that part of the remedy included placing peyote in water, she appeared so shocked that he refused to divulge any more information to her. Marcelina, hearing just this incomplete account of the "remedy," was quick to respond to María with the following: "May God not let me think of such a thing. That can't be good, that seems like devil's stuff. Let my husband do what he wants, for there is a God who is our remedy."[29]

Similarly, 20-year-old María Guadalupe Dávalos, who lived on an hacienda in Querétaro, recounted in 1792 how, seeing her in tears because her husband had just given her a beating soon after she had brought his food to him in the fields, a woman neighbor said to her: "Don't be stupid, we have a remedy, and you will see how your husband will die. Put a bucket of water under your bed when your husband is sleeping, and place a lit candle in it, and when [the candle] has gone out, your husband, too, will be gone and dead." To this María Guadalupe replied, "I won't do it. Let God, who can, kill him."[30]

Some women, hearing of this discourse, responded with a suspicious skepticism. Francisca de los Angeles, a mulatta who was married to a mestizo shoemaker in Querétaro, appeared before the Inquisition in 1692 to make a confession about "a few things that had made her apprehensive because they seemed suspicious" that she had seen while living for two years in the house of Clara de Miranda, a mestiza and an aunt of her husband.[31] Francisca noted that life with her husband was difficult, that hers was a *mala vida*. Seeing what Francisca suffered at close range, Clara de Miranda had told her that if she wanted "to change her husband's behavior and turn him into a simpleton, she should take a few of the fat worms that drag themselves along the ground on their backs, that can be found under the earth, and once dried and turned into powder serve them to him in food and drink." On two occasions Clara de Miranda went to the trouble to bring these worms to Francisca, but she refused to take them.

Another time, Francisca's husband had just combed his hair when Clara de Miranda entered the room, saying, "Your husband is a fool. Why does he leave those fallen hairs lying around? They can do him harm." Francisca asked her how such a thing was possible. And Clara de Miranda told her, "If you take a frog and tie one of those hairs around its neck and take a thorn and run it from its head to its feet, your husband will waste away." Yet another time, she offered Francisca a different remedy to pacify her husband's behavior, telling her to place a swallow in a hole in the wall above their bed, saying the words, "Here I place you, Cristóbal" (*Aqui te meto, Cristóbal)*. Clara de Miranda had told another woman that to make her husband care for her she should let a leech suck blood from her thigh and, after drying and grinding it, give it to him to drink; or she could prepare his chocolate with the water she had used to cleanse herself after having intercourse with him. Ana, an Indian woman who had been a friend of Clara's, also told Francisca that "to stupefy men and to tame them it was good to give them to drink the custom of women (*la costumbre de las mujeres*)." While Francisca had never seen Clara or Ana serve these things to men, just the mention of them in everyday conversation had made her sufficiently suspicious to go confess to a local priest who, in turn, sent her to the Inquisition for absolution.

For Marcelina, María Guadalupe, and Francisca, as for other colonial Mexican women, the discourse about the magical control of men, with its reversal of the social/sexual order and strange metaphoric practices and "cuisines," was simply diabolical, inspiring shock, fear, suspicion, and disgust. Such women seemed to think that if they had to choose between two evils—a mala vida with their husbands or doing devil's stuff—it was their obligation, as proper Christians, to choose the first.[32] Well Christianized by a church that taught the female sex to take its precepts especially seriously, these women seemed to think it was better to have the clear conscience that came from the holy martyrdom of knowing that they were on the side of God than to provoke the devil by flirting with "his stuff." In confessing to their local priests and later to the inquisitors, they betrayed themselves as well as their female friends, neighbors, and relatives, thereby giving in to the structure of male domination and turning in those women who posed a threat to that structure. Such women were their own best inquisitors.

While some women internalized the Inquisition's devaluation of female supernatural power, thereby devaluing their own and other women's efforts at resisting male hegemony, many women also openly rejected Catholic ideology and embraced the devil. Viewing themselves as beyond salvation, these women purposely chose to be connected with the Evil One. They made pacts with the devil, who, by their own accounts, acted as a kinder, more loyal, and more interested companion than their true-life husbands. Thus, María Rosa, an Afro-Indian (or *loba*) in a Zacatecan hacienda, claimed in 1747 that she had a 20-year pact with the devil, which she had entered into after her husband had run off with another woman.[33] The devil appeared to her "in the figure of a dog that hung around her skirts and cajoled her and talked to her; it would affectionately scratch her if she didn't pay attention to him." Or, Juana de los Santos, a young creole (of Spanish descent) woman from Nayarit, claimed in 1736 that she had made a pact with the devil seven years before to be able to follow the goings-on of her mulatto husband in his affairs and to take vengeance on his mistresses.[34] For her, the devil was a handsome young mulatto, a kind and loving alter-ego of her husband, who would visit her every day and ask how she was doing and who, indeed, helped her catch her husband with a mistress. Both these women made their pacts with the devil on the advice of other women, who initiated them into the counterreligious world of evil—in María Rosa's case, by being led into a room where a little dog, whose posterior she kissed, promised "to help her in any way he could," and in Juana de los Santos' case, by being given a picture of the devil by another white woman who had, like herself, had a bad marriage with a mulatto.

Interethnic Networks of Cures and Suspicions

One common feature of all of these cases involving women's use of sexual witchcraft and devil pacts is the existence of a network of women exchanging remedies and advice about marital and sexual relationships. This network was not only an interethnic one, but also an interclass one, and it included women of both the upper and lower social strata of colonial Mexico. Most typically, well-off white women, who were addressed as "doña" and lived comfortably with servants and coaches, had close contacts, even friendships, with Indian women, often cast in the role of magical specialists in the colony. The latter provided them with a cornucopia of indigenous powders and roots, as well as hummingbirds for use in love magic. In some cases, such élite white women would get Indian women to carry out sorcery for them.

Thus, in Guanajuato in 1725, doña Francisca de Parada, who lived in the house of an uncle who was a priest, asked Mathiana, an Indian woman, for help in "playing a joke" on a man who had betrayed her in a promise of marriage.[35] Mathiana was a healer who frequented the Parada household, both to provide cures and "to get something to eat of what they cooked." Out of the love she had for Francisca de Parada, Mathiana claimed that she had called upon the devil, with whose aid she would fly to the side of Francisca's ex-suitor; then she would carry him off to a deserted spot where she and another Indian woman would torture him and make him dance and kiss the devil-goat's posterior. This interesting relationship between Francisca de Parada and Mathiana, rooted in a mundane domestic reality in which an Indian woman exchanged her magical medical wares for her daily sustenance, points also to the exchange of mystical notions, so widespread in the colony, an exchange that forged a complex and hybrid religious culture. Indian women, as in this example, not only provided the paraphernalia for cures, but in the course of exchanging remedies with women of other caste and class groups acquired European ideas about the witches' sabbat and the powers of the devil. The exchanges moved in more than one direction, with creoles assimilating Indian remedies for carrying out love magic and sexual witchcraft.

Officially, the Mexican Inquisition was forbidden to prosecute Indians after its establishment in 1571, when it was decided that Indians, as neophytes, were too new to the faith to be responsible for inquisitions of their consciences.[36] Only Spanish creoles, mestizos, African slaves, and their mixed offspring were to be subject to the strictures of the Inquisition. Yet, Indians who were Hispanicized, or at least integrated into the larger community, often figured in the background of many cases and occasionally even provided testimony. When such Indians did appear, strong magical powers were attributed to them, in the general way in which those at the margins elsewhere in Spanish America were thought to hold dangerous powers.[37] Likewise, magical powers were attributed to mulatto healers in Mexico, and in southern Spain magical powers were ascribed to morisco healers.[38] Thus, women from the marginal groups in colonial society—Indians, mulattas, mestizas—who were involved in cases of sexual witchcraft had, from the point of view of men, a kind of double power: that inherent to their sex and that inherent to their caste, as the following example will show.

In 1740, Francisco Bibanco, a resident of an hacienda near Mexico City, wrote the Inquisition a letter in which he accused María Antonia de Caiseros, a mestiza, of having caused him to go blind suddenly because he had failed to marry her as he had promised.[39] Remarking "how widespread sorcery and its teachers are," especially among Indians, "who fear one another for their cunning," he explained that he had broken off with María Antonia because he had heard of her "evil deeds." Although he had provided her with a dowry, she had still taunted him, saying, "You can still see, blind one? Soon you won't." Then one day she spread flowers on the path ahead of him and immediately afterwards he went blind. Doctors could not cure him and the priest's exorcism had no effect, a clear sign that he was bewitched. He pleaded with the inquisitors to take his case seriously, because otherwise "more such evil works will be committed against our holy Catholic faith, for they have many vengeances and would bewitch whomever they want to, making a display of it, with little fear of God."

As in the opening example involving José de Ugalde, we find a man sufficiently convinced of a woman's witchcraft powers to accuse her before the Inquisition. Like José de Ugalde, who wanted to beat this uncanny power out of his wife, Francisco Bibanco, too, considered this more direct means of undoing the spell María Antonia had placed on him. When a male friend suggested to him that he simply "give that evil woman a good round of lashes," he replied that he had not done so for fear that she would go to the priest and convince him that he had made her pregnant.

Francisco Bibanco's suspicion of María Antonia, a mestiza, had to do with his perception of her as "Indian"; she was, it seems, bicultural, speaking to him in Spanish and to her mother and neighbors in Nahuatl. Bibanco viewed her as linked to an Indian world of vengeance and witchcraft that threatened, in his own words, "our holy Catholic faith." Her power, for Francisco Bibanco, seemed to reside equally in her gender and in her cultural foreignness.

Accusations by creole Spanish men against women of Indian and mixed castes come up frequently in the Mexican Inquisition records, suggesting that the discourse of women's witchcraft power became enmeshed in the colonial ideology of caste hierarchy.[40] Similarly, in southern Spain, the apparent predominance of moriscos and gypsies in the commerce of magic points to a general pattern linking magic and power to peripheral groups. Paradoxically, the powerless and the conquered, whether Indians or Moors, were viewed as having dangerous occult powers. Thus, to the intersection of gender, power, and religion we must also add caste, so that inevitably we must go beyond an analysis of women to get at the sources of women's power.

The Inscription of Sexual Witchcraft into Colonial Power

The effectiveness of sexual witchcraft, in part, grew out of a distinction between natural and unnatural illness that had roots both in pre-Hispanic and contemporaneous Castilian beliefs. This distinction was widely accepted by the general populace, as well as by priests, inquisitors, and the medical doctors of the period. Those illnesses that neither exorcism nor medicine could cure were the illnesses of evil (*maleficio*) and of witchcraft (*hechicería*). In such cases, only the person who had worked the harm could undo it. We have considered a few examples involving men who perceived that they had been made to suffer such unnatural illnesses at the hands of a woman, whether wife, rejected wife-to-be, or mistress. I have suggested that the efficacy of women's magical powers resided in the "otherness" of their sex and their race. Now, in my last example, I would like to bring together the diverse strands of gender, power, religion, race, and illness, to place sexual witchcraft in the widest possible social context—that of colonial relations of power and subordination.

In 1733 Fray Diego Núñez, prior of the monastery of Our Lady of the Assumption in Amecameca, not far from Mexico City, wrote a long letter of accusation to the Inquisition detailing how Manuela de Bocanegra, his mulatta slave, had bewitched him.[41] Manuela, he claimed, had without a doubt ensorcelled him with the help of the devil, and he had medical proof of various sorts to prove it. With this assertion he proceeded to tell the inquisitors in minute detail about the illnesses his slave had placed on him through her witchcraft.

At first his arms hurt so much that he could barely move them and no medicine could cure him, until by chance he was healed by the incense of the Agnus Dei candle. This was followed by an inability to urinate for eleven days, from which he finally recovered after another slave, a brother of Manuela, gave him a print of Saint Salvador Horta. Then he slept for six hours and upon waking expelled about "twenty or more normal measures." The worst of the illness was yet to come: the horrid aches in "the most humid and painful parts of the body" that had besieged him for eight months and made him expel more than two hundred stones in a single fortnight. Both urination and defecation had become horrendously painful, and the things his body expelled were strangely unnatural. His was not a natural illness affecting the humors of the body, Fray Diego felt certain, because his pain was continuous and vehement, and was especially awful on Sundays. What is more, with proper scientific style he had carried out experiments on the bizarre things that his body expelled and had deduced that his slave, Manuela, was at the root of them.

The stones, he explained, were all different: some were spongy, others porous, and while most were smooth and solid, they varied in color, such that they looked as if they had come not from his own body but from an anthole. And he asked: Is it natural to engender "from one and the other end: eyebrows, eyelashes, and every type of hair from my own body?" Extracted from his urine and excrement "and extremely carefully cleaned and examined they appear to be blond, thin, wavy, and a few of them greying, each of them mine according to their size, style, and arrangement as compared with those that at present are still attached to my body." Nor can the body produce, he went on, pieces of wool, a paintbrush such as those used in the art of painting, and the hair of cats, dogs, deer, and pigs commonly used to make the brushes employed for painting. Also unnatural was the shifting appearance of his excrement: at times it looked like tiny emeralds; at other times like the exact shape and style of foods he had once consumed voraciously and now hated; at times like olives from Seville; and still at other times like goat excrement that when heated would smoke and burst, giving all those present a nasty headache. These careful examinations and experiments with the products of his own body confirmed the fact that according to "medical knowledge this was diabolic maleficio." The very things expelled by his body, as Fray Diego put it, were "signs" that when read properly pointed to the person responsible for his illness: namely, his mulatta slave.

The signs inevitably pointed back, as well, to his slave's sexuality. Fray Diego was certain that the reason Manuela de Bocanegra had ensorcelled him was that he had caught her once in the sexual act, "in flagranti delicto," with a young painter who lived in the room next to hers in the monastery. At the time he scolded both of them severely, and this scolding provoked in his slave the desire for vengeance. What better way to take revenge on him than by diabolically introducing into his body the tools of her lover's craft! Thus, she had made him consume her lover's paintbrushes and the hair of which brushes were made. Since it was only from her hands that he received food and drink and had his clothes tended to, she had the advantage of being in control of the whole of his domestic life. With great cunning she had used this intimacy to gather his own hair and other of his bodily substances in order to reintroduce them into his body and thereby make him "engender" them again in wretched pain. In a later addition to his testimony Fray Diego noted that Manuela de Bocanegra had once induced her brother, also his slave, to sprinkle love powders (*polvos de buen querer*) in his chocolate, so that he would "come to love said mulatto and mulatta."

This accusation may appear to be nothing more than the ravings of a gravely ill and solipsistic priest. But placed within the context of our earlier discussion of sexual witchcraft, it becomes both comprehensible and illuminating. Indeed, Fray Diego was not the first to see an implicit parallel between the attempts of women to attract, tame, and harm men through sexual witchcraft and the magical or, in his terms, diabolical efforts of slaves to control their masters. As early as 1614 a slave owner, Leonor de Hinojosa, reported to the Inquisition that her black slave, Agustina, had in her possession a root named *pumoyate,* which was used both to attract and repel members of the opposite sex.[42] The slaveholder had made this discovery while beating her slave, who admitted that she had acquired the root, interestingly, from a Spanish healer, who told her to serve it to her master in cocoa in order to "tame" her (again, we see that the networks of magical exchange flowed in various directions). The word *amansar,* meaning to tame or domesticate, was used here as in the cases of sexual witchcraft, suggesting an explicit metaphorical connection between both the oppressive condition of being a woman and a slave and the desire to soften and "culture" the natural brutality of their husbands and masters, in what was a key reversal of the ethos linking "woman," "nature," and "slave" as wild and in need of conquest.

The relation between Fray Diego and his slave Manuela was a domestic relation, almost like that of husband and wife. She prepared his food and his clothes, and all would have been well except that her master caught her in the act of "adultery." Fray Diego's accusation against Manuela de Bocanegra is reminiscent of those accusations we encountered earlier involving men who felt they had been bewitched by women with whom they had had an intimate relationship. As in those cases, the unnatural illness Fray Diego suffered was clearly seen by him as resulting from witchcraft, and particularly from witchcraft transmitted through the medium of food. His excessively elaborated discourse about his illness, a thick Rabelaisian description of his ingestion and digestion, takes us back to our earlier discussion of how women made men "eat" their witchcraft. He highlighted not only the process of eating but also that of expelling the ensorcelled objects from the body, which became a kind of "evidence" in Fray Diego's case against his slave.

For Fray Diego, Manuela de Bocanegra's powers seemed to reside not just in her sex and in her caste but also in her position as a slave. Their relationship was made up of a series of dyads of domination: man and woman, priest and lay person, white and mulatta, and master and slave. It was as a woman, a mulatta, and especially as a slave, the most marginal and oppressed position in colonial society, that Manuela threatened Fray Diego. Hers was a supreme example of the power of the powerless, and she threatened him—as did the women who used sexual witchcraft menaced their victims—by inverting the social order and putting the dominated on top. Significantly, Fray Diego even claimed in his testimony that his slave had radically feminized his body, for in the course of his illness a wound had suddenly appeared along the length of his bottom, in the form of piles that had "transmuted the lower posterior to look like that of the female sex." His slave's witchcraft had declassed him, turning him into a kind of slave; it had re-gendered him as a woman.

Clearly for Fray Diego to have been able to fashion this accusation against his slave he had to have been familiar with the discourse of sexual witchcraft, as he most certainly was, for he explicitly said that Manuela de Bocanegra had even tried to put love powders in his cocoa. His participation in the popular beliefs of his time went further than the witchcraft accusation against his slave, however. Believing himself to be bewitched, he had taken the advice of a female neighbor, doña Josefa de Acosta, and sought out the services of a *curandera*, or healer (who was also a midwife), a mulatta by the name of Gertrudis.[43]

Gertrudis gave him an herb to drink in water and had him immerse himself in a *temascal*, or hot bath. This produced a wound in his backside that later healed with the application of a pink oil. Later she gave him two different mixtures to drink that increased his pains, and when he complained to her she told him that he would have to be patient about seeking a cure because what he had was hechizo, ensorcellment. Gertrudis then told him that Manuela was the one who had him that way, that she had in her possession a doll of him, and that she had known that he was the one who had ordered that she be beaten and sent to work in a sweatshop (*obraje*), where she had vowed to take revenge on him. Indeed, Fray Diego had sent Manuela away after becoming ill and deducing that she was at the root of his illness. The beating he ordered she be given was as routine a part of master/slave relations as it was of husband/wife relations; interestingly, Fray Diego recovered somewhat when his slave was away in the sweatshop—in her proper, subjugated position in the social structure, in other words—and he became seriously ill again when she was released. So desperate was he, in fact, that he begged Gertrudis to get the doll from Manuela, to whom he promised her liberty in exchange.

But his dealings with Gertrudis came suddenly to a halt when he discovered that she was not simply a healer and a midwife but also a sorceress and a dealer in sexual witchcraft. He made this discovery, interestingly enough, when a young Spanish woman, María Rodríguez, went to him for confession and disclosed that Gertrudis had offered her green, yellow, and white powders as well as a green porcelain "little head with little horns" so that she would have "lots of money and men would run after her." During the few days she carried around these powders and the little head, María Rodríguez said that men who had previously treated her "honestly" wanted suddenly "by force to engage in dishonest acts" and offered her lots of money; so she threw it all away and things went back to normal immediately. Hearing this, Fray Diego realized that Gertrudis was more than just a healer and that rather than curing him she was harming him further, possibly in agreement with his slave Manuela. He had found a hole in one of his shirts, as if someone had taken scissors and cut into the cloth, and ever since Gertrudis had given him the last mixture to drink he had been expelling rags and rotten hairs through his urine. Thus, Fray Diego ended up suspecting that this mulatta healer, together with his mulatta slave, were at the root of his strangely unnatural illness.

The records provide no clue as to what became of Fray Diego, or how the Inquisition reacted to his case. While Fray Diego's case is somewhat extraordinary because of the degree of his involvement in witchcraft, it does show that members of the religious élite shared in this popular discourse and could themselves participate actively in using it when illness and other misfortunes required explanation. Like the men who accused the women they had been in relationships with, Fray Diego ended up accusing his mulatta slave of having brought about his strange illness because he could find no other interpretation for his loss of control over his own body. In other words, like the French peasants who claim not to believe in witchcraft today until a series of misfortunes comes along to make them lose all sense of control, he was "caught."[44] Once "caught," only his slave's witchcraft could account for his utter powerlessness, in the same way that José de Ugalde could accuse his wife of having turned him into a fool. And again, only the church, through the Holy Office, seemed to offer the proper solace, cure, and interlocutor in these cases in which women of the marginal social classes dangerously overturned the social/sexual order.

Conclusions: The Paradox of Women's Witchcraft Powers

It is well known that women tend to exercise power in the private rather than the public domain, and in this essay we have seen how female power operated on the most private level of all, that of sexual relationships. While we tend to think of power as having to do with the control of material resources or the activities and movements of large groups of people, women's power is usually of a different, more muted, less obviously recognizable sort. As this material on women's witchcraft powers shows, control within the symbolic domain is also a form of power. While placing herbs and powders in the food they served to their husbands, or burying eggs to carry out a ligature, may seem to be trivial means of exercising power, in fact the real stakes were political, given that women's ultimate aim was to control and change the behavior of the men who dominated them. Even beyond anything women actually attempted to carry out, the cultural assignment of mystic powers to women served as a check on the excesses of male dominance.[45] Yet what was given with one hand was taken away with the other: the church's interpretation of witchcraft as superstition at once trivialized women's power and turned it into a shameful, if minor, sin.

These cases involving sexual witchcraft, which formed part of a larger corpus of "superstitions" regarded as trivial by the late colonial Inquisition because they involved the marginal social classes, were part of the everyday stuff of Inquisition proceedings.[46] The inquisitors tended to dismiss them lightly, concentrating instead, until the midseventeenth century, on the more serious religious crimes of heresy and blasphemy and, in the late colonial period, on antiroyalist clerics and other intellectual dissenters of the colonial regime. Historians, too, have tended to dismiss these cases, the inquisitorial minutiae, as not being spectacular enough to warrant investigation.

In comparing aspects of women's supernatural powers first between northern Europe and Spain, then between northern Spain and Castile, and finally between Castile and central Mexico, I have sought to shed some light on the various ways in which witchcraft was treated by the religious élite and how this affected the exercise of female power. In particular, I tried to give a sense of how an urban Spanish understanding of female power, focusing on love magic and ligature, got transfered to the New World and there became linked to the caste system and to, apparently, very violent domestic relations between men and women of different racial backgrounds.

In conclusion I want to point out the paradox of women's supernatural power, a paradox that exists in any power exercised by women. While women's witchcraft powers were thought effective on the local level, especially by men who feared they had lost the upper hand in sexual relationships, it is clear that women exercised these powers within a male-dominated system, and thus their resistance was at best limited and piecemeal, as women's own devaluation of their power showed. Even allowing for this paradox, the discourse of women's magical power made it possible for them to put into question and challenge, if unsuccessfully, the structures of inequality—the very structures that made it necessary for them to use symbolic weapons to combat real domination and oppression.

Acknowledgments

This paper is based on field and archival research carried out with the aid of a Fulbright Senior Research Award and a grant from the Organization of American States. It forms part of a larger project on witchcraft in colonial and contemporary Mexico, for which I have received generous support from the Program in Atlantic History, Culture and Society at Johns Hopkins University through a Rockefeller Residence Fellowship, the Harry Frank Guggenheim Foundation, and the Society of Fellows at the University of Michigan. To all these institutions I extend my sincere thanks. Earlier versions of this paper were presented to the Department of Anthropology at the University of Chicago, the Department of Anthropology at the University of Texas, Austin, and the Western Societies Program at Cornell University. Special thanks go to Asunción Lavrin for her comments and encouragement and to David Frye, my husband, for listening to this paper on several different occasions.

Notes

1. Archivo General de la Nación, Mexico City, Ramo Inquisición (hereafter cited as AGN, Inquisición), 894:53–54v.

2. Here I will be elaborating on ideas concerning the potential subversion of order in gender relations that appear in Natalie Z. Davis, "Women on Top," in her *Society and Culture in Early Modern France* (Stanford: Stanford University Press, 1975), pp. 124–51; Steven Ozment, *When Fathers Ruled: Family Life in Reformation Europe* (Cambridge: Harvard University Press, 1983), pp. 52–53, 71, 76–77.

3. On food magic, see Bernadino de Sahagún, *Historia general de las cosas de Nueva España,* 4 vols., ed. Angel M. Garibay K. (Mexico City: Editorial Porrúa, 1981), 2:150–51. A survey of indigenous "superstitions," incantations, and witchcraft practices in seventeenth-century New Spain is available in Hernando Ruiz de Alarcón, *Treatise on the Heathen Superstitions That Today Live among the Indians Native to this New Spain, 1629,* trans. and ed. J. Richard Andrews and Ross Hassig (Norman: University of Oklahoma Press, 1984); Noemí Quezada, *Amor y magia amorosa entre los aztecas* (Mexico City: Universidad Nacional Autónoma de México, 1975); Sebastián Cirac Estopañán, *Los procesos de hechicherías en la Inquisición de Castilla la Nueva (Tribunales de Toledo y Cuenca)* (Madrid: CSIC, 1942), pp. 81–83. For a study of a witchcraft process among the Chichimecs, see, Ruth Behar, "The Visions of a Guachichil Witch in 1599: A Window on the Subjugation of Mexico's Hunter-Gatherers," *Ethnohistory* 34:2 (Spring 1987), 115–38.

4. On metaphor theory, see James W. Fernández, *Persuasions and Performances: The Play of Tropes in Culture* (Bloomington: Indiana University Press, 1986), pp. 28–70.

5. On the ways in which the Edicts of Faith inspired confessions, see Patricia Aufderheide, "True Confessions: The Inquisition and Social Attitudes in Brazil at the Turn of the XVII Century," *Luso-Brazilian Review* 10 (1973): 208–40.

6. On the role of the church in setting rules for domestic and sexual behavior, see Lavrin's essay in this volume.

7. Michelle Zimbalist Rosaldo, "Woman, Culture, and Society: A Theoretical Overview," in *Woman, Culture, and Society,* ed. Michelle Zimbalist Rosaldo and Louise Lamphere (Stanford: Stanford University Press, 1974), pp. 17–42; Sherry B. Ortner, "Is Female to Male as Nature Is to Culture?" in *Woman, Culture, and Society,* ed. Rosaldo and Lamphere, pp. 67–87; Sherry B. Ortner and Harriet Whitehead, "Introduction: Accounting for Sexual Meanings," in *Sexual Meanings: The Cultural Construction of Gender and Sexuality,* ed. Sherry B. Ortner and Harriet Whitehead (Cambridge: Cambridge University Press, 1981), pp. 1–27; Jill Dubisch, "Introduction," in *Gender and Power in Rural Greece,* ed. Jill Dubisch (Princeton: Princeton University Press, 1986), pp. 3–41.

8. On pollution beliefs and the dangerous powers of women's sexuality, see Mary Douglas, *Purity and Danger: An Analysis of the Concepts of Pollution and Taboo* (London: Routledge and Kegan Paul, 1966). On pollution beliefs in New Guinea, see Shirley Lindenbaum, "A Wife is the Hand of Man," in *Man and Woman in the New Guinea Highlands,* ed. Paula Brown and

Georgeda Buchbinder (Washington, D.C.: American Anthropological Association, 1976), pp. 54–62; Raymond C. Kelly, "Witchcraft and Sexual Relations," in *Man and Woman,* ed. Brown and Buchbinder, pp. 36–53; Elizabeth Faithorn, "The Concept of Pollution among the Kafe of the Papua New Guinea Highlands," in *Toward an Anthropology of Women,* ed. Rayna R. Reiter (New York: Monthly Review Press, 1975), pp. 127–40.

9. On contemporary cases of food magic involving the use of menstrual blood and pubic hair (likewise part of a woman's bodily essences), see Lois Paul, "The Mastery of Work and the Mystery of Sex in a Guatemalan Village," in *Woman, Culture, and Society,* ed. Rosaldo and Lamphere, pp. 281–99. On page 198, she notes that "women know that menstrual blood is one of their own ultimate weapons against intractable husbands," citing the following informant remark: "Many men have eaten their beans with the blood of their wives and didn't know it." See also Anna Rubbo, "The Spread of Capitalism in Rural Colombia: Effects on Poor Women," in *Toward an Anthropology of Women,* ed. Rayna R. Reiter, pp. 333–57.

10. On the European witch-hunt, see E. William Monter, *Witchcraft in France and Switzerland: The Borderlands during the Reformation* (Ithaca: Cornell University Press, 1976); H. C. Erik Midelfort, *Witch-Hunting in Southwestern Germany, 1562–1684: The Social and Intellectual Foundations* (Stanford: Stanford University Press, 1972); Keith Thomas, *Religion and the Decline of Magic* (New York: Charles Scribner's Sons, 1971); Joseph Klaitz, *Servants of Satan: The Age of the Witch-Hunts* (Bloomington: Indiana University Press, 1985).

11. Christina Larner, *Enemies of God: The Witch-Hunt in Scotland* (Baltimore: Johns Hopkins University Press, 1981).

12. See Henry Kamen, *Inquisition and Society in Spain in the Sixteenth and Seventeenth Centuries* (Bloomington: Indiana University Press, 1985).

13. On the Zagarramurdi witch panic, see Gustav Hennigsen, *The Witches' Advocate: Basque Witchcraft and the Spanish Inquisition (1609–1614)* (Reno: University of Nevada Press, 1980). For a good discussion of the small-scale witch panics in northern Spain, see Carmelo Lisón Tolosana, *Brujería, estructura social y simbolismo en Galicia* (Madrid: Akal Editor, 1979), pp. 9–51.

14. Kamen, *Inquisition,* pp. 212–13.

15. Henry Kamen, "Notas sobre brujería y sexualidad y la Inquisición," in *Inquisición española Mentalidad: inquisitorial,* ed. Angel Alcalá (Barcelona: Editorial Ariel, 1984), pp. 226–36; E. William Monter, *Ritual, Myth and Magic in Early Modern Europe* (Athens: Ohio University Press, 1983), p. 102.

16. On the contrast between northern Spanish witchcraft and southern Spanish urban witchcraft, see Julio Caro Baroja, *Las brujas y su mundo* (Madrid: Alianza Editorial, 1966). For urban love magic in Italy, see Mary O'Neil, "Magical Healing, Love Magic and the Inquisition in Late Sixteenth-Century Modena," in *Inquisition and Society in Early Modern Europe,* ed. Stephen Haliczer (London: Croom Helm, 1987), pp. 88–114.

17. On the type of women involved in Spanish cases of love magic, see Cirac Estopañán, *Los procesos,* p. 215.

18. Information on Leonor de Barzana, Juana Hernández, and Catalina Gómez are found in Cirac Estopañán, *Los procesos,* pp. 210–11.

19. Cirac Estopañán, *Los procesos,* p. 81.

20. Monter, *Ritual, Myth and Magic,* p. 72.

21. On confession and sexuality, see Gruzinski's essay in this volume; Michel Foucault, *The History of Sexuality,* vol. 1: *Introduction* (New York: Vintage Books, 1980).

22. On the devaluation of women's powers by the Spanish Inquisition, see Claire Guilhem, "La Inquisición y la devaluación del verbo femenino," in *Inquisición española: Poder político y control social,* ed. Bartolomé Bennassar (Barcelona: Editorial Crítica, 1981), pp. 171–207. On the Mexican Inquisition, see Richard D.Greenleaf, *The Mexican Inquisition of the Sixteenth Century* (Albuquerque: University of New Mexico Press, 1969), and "The Inquisition in Eighteenth-Century New Mexico," *New Mexico Historical Review* 60, no.1 (Spring 1985): 29–60; Gonzalo Aguirre Beltrán, *Medicina y magia: El proceso de aculturación en la estructura colonial* (Mexico City: Instituto Nacional Indigenista, 1980); Solange Behocaray Alberro, *La actividad del Santo Oficio de la Inquisición en Nueva España, 1571–1700* (Mexico City: Instituto Nacional de Antropología e Historia, 1981).

23. The account of Magdalena de la Mata is taken from AGN Inquisición, 878:314–16.

24. Heinrich Kramer and James Sprenger, *The Malleus Maleficarum of Heinrich Kramer and James Sprenger,* trans. Montague Summers (New York: Dover, 1971 [1486]), p. 121.

25. Cirac Estopañán, *Los procesos,* p. 81.

26. Asunción Lavrin, "Women and Religion in Spanish America," in *Women and Religion in America,* vol.2: *The Colonial and Revolutionary Periods,* ed. Rosemary Radford Ruether and Rosemary Skinner Keller (San Francisco: Harper & Row, 1983), p. 45.

27. William B. Taylor, *Drinking, Homicide and Rebellion in Colonial Mexican Villages* (Stanford: Stanford University Press, 1979), p. 95; Silvia M.

Arrom, *The Women of Mexico City, 1790–1857* (Stanford: Stanford University Press, 1985), p. 232.

28. William A. Christian, Jr., "Provoked Religious Weeping in Early Modern Spain, in *Religious Organization and Religious Experience,* ed. J. Davis (London: Academic Press, 1982), p. 107.

29. AGN, Inquisición, 878:389. In this case the role of the mulatto uncle, who was clearly a healer, is significant. Like Indian men and women, mulatto men and women frequently appear in the late-colonial Inquisition cases as providers of cures and remedies for healing, magic, and sexual witchcraft.

30. AGN, Inquisición, 998, exp. 5.

31. The account of Francisca de los Angeles is taken from AGN, Inquisición, 685, exp. 10.

32. For the concept of marriage and mala vida see Boyer's essay in this volume.

33. AGN, Inquisición, 911:334–76.

34. AGN, Inquisición, 812, exp. 19. Both this and the previous case involving women's devil pacts are treated in more detail in Ruth Behar, "Sex and Sin, Witchcraft and the Devil in Late Colonial Mexico," *American Ethnologist* 14 (1987): 35–55.

35. AGN, Inquisición, 1029, exp. 9.

36. Richard D. Greenleaf, "The Inquisition and the Indians of New Spain: A Study in Jurisdictional Confusion," *The Americas* 22 (October 1965): 138–66.

37. On the shamanic power of those at the margins, see Michael Taussig, "Folk Healing and the Structure of Conquest in Southwest Colombia," *Journal of Latin American Lore* 6 (1980): 217–78; Frank Salomon, "Shamanism and Politics in Late Colonial Ecuador," *American Ethnologist* 10 (1983), pp. 413–28.

38. Richard L. Kagan, "Eleno-Elena: Annals of Androgyny in Sixteenth-Century Spain," manuscript, p. 23, notes that many popular healers were moriscos.

39. The account of Francisco Bibanco is taken from AGN, Inquisición, 929, exp. 10.

40. Examples of such denunciations abound in the records of the Mexican Inquisition. See, for instance, the case of José de Ugalde, above, and the denunciation by Lorenzo Martínez, a white farrier, against his former mistress, a mestiza, in 1709 (AGN, Inq., vol. 765, exp. 9). See also, AGN, Inquisición, 953, exp. 25 (1748). Here, a white baker from Querétaro accused his mulatta mistress of having served him ensorcelled milk that had left a ball of lead in his

stomach; the doctors who treated him could offer no cure, and one of them told him that "it didn't appear to be a natural illness but rather something they had been placed on him." Even before the mulatta ensorcelled him, however, one particular incident had made him suspicious. She had once entered the room when he had been sleeping. Having lifted her on top of him, he told her to be quiet; she had said to him, "You be quiet, because with that pig jaw of yours I could strangle you." These words, he said, had made him suspect what he later found out: that she was, indeed, a witch, because only a witch would have dared utter words as harsh as those to a man. A proper Christian woman—a proper Christian white woman?—it appears, would not have been so disobedient, so bold, or so utterly disrespectful of the order of social/sexual relations.

41. The account of Fr. Diego Muñoz is taken from AGN, Inquisición, 765, exp. 15.

42. As early as 1614 a slave owner, Leonor de Hinojosa, reported to the Inquisition that her black slave, Agustina, had in her possession a root named *puyomate,* which was used in colonial times both to attract and repel members of the opposite sex. She made this discovery while beating her slave, who admitted that she had acquired the root from a Spanish healer, who told her to serve it to her master in cocoa in order to "tame" her. This case is cited in Solange Alberro, "Inquisición y proceso de cambio social: Delitos de hechicería en Celaya, 1614," *Revista de dialectología y tradiciones populares* 30 (1974): 346–47. For the use of puyomate in colonial Mexico, see Aguirre Beltrán, *Medicina y Magia,* p. 17; Noemi Quezada, *Amor y magia amorosa entre los aztecas,* p. 96.

43. AGN, Inquisición, 765, exp. 19.

44. On the notion of how people get "caught" in witchcraft beliefs, see Jeanne Favret-Saada, *Deadly Words: Witchcraft in the Bocage* (Cambridge: Cambridge University Press, 1980).

45. For an elaboration of this idea in a contemporary account of sexual witchcraft, see Lois Paul, "Mastery of Work," pp. 281–99.

46. On the development of class ideas among the late colonial inquisitors, see Behar, "Sex and Sin," pp. 48–51.

Part II: Marriage

Susan M. Socolow

Acceptable Partners: Marriage Choice in Colonial Argentina, 1778–1810

Marriage in most societies is a mechanism by which two individuals are joined in a socially recognized union, as well as the institution through which legitimate families are formed. But it is also an institution for cementing ties between already-formed families. The choice of marriage partners is therefore of interest to more than just the bride and groom. Because of its crucial role in structuring society, in forming alliances, and in delineating kinship groups, the choice of marriage partners—so-called marriage formation—could be an area of conflict among different parties.[1]

Marriage usually occurs between individuals belonging to endogamous groups. People tend to marry those whom they and society perceive as being socially like them, from the same or contiguous socioeconomic backgrounds. But there are always important exceptions to this dictum. Despite all formal constraints some individuals violate social standards for the quite personal reasons of sexual attraction, companionship, or the desire for security and protection. A society's reactions to these exceptions helps to explain its attitude toward social mobility and social change. While few groups welcome marriage to those who are markedly different, their efforts to prevent these marriages run the gamut from lack of action to punitive legislation. Thus the response to "inappropriate" marriage partners is both a useful indication of the rigidity or openness of a given social system at a particular time and a mechanism that can be used by a social group to protect its internal cohesion. This study looks at marriage opposition in late-eighteenth-century Rio de la Plata in an attempt to analyze how legislation affecting engagement and marriage was applied. In turn, this study also improves our understanding marriage, colonial society, and the role of women.

In Roman Catholic societies marriage is one of the sacraments of the church. As such, until the end of the eighteenth century, the regulation of marriage lay solely within the legal jurisdiction of the bishop and the church courts.[2] The church, basing its decisions on canon law, decided whether a particular couple should be joined together. Church courts were free to make their decisions independent of direct civil supervision and, for the most part, free from appeals to civil courts as well.[3]

Central to Roman Catholic law was the belief that marriage could take place only between two people who had freely consented to share this sacrament. Indeed the Council of Trent decreed that couples had a right to marry of their own will and could do so without parental consent.[4] Although parents tried to prevent undesirable marriages, the church consistently held for couples, going as far as dispensing the banns so that they could marry in spite of parental opposition. Parental objections based on economic or ethnic differences between the couple (*novios*) were routinely rejected by ecclesiastical courts; as long as canon law impediments did not exist, the church's policy was pro–marital union.[5]

Royal Control

In 1776, Charles III, the Bourbon king of Spain, issued a royal Pragmática that changed dramatically both the rules and the authority governing marriage.[6] Extended to his American possessions two years later by the royal cédula (decree) of 7 April 1778, this legislation represented a departure from previous norms and demonstrated that the Bourbon reforms encompassed more than political and economic change. The *Real Pragmática,* and succeeding marriage legislation, was indeed an attempt to transform social mores at the basic level of marriage and kinship formation.[7] According to the *Pragmática,* all subjects, "from the highest classes in the State to the lowest subjects, without any exception," were to come under the law, although in America "mulattoes, blacks, mestizos and members of other similar mixed races who are publicly known and reputed as such" were to be specifically excluded.

From 1778 on, parental permission, never before required under canon law, became the sine qua non before whites (*españoles*) could be engaged to marry. Moreover any disputes over marriage were now to come before a civil court (in most cases the *juzgado de alcalde*), which would rule on whether a marriage could take place; appeal was to the Royal Audiencia. Church courts were removed from most cases involving opposition to marriage. In addition, any person marrying in spite of parental opposition could be immediately disinherited in perpetuity. Power over choice of marriage was thereby transferred from the individual exercising his or her own free will, and the church, to both the bride's and/or the groom's parents and the state.

As important as the redistribution of power enacted by the royal *Pragmática* was the redefinition of "just cause" to prevent a marriage. Although canon law impediments continued to be valid reasons to prevent a marriage, inequality between bride and groom was now enshrined as the principal cause for a successful parental dissent (*disenso*). If, after refusing to grant permission to marry, a young man or woman chose to bring formal suit against the dissenting parent, that parent need only prove inequality between the prospective spouses in order to stop the marriage.

The *Pragmática* was not the first attempt of the state openly to interfere in matters of marriage. The Spanish crown had legislated on matters of marriage concerning royal bureaucrats and military men from the sixteenth century on.[8] But this was the first time that the entire "white" population came under direct parental and royal control in these matters. The reason for this control was clearly stated in the 1776 *Pragmática* and the 1778 cédula: "to contain the lack of order that has slowly been introduced into society with the passage of time." In the eyes of the Bourbon royalists both the church and young people's individual choice had failed to produced an orderly society. It was now time to take important social matters out of their hands. Legislation during the next thirty years would only reinforce the new attitude made clear in the *Pragmática,* restricting even further the jurisdiction of the church in matters concerning child and wife support and bigamy.[9]

Although there was some initial doubt as to the effect of the 1778 royal cédula in limiting engagement and marriage, two additional royal cédulas issued in 1783 worked to check the freedom of choice of marriage partners.[10] The first, issued on 26 May, stated that if a father's opposition to his offspring's marriage was declared to be *racional* (rational) by the court, a mother could not will property to the offspring.[11] The second, published on 31 May, made parental consent or a court decision in favor of the offspring an indispensable condition for the celebration of a marriage.[12] Four years later, in 1787, still another royal cédula strengthened parental control on marriage by specifically directing all priests not to celebrate any marriage without prior approval of parents or the court.[13] In 1803, a new *Real Pragmática* on the subject of engagement and marriage restated the original principles of the 1778 legislation, while again extending the law. Blacks and *castas* (mixed-bloods) were now to be included under the *Pragmática*. Furthermore, parents could now refuse permission without specifying the reasons for their opposition. Lastly, cabildo courts were removed from hearing these cases. From then on, only the audiencia was to judge parental opposition suits.[14] Again, priests were enjoined not to celebrate any marriage in which the prospective spouses did not have parental approval. Clergymen ran the risk of losing their posts and church property if they failed to comply.

In addition to expanding his control of the church, Charles III wished to control that most dangerous force, disorder, as is clear in the *Pragmática*. The reason for this social disorder is also specified: marriage between unequals that had become so frequent that it caused "most grievous harm . . . upsetting the proper ordering of society, and [producing] continual friction and damage to families." Marriage between unequals was offensive to God because it often took place in spite of parental opposition, thereby defying "the honor, respect, and obedience that children should render to their parents in matters of such gravity and importance." The aim of the state was to control what it viewed as a dangerous confusion between social groups. To achieve this, the 1776 *Pragmática* made parental permission a prerequisite for any Spanish man or woman younger than twenty-five. The assumption was that parents and adult offspring, more aware of the importance of marriage and of the dangers produced by unequal unions, would behave in a more socially desirable fashion.

By imposing the need for parental consent for men and women up to age twenty-five, the new legislation was essentially attempting to control the marriage partner selection of a small group of men—those few who married before reaching the age of majority—and of almost all women. In eighteenth-century Río de la Plata it was rare for a Spanish woman to reach the age of twenty-five without having "taken state." Most women either married or entered a convent somewhere between the age of fourteen and twenty-one.[15] Men, on the other hand, tended to marry in their late twenties or beyond, when they were economically able to support a wife and family. Setting the age at which parental permission was required at twenty-five and below essentially meant that every women now required formal parental permission to marry.

Only in 1803 would this bias against women be corrected when a new royal cédula "on the marriage of a family's offspring" instituted a sliding age scale.[16] If his father was alive, a man now needed parental permission until the age of 25, a woman until the age of 23. If the father was deceased, but the mother alive, the man's age dropped to 24 and the woman's to 22. For orphaned children, if either paternal or maternal grandparents exercised parental authority, the age became 23 for the man and 21 for the woman. Lastly, those under the authority of a tutor could marry at 22 (man) and 20 (woman). Although the law still discriminated against women (mothers having less control than fathers), by pushing back the age of consent for females it did free a large cohort of women to marry without parental control.

The crown realized that some parents might refuse to give their permission for capricious or irrational reasons, abusing the power which the law now gave them over their progeny. Parents, or those acting in their stead, were encouraged to consent to a marriage unless they had just and rational reasons for their opposition. They were also warned not to use this law to force an offspring into a marriage that was against the minor's desire or vocation. The 1776 legislation also outlined the procedure to be followed in those cases where the prospective spouses chose to challenge parental refusal. The very existence of parental marriage opposition both before and after 1776, reflects a degree of personal independence on the part of young people of marriageable age. Although most marriages were arranged with parental intervention, these cases demonstrate that parental control was not a universal practice. Some young people were making their marital choices without parental approval.

Marriage in Colonial Argentina

By custom and tradition the marriage process in colonial Argentina, as elsewhere in Spanish America, consisted of four steps. First was the betrothal (*palabra de casamiento*), the spoken words by which a young man promised to marry a young woman, thereby establishing an espousal relationship. The betrothal could be given with a promise to marry within a stipulated period or time, or it could be open-ended. The next step was a visit to the local parish office, where the required information on the civil status of the future bride and groom (the *expediente matrimonial*) would be gathered. If one's betrothed failed to move from the first to the second step within a respectable time period, the prospective bride could begin a suit for breach of promise (*esponsales*) before the ecclesiastical authorities.

Once the marriage application was completed and the parish priest was convinced that no canonical impediment prevented the couple from marrying, banns were read, usually on three successive Sundays, publicly announcing the couple's intention to marry. Any additional information relating the possible impediments was now reported to the priest. Although parental permission was theoretically needed to become engaged to marry, it was always after the couple had agreed to marry that parents, grandparents, guardians, or other close kin refused to allow the planned union. If the couple still insisted on marrying, they could petition the court of first instance, requesting that the dissenting party be forced to present a rational reason for his or her objection to the marriage. In essence the son or daughter who had been refused permission became the plaintiff suing his or her parent, the defendant.

Although jurists and scholars disagree about whether the Pragmática limited marriage or only engagement (*esponsales*), in the Río de la Plata there is no doubt that the legislation was interpreted as controlling marriage.[17] The related question of whether the church could still perform valid marriages in spite of parental opposition is also quite clear. While in theory the church could still dispense the sacrament, any priest performing a marriage ran the risk of public sanction. Indeed, only once did a priest marry a couple without prior permission, arguing that he assumed that they were in conformity with the Pragmática, as he was acting under license from the couple's parish priest.[18]

From 1776 on, cases of marital opposition were heard before the cabildo court of first instance, the *juzgado del alcalde primero,* or that of the *alcalde segundo.* Once the Audiencia of the Río de la Plata was founded and functioning in Buenos Aires (1785), all cases generated in the cabildo courts of the audiencia's jurisdiction could be appealed to the high court. The audiencia was never the court of first instance in marriage dissent proceedings but rather the court that could review and override cabildo court decisions.

In theory the new marriage legislation would reestablish social order, but what indeed was the reality? A close reading of the cases generated as a result of the Pragmática provides us with information on how frequently offspring actually challenged their parents in the marriage arena. Moreover, the legal cases concerning marriage dissent provide valuable information about which parents were more apt to oppose the choice of marriage partners of their children, the reasons usually given for their opposition, and their degree of success. While far from numerous, the marriage dissent cases give us interesting insights into late-eighteenth-century colonial society and the social perceptions of love, sex, and sexuality in the colonial world.

I reviewed cases from the court of first instance for two contrasting urban areas of colonial Argentina. In addition cases heard before the audiencia were also analyzed. The first urban area, the city of Córdoba, was a traditional city, the center of higher education in the Viceroyalty of the Río de la Plata. The city had been closely tied to the mule trade to Potosí in the seventeenth century and had undergone a period of economic and demographical stagnation during the first half of the eighteenth century.[19] Although Córdoba experienced an economic and demographic revival under the viceroyalty, the economic base of the city was always too small to support the local population; by the mideighteenth century Córdoba became a net exporter of population both to the north (Jujuy) and to the south (Buenos Aires). While all sectors of the population had grown since 1750, the nonwhite groups had grown most quickly. A city of approximately 7,800 inhabitants in 1785, its 2,500 white citizens often behaved as though they were under siege from other racial groups.

By contrast, the port city of Buenos Aires had experienced steady economic and demographic growth since the middle of the seventeenth century. Primarily a commercial city, it had been elevated to capital of the new Viceroyalty of the Río de la Plata, taking on a host of new administrative functions. The city had a sizable artisan group and a large sector tied to the processing of hides for export. While there was great inequality of wealth in Buenos Aires, the city also provided many opportunities for the daring and the lucky. According to the evidence provided by census and parish records, the city's growing mulatto population found it relatively easy to move across blurred racial lines.[20]

How frequently did parental opposition result in legal proceedings? Although we do not have data on the total number of marriages

Table 1: Disenso Cases as a Percentage of Marriages Performed, 1781–1810

	Córdoba	Buenos Aires	Total
Number of Cases	86[a]	45[b]	131
Number of Marriages	857[c]	6103[d]	6960
Marriages/Cases	10.03	.74	1.88

a. Alfredo Pueyrredón, "Aporte documental al estudio del mestizaje en el Río de la Plata," *Revista de la Universidad Nacional de Córdoba,* "Homenaje jubilar a Monseñor Doctor Pablo Carrera" (1958), part 2, pp. 241–83. This article presents a complete list of *disenso expedientes*. See also AHPC, Escribanía.
b. See note 21.
c. Aníbal Arcondo, *Demografía retrospectiva de Córdoba, 1700–1813.* (Universidad Nacional de Córdoba, Instituto de Economía y Finanzas, 1976).
d. Nicolás Besio Moreno, *Buenos Aires: Puerto del Río de la Plata, Capital de la Argentina: Estudio crítico de su población, 1536–1936* (Buenos Aires: Talleres Gráficos Tuduri, 1939), p. 65.

performed between españoles in the entire jurisdiction of Buenos Aires or Córdoba, we can use data on the total number of marriages in the capital city as an approximate surrogate. Opposition to marriage that resulted in litigation represented approximately ten percent of all marriages in the Córdoba area, while the corresponding figure for Buenos Aires was less than one percent[21] (see table 1). Clearly, in the older, more traditional society there was more conflict between parents and children over the issue of marriage.[22]

There is no way to determine the actual number of colonial parents who objected to their offspring's choice of a spouse. Legal proceedings contain no information on how many parents successfully dissuaded their children from marrying by simply refusing to grant permission. The marriage dissent cases represent only those cases where children chose to challenge their parents' decision. Given other evidence of the power of parents and their economic control over sons and daughters, these cases might only be the tip of the proverbial iceberg of intergenerational conflict. What is obvious, nonetheless, is that the majority of offspring accepted the decision their parents had made as to their marriage plans. Only a stubborn few rejected this decision, preferring to bring their parents into court to counter their authority.[23]

Suing one's parents, grandparents, or guardians was a drastic step, especially over a matter as important and far-reaching as marriage. The crown was sensitive to the delicate nature of the testimony that might be presented in these cases. It therefore enjoined all judges to "avoid defamation of individuals and families." Because of the nature of the proceedings secrecy was of the essence. Proceedings were to be "always behind closed doors."

Although witnesses swore to secrecy, their testimony sometimes makes it evident that marriage dissent cases quickly became common knowledge, fueling local gossip with juicy information about the family or families in question.[24] Because of both the type of testimony presented and the legal strategies used, these cases were social dynamite, since they could lead to an investigation of the ethnic background of a family. Few people in colonial Argentine society could be sure enough of their social origins to weather close scrutiny back three or four generations with confidence. At the very least these cases produced "hateful testimony, evidence and legal maneuvers that are the result of the inevitable persistence of the interested parties but which usually produce lasting resentment."[25] The risks were not to be undertaken by the fainthearted.

Nonetheless several litigants did not stop with the court of first instance. They insisted on appealing negative verdicts to the Audiencia, prolonging the possibility of public airing of family skeletons and dusky progenitors. Of the forty-six cases brought to appeal before the Buenos Aires Audiencia, a majority (52 percent) had originated in the Buenos Aires *cabildo*. Next in importance (20 percent) were the northeastern sectors of the viceroyalty (Asunción, Montevideo, Corrientes, and Santa Fé), followed by the northwest (Mendoza, San Juan, Catamarca), and lastly the Córdoba region.[26] The Buenos Aires region alone appealed more cases than the rest of the viceroyalty combined.

Put another way, of the forty-five cases heard first by the Buenos Aires cabildo, slightly over half (53 percent) were appealed to the higher court. This evidence of the facility with which local residents could and did appeal to the audiencia reflects the relative advantages of living in a city where a high court was seated. Indeed, before the audiencia began to function in Buenos Aires (1783), not one of the seven marriage dissent cases that came before the cabildo was appealed. Ninety-three percent of the cases tried before the alcaldes of Córdoba were never appealed, proof of the difficulty, both in terms of time and cost, for people in the cities of the interior to avail themselves fully of royal justice. In essence the cabildos of the interior cities were far more powerful legal and social arbiters than that of Buenos Aires, where quick recourse to a higher court was the general rule.

An analysis of the Buenos Aires cases appealed to the audiencia, and those that were not, yields some provocative insights into the marriage dissent process[27] (see table 2). The lower court decisions that preceded appealed cases were almost evenly divided between "*racional*" (a decision *for the parents* or tutors) and "*irracional*" (a decision *for the couple* wishing to marry). On the other hand, an analysis of those cases not appealed presents quite a different pattern. In these cases the alcalde's decision was always for the engaged couple. In other words, while parents were evenly divided among those who accepted a decision with which they disagreed and those who insisted on pushing ahead to a higher court, young people, more determined to marry the partner of their choice, appealed all unfavorable decisions to the higher court.

Table 2: Lower Court Marriage Decisions and Appeals to the High Court of Buenos Aires, 1779–1805

Decision of first court	Case appealed	Case not appealed	Total cases
Support parents	10	0	10
Support couple	12	12	24
Case dropped	—	7	7
Unknown	—	2	2
No decision	2	—	2
TOTAL	24	21	45

Source: Archivo de la Provincia de Buenos Aires; Archivo General de la Nación, Argentina, Sección Tribunales.

The costs of bringing a marriage opposition suit were relatively high although the crown, in an effort to make this legal process available to all interested parties, had specified that "in these cases, the court is not to charge fees, expenses or any emoluments. The parties [involved in litigation] are only to pay the moderate and necessary charges for paper and for the scribe's services."[28] Cases being appealed to the audiencia also incurred "registration and assignment fees." For those cases where the total costs can be determined, the expenses ranged between 57 pesos 6 reales and 283 pesos 7 reales, averaging 123 pesos 2 reales. These costs, although high, did not prevent a wide range of litigants from appearing as plaintiff or defendant in dissent cases.

Reasons for Parental Dissent

In the case of Río de la Plata, plaintiffs, defendants, and the courts interpreted the vaguely worded royal edict as referring to one of four different types of inequality: race, social background, morality, or economic position. Given the Spanish obsession about "purity of blood," race as grounds for preventing a marriage comes as no surprise. In Córdoba as in Buenos Aires, racial inequality was the major reason for parental opposition. In 1791, for example, Pablo Beruti, a Buenos Aires notary (*escribano*) attempted to stop the marriage of his son José to María Josefa Rocha, daughter of another local notary, by claiming that the bride's father was a mulatto.[29] Although the parents of both belonged to the same occupational and socioeconomic group, Beruti argued that the bride and groom were "unequal because of blood."

Only Negro—not Indian— ancestry was an acceptable grounds for a marriage opposition based on race.[30] In addition, it was not usually the prospective bride or groom who was charged with being the source of the problem. The original transgressor, the person who had introduced the "stain" in the family was usually a mulatto grandparent. These frequent references to one mulatto grandparent (or even great grandparent) testify to a significant degree of racial miscegenation, both inside and outside marriage during the early years of the eighteenth century. In most of the cases the parent of the person charged with having a "stain" had succeeded in marrying an español, thereby further whitening his line. Indeed, if we are to believe the testimony contained in the marriage opposition cases, during the generations that preceded the *Pragmática* interracial unions and even interracial marriages were common, if not quite acceptable. As a consequence, after the Pragmática young men and women, often believing themselves to be españoles, found their racial purity under attack.

Social inequality, including inequality of birth and lineage, was the second most frequent reason for marital opposition. In these cases the dissenting parent or guardian attempted to prove that one of the betrothed was either an illegitimate child or a child born of an illegitimate parent. María Antonia Martínez, impoverished widow of Alonso Garcia, *sargento de dragones,* denied permission to her son to marry Josefa Mier, daughter of a Buenos Aires retail merchant, because she argued that Josefa's mother was born out of wedlock.[31] Charges of illegitimacy in colonial Argentina were frequent, especially since consensual unions were widespread among all urban groups below the élite before 1750, and were still the norm in rural areas. The type of illegitimacy, rather than illegitimacy itself, determined the nature of one's social disability. Indeed there was a clear distinction between "natural" children, those born to an unwed mother and an unwed father who could have married had they pleased, and truly "illegitimate" children, those whose parents would not have been able to marry because of some canonical impediment.[32] In colonial society it was far less of a social burden to be a bastard of "unwed single parents" than it was to be the fruit of an adulterous union, an incestuous affair, or a clergyman.

Still another type of social inequality claimed as the basis for a marital disenso was distinction between noble and plebeian. Spanish-born fathers pointed to their distinguished birth (*hidalguía),* arguing that this set them off from others who although "pure of blood" could not make the same claim. This was the argument presented by Pedro Medrano, minister of the Royal Hacienda in Buenos Aires, to deny permission to his son Martín to marry the creole Pascuala Iraola.[33]

Personal morality was still another reason for parental dissent. Questionable sexual morals was a charge frequently brought against lower-class young women but not against men.[34] Included were claims that women had had sexual relations with several men, that they were "common prostitutes," that their lovers had contracted venereal disease from them, and that they were publicly living with their betrothed in consensual unions. Arguments used against men as a justification for a disenso involved charges such as thievery, gambling, vagrancy, and personal dishonesty.[35] In the rare case where a father used his daughter's pregnancy as a reason to prevent her marriage, the young man was charged not with questionable morality but with seduction.[36] While this charge tended to portray the woman in question as an innocent victim, it did little social damage to the man's reputation.

Another important and acceptable reason to prevent a marriage was economic inequality. This was the most frequent argument used not only by the mercantile élite of both Buenos Aires and Córdoba in refusing to allow their sons and daughters to marry, but also the defense presented by small shop owners (*almaceneros*) and artisans. Pedro Ferreira, alternately described as a shopkeeper, a bar owner (*pulpero*), and a seller of yerba mate, went as far as kidnapping his son from the Casa de Santos Ejercicios to prevent his marriage to the daughter of an hacendado from a nearly rural area. The poverty of the family of the bride-to-be was the primary reason given for the opposition.[37] The economic inequality argument always rested on proving that one of the betrothed was from a markedly inferior economic milieu. Proof that the groom-to-be was too poor to support a wife could be included in an economic inequality opposition.

Whenever possible the dissenting parent tried to present a combination of reasons for his/her marriage opposition. Economic inequality might also overlap with noble versus plebeian lineage, or with the question of legitimacy; social inequality and moral misbehavior might both be given as the grounds for a marriage opposition. Trying to prevent the marriage of his 24-year-old daughter Dominga to José Raimundo Navarro de Velazco, Francisco Gutiérrez charged that the groom-to-be was racially unequal (mulatto), a vagrant, of illegitimate birth, economically unable to support the bride-to-be and guilty, furthermore, of seducing the innocent girl.[38] In this case the loss of his daughter's virginity and honor meant less to the father than preventing her marriage to someone deemed to be socially and economically undesirable.

A few marriage dissents were also brought on technical grounds created by the Pragmática. According to the 1778 law, couples could not be betrothed without having first obtained parental permission. In at least two cases, parents claimed to be objecting to a forthcoming marriage because their offspring had failed to adhere to this regulation.[39] Here parents, lacking any other legal reason for preventing the marriage, evoked technicalities to delay the marriage, using the time to pressure their children to change their plans.

Those marriage opposition cases that originated in the Buenos Aires court of first instance differed from those found under the Córdoba jurisdiction by the relative importance of the four major justifications for attempting to prevent an offspring's marriage. Buenos Aires litigants were far more likely to base their cases on the grounds of economic inequality, with race, social background, and morality being lesser considerations. Córdoba cases, on the other hand, put greater stress on racial and social inequalities, relegating economic considerations to third place. These differing patterns suggest that *porteños,* experiencing a degree of economic prosperity, were more willing to overlook hazy racial antecedents, concentrating instead on the economic position of the prospective spouse's family. Conversely, the *cordobeses,* inhabitants of a city in economic stagnation, concentrated on race and social rank in their defense of socioeconomic position. Nonetheless, it should be remembered that both societies were concerned with race, economic standing, social position, and morality. The difference between Buenos Aires and Córdoba was one of degree not of absolute values.

Depending on the grounds for the marriage dissent, young people had a limited choice of strategies available to counter the obstacles. In cases of opposition because of race or lineage, the most direct and difficult strategy was to present convincing testimony, in the form of baptism and marriage certificates and live witnesses, to counter the charges. Often this approach was impossible because of the rather lackadaisical manner in which parish registers had been kept.[40] Witnesses, while required by law, usually solved little. For each witness who claimed that someone's grandmother was white and a gentlewoman, there seemed to be another who would testify for the plaintiff that she was a mulatto and a common servant. Indeed, unless we are willing to believe that many witnesses with no family ties to either the plaintiff or defendant were willing to perjure themselves, we are struck by the vague racial perceptions of many colonial people. That vagueness and the ability for a quadroon or octoroon to pass into Spanish society made these people dangerous in the eyes of some members of the local élite.

Because of the difficulties involved with the direct strategy, betrothed couples attempted another set of tactics. In cases involving racial inequality they often sought to argue that the African blood found in their intended's family was in truth Indian blood, and therefore because of royal legislation on the nobility of the Indians, no stigma was involved. This strategy was all the more effective if one could prove that the ancestor in question was a noble Indian instead of a common *yanacona.*[41]

Another strategy was the "us too" approach. Here the young man or woman admitted the impurity of their intended's lineage but attempted to prove they too suffered the same blood "stain." Few people in the area were able to offer sound proof of their pure ancestry going back three or four generations, for few were the children of Spanish immigrant fathers and mothers.[42] Miscegenation had occurred to some degree in the lines of many so-called white families, with race mixture more prevalent as one went down the socioeconomic scale. In cases where the father had immigrated from Spain, the mother's creole line was fully scrutinized in a search for some touch of mulatto ancestry. Lacunae in parish registers could always be used to cast doubt on one's ancestors. The net result of this strategy, and of the marriage oppositions in general, was to uncover family skeletons that had long since been buried.

Plaintiffs and Defendants

What group or groups in society were most likely to oppose the marriage of their offspring? An occupational analysis of the heads of family for cases brought before the Buenos Aires court of first instance shows that the largest group, 39 percent of the plaintiffs, were artisans, peons, and small landowners. These were the poor whites of the colony who had the most frequent social contact with people of mixed blood, but also a group that believed it had much to lose in allowing its offspring to marry into these groups of lower racial and social status. The second largest group of plaintiffs (22 percent) were members of the merchant élite, usually engaged in suits to stop their sons from making what they perceived of as disastrous (that is, noncommercial) unions. Military officers account for 17 percent of oppositions, and small shopkeepers another 13 percent. Lastly, bureaucrats were the plaintiffs in 9 percent of the cases. Grouping individuals by élite and nonélite occupations (merchants, bureaucrats, and military officers versus artisans, small landowners, and peons, we find that 44 percent of the plaintiffs could be considered members of the local élite, while 56 percent were, although españoles, definitely considered to be among the common people. Fear of social or racial contamination was present at all levels of white society, but members of the élite also fought to protect their offspring from choosing marriage partners who were grossly economically inferior.

An analysis of the relationship of the plaintiff to the defendant shows that most frequently it was the defendant's father, as head of the family, who refused to give permission to marry (40 percent). In 27 percent of the cases a male tutor or guardian opposed the marriage. This is not surprising in a patriarchal society. What is more significant is that 27 percent of marital oppositions were initiated by widowed mothers, and another 6 percent by sisters or aunts. The relatively large numbers of women involved in preventing the marriage of their children is testimony to their interest and power, as well as indirect evidence of the considerable number of relatively young widows left to provide for their families after the death of an older spouse. Their testimony usually alludes to the economic difficulties encountered in providing for their children and their determination to fight against a marriage that would bring downward social mobility to their families.[43]

According to 1778 cédula, in the absence of parents or guardians, the state itself could step forward as plaintiff in unequal marriages involving those born in Spain. The Río de la Plata material indicates that this was a rare step. Among the marriage dissent cases reviewed, only once did the state attempt to stop a marriage by initiating the opposition process, no doubt in part because of the professional ambitions of a local bureaucrat who believed he could further his own career by preventing the marriage of a Spanish-born silk weaver to a mulatto woman.[44] In only one case was the prospective bride the defendant against the prospective groom.[45] It is clear that the groom-to-be, having promised marriage and sired a child, was no longer interested in fulfilling his pledge. His defense was that he had become engaged believing his intended was an española but had since heard rumors to the contrary. Stretching the meaning of the Pragmática, he now challenged the woman in question to prove that she was not a mulatta before a marriage could take place.

Did contested choices tend to be those made by male or female offspring? An analysis of thirty cases of parental opposition shows an almost equal division between parents of the man (sixteen cases) and parents of the woman (fourteen cases) and suggests that both men and women were making independent choices of marriage partners. A review of this sample also shows some interesting variations by social group. Among the élite cases the opposition was more likely to come from the man's parents (eleven oppositions initiated by the man's parents or tutor versus seven by the woman's). That is, the objection was to the choice by the man rather than that by the woman. Although economically or racially disadvantageous marriages of either men or women endangered a family's status and reputation, families seemed to be more on guard against their sons' mistakes, possibly because their sons had more opportunity to commit them. The above-mentioned pattern also suggests that élite men had greater opportunity to meet women from other social classes than their more closely guarded sisters.

For the nonélite groups the situation is quite the opposite. Here the parental objection was made more frequently to the daughter's choice rather than the son's (four cases begun by the man's parents versus seven by the woman's). While it is somewhat hazardous to generalize from these data because of the small number of cases involved, this difference suggests that while lower-class white women enjoyed some degree of geographical mobility and social independence, they were not encouraged to use this freedom to make marriages that frustrated their family's desire to maintain some social position. At the same time, the marriage opposition case itself demonstrates the narrow limits of all women's freedom.

Couples involved in marriage dissent cases were anxious to reach a verdict as soon as possible, in the hope that their planned marriage could soon take place. But their parents or guardians often wished to slow down the legal proceedings, betting that time itself would discourage the young couple. For those eager to prevent a marriage, questions of procedure could supply welcome ammunition. Delay as a parental strategy was more common when it was the man's parent who opposed the marriage. Long delays did not endanger the reputation of a young man, but they could be most harmful to a young woman, especially in those cases where premarital pregnancy demanded speed.

In theory speed was of the essence in all cases. The crown, realizing the social danger that these cases represented, encouraged the court of first instance to complete its hearings and present a decision within seven days after beginning the case. Another seven days were granted to begin an appeal, and the audiencia was to make a final decision within two weeks from receiving the case. The total time elapsed between the beginning of the initial process and the appeal decision was therefore to be one month.[46]

In their desire to complete proceedings within the stipulated time period, the cabildo and the royal audiencia tried to set time limits: defendants were given two to three days to state the reason for their opposition to a marriage, and an additional three to four days to present witnesses who would verify their claims. Nevertheless, for a sample of nineteen cases where elapsed time can be fully documented, the court of first instance took an average of 35.75 days to adjudicate a case. Appeal added another 53.2 days to the process. Instead of one month, the average marriage dissent ran for three months from start to finish. Moreover whenever a procedural question was raised in the course of an opposition, the case would be slowed down for at least another two months. A major jurisdictional question, such as whether marriage dissent cases involving military men should be heard by the civil court, could delay the proceedings for up to four months.[47]

The concern for a woman's honor can be seen in the few cases in which a prospective bride or her parents brought a disenso case because the groom had changed his mind about the desirability of the marriage.[48] These cases and surviving breach-of-promise cases under ecclesiastical jurisdiction suggest both the need to save a woman's honor by going through with marriage once formal espousal had been declared and the importance of marriage to a woman's social standing.

Although a woman's honor was linked to her virginity, it is clear from the marriage dissent cases that a distinction was made between sexual relations once a couple had become engaged and other liaisons.[49] For the masses sexual relations after betrothal were common. Indeed at times there seems to have been a confusion in the mind of young women between engagement and marriage, for both could be public ceremonies that created lasting obligations.[50] The acceptance of sexual relations between espoused persons also explains the large number of women with children bringing breach-of-promise suits. The two cities' élites guarded their daughters more carefully than nonélite families, but the suspicion of sexual relations between all espoused couples seems to have been general.[51]

A woman did not lose her honor as much by giving her virginity to the man she was to marry as she did by failing to marry that man. For many of the women involved in these cases, losing a marriage dissent was therefore a loss of more than a legal case. It could be at same time the loss of social position because of "inferior" racial heritage and the loss of personal honor. Furthermore, because it was assumed that engaged couples had sexual relationships, the woman who failed to marry her fiancé (whether or not it was known that she had lost her virginity) was assumed to be tarnished, inferior, dishonored.[52]

Presumably, still more dishonored was the woman who had prior sexual experiences with another man without promise of marriage. Indeed there was no clear line drawn between this woman and a prostitute, for both were considered to be "worldly, corrupt and licentious."[53] Even worse was the woman who kept any of the fruits of her scandalous behavior, publicly nursing any children who might have resulted from their liaison. This behavior was especially reprehensible for it ran counter to the ideal of feminine modesty.[54] No wonder the parish registers of Córdoba and Buenos Aires are full of Spanish *niños expósitos,* illegitimate children abandoned on the doorsteps of the leading citizens of the town.[55]

Paradoxically there could be still other advantages to abandoning a child rather than baptizing him or her as an *hijo natural.* In a 1794 royal cédula, abandoned white children were granted the same civil legal status as legitimate children.[56] In Buenos Aires at least, this cédula was interpreted retroactively and covered expósitos born years earlier.[57] In addition, as long as an abandoned child appeared to be Spanish (by phenotype), he or she would be assumed to be Spanish (by genotype) and would be duly registered in the book of Spanish baptisms. In the race-conscious world of colonial Río de la Plata, it was better to be assumed to be Spanish than to be known to be mulatto.[58]

In addition to information about concepts of honor, the disensos provide a view of colonial women and their place in society as perceived by the social élite. The ideal for Spanish women was to be protected, indeed to be subjected to the men of their family.[59] An unmarried woman was never to be left alone, even within her own home, "for one never knew who could enter and what could happen."[60] To retain their honor, women should not appear in the streets of the city without at least a servant accompanying them; to be alone in the street was a sign of either extreme poverty or prostitution. Indeed, adhering to the ideal, élite women preferred not to appear before open court, requesting instead that the judges and scribes come to their homes to question them whenever possible.

The local élite came closest to mirroring faithfully this vision of the protected sheltered female, but other social groups displayed differing realities, often in stark contrast to the ideal. Economic constraints often made it impossible for women who thought of themselves as españolas to conform to the social model. White women ran *pulperías* (saloons) and sold tripe and meat, fending for themselves while their husbands traveled to the estancias of the interior to buy cattle.[61] Poor whites and mulattas (who by definition did not have to worry about their honor) could be found peddling bread, meat pies, and other food on public squares. Still others sewed, wove linen, spun, or worked as nursemaids (*amas de leche*). White women, both married and single, worked in *trabajos mugeriles*.[62]

Other women, usually orphans of the city's middle groups, were placed with respectable older women after the death of their mothers or were sent to the Colegio de Niñas Huérfanas.[63] Even those women, española, legitimate, and brought up in a protected environment, found it difficult to make good marriages if they were from poor families.[64] Society's conception of social position, while based to a large degree on the idea of ethnic purity, also included economic dimensions.

Saving a woman's honor was intimately tied to the honor of her family. Indeed the extent to which an individual was tied to his or her family, and to which one's conduct was a reflection of that family, is made dramatically clear by the marriage dissent cases. Eighteenth-century society was organized around the family, its social position, and the preservation of its honor. Because the concept of family was wide, the choice of a marriage partner was crucial not just to one's nuclear family but also to aunts, uncles, cousins, and other members of the extended kinship group. A bad marriage to someone beneath one's social or racial standing could blemish all members of one's family, casting doubt on the entire family's claim to whiteness or hidalguía, and limiting the future marriages of first and second cousins, nieces, and nephews.[65] In the words of one witness, "equality between the marriage partners is of great importance to all the family's descendants, just like nobility."[66]

To protect their family's honor, parents often tried to use force to prevent undesirable marriages. In at least four cases, sons were imprisoned, kidnapped, or sent out of the city to separate them from their intended brides.[67] This type of force was not used against daughters in the cases reviewed. Women were, by their very nature, assumed to be more docile and malleable, and could therefore be more easily contained within the confines of their household. Some young men did request that their fiancées be removed from their parents' domain and placed in *depósito* to escape being subjected to undue parental pressure, but this was rarely granted by the court because of fear of further scandal.[68] This attitude of the civil court was in dramatic contrast to the earlier willingness of ecclesiastical officials to move young women to a safe and neutral ground, a policy that safeguarded the exercise of free will concerning marriage partners.[69]

Young men also ran away from their parents' home, usually seeking refuge with the family of their betrothed.[70] While this strategy might have produced a degree of short-term independence, in the long run it usually provided ammunition for their parents in legal proceedings. Furthermore, living in the home of their intended was always interpreted as engaging in wanton sexual relations, charges that could be used against the prospective bride. In only one case did a woman run away from home, demanding that she be deposited in a safe home, but her motives were rather dramatic—to prevent being raped by her stepfather.[71]

While the tenacity with which many prospective brides and grooms fought their parents in the marriage dissent cases, as well as an occasional love letter included in the court papers, leaves little doubt as to the existence of romantic love in the late eighteenth century, in the eyes of parents and authorities romantic attachments were "dangerous." While young people experienced romantic love, the duty of those who were older was to take a hard, rational look at the social consequences of that emotion. Love, passion, and youth had to be controlled for the survival of social order.

Both the state and parents would have preferred to avoid the question of love and marriage, arranging instead suitable partners for their children. But the continued existence of cases of filial challenge to parental choices and parental dissent to children's choices reflects the desire of young people to chose their own mates. Regardless of the desirability of parental protection of their daughters, marriage dissent cases show that young women were able to meet young men, invite them into their homes, and begin relationships without the knowledge of either or both sets of parents.[72] From the point of view of certain colonial parents any freedom was dangerous. *Mestizaje* coupled with geographical mobility had produced people who were not easily identifiable socially or ethnically, and young people, prone to fall into the trap of romantic love, were unlikely to be on guard. Those with hazy antecedents were seen as an omnipresent

threat by others of the same socioeconomic group who, no matter how poor, could at least boast of being pure white.[73]

The porosity of racial categories and the fear on the part of the whites that mulattoes would be successful in passing are illustrated by the case of Juan Bruno, a Spanish-born peddler (*tratante*) who settled in Córdoba, and Eugenia Tejada, a street vendor. Although it was never clear whether Eugenia was a mulatta, a quadroon, or a mestiza, the couple was married by the church after a lengthy, rather public, and tempestuous love affair. Hearing of this marriage, the Córdoba cabildo devoted an entire session to censuring the couple and forbade Eugenia to dress like an española under the threat of fine and corporal punishment. This prohibition on dress is especially interesting, for clothing was an essential marker, a way to distinguish the whites from the mulattoes and the blacks, in a society characterized by widespread racial confusion.[74] The ferocity with which the élite of Cordoban society attacked the couple for their marriage suggests a socioracial paranoia heightened because of the bride's ability to pass for a white woman. Eugenia Tejada was not the first mixed-blood to marry a Spaniard, but this marriage represented a dangerous precedent because of the bride's phenotype; the couple, therefore, had to be punished in an exemplary fashion.[75]

Racial barriers were more difficult to overcome in traditional societies such as that of Córdoba than in more dynamic Buenos Aires. In the rural backlands of both Buenos Aires and Córdoba, poverty and military service tended to lessen racial distinctions between españoles and mulattoes or mestizos. The extent to which this melting had occurred can be seen not only in the difficulty that witnesses often had in agreeing on a person's race but also in the rather cavalier fashion in which rural parish records were kept. By 1770 priests serving rural parishes no longer attempted to enter their flock in ledgers that corresponded to race; instead all were inscribed in the baptism and marriage books reserved for españoles.[76] Much the same process seems to have gone on in the semiurban outskirts of the city.

The high level of geographical mobility through the entire Buenos Aires–Córdoba area also added to the vagueness of racial identification. By changing residence, one could often also change racial, if not social, categories.[77] It is no accident that the abovementioned interracial couple, shamed by the Córdoba cabildo, quickly left the city, seeking refuge first in the countryside near Río Segundo and then in Luján, along the Buenos Aires frontier. Juan

Bruno, like many others, realized that his wife's life would be better in Buenos Aires, "because in Córdoba, people like her are not allowed to be treated like ladies."[78] He eventually rose to the rank of *comandante del río* and *administrador principal* of the town. As the wife of a local official and a man who owned a farm (*quinta*) outside Buenos Aires, Doña Eugenia, while never accepted in the highest spheres of porteño society, was nonetheless accorded the respect due an española.

The ability to move from one socioracial group to another could be found to a lesser degree in the urban setting. Movement was not necessarily upward, and there is some indication that in the case of women, not only their social but also their racial category was determined by their husband's group. The case of Ana María Josefa Rodríguez, a poor Spanish woman who married the free mulatto, Francisco Pozo, is instructive.[79] In the eyes of the census taker, and indeed in society in general, Ana María had in effect become a mulatta herself.[80]

The Legal and Social Reality

Parents and tutors fully expected to be vindicated in a court of law. Surprisingly, the decisions reached by the lower and upper courts did not usually support parental opposition. Of eighty-three cases heard in Buenos Aires, Córdoba, or before the audiencia, the judges found parental opposition to be *racional* in twenty-six cases, while their decisions favored the marriage of the betrothed couple in thirty-seven cases.[81] Although armed with greater power than ever to decide in cases touching one of the most personal areas of people's lives, the judges in Río de la Plata tended to insist on proof of inequality (the letter of the law) in reaching their verdict. Although they reflected the biases of their class, they were not neglectful of the law.

In reaching their decision, the court of first instance of Buenos Aires tended to decide more frequently against the parent or tutor opposing the marriage than did the Córdoba court.[82] In addition, 19 percent of Córdoba's first instance cases were dropped by either the prospective bride or groom before completion of the court proceedings, while all Buenos Aires cases were seen to completion. Both trends suggest a greater degree of social and parental intransigence in the more traditional society.

In those cases that came to appeal, the audiencia proved generally supportive of lower court decisions. Only one out of five of the cases appealed to the high court was overturned, but in overturning lower court decisions the audiencia proved as likely reverse a decision favoring the young person as the other way around. The audiencia ruled in favor of the parent's opposition in less than one of every three cases which it reviewed.

In general the courts paid little attention to extenuating circumstances that in earlier times might have hastened marriage. A premarital pregnancy or the need for a "marriage of conscience that demands quick resolution" little swayed the judge.[83] Neither did a long-standing union that had already produced several children.[84] While the church had been ever eager (although not always successful) to legitimize unions, the state had other priorities. Even in those cases where it was clear that an illegitimate union would continue if permission to marry was denied, the state defended the concept of equality above all else.

Indeed the new state policy vis-a-vis marriage might have contributed, at least in part, to driving a high illegitimacy rate even higher. The percentage of "white" illegitimate births, as high as 19 percent in the years before 1778, gradually moved upward, reaching 32 percent in the 1780's.[85] Although illegitimate "white" births were never at the same level of illegitimate "black" births (the latter averaging 44 percent), the weight now given to parental opposition might have dissuaded some people living in consensual unions from even considering marriage. What is nonetheless clear is that premarital or extramarital relations continued to be fairly common.

The marriage opposition verdicts are an important source of information on élite perceptions of society. In the case of Buenos Aires, the *alcaldes de primer* or *segundo voto,* the men who made the initial determination in the cases, were without exception powerful local merchants. During the years 1785–1805, when the alcaldes tried these cases, all but one of them were also Spanish-born.[86] In essence, the way in which they applied the law reflected the world view and priorities of a commercial peninsular élite. Needless to say, application of the *Pragmática* was not uniform. The tendency of parents or tutors to refuse permission to marry on a combination of grounds (i.e., race and economic position), along with lacunae in local records and conflicting testimony, provided the judges with great latitude in reaching their decisions.

In Buenos Aires, as in Córdoba, the central concept in all marriage dissent cases was that of "equality"; parents and guardians always justified their oppositions because the betrothed were unequal. In a handful of cases the evidence as to inequality was clear and overwhelming, and the alcaldes applied the corresponding legislation. But the majority of cases were more complex, the evidence more contradictory. In these cases the alcaldes of Buenos Aires—more than those of Córdoba—always considered economic inequality as a factor, even when neither plaintiff nor defendant chose to base their case on these grounds.The merchant city fathers of Buenos Aires showed time and time again that economic position in porteño society overrode race, legitimacy, and upbringing in difficult cases.

Compare for example the case of García versus Martínez with that of Castro y Ulloa versus Rubio. In the former case the alcalde de primer voto found the parents' opposition to be groundless. Although the bride's mother was clearly an illegitimate child (sufficient reason for claiming inequality of birth), her family enjoyed a moderate economic position. In the latter case, the marriage opposition was supported by the court. The bride was española, legitimate, well brought up, but from a family "notorious for its poverty," and therefore an unacceptable wife for the son of a Cádiz merchant.[87]

Not only did the alcaldes interpret the law to fit their conception of equality, but they also quickly closed ranks when any member of the local élite was involved in marriage opposition proceedings. Important merchants or bureaucrats who objected to their child's choice of a marriage partner were assured of the support of the alcaldes even when the reason for the opposition was as vague as "the groom-to-be is from an unknown family."[88] In at least two cases the merchant alcaldes of Buenos Aires supported their peers when they prevented young Spanish clerks from making marriages that would have seriously limited their commercial futures.[89] While the alcaldes were probably acting on the advice of the Cabildo's legal counsel, this *asesor,* a lawyer by training, reflected the same social bias as the judges.

Race and social position were important variables vis-a-vis their own group, yet the merchant alcaldes were little moved by these variables in marriage opposition cases involving others. The scant interest in race can be seen in the case of Casco versus Aramburu, in which a chair maker (*silletero*) refused to give permission to his daughter to marry a journeyman silversmith (*oficial de platería*).[90]

Although the father's opposition was based in part on the race of the groom, the court did not gather testimony on the issue. This oversight did not stop the *alcalde* from declaring the marriage dissent to be without merit. The verdict reflected the social conceptions and prejudices of an élite that, while defending its own social position and racial purity, failed to support poor artisans in their attempt to do the same.

A study of court verdicts corroborates the influence of social standing and occupation on the decision of the local court. Merchants were the most successful plaintiffs, winning all opposition, while small shopkeepers and bureaucrats were successful in only 50 percent of the cases involving their children or wards. Artisans, peones and small landowners won only one-third of their marriage oppositions. Military officers fared even less well, supported by the court in only 25 percent of their actions. They were the group whose arguments were most likely to be judged "irrational" and "authoritarian."[91]

The fact that cabildo justice tended to reject their arguments based on race did not mean that white artisans calmly accepted race mixture for their children. While there seems to have been little difference between one artisan and another in the eyes of the local élite, the artisans themselves, especially those who had immigrated from Spain, fought to remain separate from the mulatto masses.[92] The strong racial prejudices of the artisans are reflected in several marriage dissent cases, as is their attention to emblems designating race and class.[93] The general racial confusion in the Río de la Plata made it all the more important that one be on guard against unequal marriages.

In both Buenos Aires and Córdoba, marriage opposition decisions not only reflect the élite's attitude toward the race; they also show their expectations of sexual behavior. For the alcaldes, poor girls, regardless of their race, were presumed to be sexually experienced past the age of puberty. Indeed in the face of evidence to the contrary, the judges could not conceive of poor girls maintaining their purity.[94] The poor were by definition licentious.

How successful was the *Pragmática* in preventing the social disorder caused by interracial marriage or marriage between social unequals? To judge from the cases considered here and from later legislation, it was less than totally effective, and eventually more draconian measures were enacted. In 1805, a royal cédula prohibited the marriage of any Spaniard regardless of his or her age to any casta without the prior authorization of the viceroy or audiencia.[95] Clearly, earlier legislation had failed to establish order, and it was now time for the state to take an even more active role in controlling social behavior.

A survey of marriages performed from 1750 to 1810 in three of the six parishes in Buenos Aires suggests that the *Pragmática* had an effect that, although not total, was nonetheless important.[96] Before 1778, the year of the enactment of the *Pragmática*, the total number of marriages between obvious social unequals (marriages between whites and other races or marriages between legitimate and illegitimate persons) averaged 23.4 per one hundred. The rate of these marriages after 1778 fell to 10.1 per hundred. Parents, tutors, and *platense* society as a whole increasingly found unequal marriages objectionable, even though the courts did not necessarily agree.

The Bourbon reforms and legislation such as the *Pragmática* served to intensify racial categorization. Earlier, both in urban and in rural areas racial labeling had been vague. In a society where many people of mixed race had been able to drift from one category to another, where country people could migrate to the city changing their occupations and perhaps forgetting certain details of their background, people were now made increasingly aware of their racial inferiority. Race had always been important, but the categories had blurred before the *Pragmática* allowed parents and the state to redraw the lines.

In the Río de la Plata, the *Pragmática* tended to encourage the tightening of social and racial mobility at the very moment when the area as a whole was experiencing economic and demographic growth. This aspiration to narrow acceptable marriage partners was not without its blatant ironies. Consider for example the case of Francisco Ramos, a brick maker who married a woman reputed to be *mulata* in the early 1770s. In 1796 the same Francisco Ramos was engaged in a marriage dissent case with his son because the latter wanted to marry a supposed mulatto.[97]

New marriage legislation did not produce a uniform reaction throughout the colony. In the case of Córdoba, the large number of marriage opposition cases in proportion to the total number of marriages performed suggests that inhabitants of urban areas that experienced little or no economic expansion were more likely to engage in this type of litigation than those living in zones undergoing economic growth. This, alternatively, suggests that in economically stagnant areas there might have been a greater tendency for people to choose prospective mates from among those who were economically or racially dissimilar and/or a greater willingness to challenge parental authority to defend that choice. Both the Buenos Aires and Córdoba cases also hint that economic cycles do not necessarily correspond neatly to changing patterns of racial and marriage control.[98]

In America, the *Pragmática* of 1776 provided legal justification to construct racial and economic barriers in the most personal domain, that of family and marriage. Moreover, because the legislation was a valid reflection of the social philosophy of the times, its effects were felt beyond the institution of marriage. Social and religious organizations such as Third Orders, which already practiced a socioracial discrimination, limiting membership to whites of certain social standing, now justified their conduct by turning to the Royal Pragmática.[99] The Pragmática did not create the attitudes that produced social and economic discrimination; rather, it legitimized already existing prejudices and biases.

Notes

1. Much work on marriage and the family has been done in French and English history. See for example the essays by Robert Wheaton and Beatrice Gottlieb in *Family and Sexuality in French History,* ed. Robert Wheaton and Tamara K. Hareven (Philadelphia: University of Pennsylvania Press, 1980); Lawrence Stone, *The Family, Sex and Marriage in England, 1500–1800* (New York: Harper and Row, 1977); Gerald L. Soliday, ed., *History of the Family and Kinship* (Millwood, N.Y.: Kraus International Publications, 1980). In Latin American history, although much recent work has concentrated on family and kinship, relatively little has been written on the social role of marriage. Exceptions to this include Robert McCaa, "Calidad, Clase, and Marriage in Colonial Mexico: The Case of Parral, 1778–90," *Hispanic American Historical Review* 64, no.3 (August 1984): 477–501; María Beatriz Nizza da Silva, *Sistema de casamento no Brasil colonial* (São Paulo: T. A. Queiroz, Editor, 1984). In addition the following studies have made use of cases of marital opposition: Verena Martínez-Alier, *Marriage, Class and Colour in Nineteenth-Century Cuba: A Study of Racial Attitudes and Sexual Values in a Slave Society* (Cambridge: Cambridge University Press, 1974); Patricia Pau-

line Seed, "Parents Versus Children: Marriage Oppositions in Colonial Mexico, 1610–1779," Ph.D. dissertation, University of Wisconsin, 1980; Patricia Seed, "The Church and the Patriarchal Family: Marriage Conflicts in Sixteenth-and Seventeenth-Century Mexico," *Journal of Family History* 10 (1985), 284–93.

2. Justo Donoso, *Instituciones de derecho canónico americano,* 2 vols. (Valparaiso, Chile: Imprenta y Librería del Mercurio, 1849), 2:155.

3. Seed, "Parents vs Children," pp. 31–32.

4. Domingo Cavalario, *Instituciones del derecho canónico,* 3 vols. (Paris: Librería de Don Vicente Salva, 1846), 2:168; Donoso, *Instituciones,* 2:152–53.

5. Canon law impediments fell into two categories. The first group, unsurmountable obstacles (*impedimentos dirimentes),* were by far the more serious, being just cause to annul any marriage. These impediments included age (younger than 12 for the bride and 14 for the groom), existing prior marriage (bigamy), and kinship (both affinal and spiritual). The second group of impediments, called constraining obstacles (*impedimentos impedientes*), prohibited marriage during certain days in the religious calendar, or marriages performed in the absence of banns. These obstacles were of a lesser order of importance, and marriages incurring these impediments, while illegal, were not automatically annulled. These canon laws governed marriages in Spain and her (ex)-colonies until the middle of the nineteenth century. Opposition to marriage had to be made on one of two principles: (1) either lack of free will of one or both of the parties in contracting the marriage or (2) the existence of an impediment that would render the marriage invalid should it take place. For more information on canon law see Jaime Mans, *Legislación, jurisprudencia y formularios sobre el matrimonio canónico* (Barcelona: Casa Editorial Bosch, 1951). The Latin and Spanish texts of the Council of Trent are found in Ignacio López de Ayala, *El sacrosanto y ecumenico concilio de Trento* (Madrid: Imprenta de Repulles, 1817). For the English text see, H. J. Schroeder, trans., *Canons and Decrees of the Council of Trent,* (St. Louis, Mo.: B. Herder, 1941). See also Daisy Rípodas Ardanaz, *El matrimonio en Indias: Realidad social y regulación jurídica* (Buenos Aires: Conicet, 1977), pp. 85 ff. At least one historian has suggested that the decisions of ecclesiastical courts contributed to the rate of interracial marriage and miscegenation (Eduardo R. Saguier, "Church and State in Buenos Aires in the Seventeenth Century," *Journal of Church and State* 26, no.3 [Autumn 1984], 508–13).

6. The "Pragmática sanción para evitar el abuso de contraer matrimonios desiguales," issued on 23 March, has been published in Richard Konetzke, *Colección de documentos para la historia de la formación social de hispa-*

noamérica (Madrid: Consejo Superior de Investigaciones Científicas, 1962), 3:406–13. Konetzke also reproduces the Junta de Ministros royal cédula that led to this pragmática in *Colección de documentos,* 3:401–5, as well as the 1778 royal cédula extending the Pragmática to America (*Colección de documentos,* 3:438–42).

7. The *Pragmática* would be clarified and reiterated several times in the next twenty years. See royal cédulas of 26 May 1783; 19 April 1788; 8 February 1790; 27 February 1793; 17 February 1798 in Konetzke, *Colección de documentos,* 3:527–29; 625–26, 670–71; 711–14; 759–66. In 1792 still another cédula would require a royal license for all students studying in institutions of higher education under royal patronage. Included under this rubric were female institutions (Konetzke, *Colección de documentos,* 3:706–7, royal cédula of 11 June 1792).

8. Rípodas Ardanaz, *El matrimonio,* pp. 317–60.

9. The royal order of 8 March 1787 forbade any church court from trying a case of broken engagement if that engagement had been made without prior parental permission (Konetzke, *Colección de documentos,* 3:623–25). The royal cédula of 22 March 1787 limited the jurisdiction of the church court in matters concerning "alimentos y tenencia de hijos" to divorce cases only. The next year bigamy was placed under civil rather than ecclesiastical jurisdiction.

10. Rípodas, *El matrimonio,* pp. 270–72.

11. Konetzke, *Colección de documentos,* 3:527–29.

12. *Cedulario de la Real Audiencia de Buenos Aires* (La Plata: Archivo Histórico de la Provincia de Buenos Aires, 1929–38), 1:6–8.

13. Royal cédula of 8 March 1787, in *Cedulario de la Real Audiencia de Buenos Aires,* 1:158–60.

14. Konetzke, *Colección de documentos,* 3:794–96, royal cédula of 1 June 1803. The crown stopped short of making disinheritance mandatory when children married without parental permission, or of forbidding these offspring to hold public office. However, this more draconian stance had been included in the draft of the Nuevo Código presented to Charles IV in 1790. See Rípodas, *El matrimonio,* p. 272.

15. Susan Migden Socolow, *The Merchants of Buenos Aires, 1778–1810: Family and Commerce* (New York: Cambridge University Press, 1978), pp. 39–40. Comparable data for a small commercial town in eighteenth-century Chile (San Felipe) suggest a median marriage age for women of 22.1 years and 26.1 years for men. See Eduardo Cavieres, "Formas de vida y estructuras demográficas de una sociedad colonial: San Felipe en la segunda mitad del siglo XVIII," *Cuadernos de Historia* (Santiago de Chile) 3 (July 1983): 90. Nine-

teenth-century data, again for Chile, present much the same pattern. According to Sergio Vergara Quiroz, "for women the modal age of marriage was 17. Forty percent of all brides were married between 15 and 18 years of age and, furthermore, sixty-five percent were married by age 22." See his "Noviazgo y matrimonio en Chile durante el siglo XIX; Mujer y sociedad en los años 1819–1831," *Cuadernos de Historia* 2 (July 1982): 138. I thank Asunción Lavrin for calling my attention to these sources.

16. Konetzke, *Colección de documentos,* 3:794–96, royal cédula for 1 June 1803.

17. For a discussion of the juridical arguments see Rípodas, *El matrimonio,* pp. 292–307.

18. Archivo de la Provincia de Buenos Aires (hereafter cited as APBA), Martínez vs. Guerrero, 7-5-14-101.

19. Aníbal Arcondo, *Demografía retrospectiva de Córdoba, 1700–1813,* Serie Material de Trabajo No. 16, Universidad Nacional de Córdoba, Instituto de Economía y Finanzas, 1976.

20. For additional information on the racial composition of Buenos Aires see Susan M. Socolow, "Buenos Aires at the Time of Independence," in *Buenos Aires: 400 Years,* ed. Stanley R. Ross and Thomas F. McGann (Austin: University of Texas Press, 1982), pp. 18–39; Susan M. Socolow and Lyman L. Johnson, "Population and Space in Eighteenth-Century Buenos Aires," in *Social Fabric and Spatial Structure in Colonial Latin America,* ed. David J. Robinson (Syracuse and Ann Arbor: Syracuse University Press and University Microfilms, 1979), pp. 339–68.

21. Dissent cases for Córdoba are found in the Escribanía section of the Archivo Histórico de la Provincia de Córdoba (hereafter called AHPC). The Buenos Aires *disenso* cases of first instance are scattered through *legajos* found in the Tribunales section of the Archivo de la Nación Argentina (hereafter referred to as AGNA). These cases have also been studied by Nelly R. Porro in the following articles: "Conflictos sociales y tensiones familiares en la sociedad virreinal rioplatense a través de los juicios de disenso en el Río de la Plata: Nuevos aportes sobre la aplicación de la pragmática de hijos de familia," *Anuario Histórico Jurídico Ecuatoriano* 5 (1980): 193–229; "Estrañamientos y depósitos en los juicios de disensos, " *Revista de Historia de Derecho* 7 (1980): 123–50. The total white population of the two intendancies during the decade 1785–95 was approximately 18,000 for Córdoba and 25,000 for Buenos Aires. Approximately 2,500 whites were found in the city of Córdoba while the city of Buenos Aires boasted approximately 16,000 españoles. These numbers are based on data reported by Jorge Comandrán Ruiz, *Evolución demográfica argentina durante el período hispano (1535–1810)* (Buenos Aires:

Eudeba, 1969), pp. 80–81. For further discussion of the population of the city of Buenos Aires see Lyman Johnson, "Estimaciones de la población de Buenos Aires en 1744, 1778 y 1810," *Desarrollo Económico* 19–23 (April–June 1979): 107–19; Johnson and Socolow, "Population and Space," pp. 341–53.

22. Both the cases from Córdoba and those from Buenos Aires demonstrate the same general periodicity although the specifics differ somewhat. In Córdoba the first disenso case was presented in 1781; the decade of the 1790s was by far the most litigious with two years, with 1794 and 1795 presenting dramatic ratios of disensos per total number of marriages performed (.32 and .42 respectively). In addition the highest annual number of cases (ten) came before the Córdoba alcaldes in 1797. The Buenos Aires cases occurred over a period from 1779 to 1807. These disensos peaked in the first half of the decade of 1790.

23. According to a royal cédula issued on 18 September 1788, only a son or daughter could be party to a disenso against his or her parents. In effect this meant that a dissent was raised by the son or daughter prevented from entering into marriage by his or her own parents. The prospective spouse had no right to join the suit if his or her parents did not disapprove. See APBA, Espinosa vs. Ferreira, 7-5-16-35.

24. In almost very disenso case studied, several witnesses stated, "I know the parties engaged in this litigation and I have heard about the matter under consideration." In addition several cases contain evidence that even the most confidential details of the proceedings were often well known to the general public (AGNA, Galeano versus Berza, Tribunales, Legajo M-17, Expediente 7, IX-41-8-1; Lasaga versus Lasaga, Tribunales, Legajo 208, Expediente 12, IX-38-6-3; Porro, "Los juicios de disenso," pp. 211–12).

25. APBA, Quesada versus Quesada, 7-5-15-71.

26. Origin of Cases Brought on Appeal to Audiencia Court

Region	Number of Cases	Percent
Buenos Aires	24	52
Córdoba	6	13
Northwest	7	15
Northeast	9	20
Total	46	100

A list of cases can be found in Zulema López et al., "Aplicación de la legislación sobre matrimonios en hijos de familia en el Río de la Plata," *Tercer Congreso del Instituto Internacional de Historia del Derecho Indiano* (Madrid, 1973), pp. 779–99. These cases are found in the Archivo de la Provincia de Buenos Aires.

27. Twenty-two of the twenty-four cases that were appealed were done so at the bequest of the litigants; in the two other cases the cabildo failed to reach a decision and voluntarily turned the case over to the Audiencia. Of the twenty-

one cases not appealed, two must be excluded because it is impossible to determine the cabildo's court of first instance decision. Seven more cases were never appealed because the parties to the case, usually the dissenting parent, experienced a change of heart and dropped the case before it came before the magistrates. Of the remaining twelve cases that were not appealed, the alcalde's decision was for the couple.

28. Konetzke, *Colección de documentos,* 3:441, royal cédula of 7 April 1778, article 7. The most costly case found was APBA, Balcarce contra Martínez, 7-5-17-4. The least expensive was APBA, Luque contra Luque, 7-5-14-103.

29. APBA, Beruti versus Beruti, 7-5-16-23. Other cases in which race is the major grounds for disenso included AGNA, Aizpurúa versus Aizpurúa, Tribunales, Legajo A-17, Expediente 4, IX-40–33; Troncoso versus Carvajal, Tribunales, Legajo C-14, Expediente 9, IX-40-7-1; APBA, Santucho versus Ríos, 7-5-14-100; Baylón Pineda versus Belgrano Pérez, 7-5-16-20; Martínez versus Guerrero, 7-5-14-101; AHPC, Icea versus Rosas, Escribanía 2, 75, 24; López versus Romero, Escribanía 2, 98, 22.

30. María Rosa Quintana, Indian, and widow of Miguel Salazar, *español,* successfully prevented her son from marrying a mulatto woman by arguing that this marriage would prejudice her descendants (APBA, Salazar versus Quintana, 7-5-16-24). For cases where Indian blood was ruled insufficient grounds for opposition to a marriage, see AHPC, Peralta versus Bernal, Escribanía 2, 84, 18; Cabrera versus Peralta, Escribanía 2, 84, 1; Baigorrí versus Baigorrí, Escribanía 4, 46 (11), 10; AGNA, Arias versus Flores, Tribunales, Legajo 141, Expediente 24, IX-37-5-5.

31. APBA, García versus Martínez, 7-5-14-37 and 7-5-16-21. Cases based on illegitimacy also include AGNA, Cañete versus Yegros, Tribunales, Legajo 208, Expediente 7, IX-38-6-3; Arroyo versus Arroyo, Tribunales, Legajo 120, Expediente 15, IX-37–2-4; APBA, Gardel versus Gardel, 7-5-15-38; Navarro versus Gutiérrez, 7-5-16-27.

32. For a more detailed description of the various types of illegitimacy in Hispanic society see Woodrow W. Borah, "Marriage and Legitimacy in Mexican Culture: Mexico and California," *California Law Review* 54 (May 1966): 946–1008. See also Ann Twinam's essay in this volume.

33. APBA, Medrano versus Medrano, 7-5-17-3. For additional examples of cases that used a noble versus plebeian argument, see APBA, Quesada versus Quesada, 7-5-15-71; Azcuenaga versus Azcuenaga, 7-5-16-38; AHPC, Días versus Alday, Escribanía 1, 410, 6.

34. The sexual morality of the bride-to-be was attacked in AGNA, Ochagavia versus Ochagavia, Tribunales, Legajo E-6, Expediente 12, IX-40-9-2; Ocampos versus Pérez, Tribunales, Legajo 0-4, Expediente 17, IX-41-9-3; Alvarez versus

Camargo, Tribunales, Legajo 208, Expediente 11, IX-38-6-3; APBA, Espinosa versus Ferreira, 7-5-16-35; Galain versus Sosa, 7-5-16-25; Quesada versus Quesada, 7-5-15-71; Merlo versus González Movellán, 7-5-15-41 and 7-5-15-64; Paulet versus Ortuña, 7-5-16-26; Ramos versus Ramos, 7-5-14-38.

35. Among these cases are APBA, Quesada versus Quesada, 7-5-15-71; Luque versus Luque, 7-5-14-103; and Azcuenaga versus Azcuenaga, 7-5-6-38.

36. See APBA, Navarro versus Gutiérrez, 7-5-16-27; Casco versus Aramburu, 7-5-16-22.

37. APBA, Espinosa versus Ferreira, 7-5-16-35. Cases where economic inequality was the prime justification for the marriage opposition also include AGNA, Candelaria versus Candelaria, Tribunales, Legajo T-6, Expediente 6, IX-42-7-6; APBA, Castro y Ulloa versus Rubio, 7-5-15-68; Casco versus Aramburu, 7-5-16-22.

38. APBA, Navarro versus Gutiérrez, 7-5-16-27. Approximately 40 percent of all marriage dissent cases contained overlapping charges.

39. APBA, Salazar, 7-5-16-24; Paulet versus Ortuña, 7-5-16-26.

40. See APBA, Merlo versus González Movellán, 7-5-15-41 and 7-5-15-64 for reference to vague way in which the church inscribed people in baptism and marriage books of Spaniards.

41. In APBA, Balcarce versus Martínez de Bustamante, 7-5-17-4, the bride-to-be claimed to be a descendant of a cacique.

42. APBA, Cuello versus Gauto, 7-5-14-107.

43. APBA, Galain versus Sosa, 7-5-16-25.

44. APBA, Guerrero versus Martínez, 7-5-14-101. The bureaucrat, don Rafael Guerrero, treasurer of the Royal Exchequer office in Santa Fé, acting as self-appointed "*padre de forasteros,*" quickly become embroiled with a local parish priest who performed the marriage because both parties were adults with no canonical impediment preventing their union and because no parent protest had been voiced.

45. APBA, Merlo versus González Movellán, 7-5-15-41 and 7-5-15-64.

46. See the royal Pragmática of 23 March 1776, article 9 in Konetzke, *Colección de documentos,* 3:409–10.

47. See, for example, APBA, Quesada versus Quesada, 7-5-15-71.

48. Ibid.; Merlo versus González Movellán, 7-5-15-41 and 7-5-15-64. On the importance of virginity see Asunción Lavrin, "Aproximación histórica al tema de la sexualidad en el México colonial," *Encuentro* 2, no.1 (October–December): 29.

49. APBA, Espinosa versus Ferreira, 7-5-16-35. According to Lavrin, in Mexico "the practice of giving a promise to marry was used frequently . . . to

initiate physical relations" (Lavrin, "Aproximación histórica," p. 30). See also Lavrin's and Twinam's essays in this volume.

50. APBA, Merlo versus González Movellán, 7-5-15-41 and 7-5-15-64.

51. See the testimony in APBA, Cuello versus Gauto, 7-5-14-107.

52. APBA, Cuello versus Gauto, 7-5-14-107.

53. APBA, Ramos versus Ramos, 7-5-14-38.

54. APBA, Espinosa versus Ferreira, 7-5-14-38: "She has not even shown the modesty that is natural to her sex and has publicly raised a child that she had by another man."

55. A review of the baptism records of the *porteño* parish of San Nicolás de Bari for the years 1750–53 shows that approximately 28 percent of all births were illegitimate. In addition, one out of every eight legitimate children was abandoned. In an attempt to cope with this problem, a *casa cuna,* later called a *casa de niños expósitos,* was set up in Buenos Aires in 1765 (Socolow, *The Merchants of Buenos Aires,* p. 222). For further information on illegitimacy elsewhere in the Spanish empire, see Calvo's essay in this volume.

56. Royal cédula of 19 February 1794, in Konetzke, *Colección de documentos,* 3:723–25.

57. APBA, Gardel versus Gardel, 7-5-15-38.

58. APBA, Ramos versus Ramos, 7-5-14-38.

59. APBA, Castro y Ulloa versus Rubio, 7-5-15-68, describes a virtuous woman as one who is "sheltered, chaste, and obedient."

60. APBA, Espinosa versus Ferreira, 7-5-14-38; Ramos versus Ramos, 7-5-14-38.

61. APBA, Baylón Pineda versus Belgrano Pérez, 7-5-16-20; AGNA, Lasaga versus Lasaga, Tribunales, Legajo 182, Expediente 2, IX-38-2-4; Fonseca versus Fonseca, Tribunales, Legajo 208, Expediente 6, IX-38-6-3.

62. APBA, Casco versus Aramburu, 7-5-16-22.

63. APBA, Castro y Ulloa versus Rubio, 7-5-15-68; Baylón Pineda versus Belgrano Pérez, 7-5-16-20. For the orphans' school, see also Pedro Cabrera, *Cultura y beneficiencia durante la colonia,* 2 vols. (Córdoba: Talleres Gráficos de la Penitenciaría, 1928), 1:59–65. Information supplied by Asunción Lavrin.

64. APBA, Castro y Ulloa versus Rubio, 7-5-15-68.

65. APBA, Galain versus Sosa, 7-5-16-25.

66. APBA, Quesada versus Quesada, 7-5-15-71.

67. APBA, Castro y Ulloa versus Rubio, 7-5-15-68; Quesada versus Quesada, 7-5-15-71; Espinosa versus Ferreira, 7-5-16-35.

68. APBA, Calancha versus Delgado, 7-5-16-34; Casco versus Aramburu, 7-5-16-22.

69. Saguier, "Church and State in Buenos Aires," p. 510.

70. APBA, Paulet versus Ortuña, 7-5-16-26; Ramos versus Ramos, 7-5-14-38.

71. APBA, Cuello versus Gauto, 7-5-14-107.

72. In at least one case the woman and her family were totally unknown to the man's tutor (APBA, Paulet versus Ortuña, 7-5-16-26).

73. APBA, Baylón Pineda versus Belgrano Pérez, 7-5-16-20.

74. Clothing in and of itself was a crucial symbol to colonial society. One's dress reflected one's racial status. Only white women could dress in silk garments or use silk shawls (*mantas*) and aproned skirts (*delantales*). Mulattas, on the other hand, wore clothing made of *picote*, a coarse, glossy fabric. Just as dress was an emblem used to separate races, the use of prescribed forms of social behavior filled the same function. Because mulattos were enjoined from eating at the same table with whites, any person who consistently refused an invitation to sit and dine was suspected of being mulatto. The same assumption was made if one was publicly addressed as "aunt" or "uncle." See APBA, Ramos versus Ramos, 7-5-14-38. Only white women could appear in church accompanied by a slave carrying their church rug. See APBA, Balcarce versus Martínez de Bustamante, 7-5-17-4. Furthermore, all españolas, regardless of social origin or economic situation, insisted they be called *doña* to underline their superior status. For information on dress and other social conventions, see AHPC, Acuerdos Municipales, Libro 28, folio 162, *acuerdo* of 2 April 1746; and APBA, Balcarce versus Martínez de Bustamante, 7-5-17-4; Baylón Pineda versus Belgrano Pérez, 7-5-16-20.

75. APBA, Balcarce versus Martínez de Bustamante, 7-5-17-4. The alcaldes of Córdoba would again order a woman of doubtful racial origin not to wear silk in 1785. See AHPC, Escribanía 2, 64, 6.

76. APBA, Merlo versus González Movellán, 7-5-15-41 and 7-5-15-64.

77. APBA, Merlo versus González Movellán, 7-5-15-41 and 7-5-15-64; Balcarce versus Martínez de Bustamante, 7-5-17-4.

78. APBA, Merlo versus González Movellán, 7-5-15-41.

79. APBA, Galain versus Sosa, 7-5-16-25.

80. Facultad de Filosofía y Letras, Universidad de Buenos Aires, *Documentos para la historia argentina*, vol. 11: *Territorio y población, Padrón de la ciudad de Buenos Aires, 1778* (Buenos Aires: Compañía Sud-Americana de Billetes de Banco, 1919), p. 601.

81. In the remaining twenty cases the verdict is unknown in seven; the case was dropped before a verdict was reached in eight; and the couple managed to marry before a verdict was delivered in three. Two cases were judged to be within the church's domain and were transferred to an ecclesiastical court.

82. Buenos Aires decisions were in favor of the couple in 55 percent of the cases, and against them in 36 percent. Córdoba decisions were against them in 34 percent of the decisions.

83. APBA, Galain versus Sosa, 7-5-16-25.

84. APBA, Martínez versus Martínez, 7-5-17-1.

85. These rates have been calculated from the Buenos Aires cathedral baptismal books (*libros de bautismo*), currently found in the archives of La Merced church.

86. Before 1785 Buenos Aires marriage dissent cases were routinely heard by the viceroy; cases outside the city's jurisdiction were heard by the local intendant. After 1805 the viceroy again served as court of first instance for marriage oppositions. For Buenos Aires only eight cases fall into either of these time periods (Porro, "Los juicios de disenso," 203–4).

87. APBA, García versus Martínez, 7-5-14-37 and 7-5-16-27; Castro y Ulloa versus Rubio, 7-5-15-68.

88. This was the reason for refusing Magdalena Somalo permission to marry Santiago Costa (APBA, Somalo versus Somalo, 7-5-17-25, 7-5-17-26 and 7-5-17-60). See also Azcuenaga versus Azcuenaga, 7-5-16-38; Balcarce versus Martínez de Bustamante, 7-5-17-4; Medrano versus Medrano, 7-5-17-3; AGNA, Gregorio de Espinosa versus Belgrano Pérez, Tribunales, Legajo E6, Expediente 11, IX-40-9-2.

89. APBA, Castro y Ulloa versus Rubio, 7-5-15-68; Merlo versus González Movellán, 7-5-15-41 and 7-5-15-64. In the second case don Manuel Ribas, a merchant who employed González Movellán as an agent-clerk in Los Arroyos, used economic pressure in the form of money that González Movellán owed him for goods received (*cuentas pendientes*) to prevent the young man from going through with the marriage.

90. APBA, Casco versus Aramburu, 7-5-16-22.

91. APBA, de la Valle versus González, 7-5-18-115 and 7-5-14-53. Juan González, an army captain, was declared to have no basis to oppose the marriage of his daughter María Mercedes to Manuel de la Valle, accountant (*contador*) in the Royal Tobacco Monopoly.

92. Lyman L. Johnson, "The Impact of Racial Discrimination on Black Artisans in Colonial Buenos Aires," *Social History* 6, no.3 (October 1981): 301–16.

93. APBA, Ramos versus Ramos, 7-5-14-38; Baylón Pineda versus Belgrano Pérez, 7-5-16-20; AHPC, Basualdo versus Gómez, Escribanía 2, 94, 12.

94. APBA, Castro y Ulloa versus Rubio, 7-5-15-68.

95. Royal cédula of 27 May 1805, *Cedulario de la Real Audiencia,* 3:293–95.

96. The three parishes reviewed are Cathedral North (La Merced), San Nicolás de Bari, and Nuestra Señora de la Concepción.

97. APBA, Ramos versus Ramos, 7-5-14-38.

98. This hypothesis about the effect of economic decline on demographic patterns is different from that presented by Marcelo Carmagnani, "Demografía y sociedad: La estructura social de los centros mineros del norte de Mexico, 1600–1720," *Historia Mexicana* 21, no.3 (January–March 1972): 441. Carmagnani finds that "when the period of decline in mineral production begins . . . the Spanish group tends to close in upon itself more and more."

99. APBA, Balcarce versus Martínez de Bustamante, 7-5-17-4.

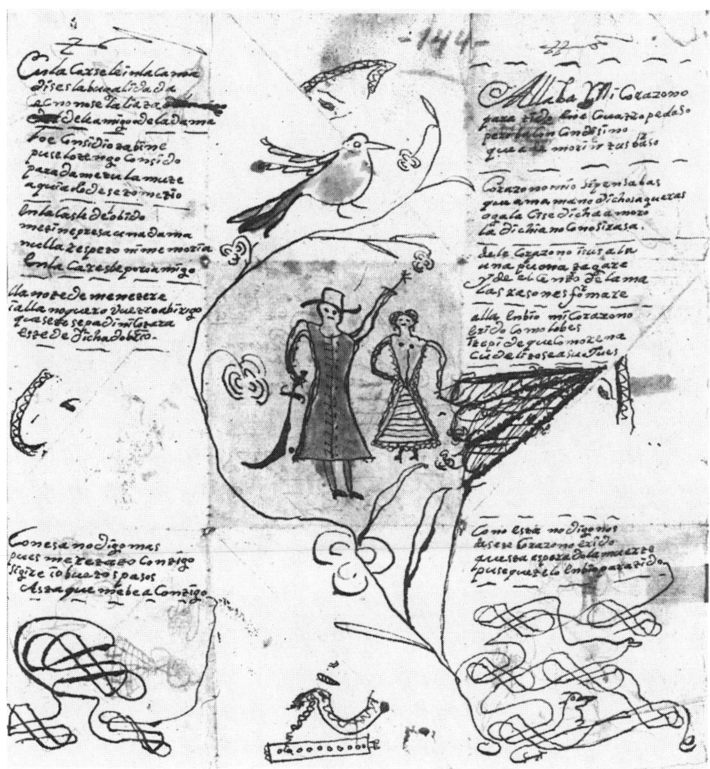

15. Love letter found in a criminal process. Poem describes a wounded heart that a man sends to his lover. Source: Archivo General de la Nación, Mexico City, Criminales, vol. 8, fol. 144 (1743).

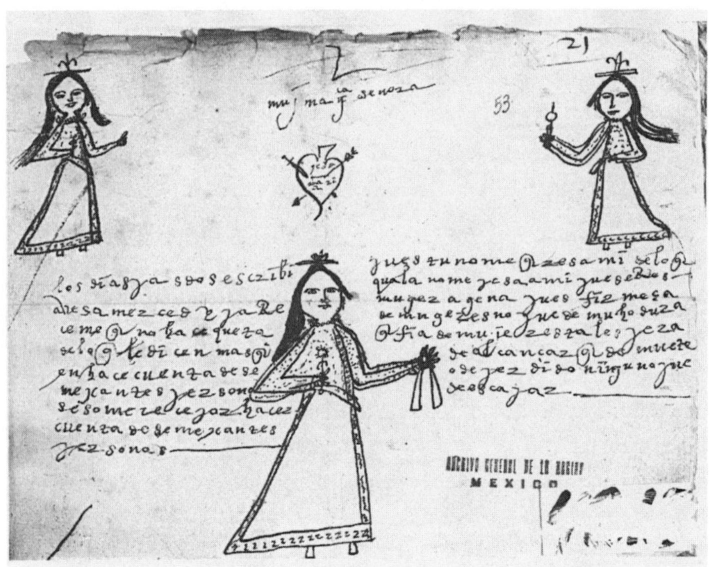

16. Love letter addressed to "Most magnificent lady." Source: Archivo General de la Nación, Mexico City, Inquisición, vol. 100, exp. 2 (1571).

17. Northern Peruvian Indian couple exchanging gifts before their wedding. Source: Bishop D. Baltasar Jaime Martínez Compañón, Trujillo del Perú a fines del siglo XVIII, ed. Jesús Domínguez Bordona (Madrid, n.p., 1936).

18. Spanish *corregidor* and his wife in bed. The representation of couples sleeping together was extremely unusual during the colonial period. Source: Felipe Guamán Poma de Ayala, *Nueva corónica y buen gobierno* (Paris: Musée d'Ethnologie, 1936), p. 496.

Caussa Matrimonial del Año de 1679

Doña Catalina de Caseres Sotomayor

Contra

Don Josef Vasquez de Guzman

Juez el S.r Provisor Notario el secretario Pedro
Carrillo de Guzman

19. Cover of the annulment of marriage suit of doña Catalina de Caseres Sotomayor *vs.* don José Vásquez de Guzmán, Cuzco, 1679. Note symbol of either love or woman restrained in captivity. (Courtesy of Professor Bernard Lavellé.)

Richard Boyer

Women, *La Mala Vida*, and the Politics of Marriage

The politics of marriage in early modern times was played out against the backdrop of patriarchalism. I begin this essay, therefore, with a brief sketch of patriarchalism as a cultural assumption and as an ordering principle in western Christendom and the Spanish peninsula. This section is based on theoretical and normative materials; a second section, based on Inquisition files, approaches domestic politics more immediately by looking at couples in conflict.

Patriarchalism: A Cultural Assumption

From the days of the primitive church to early modern times, patriarchalism was the underlying principle of all social relationships.[1] Its fundamental expression was the family, with husband dominant over wife, children, and any others in the household; they, in turn, freely subordinated themselves to his authority. Because it was "the original social institution," the family was the primary manifestation of "the pattern of the Divine Plan for the whole formation of society from the smallest beginnings to the formation of a nation."[2] This is not to imply that patriarchalism did not predate Christianity. Obviously it did. Indeed it could hardly have been imbedded more deeply and passed on more directly, given the patriarchal character of Judaism. The important point here, however, is that Christianity modified it. Focused on the family, "the original form of, and preparation for, all social relationships," the church called for an infusion of "the Christian virtues of love."[3] If this implied a softening of patriarchal authority, the new emphasis did not affect the "fundamental law" [of] organic inequality."[4] Women and children were always minors under the tutelage of the senior male, who in Spanish law, for example, retained administrative control over his wife's property and the right to discipline.[5]

Under the influence of Christianity, the patriarchal principle evolved from an absolute "natural authority" to "the duty of looking after the welfare of others."[6] For Saint Augustine this duty was a solemn charge: "the masters are to endure more labor in their government than the servants in their service."[7] By the time of the Carolingian kings, the duty of just government was firmly attached to the institution of Kingship, and the power to rule was conferred not by the ruled but by the "grace of God." With such theocratic underpinnings, kings were to act as "tutors" and guardians of a people who were perpetual minors. In effect, the relationship was of the order of parent to child or husband to wife.[8] By about A.D. 800, churchmen were applying the vocabulary of Christian patriarchalism to Charlemagne as the embodiment of the kingly ideal: "involved in a fatherly way in the lives of all his subjects—*subjecti* though they be," the warrior, judge, father, prince, who brought peace and harmony to the kingdom.[9] But however benevolent such authority, its direction was always from the top down. "The people," said Charlemagne's adviser, "are not to be followed but are to be taught."[10]

The paradox, however, is that kings, whose legitimacy rested on theocratic principles, enjoyed unfettered authority over their subjects but submitted to "religious norms and laws . . . manipulated by ecclesiastics [which] were not only prior to . . . but entirely independent of" the monarch.[11] "You have not created me archbishop of Rheims," the prelate reminded his king in 860, "but I, together with my colleagues, have elected you to the government of the kingdom, on condition that you observe the laws."[12] The benevolent patriarchy of Christianity was an ideal and an expectation. Churchmen could define and manipulate it but, more importantly for our purposes, the ruled might also seize it as a "critical principle of Christian sociology" by which to judge the performance of their ruler.[13] Eventually resistance and rebellion could be a right, and sometimes a duty, if monarchs tyrannized rather than looked after their subjects.[14]

Christian patriarchalism informed equally the notion of authority and rulership at the scale of both family and state. What matters most is that Christianity was a total system that transcended categories such as "state" and "politics" until they entered European discourse in the thirteenth century with the rediscovery of Aristotle.[15]

In strictly chronological terms, kingship was a secondary application on a larger scale of the antecedent family patriarchalism. But once political structures were in place, once the succession of kings was institutionalized, the original priority of the family as model for the state was reversed. "The head of the household ought to take his principles from the law of the city," Augustine wrote, "in order that . . . he may so rule his own household as to bring it into harmony with the peace of the city."[16] Even so, kings did not cease to be examples in their domestic sphere.[17] "A king who honors, loves, and watches over his wife," intones Spain's thirteenth-century code of laws, "will offer a good example to the people of all his country."[18] In the Spanish case, perhaps more than "an example," for the quality of the king's family relations tested his legitimacy to be patriarch of all of society. This moral test had been in place from the ninth century: "A pious and wise king performs the office of ruling in three ways," wrote Sedulius Scottus: "He should first rule himself with reasonable and meritorious discipline; second, his wife, his children, and his own household; and third, the people entrusted to him."[19] The very notion of kingship as rooted in the patriarchal ideal never ceased to be rooted in its original source, the family. Much later, in New Spain, church ideology made the same connection in the iconography of altar pieces and in the pastoral letters of bishops.[20]

Its origins notwithstanding, the kingship stood for all subordinate patriarchal authorities; it defined, qualified, limited, and sometimes revoked lesser *patria potestas* (paternal powers).[21] As is often noted, vassalage, the organizing principle of early kingship, is little more than a pyramid of familylike patriarchies differing from one another only in scale, not in kind. The *Siete partidas* cites five levels of authority: 1) the king, in possession of "the clear and absolute right to judge and command the people of his country"; 2) lords of regions; 3) lords of estates; 4) the "authority that fathers have over their children" and wives; 5) the "powers" of masters over slaves.[22] But surely such a legal formulation was more refined than actual practice. Apart from Catalonia and Aragon, the Christian societies of the Iberian peninsula in early modern times evolved a more informal and more fluid pattern of patriarchal relations, shaped, above all, by the Reconquest and the reoccupation of Moorish territory.[23]

As the patriarchal authority of the family became dependent on that of the state, so too it came to model its politics *qua* politics on the state. The ideal of an organic unity between rulers and ruled, between greater and lesser, could be seen to be more than ever a process, rather than a given. The reason, at least in part, is that organicism was above all a union of the unequal. But the behavior of kings, governors, judges, and bishops demonstrated that, far from being a static and uncontested ordering, Christian organicism involved protest, struggle, and alliances. Bishops or governors, on occasion, even resorted to the dangerous tactic of using the common people to gain advantage over one another.[24] For ruled as well as for rulers, the ideal of reciprocity, expressed in mystical and metaphorical images, did not, of course, question patriarchal authority as a norm; it did, however, provide a vantage point for judging how a patriarch exercised his power and a logic for resisting an autocrat when he lost sight of peace and justice.

The politics of the family, then, are informed by two sources: one theoretical, the other practical. The latter shaped experience more directly, for, however persuasive ideas refined by intellectuals, practice and example transmit directly to daily life. Then as now, people learn the process of politics by discovering that power is contested—however cynically—over ideals; politics takes on meaning in the interaction between the people and institutions that actually impinge on their lives.

The arena where this took place was the family. It is appropriate, therefore, to examine material so focused in the form of guides written to instruct parish clergy in hearing confession and administering the sacrament of penance. A drawback of these manuals is that they were normative, at least once removed from actual experience. Nevertheless, they had to approximate real life in order to accomplish their purpose: to prepare priests for situations that they would actually encounter. True, norms are stressed, but not in isolation; instead, one sees them interacting with a whole range of circumstances and variations of sins. The manuals that I have seen proceed by a simulated conversation between priest and penitent and are followed by didactic asides addressed to the priest. Such a format was in fact "political," if you will. If the interactions were hypothetical, they nonetheless represent the author's experience and knowledge of how penitents engaged religious norms. With caution, therefore, one can infer some patterns of actual behavior. Equally important, assuming that these books guided pastoral practice, priestly behavior may also be inferred from them. In the confessional the priest had a delicate task. He had to probe behavior sufficiently to bring sin fully into the open, but not to the degree that details and embellishments, actual or imagined, became a lascivious meditation, tantamount to instruction in new ways to sin.[25]

Confessional manuals, then, come at least a step closer to that elusive "actual behavior" of parishioners by dramatizing plausible interactions between behavior and norms. As for the latter, it can come as no surprise that, in a manual published in 1689, Fr. Jayme de Corella made patriarchal authority the basis for the family structure. "The father," he said, "is the true head of his family."[26] But because authority always carries responsibility, an obligation that applies to "any person in a superior station," that person "must be an example of good to his subjects," for otherwise he sins against justice.[27] Patriarchal authority, therefore, had limits. But how, given its discretionary nature, were they to be effected? The problem comes up in a dialogue between penitent and confessor:

> P: Father, sometimes I lose control when I punish her [his wife]; otherwise I cannot control her and she doesn't carry out her domestic duties. Other times I just treat her badly for no particular reason.
> C: When there is a legitimate reason it is lawful for the husband to punish and even to strike his wife, but with moderation and to the end that she mend her ways.

Nevertheless, Corella warns, all authorities agree that a husband may not punish his wife without reasonable (*razonable*) cause, for arbitrary punishments severely administered are a mortal sin.[28] Needless to say, Corella allows the husband a great deal of room to maneuver in disciplining his wife. Whatever the personal qualities of the family patriarch, he in effect acted as his own judge of what "moderate" and efficacious punishments consisted of. In practice arbitrary treatment was checked only by the stipulation that it not be too severe. There is little leverage here to control the frequency and extent of beatings of wives by husbands.

What recourse did a woman have with such an arrangement? Her best strategy, perhaps, was to seize on the ethical basis of the patriarchal "contract"—however negligent its enforcement—and affirm that "punishment" had been immoderate or arbitrary, that therefore she had been treated unjustly. Such a judgment by a woman was the basis for further steps, as we shall see below, that ranged from seeking outside help to running away. For Corella, then, the husband's authority is the keystone of family structure, and the duty of the wife is to obey him, "her true superior." But just as the authority of the husband is not without conditions, neither is the obedience of the wife. Corella goes so far as to call the marriage relationship a "virtual contract . . . in which the husband is obliged to maintain (*sustentar*) her, and she, to obey him in what is rational and just."[29] In marriage, as in the state, order must not compromise justice; exercising tyranny is no less a sin than yielding to anarchy.

The contractual nature of marriage can also be seen in Fray Alonso de Herrera's celebrated and widely circulated *Espejo de la perfecta casada,* a work addressed to women.[30] In setting forth "the conditions necessary for good marriages, for domestic peace, and for the proper bringing up of children and the governance of her family in love and the fear of God," Fray Alonso stresses that man and wife are equal, that their love and loyalty must be mutual.[31] In an exegesis of the Biblical account of creation, he notes that God *might* have created man and woman of different materials, or woman of a part of man other than his rib. That woman was shaped from a part of man close to his heart is proof for Fray Alonso of a natural "affinity and bond leading . . . to greater intimacy and a more intense love whereby man looks at woman not as something apart but as a piece (*pedazo*) of his very person."[32]

Fray Jayme de Corella argued that marriage was a contract, Fray Alonso that it was a mystical union. Nevertheless, each stressed a reciprocal dynamic, based on justice and reason in one case, on the bonds of love in the other. Love is "perfect," according to Fray Alonso, when it is "reciprocal and mutual." The mystery that man and wife become "one flesh," separable only by death, becomes a metaphor for the union of individuals in the "mystical body of the church," with Christ the head.[33] Fray Alonso considers reciprocal demands so central to marriage that patriarchal authority is drastically transformed. "A married man," he writes, is at once "lord and slave of his wife: lord in that he orders and governs her; slave in that he serves and esteems her and would sacrifice himself for her."[34]

The moral economy of marriages, then, is based on an ideal of reciprocity, transmitted to families through secular and cultic means. The ideal must be stressed, for—however theoretical, however imperfectly understood—it is the basis for the exercise of power. If the practice of politics concerns above all the interplay of greater and lesser forces, the agent that dominates must do so with legitimacy, on grounds other than naked power.[35] And even when ideals are used cynically merely to cloak raw force, that they *are* used gives an opening for the dominated to criticize, to resist, to oppose, or to modify the behavior of a tyrant. In this way the oppressed engage in a political process, comparing the conditions of their lives with the supposed terms of reference of those in authority over them.

The normative literature recognized that domestic life involved a give-and-take in which discord had to be resolved by means other than force. Yet Fray Vicente Ferrer, in a work published in Mexico late in the eighteenth century, urged that "the conjugal act," so often used as a means "to dissolve quarrels and disagreements," not be so used; "other means," he said, are more appropriate.[36] The context for his advice is a discussion of when sexual intercourse is more, and when less, licit. His passing reference to the ordinariness of domestic quarrels and of sex as a solution to them suggests that the church was still embattled in the campaign to control the sexual practices of parishioners. Taking a more general tone, Fray Jayme de Corella also pointed to the banality of "domestic differences that occur frequently between husbands and wives." Such matters are "ordinarily only venial sins," he says, even though occasions for angry words.[37]

Thus priests concerned with pastoral theology accepted that domestic skirmishes were a normal part of married life. But divisions within marriages could also be more serious, to the point that they overshadowed the spirit of reciprocity. Fray Alonso refers to married partners in such a predicament as delivered over to *la mala vida,* or bad life, and suffering great torment.[38] He proposed that couples be encouraged to discover in practice the mystical union that was the ideal of marriage.

La Mala Vida and Domestic Politics

In real life, couples fought and struggled, engaged in a politics of marriage in which power and resentment, alliances and isolation, practicality and idealism were jumbled up. It is to this politics, practiced in the rough and tumble of day-to-day living, that we now turn by examining bigamy records of the Holy Office of the Inquisition from New Spain.[39] These records are anecdotal and circumstantial as well as a continuous series running for some 250 years. By definition, judges trying an alleged bigamist sought to determine whether he or she had contracted a second marriage illicitly while the original and legitimate spouse was alive. To admit or dismiss such a charge, they, at the very least, had to compile material establishing when, where, and with whom the accused had contracted two or more marriages and what precisely were the present circumstances of the alleged spouses, especially the legitimate one. Clerks compiled files relative to these matters, consisting mainly of affidavits taken from the accused and his network: spouses, godparents, family, friends, neighbors, and work acquaintances. This material, therefore, systematically focuses on domestic life—its genesis, evolution, and disruptions; it also points to some extra-domestic intrusions affecting marriages, such as debt, crime, or work.

From the study of this source I am convinced that the politics of marriage can best be understood from the standpoint of women. The reason is obvious: women had less power and little claim to outside intervention when husbands abused patriarchal authority. They did have, however, as we have seen, strong moral grounds to claim just and loving treatment. When the reality of married life diverged too far from their ideal of it, they acted. The alternative was to acquiesce in a husband's tyranny and settle for skirmishes that preserved some dignity, perhaps, but did not question that the larger compact of marriage had been violated. The two are not mutually exclusive, as will become clear, but marriages that manifested only a politics of skirmishing with no formal complaints lodged were not looked into by the Holy Office and are therefore beyond our purview here.[40]

María de Itá, like so many other women of Spain, saw her husband embark for the New World with the expectation that he would return shortly or send for her. But Agustín, like so many men who went to the New World alone, dropped from her view. As the years passed, María concluded that Agustín had abandoned her and thereby had violated their marriage contract. For her view it is best to turn to her own words, recovered from a letter she wrote to Agustín in 1746 from Cádiz:

> Husband and dearly beloved of my heart, it will be a great joy to me if this arrives in your hands and finds you enjoying the health that my good wishes would want. I urge you, as is my duty, to benefit from it, for I am trying to make you aware of your bad will. I would like to know, Agustín, why you have not remembered a daughter and a wife whom God has given to you; I would like to know if ill health turned you away from taking the slightest bother. It falls to me to make you aware that you have gone astray. Do not forget that you have only one soul, that you are about to lose it by ignoring your

obligations. If that is not your wish, send word to say why you have not troubled yourself. I pray to God that you are not living as I am, going from door to door asking for alms; the days pass and your daughter and I go without breakfast (*sin desayunarme*). And yet I rest everything with God, confident that the remedy is in his hands. However bad things are, however delayed the remedy, I do not believe that you are dead. I have no friends but I realize that God will hold you accountable, for there are no excuses. But for so much to do, I would go myself and look for you. I ask you, for God's sake, to return; every day I do novenas asking him to bring you back. I have shed so many tears that I think I shall become blind. With this I stop, begging God to keep you many years.[41]

In María's artless jumble of greeting, scolding, and news, there is, above all, a wife communicating with her husband. The tone is familiar, the setting and circumstance presumed rather than elaborated. Her basic message, "come home," is assumed to solve all the problems: María's poverty, isolation, personal anguish, and anxieties about her daughter's future. Yet, these factors are not central to *la política* of her reproaches. However pitiable her own distress, María's more powerful point was that Agustín must now consider that his soul was in danger. And if evading his duties as a husband and father violated his commitment to God, it followed that God, not Agustín, was her hope.

Is this merely a tactic, or has María displaced the immediacy of her personal distress with religious discourse? The former construction is too cynical. Yet, in these circumstances her attempt to awaken Agustin's conscience was not disinterested. It was a means not an end. Whether she consciously saw it this way or not, she attacked more powerfully with the threat of eternal damnation than with the appeal to pity and humanity. The return to a state of grace depended on his returning to her.

Yet, I consider this tactical advantage somewhat accidental. María's fixation on the sacramental and contractual character of matrimony shows how deeply she had internalized church teachings. Possibly they were a consolation, but one with a dear price: alienation from direct contact with, and immediate solutions for, her own distress. In exchange, the church gave her a religious language for explaining suffering and assessing responsibility. Agustín's reaction to all this has been lost, but time, distance, a new life in the

Indies, and possibly a more imperfect religious imprinting must have blunted its effect. One may say that, rhetorically, María got the better of Agustín, but to no advantage, for he frustrated her by refusing to come home and end her mala vida. As the years passed, perhaps she felt consoled that he would ultimately answer for his neglect.

María's letter introduces the notion of marital politics by linking her mala vida to theology. The mala vida occasioned a political response in other cases. Take Francisca de Torres, for example, who had the misfortune to marry Gómez de León (b. ca. 1545 in Seville).[42] Gómez was abusive, unfaithful, profligate, and selfish, qualities neither his wife nor his mother could moderate. Witness, for example, his callousness in selling his mother's house slave to obtain gambling money. She was closely attached to the young black girl, but that was of no concern to Gómez. At best, he may have intended to buy the girl back with his expected winnings. In any case, the girl was gone and Gómez's mother, shattered by her loss, committed suicide by hanging herself.

Francisca's parents, shopkeepers of Portuguese origin, did their best to find mediators who would intercede with Gómez on their daughter's behalf. They complained that Francisca suffered the mala vida with this man. He failed to support her and had even gambled away her dowry of seven hundred ducats, property that under Spanish law was supposed to remain inviolably the woman's. In spite of everything, Francisca did her best to be a wife to Gómez. She tolerated him for twelve years and bore two children. Unhappily for her parents, however, Francisca and the children depended on them for ordinary maintenance. They, in turn, called this burden a continual tax (*siempre eran pecheros*) and complained about their son-in-law to whoever would listen. This was about all they could do, for they were afraid to reproach Gómez directly because, "calling them scoundrels, Jews, shopkeepers, and other insulting words," he silenced and intimidated them (*llamándolos de vellacos, judíos, especieros, y otras palabras afrentosas*).

Gómez can be viewed as a particularly hardened type who in word and deed showed no regard for family sensibilities, for customary behavior, or for legal restrictions. A major component of the mala vida in this case was the failure of Gómez to support Francisca and the children. Although not indicated in the documents, Francisca surely would have felt that some of the money Gómez spent on his mistress, what there was after gambling expenses, should have gone to her.

Violante Pizarro, at least, thought so.[43] After some years of married life, her husband Francisco (b. ca. 1523) left her in their home village of Campomayor (near Badajoz) and went to Seville. Francisco was looking for jobs hauling freight with his four mules and, presumably, was supposed to return after a time or, if he resettled, to send for Violante. She was never sure where he was because he went wherever his jobs took him. Later she disparaged his lack of a settled existence as "gypsy-like." Eventually she tracked him down in Seville, where he was living with a mulatta. She moved in too. Perhaps she thought that she could claim priority as Francisco's legitimate wife, but after three months she realized that she could not. She left saying that she could no longer "endure the mala vida with him caused by his love for the mulatta "(*que no lo podía sufrir por la mala vida que con el tenía por amor de la dicha mulata*). She returned alone and pregnant to Campomayor. She broke off her attempt to resume married life at the moment when her life as an abandoned wife was about to become more difficult with another child to raise.

Both Violante and Francisca came to a point where they could expect no further support from their husbands; both saw their marriages break up as the husband attached himself to another woman; both had seen their husbands pulled from a provincial town to the metropolis of Seville, whence both men eventually went to the Indies; both considered their errant husbands responsible for their malas vidas. It would be impossible to order various factors into a causative chain to know, for example, whether the intrusion of a second woman was cause or result of the husband's abandonment of the marriage. Nevertheless, remembering that politics is at bottom a matter of power, both women did what they could to win their husbands back. Francisca and Violante each had a strong moral case, but neither could turn this to enough political leverage to reestablish married life. Gómez was simply oblivious, not in the least affected by his wife or anyone else; Francisco physically removed himself from the place where Violante's natural allies—family, relatives, godparents, parish priest, municipal officials—could influence him.

In rejoining Francisco, Violante assumed, perhaps, that she could hold him to his responsibilities as a husband. But the political process was more complex, for it included another woman. Moreover her status as legitimate wife had no affect whatsoever on his attachment to his mistress. From the vantage of their common living quarters, she had daily evidence of his affection for the other woman in spite of, or perhaps because of, the fact that she and Francisco also reestablished a sexual relationship of some sort (to judge by her pregnancy).[44]

Finally, both women were contending with the larger realities of economic and demographic shifts that saw large numbers of people moving to Seville and its region and, from there, sometimes to the Indies. These trends are often noted in, but seldom illuminated by, the stories of individuals caught up in that flow. Francisco clearly was so caught, and, to some degree, everything else followed from his apparently innocuous decision to head with his mules south, where the economy was booming. Without pretending to disentangle the infinite, mostly secret, and unrecorded possibilities, let us note simply that these women could trace the mala vida to the presence of another woman and that they defined it mainly as the cessation of support from their husbands. In a sense, the political process ended when each man removed himself from reach of his wife by embarking for the Indies.

The mala vida took other forms. In New Spain, María Guadalupe Delgadillo (b. ca. 1760), an orphan of European descent (*española*), married José Antonio Santos, a mestizo.[45] María remained with José for ten months but then ran away to Mexico City to escape the harsh treatment meted out by José and his mother. In Mexico City, she obtained shelter at the convent of San Lorenzo, where, for six months or so, she earned her keep by working as a servant. Then, relatives of her husband spotted her on the street, took her into custody, and "advised" her to return to him. She did, but nothing had changed. As before, José and his mother accorded "punishments and bad treatment," and María ran off again to Mexico City.

During this second bout of married life María was far from passive. As the pattern of mistreatment was renewed, she protested by threatening to leave again. But her militancy had no effect. In fact, husband and mother-in-law hounded her out of the house when she stood up to them. María blamed her mala vida mostly on her mother-in-law, who insisted on complete subordination. María was to be servant more than family. José seemed to have no independent views but simply echoed the attitudes of his mother. She ordered

José around too, María charged, forbidding him to give her money, at times not even permitting him to sleep with her.

When María ran away from this treatment she was not abandoning the marriage but engaging in a *política* to correct it. In a letter from Mexico City, she exhorted José in "remonstrance of the obligations of matrimony . . . that he would be *responsible before God* for *this* abandonment [emphasis added]." She had run away but he had abandoned her. How could this be? The answer lies in María's view of marriage. The mala vida was in effect an abandonment and a desecration of marriage. It fully justified withdrawing and taking refuge in Mexico City.

María's message was not a taunt but an invitation to reestablish the marriage. But correctly. The mala vida of her servantlike condition within marriage had to change. As we have seen, even before running away she had tried to effect such a change with whatever arguments and resources she had. At least once, she asked the parish priest to help. But this only made matters worse. Angered and embarrassed, José and his mother "doubled her tribulations," he becoming more authoritarian, she more like a jailor as she restricted María to the house (*la colgaba su marido y encerraba su suegra*).

With María and José one can follow the breakdown of a marriage. It was troubled from the first because they disagreed as to what marriage was. Mutuality, the view of María, conflicted with authoritarianism, the pattern of José. Her view was more correct, his more prevalent. Moreover, to judge by the way his mother reinforced and even outdid José, women participated fully in oppressing other women, especially "aliens" brought in as the wives of sons or brothers. María's attempt to alter the conditions of her life led her to mount a political campaign, now focused on José, now on his mother. Increasingly she saw that the mother-in-law was the main problem, but she could neither change the older woman nor undermine her control over her son. José's behavior might have been open to challenge and modification had the politics of this marriage involved only husband and wife. But here a third party subverted flexibility, closing ranks with José before the appeals of an outsider. In the end María was isolated and had to choose between the mala vida or flight. She decided to leave José a second time only after she had confirmed and reconfirmed that he and his mother would not budge. She failed to change the role they assigned to her; but they also failed to break her insistence that she, as wife, should be treated as a partner and companion.

Mariana Monroy (white, b. ca. 1649 in New Spain) also married a man who treated her as a servant.[46] Manuel Figueroa, her peninsular husband, forced Mariana to begin household work at one o'clock in the morning. When she did not execute tasks to his satisfaction, she said, he abused and beat her—treatment that she suffered at his hands many times (*sino acía las cosas a su gusto como él quería la maltratava y aporreaba muchas vezes*). One day, after three years of this, Mariana fled. The occasion was another beating; Mariana had failed to carry out Manuel's orders quickly enough. The episode was only another in a series, but this time something had snapped. So much servility, Mariana decided, was not appropriate for a wife, perhaps not even for a servant.

That Mariana tolerated such conditions for three years must not be construed as docility or the inability to conceptualize the injustices of the mala vida. When the time came she had a plan that showed her to be confident and prepared. She went directly to the house of Manuel de Escalante, a prosecuting attorney of the high court of Mexico City, and asked for an audience. She intended to sue for damages for the beatings, it seems, but he was out and she changed her plan after waiting all day for him. For some reason he failed to appear and, at least for the moment, Mariana gave up the idea of a legal suit. She withdrew to the convent of Santa Catalina, where she remained from Shrovetide until Holy Week, a period of about six weeks. Only then, because she believed—wrongly as it turned out—that the viceroy himself had interested himself in her case, did she reappear in public.

The story that brought Mariana from refuge was passed on, probably at the behest of Manuel, by Francisca de Garibay, a friend who visited her at the convent. However improbable it seems in the retelling, what matters is that Mariana believed it and acted on it. Why? Because it rang true and was consonant with what she thought possible and probable. It can serve, therefore, as an indicator of Mariana's mentality. Francisca told Mariana that she had "complained to the viceroy that Manuel Figueroa had inflicted the mala vida on Mariana [and that he claimed] that he was going to send Manuel to China [i.e. the Philippines]." Since the abuse was true and so much on Mariana's mind, the punishment seemed welcome and appropriate. It was what she wanted to hear. More striking is the fact that Mariana showed no surprise that the highest official of the kingdom, proxy of the king himself, would personally see to the exile of her husband and would do so solely on the basis of her friend's interview. At this remove one is struck by Mariana's trust in governmental paternalism. But however naive her assumption that the viceroy would intervene, that she looked to him to end her mala vida assumes the political nature of marriage. By her linking of the viceroy with her domestic problems, demonstrates the importance she attached to marriage in a general way. Unlike María, who appealed to a priest for help, Mariana appealed to secular authorities.

Additional information can be gleaned from Mariana's statements to the inquisitors. In the first place, the marriage had been her mother's idea, she said, and against her own inclination. She had been fourteen at the time, not excessively young, but too inexperienced to veto the match against her mother's wishes. Her mother, a widow, worked as a seamstress to support the two of them; she assumed, perhaps, that marrying Mariana to a recently arrived peninsular Spaniard would be a social and economic advantage. But the genesis of the marriage does not explain why Mariana found it intolerable. For that one must examine the character of Manuel, whose brutishness became unbearable as soon as Mariana consummated her marriage to him. He beat her and worked her to exhaustion, and she detested him (*le aborrecía*). Her loathing proved her lack of subservience and fueled their discord. The relationship, Mariana said, was one of "continuous war, disagreement, and disunion" (*una continua guerra, discordia, y disunión*).

Yet Mariana's view of Manuel went beyond feelings. The bad opinion (*mal concepto*) she had of him, she said, stemmed from his twisted and defective character. His "perverted nature [was] so bad and so disturbed" that she decided that her marriage to him was "null, invalid, and no longer binding." Mariana, in effect, placed Manuel in a category with heretics (*en su concepto como si fuese un hereje*), grounds for declaring a marriage invalid. However "true" this analysis in some objective sense, it is most remarkable because it was a legal argument for obtaining a divorce, given, of course, that she could convince the authorities that her report was accurate and its implications correct. Whether by legal or extralegal means, she meant to escape and remained single-minded in her efforts to do so. We have already seen her trying to get her case into the courts. She paid for legal counsel by selling her possessions. Although Mariana does not specify the nature of this counsel, she indicates that her efforts were frustrated because complications and impediments of one sort or another—not described, unfortunately—frustrated the suit (*siempre se ofrecían embaraços y se allava con imposibilidad de fuerzas para ello . . .*).

Mariana provides us with a vivid picture of the mala vida but, more importantly, her statements document her intolerance of it. Other cases touch on similar situations but in less detail. María de Villagrán (b. ca. 1552 in Mexico), a mestiza daughter of a Spanish father and Indian mother, married Domingo, a mulatto, when she was fourteen or fifteen.[47] It all began when he simply took her from the home of the storekeeper (*tendero*) in Mexico City who had raised her (probably as an orphan) and began to live with her. But that was not acceptable. Officials placed Domingo in jail until a priest came to witness and bless the marriage properly. Domingo and María then went to Cuernavaca, where they lived as man and wife, somewhat stormily it seems. Over fifteen years they had two children and María ran away three times, almost surely on occasions when Domingo had beaten her. On the third occasion, she said, he had lashed and wounded her so severely that he left her for dead. At this point he ran away, probably to avoid being charged with homicide. But María recovered and, now abandoned, returned to Mexico City. To what extent did Domingo's violent outbursts poison this marriage? The answer can only be inferred from María's running away, surely only a hint of the scores of lesser beatings that she endured during this long marriage.

If some women tolerated considerable violence, then, what were the limits and when were they reached? We will never know from the fragmentary materials left in archives. Nevertheless, another example can be offered, that of María Jesús de Encarnación (b. ca. 1750 in Lagos, Mexico), daughter of a mulatto father and an Indian mother, married at nineteen to José Vicente, a mulatto.[48] María and José had one child and lived as man and wife for seven or eight years. Then, because José "punished her," María ran away, leaving her son with his grandfather (her father-in-law). María's terse account omits any circumstantial details leading to her departure. Note, however, that a beating occasioned her flight and that she left only after a considerable time. From the two Marías one infers that relations between men and women could smoulder for years until habitual abuses, normally tolerated from time to time, flared into excesses that could be borne no longer. Such occasions might involve alcohol and a fiesta, and be precipitated by unfaithfulness—real or imagined—insubordination, an alleged neglect of household duties, or no particular reason at all.

María Jesús's use of the word *castigar* or "punish" is a clue to at least part of the mentality of husbands beating wives. As we have already observed in confessional manuals, the convention existed in pastoral theology that beatings were punishments administered by men and tolerated by women because they were corrective and therefore edifying. The context for such acts is, of course, the ideal of male patriarchy; the arena for them, the politics of marriage. The strategy of the wife was to appeal to the moral restraint inherent in the marital convention to counter "irrational" and arbitrary violence. But the problem always remained that in this politics men had most of the power. They controlled the occasion and the administration of the blows; if anger, jealousy, alcohol, or sadism clouded judgment and led to excesses, no machinery was in place to intervene decisively.

Our cases so far have indicated that women monitored, analyzed, complained, and resisted the mala vida, as received in a variety of forms. The politics of the resistance was this: if beatings were supposed to be edifying, they had to seem to be corrective and not merely arbitrary abuse. A victim of simple abuse had grounds to say that "correction" was mistreatment and unjust. And women did make such judgments. Witness Mariana Monroy, who, as we have seen, said that her husband had a perverted nature.

Neighbors and other members of a common household formed similar opinions, as in the case of Rosa Maldonada (b. ca. 1742 in Sierra de Pinos, Mexico).[49] When Rosa was a young widow, Juan Nicolás took her away (*hurtada*), began to live with her, and eventually married her. Afterward they moved to a rancho owned by Juan's mother near Guadalcázar. Juan's brother and his wife María also lived there and therefore had a close view of Juan's relationship with Rosa. María noticed that Rosa developed reddish bruises "especially when she fought with Juan." Francisco Xavier Albiro, a hired hand, described Rosa's face as free of any markings whatsoever—unusual given the ubiquity of scarring from smallpox—except that periodically she appeared in a bruised and battered condition. The reason, invariably, was that she had fought with Juan and been beaten brutally to the point where she was "wrecked completely, speechless, and unconscious" (*principalmente quando se peleaba con su marido, que se torcía toda, se le quitaba el habla, y privaba los sentidos*). Francisco linked the beatings to Juan's "excitable and choleric temperament" (*genio inquieto y colérico*), without judging whether it seemed excessive or not. Local officials, however, seemed to consider Juan dangerous and a serious enough threat to Rosa that, for a short time at least, they "deposited" her in the household of a third party to protect her.

But there could be no effective way to protect women with "excitable and choleric" husbands. Except in the most extreme cases, wives were always delivered back to their husbands. So was Rosa. For her, however, two factors may have made things worse. First, she was a very attractive woman and Juan, at times, might have perceived her as behaving flirtatiously. Francisco, the hired hand, mentioned Rosa's beautiful olive-skinned complexion, curly hair, full figure, small nose, and nicely proportioned eyes. She was also known, he added, for her lively singing and dancing at parties (*muy cantadora y bailadora en los fandangos*). One can surmise that Rosa's behavior at the fandangos spurred Juan's outbreaks of violence, for jealousy and homicide were closely linked in colonial Mexico.[50] Certainly they were in this instance as well, for later, when Rosa ran away with another man, Juan gave chase intending to kill them.

A second factor that caused additional grief was Rosa's tendency to fight back. Because men expected submission from women, Rosa's resistance fueled Juan's violence. Partly, she must have been just trying to defend herself, but doing so denied Juan the degree of control over her that he presumed. That the cost of such resistance was inevitably a brutal beating underscores how strongly she must have felt. In her politics with Juan, Rosa tolerated his brutality, somehow expecting that the influence of family, friends, and local officials might moderate it. But only up to a point, for some times she hit back. And when the chance came, she sublimated her unhappiness by joyously coming to life at dances. But in the end she was reduced to just one tactic: running away.

María Ygnacia Cervantes (b. ca. 1753 in Guanajuato, Mexico), although born of parents of mixed Spanish and Indian stock, was called mulatta by the notary of the Inquisition.[51] She herself specified that she was "of the same quality" (*su igual en calidad*) as her mestizo husband, Ramón, a tanner. By this she may have meant similar social or racial status, or both. María married Ramón when she was fourteen and "within two weeks," she said, "began to suffer the mala vida." For María this meant "bad treatment from a husband, a mother-in-law, and from two sisters-in-law." It also consisted in Ramón's "great cruelty, " proof of which she carried on her body in the scars of eight wounds. The beatings and bad treatment caused María to abort six of seven children. After five years of this, and left on her own for a time in Marfil, María decided that she had had enough of the mala vida with Ramón (*aburrida de la mala vida que le daba su marido*). She took up with a young, unmarried soldier, Raymundo, whom she described as a *pardo* (light-skinned mulatto). María lived with Raymundo for five months until Ramón returned and took her to Guanajuato with him. Six years later María took up with Raymundo once again—in the meantime he had married—this time for nine months. All of this remains hazy and ill-defined because file references to this period of María's life are brief and not mentioned in context. What is clear, however, is that María was brutally treated by her husband and on at least two occasions lived apart from him with another man.

A political process as such is not evident in María's dealings with Ramón. Yet, we can infer it. She, like Rosa and other women with particularly violent husbands, engaged in a politics to relieve the mala vida. Note, for example, the pattern of long endurance. Note, too, María's initiative in attaching herself to Raymundo, in part, surely, to escape Ramón. But nothing worked, and at age thirty María left Ramón—this time permanently and without a companion. Her first destination was the town of Silao, where she hoped "to change her luck," for in Guanajuato, she said in an understatement, "she found herself held back (*atrazada*)." Although María's departure must be seen against the backdrop of her mala vida, it is remarkable that her intent was not merely to escape what she could no longer tolerate, but also to discover and experience a more satisfactory life. This spirit is evident in María's first job in Silao, where she contracted to be a servant in the house of a señora Françās. María quit after one week "because she did not like the arrangements" (*porque no le agradó la conveniencia*). One could follow María's steps further as she moved from place to place and found another man to live with. However, this much of her life has shown something of the content of her mala vida with her first husband and how she broke away after sixteen years.

The women we have seen so far resisted what they considered excessive abuse and control with few resources but their wits and, perhaps, a reluctant neighbor or priest. The case of Pedro Matheo (b. ca. 1642 in Xalostotitlan, bishopric of Guadalajara) shows that the authority of a husband over his wife could be severely checked if a couple remained in residence with the woman's family.[52] Pedro was a young mestizo of Indian mother and unknown father who was approached by his future father-in-law, an Indian, to marry his daughter, Francisca. Because Pedro had no money, Francisca's father took care of all arrangements and settled the couple in his household. After a year Pedro decided to look for a new employer. Not surprisingly, he presumed that Francisca would go with him. But she did not want to leave her family and home village, and her father refused to let her go. The two men came to blows but in the end Francisca's father had his way. He ordered Pedro to leave, saying that "he would support his daughter as he had in the past when he raised her."

Humiliated by his loss of control over Francisca, Pedro departed silently, without even a word of goodbye. Later he viewed defeat as a "weakness," caused by his youth, since he had only been a "*muchacho.*" It was a bitter memory, for he must have become increasingly aware that law and custom made a husband's claim to a wife prior to a father's over a daughter. Underlying the question of dominance, the issue between the two men was also partly economic. Pedro's father-in-law stood to lose two subsistence workers from his household. The younger man's stamina and strong physique were valuable qualities for a household economy as long as he remained docile. Because Francisca and her family were Indians and therefore, perhaps, more likely than Pedro to be rooted in their community, they may have imposed an uncomfortable immobility on Pedro, who, as a mestizo, was less likely than they to be so strongly attached to one place.

Similarly, Joseph Antonio Galbes (b. ca. 1733 in Tepetlapa), a mestizo, had a problem with his wife Martina, also an Indian, as to whether they would live in his territory or hers.[53] A carter and mule driver, Joseph was constantly on the move but always in the employ of others, for he owed no mules. When he had occasion to pass through his home area of Huexosingo, his uncle, owner or renter of a rancho, took Joseph in, outfited him with four mules, and put him to work hauling freight. But before the arrangement could be permanent, Joseph had to convince Martina to relocate. He knew that this would be a delicate matter, for, as he recalled later, "I had to rekindle her love anew and win her over in order to take her back to my district" (*ube de enamorarla nuevamente y benserla para trasportarla a mi tierra*).

Joseph realized that Francisca might veto his good opportunity. But he persuaded her to go. They joined the uncle's household and Joseph worked freighting goods under his uncle's patronage. The arrangement seemed fine to Joseph but, within two weeks, Martina's dissatisfaction surfaced. Joseph was getting ready to take a load of molasses (*miel*) from San Juan to Jalpa and told Martina to pack his provisions for the journey. Martina, in a not-so-oblique reference to Joseph's infidelities—real or imagined—replied defiantly that maybe he should ask one of his other women to do it. Embarrassed by Martina's disrespect in front of his relatives, Joseph unraveled a cord that he had been braiding and began to lash her. But before Joseph had done much damage, his aunt intervened and attacked Joseph in turn. In the confusion, Martina slipped out of the house and made her way to a nearby inn, eventually to be pursued and located by Joseph on horseback.

At this point Martina was under protection of the innkeeper, who refused to allow Joseph to take his wife away unless ordered to do so by judicial officials. He did allow the couple to converse, however, and Joseph, apparently assuming that the lashing of Martina and his infidelities could not be the reason, asked Martina why she had run away. Not dealing with specifics, Martina said simply that he had made her want to leave and that she intended to return to her own land. Joseph pressed, trying to convince her to return with him, but his plea only agitated and angered her. She repeated that she would not return and, as Joseph recounted later, "that I was not her husband and neither did she even know me" (*respondió con mucha ira que no tenía para que bolber que ni llo era su marido ni me conosía tampoco*). Her strong language, perhaps also meant for the ears of the innkeeper, did not deter Joseph and he tried again the next day. This time he came supported by his uncle and some relatives, but, if anything, Martina had strengthened her resolve. Even if they killed her, she shouted, she would not return. At this impasse, Joseph loaded the molasses and went to deliver it, a job that took four days. On returning he went to the inn a third time to try to bring Martina home (*por ber si la redusía para mi casa*). This time Martina was less impassioned but no less resolute. Calmly, she laid down her condition for resuming married life: Joseph would have to take her back to her land because she could not be content in "these territories." Joseph capitulated and the couple slipped out of the inn under cover of night to avoid the surveillance of the local governor's lieutenant, who had been protecting Martina. Once they were back and settled on a sugar plantation in Chetla, however, Joseph took stock of his life. He now realized, he said, that labor on a sugar estate "was not my craft [and] because of what had happened with my wife my love became cold" (*aquello no era mi oficio . . . [y] porque con lo que me abía pasado con dicha mi muger me resfrió la boluntad*).

With Martina and Joseph one sees a political process that modifies the expected pattern. First, in Martina's disputes with her husband she was less isolated than other women we have seen. Her husband's aunt protected her, as did an innkeeper and a local official. Secondly, Martina commanded such a forceful personality that Joseph could not order her about arbitrarily and treat her with brute force on a whim. Moving her in the first place required a gentle and seductive approach; her refusal to stay in his territory led to his giving in and returning to hers. Because this file contains no affidavit from Martina, it is not clear whether she viewed her existence with Joseph's relatives as a mala vida. From Joseph's testimony, however, two points can be inferred that suggest that she did: he may have had one or more mistresses, and he was capable of outbreaks of violence. Yet the thrust of the testimony in the file is not that married life with Joseph was intolerable for Martina, but that life away from home was. Perhaps most interesting is the way Joseph took stock of his life after returning with Martina to her home region. She had somehow emasculated him in his own eyes by imposing her will on him; his honor and his work prospects had both been reduced. Wives were supposed to be obedient to husbands, but instead of dominating he had been dominated. Now the mules were no longer at his disposal and his prospects were tied to the work gangs of a sugar plantation. And, perhaps worst of all, Martina's assertiveness had cooled Joseph's ardor. His self-confessed failure to conform to a cultural expectation also affected his private feelings.

Martina is an example of a woman attempting not merely to stop abusive treatment but to restructure the context of married life: residence, work, family alignment, and contact with friends. True, a lashing was the occasion for her flight, but her willingness to negotiate a reconciliation indicates that the objective conditions of the mala vida had not reached a point of no return. And even if Martina had arrived at such a judgment, it would be almost impossible to document now.

The case of Hypólita de Alcántara (b. of Indian mother and Spanish father, ca. 1676) allows for some glimpses of intolerable factors.[54] Hypólita married Mathias Cortés, a servant of the alcalde mayor of Colima. Mathias robbed his master of a mule and other property worth one thousand pesos, for which he was confined to a workhouse (*obraje*) in Mexico City for four years. Hypólita claimed that she had stayed with him for a year; Mathias said it had been just two months. In any case, Hypólita left Mathias for "the mala vida that he gave her" in the workhouse. And no doubt the conditions there were dreadful. But the mala vida was nothing new for Hypólita; it had characterized her life with Mathias from the beginning. Witness her summary of six or seven years with him: "coming and going without any permanent existence and [with] incessant abuse in word and deed" (*sin hazer pie fixo sino yendo y viniendo y maltratando mucho a esta de obra y de palabra*). The obraje, then, was only the last straw. Leaving Mathias, Hypólita stayed in Mexico City and went to the convent of San Bernardo, where she served for a month before she obtained a position as a household servant with the countess of Peñalba. She did not resume her marriage with Mathias when he completed his sentence, although, while avoiding contact, she occasionally saw him. Even in a crowd Mathias was easy to spot, she said, because his face was so ugly. His appearance had indeed suffered some degeneration, to judge from a more clinical description by the notary of the Inquisition: "a small, thin man, his face dark, long, and withered, his beard grayish with a moustache, a scar in the middle of his forehead, dark eyes, his lower teeth rotten, his upper ones missing." Hypólita's personal revulsion for Mathias was not the original reason for separating from him, it seems, but that plus the positive aspects of a life without him became the basis for remaining separated.

Other glimpses can be seen of spouses actively disliking one another. Angela Muñoz, the wife of Juan de Lizarraburo (b. ca. 1640 in Villa de Rentería, province of Guipuzcoa, Vizcaya), was, in his opinion, a difficult woman to get along with—strong, rude, harsh.[55] For example, in 1689, Juan recalled for the inquisitors Angela's outburst of the previous Easter. "Get lost, you Jewish dog" (*anda, perro judío*), she had shouted. Even before that, Juan said, he had separated from Angela and moved to Copandaro, an Indian village four leagues from San Juan Zitáquaro, because he could not stand her shrewish personality and "the little or no attendance [that she paid] to his person."

Because Juan's file does not include testimony from Angela, one can only infer the reasons for her neglect and peevishness. Firstly, Angela's temper and insults manifested a forceful personality. These qualities, however, may have been exaggerated by a corresponding weakness in Juan that undercut his ability to defend himself. Physically, his debilitation had reached the point where he could no longer work as an itinerant peddler. He had picked up syphilis (*gálico*) years before when, as a seaman, he had plied the Atlantic between Spain and the Indies for some twenty years with long stays on the isthmus of Panama. The disease slowly weakened him over the years in spite of mercurial ointment treatments (*unciones*) in Mexico City. At the time of his arrest he was suffering from attacks of fever, weakness, runny bowels (*cursos*).

Angela's strength in conjuncture with Juan's weakness explains how she dominated the politics of their marriage. She controlled their verbal exchanges and gave Juan a mala vida by refusing to sustain him in a wifely way. As a result, Juan retreated, leaving Angela in control of their common property and in possession of their house. Here the politics utilized by a woman in marriage did not require the refinement of moral suasion: she held the power. Her outbursts were as gratuitous as they were unrestrained and, in Juan's view at least, not connected with any particular grievance. In this regard, Angela behaved more like a husband to a wife than vice versa. And indeed, perhaps even more harshly, for she mixed contempt for Juan's weakness even as she dominated him. It would be wrong, however, to view Angela as a sadist. Her behavior, in fact, points to a major grievance: Juan did not contribute to their living. In refusing to serve him, she was retaliating in kind. In a society that expected men to be strong and dominant, Angela must have lost respect for Juan as she saw him increasingly unable to play his expected role.

Juan's mala vida at the hands of Angela underscores the fact that the politics of marriage was about power more than gender. Normally men held the upper hand because they had greater brute strength and because they were playing out the patriarchal role expected of them in custom and in law. María Micaela, born in the mining district of Pachuca (ca. 1705?), also drove her husband away, again illustrating that one's power more than one's sex mattered most in domestic politics.[56] There are, however, interesting differences. María was brought to Mexico City by her mother and placed as a servant in the household of don Joseph de Abendano, auditor of the tribunal of accounts. Two developments can be traced to María's term of service with don Joseph: she acquired a taste for expensive clothing and she became pregnant. It is plausible that both could be traced to don Joseph, for a status convention of wealthy men of the capital at this time was to dress their mulatta mistresses as elegantly as possible.[57] A circumstantial point, the timing of María's pregnancy, supports such a connection. In her declaration to the inquisitors, María said that she gave birth to a child "three or four months after marrying Joseph Francisco (b. ca. 1706 in Pachuca), a young mulatto coachman, shoemaker, and all-purpose laborer. Joseph, however, said that his "illicit friendship" with María Micaela had gone on for only a month and that "a little more than two months later" he and María Micaela had married. If accurate, this chronology points to don Joseph as a more likely candidate than Joseph Francisco as the father of the child. Finally, one other small point is of interest. The level at which don Joseph patronized the marriage—making his coach available to the couple and hosting a celebration at his house—seems excessive unless one assumes a closer tie between him and María Micaela than merely master-servant.

After the marriage, the couple moved in with María Micaela's parents, but all was not well. Joseph tried to make a go of it for four years but, in his words, chafed at "the mala vida that he suffered with his wife because his energies were insufficient to give her all that she wanted." Finally he ran away to Zacatecas with a troupe of actors. The tension, it seems, was simply a conflict between limited means and high expectations. María resented the straitened circumstances that came with marriage to Joseph; rather than keep her demands within bounds, she railed at him. She would complain and pester him, he said, with angry and insulting importunities, insisting that "she had to be able to wear clothing of the finest quality and various other things that he was not able to acquire with only his labor" (*impertinenzias y desazones que le daba dicha su muger no dexándole en paz sobre que la havía de traer con bestidos muy de sobra y otras diferentes cosas que no podía adquirir con solo su trabajo . . .*).

Joseph Francisco may have exaggerated, but in outline his characterization seems accurate. María Micaela's own testimony is an indication. She told the inquisitors of a temporary reunion with Joseph Francisco after he had left her. He had returned to Mexico City employed as a coachman in the service of a priest and María spotted him in a crowd witnessing a public execution. At first she confronted him with the rumor that he had married a second time. Joseph denied the rumor and implied that it must have sprung from his having had his "weaknesses as a man with another woman." But a more important grievance to María than possible adulteries was that she could not pry any money out of him. Although he visited her several times at her house, she complained, he did not "help her with anything whatsoever, although he had money." As Joseph's wife, María of course had a legitimate claim on his resources, but she may have expected too much. Joseph clearly thought she was insatiable. The most telling comment on his experience of the mala vida with María Micaela came years later when Joseph explained why he married a second time: it was to see, he said, if he could not "experience a better life than in the first marriage."

In Joseph Francisco and Juan de Lizarraburo one can see the unusual circumstance of men claiming to be subjected to the mala vida by their wives. María Micaela's demands on Joseph Francisco for a standard of living beyond his means were a matter of her acquired taste. But surely she could not have indulged it and pressured her husband so mercilessly if her parents and don Joseph had not been on her side. Perhaps this was the reason that Joseph Francisco did not try to cow her with brute force. Instead, he adopted the tactic of the weaker party, one more commonly used by women to counter violent husbands. He endured for a time, and then ran off. In both cases the wives controlled the politics of their marriages; when the men reached the limits of their endurance, they extricated themselves by flight rather than face an unequal and potentially humiliating confrontation.

A final form of the mala vida, desertion, can be mentioned to bring us full circle to the letter that began our cases. It could occur for personal or structural reasons, with or without planning, within months of a marriage or after many years. It could result in husbands and wives having no contact for years at a time. Yet it was risky for either of them to conclude that the marriage bond was therefore severed. Witness the remarkable marriage of Inés de Espinosa and Jacobe Luxeri (m. ca. 1548 in Veracruz).[58] The couple lived six years in Guatemala City and then Jacobe went to Peru for twenty years, during which time Inés had no word of him. When a rumor reached her that Jacobe had died, Inés sent their son, Christóbal, to investigate. Christóbal found his father very much alive in a mining camp near Popayán and stayed with him for two years—"getting reacquainted as father and son," as Christóbal put it.[59] Christóbal returned and Jacobe again dropped from sight, this time for ten years. He then saw Inés briefly ("three or four days") in Guatemala City while on his way to Mexico City to take up "a certain employment." He stayed away for three or four years and once again stopped in for a few days as he headed back to Perú. Another "twelve to fifteen years" passed, Inés said, without news. Then, probably to her relief, travelers told her that Jacobe was dead—falsely, as it turned out, for she got into trouble when authorities determined that she had remarried before Jacobe's death.

Inés's problem was shared by many women: how long was one to wait before remarrying? We have seen that Inés tried to find out news of her husband and sent her son to verify his rumored death. But for all those years before she thought she had such a reliable report, she remained faithful. Beatriz González (b. ca. 1503?), who left behind an articulate statement of her view, was less patient.[60] Her husband, Juan González, embarked for the Levant from Málaga in 1521, she said, and "left me with two daughters in the village of Guadalcanal, where I was waiting for him and I raised my daughters with much labor and fatigue to my person until 1530 without compromising the honor of my person or my life."

During Juan's ten-year absence, she added, neighbors and relatives (including in-laws), would "say to me every day that the said Juan González was dead or that he had died in Italy." Finally, she decided that ten years was enough; she determined to go to New Spain to remarry in order to improve the chances of her two daughters. Beatriz carried out her plan, although not without misfortune, for one of the daughters became ill and died on the road from Veracruz to Mexico City. Were emigration and the plan to find a second husband in the Indies justifiable? Beatriz thought so "because by right all those that are absent in distant and remote places should be presumed dead so that their wives can remarry without penalty" (*porque de derecho todos los que están ausentes en partes longincuas y remotas son avidos por muertos la muerte de los quales para que sus mugeres se pueden casar sin pena*).

The situation of Beatriz, of María de Itá, whose letter began this section, and of several others could be characterized in simplest terms as the mala vida as a result of an absent husband. The grievance in part was lack of support, a complaint that did not imply that women expected not to work. It did imply hardship, loneliness, and lesser levels of respect in their communities. Husband and wife both expected to work, most typically perhaps, in a single household under a common master, assigned to tasks according to the usual domestic division of labor by sex.[61] We have seen, moreover, that single women seemed to have little trouble getting work, especially of a servile kind, when they left their husbands. Also, if there were children, desertion added the extra burden of raising them, giving them proper rites of passage, and launching them as best one could into adult life. Deserted wives did all of this less successfully and with greater sacrifices without a husband in residence. Material and personal needs, then, could be frustrated by legal and religious restrictions on divorce and remarriage if confirmation of the death of a missing husband could not be confirmed. Beatriz's ten-year rule was her reasonable compromise. Let us note that it was not extreme or stated out of isolated desperation, but a view urged by friends, neighbors, and relatives. One can see it, therefore, as a reflection of community norms.

With our cases from the Inquisition we have ranged from the sixteenth to the eighteenth century, from Spain to New Spain, from ranchos in the countryside to Mexico City. Over this time and in scattered places we have observed people of various racial and ethnic categories and economic standing. The constant running through these variables is the notion of the mala vida as a window on the politics of marriage. It may seem paradoxical, at first, to be trying to learn something of marriage by looking at troubled ones. In fact, however, "trouble" is the catalyst that moves us to order our thoughts about most matters. As long as norms and experience roughly coincide, one is unlikely to change course or to analyze experience; the awareness of a disparity between them is what spurs thought and action. Statements about the mala vida point to the perception of such a disparity in married life. They, in turn, spurred political actions designed to correct it. Of course, assumptions about norms can be eccentric or "representative," distorted or accurate. But this essay is not concerned with making those distinctions. Rather, it embraces all phenomena that have been documented as within the range of possible human experience, and therefore as deserving of incorporation in historical discourse.

Silvia M. Arrom has summarized the essential basis of marriage for a woman in the Hispanic world: "In return for the support, protection, and guidance her husband was legally required to provide, a wife owed him nearly total obedience."[62] This legal characterization, and others discussed at the outset of this essay, stresses both the husband's dominance and his obligations. Our cases of the mala vida have shown that to the degree that obligations were neglected, the logic of obedience was undercut. However slanted in favor of the husband, there was an aspect of marriage that insisted on a degree of reciprocity. This provided women (and occasionally men) with a basis for evaluating their lot within the bonds of marriage; it gave them the leverage to counter mistreatment by engaging in a political process.

Although there were wide variations in how much women would tolerate, the tendency was to endure the mala vida for long periods before acting drastically, for example by running away. Short of that, they used whatever tactics and resources were at hand to defend themselves and try to modify their circumstances. Potential allies might be friends, a priest, or an official; but, above all, family. Even so, the key ingredient was the persistance and forcefulness of the woman herself, for outsiders interfered with a husband's prerogatives only with reluctance. When women did run away it is notable that they frequently took first refuge in convents, where their safety was assured and their labor needed.

Were the women who turned up in the records of the Inquisition *particularly* badly married? I think not. Whether they were or were not, however, it is important to remember that they drew upon the larger culture to identify, speak about, and contest the conditions under which they lived. Their stories, therefore, reflect the assumptions and conventions of society even as they tell of their personal circumstances and the distress of individuals. The latter are not merely a way to view the former; they are inseparable from it.

Acknowledgments

The research for this essay was supported by a fellowship from the Social Sciences and Humanities Council of Canada. I am grateful to Philip Amos, Paul Edward Dutton, Michael Fellman, Steve Stern, Michelle Metcalfe, Catherine Le Grand, and above all, Asunción Lavrin for comments on one or another draft.

Notes

1. Ernst Troeltsch, *The Social Teaching of the Christian Churches,* trans. Olive Wyon (New York: Harper, 1960 [1931]), 1:186–315 passim, 418.

2. Theodore Meyer, *Die christlich-ethischen sozial Prinzipien und die Arbeiterfrage* (1904), p.78, quoted in Troeltsch, *Social Teaching,* 1:418n. Meyer seems to be drawing on Saint Augustine and possibly Aristotle. Augustine not only considered the peace of the family under patriarchal authority integral to that of the city but also supposed that the former is drawn from the latter and composed of the same dynamics. In that sense he goes beyond Aristotle, who argued that "the state . . . was the consummation of all other natural unions, such as the family, the village, the town, etc." (Walter Ullmann, *Medieval Political Thought* [Baltimore: Penguin, 1975, originally 1965], p. 168); see also Saint Augustine, *The City of God,* trans. John Healey, 2 vols. (London: J. M. Dent, 1931), 2, book 19, chaps. 14–16.

3. Troeltsch, *Social Teaching,* 1:313.

4. Meyer, *Sozial Prinzipien,* p. 418n.

5. *Las siete partidas,* trans. Samuel Parsons Scott (Chicago, New York, Washington: Comparative Law Bureau of the American Bar Association, by Commerce Clearing House, 1931), Partida 4, title 11, pp. 930–44.

6. Troeltsch, *Social Teaching,* 1:287.

7. Saint Augustine, *City of God,* 2, book 19, chap. 16.

8. Ullmann, *Medieval Political Thought,* pp. 55–56.

9. J. M. Wallace-Hadrill, *Early German Kingship in England and on the Continent* (Oxford: Clarendon Press, 1971), pp. 98–123, especially 104. Emphasis is added. I am grateful to my colleague Paul Edward Dutton for bringing this reference to my attention.

10. Ullmann, *Medieval Political Thought,* p. 57.

11. Walter Ullmann, *The Carolingian Renaissance and the Idea of Kingship* (London: Methuen, 1969), p. 187.

12. Quoted in Ullmann, *Medieval Political Thought,* p. 88.

13. Troeltsch, *Social Teaching*, 1:34.

14. Troeltsch, *Social Teaching*, 1:289; *Las Siete Partidas*, Partida 2, title 1, law 10, pp. 274–75.

15. Ullmann, *Medieval Political Thought*, pp. 16–17.

16. Reginald H. Barrow, *Introduction to St. Augustine, The City of God* (London: Faber and Faber, 1950), Book 19, chap. 16, pp. 102–4. I am grateful to Richard Sullivan for critical commentary on Barrow's and Healey's translations of this passage (see citation in note 2).

17. J. A. Fernández-Santamaría, *The State, War and Peace: Spanish Political Thought in the Renaissance, 1516–1559* (New York: Cambridge University Press, 1977), p. 246.

18. *Las Siete Partidas*, Partida 2, title 6, law 2, p. 199.

19. Sedulius Scottus, "On Christian Rulers," chap. 5, trans. E. G. Doyle, in *Medieval and Renaissance Texts and Studies*, vol.17 (Binghamton, New York: State University of New York at Binghamton, 1983), p. 59.

20. William B. Taylor, "Between Global Process and Local Knowledge: An Inquiry into Early Latin American Social History, 1500–1900," in *Reliving the Past: the Worlds of Social History*, ed. Olivier Zuns (Chapel Hill: University of North Carolina Press, 1985), pp. 148–49

21. *Las Siete Partidas*, Partida 4, titles 17, 18, pp. 960–71.

22. *Las Siete Partidas*, Partida 4, title 25, especially laws 1 and 2, p. 992.

23. A military chief, for example, called on his own group of retainers, *criados*, linked to him by personal loyalty and the common enterprise of booty and war, rather than by ceremonial contracts. Even when small landowners commended themselves to a powerful lord in Castile and León before the twelfth century, they chose him freely and, if the arrangement did not suit them, they could "seek a new lord 'from sea to sea.'" Eventually the terminology of Europe north of the Pyrenees entered Spain, but even after a word such as "fief" achieved currency in Spain, its Spanish equivalent, *préstamo*, was the more common term. In spite of sharing a common ethos with the rest of Christian Europe, Spanish patterns of patriarchalism were less rigid. This has been worked out for the roles and status of women by Heather Dillard in her *Daughters of the Reconquest: Women in Castilian Town Society, 1100–1300* (New York: Cambridge University Press, 1984). See also A. MacKay, *Spain in the Middle Ages: From Frontier to Empire, 1000–1500* (London: Macmillan, 1977), p. 42; Marc Bloch, *Feudal Society*, trans. L. A. Manyon, 2 vols. (Chicago: University of Chicago Press, 1961), 1:184–87.

24. An example from the seventeenth century is discussed in Richard Boyer, "Absolutism versus Corporatism in New Spain: The Administration

of the Marquis of Gelves, 1621–1624," *International History Review* 4, no.4 (November 1982): 501.

25. Thomas N. Tentler, *Sin and Confession on the Eve of the Reformation* (Princeton: Princeton University Press, 1977), pp. 48–133.

26. Jayme de Corella, *Práctica de el confessionario y explicación de las 65 Proposiciones condenadas por la santidad de N. S. P. Inocencio* XI: *Su materia los casos más selectos de la theología moral: Su forma un diálogo entre el confesor y penitente* (Valencia: Imprenta de Iaume de Bordazar, 1689), p. 62. I am grateful to Asunción Lavrin for calling my attention to this work and for providing me with copies of works by Ferrer and Herrera that will be discussed below.

27. Ibid., p. 62.

28. Ibid., pp. 65–66. In his commentary, Corella cites Tiraquel, who says that a husband may not strike his wife under any circumstances. But Corella has three other authorities who disagree. The juggling of authorities is, of course, a method of proof. More important for our purposes is the range of opinions available on questions of moral theology from which Corella, and others writing books of application, might choose. In spite of the variations in both the theoretical and applied literature, I assume that applied moral theology as represented in the confessional manuals does not stray far from consensus on fundamentals, for example relative to patriarchal authority. The important principle here, however, was that "in a Christian society it was the priests alone who were qualified to pronounce upon the bond that brought society into being, to pronounce on the faith." See Ullmann, *Medieval Political Thought,* p. 81. Secular law mirrors the ecclesiastical perspective, not expressly allowing for physical correction but condoning it if it were moderate or provoked. See Silvia Marina Arrom, *The Women of Mexico City, 1790–1857* (Stanford: Stanford University Press, 1985), p. 72.

29. Corella, *Práctica,* p.66. In a study of canon law published in the nineteenth century, Justo Donoso says in no uncertain terms that marriage is equally a contract and a sacrament. As for the former, marriage has held that status "since the origin of the world." See Justo Donoso, *Instituciones de derecho canónico americano,* 2 vols. (Valparaiso: Imprenta y Librería Mercurio, 1849), 2:148.

30. Alonso de Herrera, *Espejo de la perfecta casada* (Granada: Blas Martínez, 1636). The author lived in Peru and may have published a first edition of the work there (Asunción Lavrin, personal correspondence).

31. Herrera, *Espejo,* title page. It is notable that Herrera dedicates Espejo to a woman, the "illustrious señora doña María Zapata, wife of don Juán de

Quesada, knight of the Order of Santiago and brother of the Conde de Garcies."

32. Ibid., p. 114.

33. Ibid., pp. 114–15; *Las Siete Partidas,* Partida 4, title 1, law 5, p.881. The source for the point is, of course, ultimately to be traced to the Apostle Paul, Ephesians 6:21–33 and 1 Corinthians 12.

34. Herrera, *Espejo,* p. 115.

35. Antonio de Guevara (b. ca. 1480) advises the prince to "love your subjects and be beloved of them, for much greater is the effort of the man who labors through love than the toil of the man who merely serves" (paraphrased in Fernández-Santamaría, *The State,* p. 259).

36. Vicente Ferrer, *Suma moral para examen de curas y confesores* (México City: Imprenta Nueva Madrileña de D. Felipe de Zúñiga y Ontiveros, 1778), p. 381.

37. Corella, *Práctica,* p. 66.

38. Herrera, *Espejo,* p.114. In a case involving Teresa Romero, a fake midseventeenth-century religious visionary, the inquisitors used "mala vida" to characterize her libertine ways. See Solange Alberro, "La licencia vestida de santidad: Teresa de Jesús, falsa beata del siglo xvii," in *De la santidad a la perversión,* ed. Sergio Ortega (Mexico: Grijalbo, 1986), p.229. A slave may use the term "mala vida" in the same way that women used it: to denote ill treatment, lack of support, and overwork. In such a manner, a woman recalled her runaway slave husband, who "about six years ago . . . ran away from his master's house, fed up with the mala vida that they gave him." See María Elena Cortés Jácome, "No tengo más délito que haberme casado otra vez . . ." in *De la santidad,* ed. Ortega, p. 171.

39. This essay as well as a larger work in progress is based on my analysis of 214 bigamy files from the Mexican tribunal of the Holy Office. Some of the files contain depositions taken in Spain that document events in the lives of immigrants before they arrived in New Spain.

40. Ruth Behar, in an essay published after I prepared this one, discusses magic and witchcraft in eighteenth-century Mexico, a crime three times as common among women as among men (224 vs. 79 cases). Women used witchcraft mainly to overcome problems with men and were motivated by their desire to counter mala vida. Her materials, and others from the *Brujería, Hechicería,* and *Maleficio* section of the Inquisition records, complement this essay. See Ruth Behar, "Sex and Sin, Witchcraft and the Devil in Late-Colonial Mexico," *American Ethnologist* 14, no.1 (February 1987): 34–54, especially, pp. 41, 46, and 52n. See also her essay in this volume.

41. The account of María de Itá is taken from the Archivo General de la Nación (Mexico City) [hereafter AGN], Inquisición 820, pt. 1, exp. 6, fols. 1–52. This, as well as all other passages from the Inquisition files, is my translation.

42. The account of Francisca Torres is taken from AGN, Inquisición, vol. 91, exp. 5. Approximate birth dates will be placed in parentheses in the text whenever possible in order to locate the cases chronologically. Normally such dates can be known for the accused but less frequently for his or her spouse.

43. The story of Violante Pizarro is taken from AGN, Inquisición, vol. 526, exp. 2, fols. 37–151.

44. Another possibility is that Violante put herself through this humiliating situation because she was already pregnant and wanted to establish a circumstantial case for Francisco being the father of the child.

45. The story of María Guadalupe Delgadillo is taken from AGN, Inquisición, vol. 1192, fols. 1–85.

46. The account of Mariana Monroy is taken from AGN, Inquisición, vol. 441, exp. 2, fols. 356–411.

47. The account of María de Villagrán is taken from AGN, Inquisición, 137, exp. 5.

48. The account of María Jesús de la Encarnación is taken from AGN, Inquisición, 1292, exp. 7, fols. 1–101.

49. The account of Rosa Maldonada is taken from AGN, Inquisición, 1180, fols. 14–98.

50. William B. Taylor, *Drinking, Homicide, and Rebellion in Colonial Mexican Villages* (Stanford: Stanford University Press, 1979), pp. 83–97, 153.

51. María Ygnacia's account is taken from AGN, Inquisición, 648, exp. 7, fols. 497–593.

52. The account of Pedro Matheo is taken from AGN, Inquisición, 605, exp. 2, fols. 189–278.

53. The account of Joseph Antonio Galbes is taken from AGN, Inquisición, 1062, exp. 2.

54. The account of Hypólita de Alcántara is taken from AGN, Inquisición, 547, exp. 8.

55. The account of Angela Muñoz is taken from AGN, Inquisición, 657, exp. 3, fols. 300–323.

56. María Micaela's story is taken from AGN, Inquisición, 794, exp. 24, fols. 226–332.

57. J. Eric S. Thompson, *Thomas Gage's Travels in the New World* (Nor-

man: University of Oklahoma Press, 1958), pp. 68–69.

58. The account of Inés de Espinosa is taken from AGN, Inquisición, 134, exp. 7.

59. By this time Christóbal was about twenty and it is quite likely that he had never seen his father, certainly not to remember him.

60. The account of Beatriz González is taken from AGN, Inquisición, 22, exp. 12.

61. I discuss work in some detail in a book in preparation.

62. Arrom, *Women of Mexico City,* p. 65.

Thomas Calvo

The Warmth of the Hearth: Seventeenth-Century Guadalajara Families

The specific studies of the phenomena surrounding family cohesion—sexuality, love in all its various guises, the couple's stability or lack thereof—have received a great deal of analysis and discussion.[1] The scholarly harvest in regard to Latin America's colonial period is meager, with the exception of Gilberto Freyre's classic work. Even in Mexico the gap has yet to be bridged.[2] Joining the ranks of Western historiography will not be mere scientific mimicry. Sexuality and love lie at the heart of family sociology, which is the centerpiece of sociology itself. At a time when the concept of a "cultural area" is fashionable, it is not quite certain whether Latin American belongs to the Hispanic, and therefore Western world, or whether it should be assigned a place of its own. In any case, an in-depth study of the family and its composition will shed light on a determinant criterion.

Such an ambition can be achieved only under a twofold condition. The family fabric is so complex, and the risk of confronting a diversity of family situations so obvious, that the subject of study must be circumscribed to the utmost and viewed from the confines of a microcosm. The one we have chosen—Guadalajara in the middle of the colonial period—is first and foremost representative of itself: urban, creole, mestizo, and Afro-Mexican.[3] At the outer edge of New Spain, it could hardly speak for all of Mexico, although it foreshadowed the mestizo Mexico of today. Over the centuries it has become a richer and more fruitful source of knowledge than the several thousands of inhabitants then living in a fringe area would have forecast. No single approach would suffice to provide access to such a polymorphous reality. The researcher is compelled to leave no stone unturned and to sift through the entire gamut of quantitative and qualitative sources. They complement and clarify each other, although sometimes they also contradict. To avoid too striking a contrast and overly flagrant contradictions, one source has been given priority: the parish records of Guadalajara's Cathedral Church (Sagrario Metropolitano), which will highlight historical quantification. Its marriage records seem to provide a reassuring portrait of the Guadalajara family. The initial perceived coherence, however, becomes blurred when one dips deeply into the more troubled waters of the baptismal registry, finding legitimate and illegitimate births equally divided. Thus, as often, the quantitative approach is unsettling. It destroys certain preconceived ideas and poses as many questions as it answers. It requires evaluation in the light of other sources that are less massive, while more subtle and subjective. This is desirable, because sexuality and love cannot be assessed in terms of numerical indices.

Marriage and Family: Reassuring Statistics?

Elsewhere I have described the difficulties encountered, and the tortuous path followed, in reconstructing some two hundred seventeenth-century Guadalajara families.[4] The details are not germane here, but it is appropriate to note that our sample, based on the marriages that took place in the Sagrario between 1666 and 1675, covers the most stable segment of the population. The elusive data single out the creole population from all the rest: *español* couples account for 52 percent of the marriage sample (other ethnic groups constitute 32.2 percent), while in the aggregate they represent only 30.2 percent of the total, as compared with 33.6 percent for the mestizo and indigenous segments (the remaining segment was not determined). We must, therefore, anticipate findings somewhat more consistent with our Western ethnocentrism (stemming from their Hispanicism and the greater space they occupy in the permanent records) than they probably were in actual fact. This is an unavoidable corollary to the adoption of Christian marriage—the basis of western family—as our starting point.

The findings are, nevertheless, quite different from those that characterized the European world, even Spain, at that time. The focal point is the age at which women married, the determining factor in so-called "natural" demography. The Guadalajaran average taking the nuptial vows was 25 years old.[5] In Western Europe (Protestant as well as Catholic), it ranged between 25 and 28 years in those days.[6] Equally important for our purposes was the observation of a bifurcated path at both sexual and ethnic levels: the "elderly" peninsulars, over 25 years of age, married young creole girls under 21, while the mulattos and natives did not wait that long. After all, what had the latter to gain from a society that limited their upward mobility? If the men waited, they found their options limited to *castas* well along in years (around 25), burdened with children and experience, and for whom marriage was a convenient solution.[7] At least, that might have been the attitude adopted in the middle of the century by *coyote* Xacinta Bernal, whose marriage to mulatto Phelipe Plasencia made him the head of a noisy household, since her "dowry" included seven children, a daughter-in-law, and a grandson.[8]

The above is, of course almost a caricature, and not a typical example. But one first irreducible conclusion stands: it would be illusory to look for a single prototype family in seventeenth-century Guadalajara, even in the midst of "legalist" families playing the game of marriage. For the *españoles* marriage was one possible means of preserving ethnic virtues and privileges. Establishing a bond with a young criolla bride helped in the process of either founding or stabilizing a patrimony—since we must not forget the importance of the dowry brought by the wife. For the castas it offered social

Table 1. Age at First Marriage among Neo-Galicians, 1666–90

			Men				
Age	under 15	15–19	20–24	25–29	30–34	35 & older	Total
Cases	1	14	25	5	7	4	56
Percent	1.8	25.0	44.6	8.9	12.5	7.1	
			Women				
Cases	4	24	20	15	5	4	72
Percent	5.5	33.3	27.7	20.8	6.9	5.5	

Source: Archivo Sagrario Metropolitano, Guadalajara, Baptismal and Marriage Books, 1666–90.

upgrading, since marriage meant escaping certain social stigmas such as nonlegitimate births and concubinage. Obviously it could be a moral imperative (among the reconstructed families I had to include three marriages legitimized on the death bed, *in articulo mortis*).[9]

By marrying three years earlier than her European contemporary, the Guadalajaran wife might be expected to have produced more offspring. My findings are just the opposite. The complete families (according to research that followed the spouses beyond the female fertility period) had fewer than six children as an average. I would have expected at least seven or eight. The source might be challenged, given the limited size of my sample. The explanation, however, seems to be more deep-seated: the interval between births was relatively long, usually between 20 and 22 months until the arrival of the fourth child, and 28 months thereafter. These figures are typical, and can take place in a specific demographic and social context only assuming a relatively low infant mortality rate. Does this factor stem, in this still underpopulated area, from satisfactory economic and sanitary conditions? No doubt it does in part, especially since my sample is restricted to the upper social brackets. Can it be also explained by more diligent care for the child? The questions are challenging, and a conclusion may not be reached until more research is carried out.

The long average natality interval can also be attributable to the limited use of wet nurses. This remains a ticklish question. Most of the español families included in my survey did not seem to have adopted this practice. Yet, in 1616 the Franciscans of Guadalajara blamed the progressive disappearance of the Indians on this "nefarious" practice:

> They abandon their towns, going far away from their regions and leaving behind their wives who, together with other women, are compelled by the *repartidores* and other officials to serve not only as domestics in the households of Spanish women, but also as nurses to their children, at times even suckling the children of servants with their own milk, deeming it better and more equitable that the poor Indian woman should nurse other people's children, abandoning her own, or at least depriving them of much of the sustenance she owes them as their mother.[10]

Did the Franciscans paint too black a picture? Did the sharp drop in the native population until 1640–50 limit this form of exploitation? Evidence of this practice is found throughout colonial times. Toward the end of the seventeenth century the children of don Luis de Hijar Palomino freed Gertrudis, a "mulatto slave who belonged to our aforesaid parents, for having suckled us at her breast as our wet nurse."[11] Later still, in 1795, María Victoria Hernández presented a claim against her former master:

> Ten years ago, don Sebastian Moyeda, a resident of this place, hired me as a wet nurse at a salary of four pesos a month, and I gave his daughter all of my milk for a year and eleven months, sacrificing the life of my own son and leaving the rest of my family to fend for themselves, working not only as a nurse to the child, but also washing, ironing, milking, and doing other housework for which I was not hired, and thus was overworked and beaten by the aforesaid don Sebastian and his wife, to the point where I was often bathed in blood.[12]

Is it a coincidence or simply a reflection of reality that these three texts seem to summarize the history of wet nursing in Guadalajara? During the sixteenth century a still plentiful and subjugated native population, along with a small white and mestizo group, fostered the practice down to the lowest strata of the mixed-blood segment. In the seventeenth century, the demographics are reversed. With female African labor on the rise, the role of nursing mothers was assigned exclusively to slaves, thus serving only the wealthiest families. When slavery declined in the eighteenth century, preference was given to hired nurses, such as the aforementioned María Victoriana, thereby perhaps making the option more democratic. Whatever the era, an essential constant distinguishes this practice from that of northern Europe (France, at least) and ties it to Mediterranean Europe (as in Florence). The infants were suckled at the parents' home and under their close surveillance, forestalling any number of mishaps that could befall them. Conversely, wet nursing represented both a terrible danger, as the example of María Victoriana illustrates, to the child of the hired nurse, and a source of overexploitation for the nurse, bordering on violence and suggesting an atmosphere of harshness within the household.[13]

But neither the low infant mortality rate nor the limited use of wet nurses can adequately explain why the reconstructed families in our sampling should have an average of four children, or why nearly one-fourth of these marriages were sterile. Here, again, we must address the social context: the existence of extensive polygamy in a female-dominated city. For every hundred women who died in the city there were only seventy-two men. This chronic gender instability meant that when María de Cárdenas, who married in 1671, died in 1709, her husband had long since abandoned her (*se ausentó el contenido*). We should not forget the numerous couples practicing concubinage who eventually married, having had some of their offspring before doing so. This is a paradoxical situation in an eminently Roman Catholic region. The limitation of family size takes place among the legally married couples, perhaps for economic reasons (such as the division of the patrimony). An element in that pattern is the age of marriage: rather late among the social élite. By mid-century, when illegitimacy swelled the birth rate and produced 58 percent of all offspring, the correlation (*coeficiente*) between baptisms of legitimate children and marriages is extraordinarily low (2.63 for 81660–69).[14] Creoles had an average of only 4.5 children, as compared with 5 for the *castas*. It would be foolhardy to place all the blame on the use of contraceptives or abortion, but the issue cannot be lightly dismissed.[15]

The biological families were rather small. In the center of the city, where the élite resided, the median was 5.3 persons per household. On the southern side of the city, which was more densely populated, more mestizo, and closer to the Indian sector of Mexicalcingo,[16] the size of the household was smaller, 4.1 persons. The household seems reduced to parents and children, suggesting a strong family cohesion. But we must use caution with these numbers. One hundred sixty-three of the 346 households studies were headed by women; in other words, the paternal influence was missing in nearly half the households. We should not mistake this situation for one of female independence. These women, first and foremost, lived alone or were heads of very small homes of two or three persons. They also presided over households whose members were older than the average.[17] This did not really mean a greater autonomy for women, since the female heads of households were often condemned to such a status once they stopped being concubines due to old age or became isolated widows, thus creating many pockets of poverty in the city.

The situation reveals a paradox. Cohesion undeniably existed within urban families, but it was disrupted by the racist and class-oriented nature of society and by the weakness of the tridentian marriage model. Children were cared for, as the low mortality rate indicates, but those receiving the best care were the scions of the master. In élite marriages the advanced age of the husband acted as a deterrent to fecundity.

And what is the role played by the church in all of this? Even in this Episcopal See, the church had its rearguard skirmishes while it fought on other fronts to establish its political and economic power and to end internal rivalry. At best, it sought to impose a genuine marriage ritual.[18] It also engaged in sporadic attempts to stem the rising tide of concubinage and illegitimacy that characterized two thirds of the century.

Concubinage and Illegitimacy: A Disturbing Reality?

The external reality of illegitimacy may be conveyed in statistics (see tables 3, 4). In a city of tertiary activities it can be explained by a sharp sexual imbalance that overrepresents the female group. Socially, it is linked to the presence of an entire Afro-Mexican sector consisting largely of female slaves. The rising curve of illegitimacy in midcentury is due to the mass importation of African slaves during the preceding decades.

More than the facts—and their somewhat mechanical explanations—what strikes us here is the way this situation could be either experienced by some or resented by others, while becoming a part of the family reality. Concubinage could be found in all forms. Prudence advised social discretion in some instances. Such was the case of the parish priest of Jeres, Lorenzo Carvallo, who put a sudden end to his public liaison with a mestizo woman when he learned that the *visitador* was heading toward his jurisdiction. Another skillful maneuver was executed by "Francisco Gallegos (*vecino* of Tonalá), who for seven years has lived in sin with a mestizo woman named Juana Saldana, and although it is true that she does not reside in his house, wherever she is he provides for her living."

The powerful could go so far as to show a supreme disdain for laws and the public. At the apex of the social pyramid, don Tomás Pisarro, *oidor* of the Audiencia of Guadalajara, "has for years had a liaison with a married woman, parading and flaunting his sin, taking his "friend" to church all or most of the holy days, attending the same mass at the Soledad hermitage, and getting her a box at the public bullfights." Nothing stopped him. Excommunicated, he had

Table 2. Marital Status of Deceased Persons in the Sagrario of Guadalajara, 1685–99

	Married or Widowed	Single	Unknown	Total
Men				
Peninsulars	29	15	3	47
White Mexicans	114	51	19	184
Blacks and Mixed Bloods	111	56	23	190
Indians	18	8	8	34
Not determined	58	25	30	113
Total	330	155	83	568
Women				
Peninsulars	—	—	—	—
White Mexicans	169	114	10	293
Blacks and Mixed Bloods	117	202	43	362
Indians	24	12	5	41
Not determined	76	48	9	133
Total	386	376	67	829

Source: Archivo Sagrario Metropolitano, Guadalajara (ASMG). Burial Books. The deaths recorded in this table and the archival source consulted comprised the adult population only. This table appeared in Thomas Calvo, "Concubinato y mestizaje en el medio urbano: El caso de Guadalajara en el siglo XVII," *Revista de Indias* 44, no. 173 (January–June, 1984): 205. "Single" simply means unmarried. Such women could have been either concubines, unwed mothers, or spinsters. This applies equally to men. However, the number of women reported as single at their death is significantly high. Ecclesiastic censal reports for the second half of the century indicate that the masculinity index in Guadalajara was low. For further discussion see Calvo, "Concubinato y mestizaje en el medio urbano."

no scruples about walking on the Alameda with his mistress. When a merchant came too close to her, he shot at him to drive him away. For sheer sacrilege, however, the prize went to Fr. Juan de Abrejo, custodian (*guardian*) of the Franciscan monastery in Jalisco, who was reported by oidor Arévalo Sedeño as "well known for having lived in sin with a beautiful Indian girl known as "The Serf" (*la sierba*).

Table 3. Recorded Out-of-Wedlock Births in Guadalajara, 1600–99

	Foundlings or of Unknown Parents	Undetermined Affiliation	Total No. of Births and % Illegitimacy		
				Deficit (%)	Excess (%)
1600–1609	222	4	560	39.6	40.3
1610–19	381	16	798	47.7	49.7
1620–29	593	30	1068	55.5	58.3
1630–39*	599	9	1002	59.7	60.6
1640–49	706	59	1308	53.9	58.4
1650–59	780	161	1467	53.1	64.1
1660–69	898	294	1880	47.7	63.4
1670–79	1064	142	2077	51.2	58.0
1680–89*	1015	2	1934	52.4	52.5
1690–99	1348	16	2806	48.0	48.6

Note: Since the majority of "undetermined affiliation" parents were slaves, many of whom where illegitimate themselves, the percentages under Excess (which assumes that all the "undetermined" were illegitimate) are closer to reality.

Source: ASMG, Baptismal Books. The terms "of unknown parents" (mother or father, or both), *hijos de iglesia,* and *expósito* were those commonly used by parish priests for recording illegitimate births in the seventeenth century.

*Decades with information for only eight years.

Among many public appearances, she went out one day wearing a handsome blouse and a velvet skirt . . . and that same day the aforementioned custodian said mass in a new chasuble and placed a new frontal on the altar made of the same velvet as the woman's skirt."[19]

These may be extreme cases of impunity, but at the other end of the social scale, protected by their very anonymity, the mass of mestizos availed themselves of the same opportunity. All those men enjoyed another form of effective protection: in that male-oriented society, the onus (read responsibility) was almost systematically laid at the door of women. The lingering emotional memory left in the mind of Thomas Gage by mulatto women and "their provocative walk sway" is well known. In 1636 rumor had it that a certain Beatris de Rivera, a creole woman from Guadalajara, had bewitched the priest Pedro Avila Cepeda. Since he was known, among other things, to have deflowered his niece, Isabel de Avila, he had no need of magic to fall under Rivera's spell. The mistress of prosecutor (*fiscal*) don Luis Martínez Hidalgo was nicknamed "The Witch," but again the prosecutor, adept in "bad habits" (*malas costumbres*), was surely led by his own inclination, rather than the dictates of the woman.[20] Consciously or not, the female sex left itself open to criticism and molded itself to the role the other sex liked to see them play. Around 1620–23 a wave of accusations of witchcraft practice (about one-third of them of an erotic nature) swept over the city. Allegedly, more than three-quarters of the victims were men, and the women were almost exclusively the instigators and "practitioners."[21]

More than the image of women as miscreants and sorceresses (with which the Virgin could be contrasted), the shocking factor in the examples cited is the social distance between the two accomplices or partners, which from the standpoint of the period could be explained only by the man's "blindness."[22] When the couples appeared to be social equals, however prominent, the irregularity of the situation was largely accepted, almost condoned by general complicity, even on the part of the religious authorities. By the time their first legitimate daughter was born in 1696, physician don Domingo Guerrero and doña Ana de Padilla had known the joys of parenthood since 1688. Their three children, born out of wedlock, were later legitimized.[23]

This understanding had its limits, established as much by the circumstances as by deliberate intent. The ongoing conflict between Bishop Garabito and his *provisor,* (vicar general) on the one hand, and President Cevallos and the courts, on the other, shed considerable light on the misadventures of don Luis Hurtado and his concubine, doña Francisca Chumazero. Don Luis was a protégé of the president, who appointed him *alcalde mayor* of the wealthy province of Aguacatlán. Already married in Puebla, he established an illicit relationship with Francisca and became the target of the provisor, who was at sword's points with the civil authorities. While ecclesiastic justice acted in all haste and demanded on 8 April 1686 that don Luis be thrown into prison, the audiencia asked for action with "moderation, charity, and the secrecy required by the status and the reputation of virginity of the aforesaid maiden," comparing the attitude of the Guadalajara clerics with that of the "great prelate" of Michoacán, don Juan de Ortega y Montañés, who recommended that action in such cases be tempered "with gentleness." Finally, in 1689, the two lovers fled and lived happily in New Spain. This was the only way to escape a situation in which a jurisdictional friction between civil and ecclesiastical power complicated the couple's original intentions.[24]

Did the indulgence of the authorities cause a hardening of social repression? In 1584 the visit of the bishop of Zacatecas was marked by a confrontation with the *corregidor* that benefited the numerous concubines in that city, but not everyone was happy about it. The following year, when it was his turn to visit the city, oidor don Fernando Altamirano had to deal severely with three instances of cuckoldry that befell "an honorable citizen and attorney of those mines."[25] Only thirteen of the hundreds of cases before the audiencia during the six years of the 1612–20 period for which records are available have a sexual connotation: two were confirmed cases of concubinage, but four criminal suits were designed to curb the excesses of the people's "honor codes" that had led betrayed spouses to kill the adulterous lovers. When the community attempted to impose its own interpretation of punishment (*charivari*), the task of the representative of royal authority was to prevent or curb such appropriation of power from the family itself.[26] Need I add that the authorities dealt more severely with any hint of charivari (twelve years of exile and a 400-peso-fine) than with concubinage (two silver marks)? In the eyes of the judges, *pundonor* constituted ample justification for the crimes of murderous husbands and "physicians of their honor," who were sometimes sentenced only to defray the costs.[27] These incidents were not infrequent in Zacatecas, Ramos, New Biscay, and Lagos; in other words, rustic milieux where the failure of the judiciary to act pushed society to do so itself. Guadalajara, as a major urban center, was possibly sufficiently policed to escape that type of "personalized" justice.

Did the social climate affect the cohabiting couples? Nearly half the households were under suspicion of having been formed irregularly. This is a situation that begs to be examined, primarily from within. But many of the pieces are missing, and we can approach the subject only tangentially. At the time, society's attitude, hence that of the unwed couple itself, was undergoing a change, and premarital cohabitation seems to be progressively less associated with slavery and Afro-Mexican miscegenation.[28] Around 1600, almost 75 percent of Afro-Mexicans (primarily slaves) were illegitimate, and this group alone accounts for more than half of the offspring—but only one-third of those baptized. At the two extremes of

Table 4. Population of Guadalajara
Legitimacy and Ethnic Origins, 1692–93, 1698–1702

	Legitimate	Foundlings	% of foundlings	% among all foundlings
Españoles	411	263	39.0	27.2
Mestizos	124	93	42.9	9.6
Mulattoes	248	381	60.6	39.4
Other castas	31	22	41.5	2.3
Blacks	5	4	44.4	0.4
Indians	22	22	50.0	2.3
Not determined	204	182	47.2	18.8
TOTAL	1,045	967	48.1	

Source: Archivo del Sagrario Metropolitano de Guadalajara, Baptismal Books. This table appeared in Thomas Calvo, "Concubinato y mestizaje," p. 211.

the social spectrum, Spaniards and Indians were the mainstay of stability and formalism. Toward 1700, however, the features of the young illegitimate child were less marked, even growing lighter. The observer looking at a young creole might now wonder: legitimate or illegitimate? (See table 4.)

At the beginning of the eighteenth century, between 1720 and 1730, we witness a contradictory evolution in the practice of concubinage. On the one hand it lost some of its negative connotations. It would be premature to assume the disappearance of concubines and illegitimates, a considerable segment of the population. At the same time, however, the church began to succeed in imposing its tridentine model of marriage on the population. The rates of illegitimacy begin to decline significantly.

A scrutiny of the attitudes toward the "end product" of concubinage, the child itself, may allow us to understand the direct impact of this situation. Generally speaking, attitudes about illegitimate children were ambiguous. If since the early Middle Ages the church discouraged illegitimacy in candidates for the priesthood, it did not really make an issue of it and, at least until the end of the seventeenth century, kept its doors partially open by means of subtle distinctions.[29] The position adopted by the crown was equally confused. In the sixteenth century, faced with a critical mestizo problem, its main concern was the social assimilation of the offspring of the conquistadors and Indian women. Thus, in 1591 it authorized the Viceroy of Mexico to legitimize the "natural and bastard" children of mixed blood. Later on, influenced by the fear of certain jurists regarding an excess of mixed breeding, it rescinded that measure with a firm ban in 1625 on legitimization in the Indies of "children not born to married couples."[30] Baptismal records, and doubtless public opinion in Guadalajara as well, reflect this shift, for around this time illegitimate or bastard children became "offspring of unknown parents," thus putting a damper on possible subsequent legitimization.

These tergiversations, which have a bearing on principles, leave enough flexibility to cover every possible contingency, starting with examples of obvious social success. Honor to whom honor is due. Bernardo de Balbuena, natural son of one of the oldest settlers of New Galicia, troubador of the "Mexican springtime," later became bishop of Puerto Rico without any problem. Others who succeeded were more humble, such as the priest, natural son of a peninsular deceased in Guadalajara in 1680, or the *bachiller* Nicolás Xoares, local physician and "son of unknown parents."[31]

But, in trying to prove too much one runs the risk of losing sight of the contemporaries' real misgivings about illegitimacy, which was something that weighed very heavily on the future of children, and on society, but first in the very heart of the family. Their potential share of the family inheritance reflected their inferior status. A nonlegitimized child born out of wedlock might inherit the entire patrimony unless opposed by a legitimate heir, but even then he/she faced considerable obstacles.[32] The inheritance left by Captain Pedro de Anda, who died intestate in January 1619, is from many angles exemplary, although it is only indirectly relevant to Guadalajara, since this New Galician was a resident rancher at Sierra de Pinos.[33] His three natural daughters were first obliged to submit evidence that they were

> the natural children of the aforesaid Captain Pedro de Anda, (who) brought them up in his household, educating them, feeding them, and marrying them off; and that they had always heard the said Captain Pedro de Anda say that as his daughters they would inherit all of his estate since he had earned it and

worked to provide them with dowries and that they would inherit it in equal shares.[34]

They were also forced to rebut the claims of other relatives, particularly those of their uncle, Estevan de Anda, natural half-brother of the deceased; and of María Ortiz, fruit of Pedro's love affair with a slave women. Her indignant half-sisters did not agree with her inheriting from their father, dryly arguing that "for reasons established by the law, the aforesaid (María), if she were his daughter—which we deny—is barred from inheriting, being, as she is, the daughter of a black slave." It ill-behooved them, as the daughters of an Indian woman, to quote the law. The attack on the daughter fell like an ax from the pen of the district attorney responsible for "defending" the estate of the deceased. He dismissed the uncle, made no mention of María, and declared about the three sisters:

> and had they not been acknowledged as [the deceased's] natural daughter, they would receive only one-fifth of the estate and nothing else, and this is because they neither should nor can enjoy the same privilege as the legitimate children, as this would be tantamount to becoming their equals.

Having received most of the estate in trust with the complicity of the local authorities, Estevan de Anda managed to delay the final sale until 1631. His own son-in-law was the buyer, paying 2,400 pesos with a down payment of some 1,000 pesos to the tax collector. The daughters of the deceased, married to poor men, widowed, or not yet of age, could do nothing to stave off this usurpation. This epilogue shows how precarious the status of natural children was, despite all the love their parents might shower on them. The few letters from Pedro de Anda to which I had access are brimming over with tenderness and solicitude about his daughters. However, such circumstances as the absence of a will, the greed of all parties, and the natural weakness of the bereft young girls contributed to their undoing. The stigma of illegitimacy was adduced by the vultures—the bastard Estevan and the tax collector—as the final pretext to disinherit them.

The illegitimate child might also find a rival in the guise of the church. This was the case of the daughter of María de Guillén—herself born under irregular circumstances—who had to be content with the crumbs when her mother donated her house and shop, the bulk of her estate, to various religious institutions. Truly, the sacrifice was mitigated by the maternal offer of "God's blessing and my own," but that was the sum and substance of the unhappy girl's inheritance.[35] There being legitimate heirs, the illegitimate child received, at best, a sixth of the estate. In 1693, a merchant divided his worldly goods between his wife (five-sixths) and his natural son (one-sixth). The same formula was adopted by notary Pedro de Agundis, this time in the case of two daughters. The portion of the illegitimate one was limited to the one-sixth recognized by the law. And yet the young girl appeared to have been warmly accepted by her father's legitimate family, with whom she lived and was raised with all the love due to a daughter, as attested in a statement signed in 1695 by the notary's wife herself. It is true that the statement in question underscored the distance between the two heiresses, for the legitimate sister's dowry was 2,311 pesos, whereas our heroine had to be content with 550.[36] When the illegitimate offspring competed with the various statutory heirs, their portion was still smaller, often bordering on alms. When he died in 1671, ensign (*alférez*) Francisco de Mendoza divided his estate among his four legitimate offspring, leaving only 300 pesos to his natural daughter, scarcely more than the amount needed to bury him and cover his several pious bequests.[37]

All these examples apply exclusively to the so-called white population, since this research is based on their wills. Among the mestizos, as I suggested earlier, the stigma of illegitimacy was less distinct, and the status of the natural child more privileged. Hence precautions were taken by numerous mulatto women who left a written record of their last wishes, bequeathing their property, however small, to their natural children. Sometimes the rules governing such transfers were the reverse of the whites' practice. Juan de Arteaga made his illegitimate daughter Brixida his universal heiress at the expense of his wife. He himself had been born in wedlock. But he was also a mulatto, and perhaps when the crucial moment arrived, it was the second determinant—vector of more spontaneous forces, less rooted in the incipient social, religious, or any other tradition—that ruled him.[38]

It was not a question of inheritance alone, however. To stop there would be an oversimplification, assigning purely materialistic bases to highly complex phenomena. A case in point is the complaint lodged with the *juez de residencia* in September 1650 by Diego de Vargas, accusing the president of the audiencia, Fernández de Baeza, and his wife of literally kidnapping Vargas's daughter, then six years old, keeping her working for them without wages and abusing her for seven years. It is rather surprising, however, to learn that the child had not been living with him, but staying with a widow at the time. The reasons he adduced are quite obscure at first glance: "so that she could be company [for the widow] out of proper respect." The mystery is cleared up by his wedding certificate, dated a month earlier. For fifteen years, the child was merely the natural daughter of a couple who, for economic and social reasons in addition of lack of interest, paid little attention to her. As such, she was put out to work, and shunted from pillar to post working for others, and her flesh attested to the brutal treatment she received. The adolescent Juana de Vargas finally became the legitimate daughter, and her father and his witness averred that he had always recognized her as his child. But I wonder whether those factors effaced the physical and moral scars she bore.[39]

Thus far I have avoided the use of the word "marginal" to describe the illegitimate population, and yet it comes readily to mind. Can half of the population be "marginal"? Did not its own behavior set aside the illegitimately born, particularly in the face of marriage, the institution that was in spite of everything one of the pillars of the established order? (See table 3.) The term "marginal" may be assumed to refer to the nonwhite free population, born in Guadalajara around 1690–94. Forty-five percent of the baptisms from this group were out-of-wedlock baptisms. Having grown up outside the institution of marriage, most of these children, in turn, slipped through the meshes of the matrimonial net, since they accounted for a mere 23 percent of the newlyweds in 1715–19[40] (see table 5).

In the Manner of a Conclusion: Where Is Family Cohesion?

What good are all these statistics? Why bring up so many tragedies, petty actions and anonymous fates unless we can answer the essential question posed by our study: What happens in the midst of all this to the family cell and its most precious attribute, the warmth that is the product of its cohesion and tenderness?

In this effervescent colonial slaveholding society—partly of Iberian origin and revealing the corresponding influences, brimming over with vitality and stirred by Brownian movements—cohesion was difficult to maintain.[41] Periodically, the crown sent summons to

Table 5. Legitimacy of Couples Marrying at the Sagrario of Guadalajara, 1715–19

Legitimate	Unknown Parents	"Natural" Children	No Information	Foundlings	Total
496	116	20	11	5	648
(76.5%)	(17.9%)	(3.1%)	(1.7%)	(0.8%)	

Source: ASMG, Books of Marriage. Widows and slaves were excluded. The couples are natives of either Guadalajara or unknown provenances.

the courts to ship back to Spain certain husbands who had forgotten their peninsular spouses.[42] Conversely, María de Herrera married an Iberian who soon deserted her to go back home. Captain Juan Baptista, deputy mayor of Xeres in 1648, had left a wife and children in China [the Philippines?] and was subtly blackmailed for it by a priest who was himself living in sin. Others went even further and became polygamists. Francisco de Lagandara, a sculptor, fickle of heart and fleet of foot, had a wife in every port: first in Sevile, where he was born, then in Rome, and finally in Guatemala. He was about to repeat the offense in Guadalajara when he was denounced.[43] One of the oldest Guadalajara wills on record provides a striking, but not unusual, example of the dissolution of a homestead in this milieu straddling two and sometimes three continents. In 1575, Alonso de Segura, a native of Segura de León, wondered about his progeny on his deathbed. One of his sons had been married in Mexico, but the father was not too sure what had happened to the others, particularly "another son, the youngest—I do not know his name because he was quite small when I left him in the city of Se[ville?] when I came to these parts."[44]

At the other end of the chain, Bartolomé Bennassar's research in the records of the Spanish Inquisition give us an inkling: the husband and father of Claudia and María Chaves, respectively, sailed off to the Indies and was never heard of again. Left to fend for themselves, the two women had no choice but to live, fairly well at that, off their charms in Toledo.[45]

Because of the mixing it fosters, the promiscuity it imposes, and the fundamental imbalance it creates between men and women, the urban milieu itself spawns illegitimacy. Most importantly, the surrounding countryside already showed evidence of the corrupting power of the city, a modern Babylon whither people came during the Holy Week and Easter to find cut-rate absolution. Pedro Rochin chose the city for his escapades, seeking to make them more plausible to a young and credulous country girl from Ahuacatlan.[46]

In the orthodox view, corruption and instability are the end products of concubinage and fluid marital patterns. But the undeniable and indispensable flexibility of the urban family may have well prevented tragedies from too strict an application of tridentine precepts when society itself had not yet stabilized. From the outset, the church had imposed a constraining and indissoluble model of marriage on all of New Spain. In the mining territories of the north, the influx of uprooted natives, *forasteros,* led to widespread concubinage and even adultery. What powered the immense tide of wanton living? It was driven by rejection, frustration, and flight on the one hand, and exploitation and inequities on the other. Since the communities of origin could not accept extramarital cohabitation, emigration was the only solution. In the north, the need for men, and women in turn, served as a suction pump whose least concern was the stability so greatly desired by the church. These extremes were perhaps what the urban world, easy-going and tolerant of mixed-blood populations, managed to avoid.[47]

But then, the essential question arises as to the relation between consecrated union and family: does the latter suffer from the depressed status of the former? Apparently so, for the indissoluble nature of the Christian marriage may be a fine guarantee of family stability, at least at the outset. There was no dearth of matrimonial failures, or of husbands breaking their vows: don Luis Hurtado of Puebla, numerous Iberians, the Mazapil Indian women, and scores of others. That failure may assume a wide range of guises, however, and curiously the most dramatic example was to be found in the family of don Luis Hurtado. The couple formed by doña Jacinta de Vidarte y Pardo and don Pedro Hurtado de Mendoza foundered on the young wife's excessive self-imposed physical penance. When she died at the age of twenty-three, the impact on her husband was so great that he resigned as alcalde of Puebla and became a priest.[48] Unquestionably, the failure and flight that brought certain marriages to an end were all the more irreparable because the sanctification of marriages made them indissoluble.

The family should constitute an affectionate household. It is true that we have encountered passion, especially because it was frustrated, as for don Luis Hurtado. We have even seen instances of homicidal mania when, in the case of the clergy, the union was impossible and sacrilegious.[49] But, it is in marriage that esteem and confidence are to be found. No one can doubt that doña María de Angulo and Diego Cabello Sotilli, her "dear and esteemed spouse," were a devoted couple, judging from the will of the dying woman.[50] Such affection was doubtless predicated on social and economic realities as much as, or more than, on sanctification. Was not the agreement between Inés de Saavedra and her husband based primarily on "the sweat and the toil" they expended together to build up their meager estate?[51] A number of couples living in concubinage must have found themselves in less sheltered emotional shores; otherwise why seek the haven of marriage sanctification, and ratification, at deathbed? Marriage never gave an ironclad guarantee of affection, let alone stability, and battered wives were legion, wife-beating being one of the most common events in the city's everyday life. Such violence must literally have rotted away conjugal ties, bringing in its wake resentment and a desire for vengeance, if we are to believe some thirty-three depositions presented to the Inquisition. Nearly a fifth of the denunciations involved practices designed to subdue a husband, a son-in-law, or a particularly irascible master.[52]

In the end, a relative indifference to marital sanctification developed. This autonomy from socioreligious rules reflects greater solidity than would appear to be indicated by our statistics on illegitimacy and orphans.[53] It is significant that no orphanages (*casa cuna*) were needed here. The combination of hospitality and charity with the feeling for the family, all deeply rooted in Hispanic society, explains the presence of orphans in numerous families. Those children at times achieved a status superior to that of "natural" children begotten of slaves or maids. Agustín de Gamboa, the most important merchant in Guadalajara in the seventeenth century, had no legitimate offspring, but he sheltered seven girls whom he married to trusted men.[54] If the church tried to guide and direct, it did not, as an institution, have to make up for family shortcomings in this domain. Certain indicators tend to show that the situation of children was more enviable than that of their Western counterparts of the same era, hence the far more limited recourse to wet-nursing. Female heads of households provided an additional guarantee of stability.

We have found paternal love expressed with the utmost clarity, even by particularly unpolished men. One of them was Captain Pedro de Anda, shaped by the terrible reality of the Chichimeca wars. His main concern was always for the three daughters whom he had left alone at the *estancia* and whom he showered with advice in his letters from afar. The example is all the more interesting because there was no wife at home, and single-parent households were not the exclusive prerogative of women. For some men a sense of family and love of children was stronger than their assumed proverbial thoughtlessness.[55]

In another remarkable instance of a single parent family, Gaspar de los Reyes, an Indian from Mezquitan, near Guadalajara, wrote to his brother from San Luis Potosí in 1708, begging him to find "my daughter Manuela . . . and if by chance she is lost and is no longer a maiden, she shall not lose my blessing. She is my daughter, and I love her. What else can I do? It must be my fault, for having left them."[56] A trained artisan, he worked as a stonecutter at the Jesuit church in San Luis. He had manifestly assimilated the Spanish system of values, evident in the concepts and words he used, but was able to put his fatherly love before the Hispanic obsession with the stigma of lost virginity (*mancilla*).

That love is also evident in the information gathered about various neo-Galician sanctuaries, particularly that of San Juan de los Lagos, whose first miracle brought a mortally wounded little girl back to life. Before 1668, thirteen of the sixty-four miracles attributed to San Juan involved children, suggesting that the Virgin worshipped there was particularly sympathetic with the grief expressed by mothers over the small lifeless bodies.

Several years ago, fascinated by the demographic reality and the baroque rate of illegitimacy, I wondered whether it made sense to speak about "family" in such a disjointed environment. Today I think that an element of cohesion always existed: sometimes it was the father, almost always the mother, not to mention relatives. The family model discussed here, despite its archaic nature, did not differ much from the contemporary model, combining instability and love in degrees that the traditional Western family never experienced.

Notes

1. See Philippe Ariès, *Centuries of Childhood: A Social History of Family Life* (New York: Knopf, 1962); Peter Laslett, *Household and Family in Past Time* (Cambridge: Cambridge University Press, 1972); Jean Louis Flandrin, *Le Sexe et l'Occident: Evolution des attitudes et des comportements* (Paris: Seuil, 1981), and *Families in Former Times: Kinship, Household and Sexuality in Early Modern France* (New York: Cambridge University Press, 1979); Elisabeth Badinter, *L'amour en plus: Histoire de l'amour maternel* (Paris: Flammarion, 1981). See also the special number of *Annales, Economies, Sociétés, Civilisations* on Family and Society, July–August 1972.

2. Among the pioneering works, see those of Gilberto Freyre, *The Masters and the Slaves* (New York: Samuel Putnam, 1946); Mentalité Seminar, especially, *Familia y sexualidad en Nueva España* (Mexico City: Fondo de Cultura Económica, 1982); Gonzalo Aguirre Beltrán, *Medicina y magia* (Mexico City: Instituto Nacional Indigenista, 1973); Asunción Lavrin, "Aproximación histórica al tema de la sexualidad en el México colonial," *Encuentro* 2, no.5 (October–December 1984): 29–39; Thomas Calvo, "Familia y registro parroquial: El caso tapatío en el siglo XVII," *Relaciones* 3, no.10 (Spring 1982): 53–67. See also the essays by Sergio Ortega Noriega, Cristina Ruiz Martínez, Ana María Atondo Rodríguez, María Elena Cortés Jácome, Dolores Enciso Rojas, and François Giraud in *De la santidad a la perversión*, ed. Sergio Ortega Noriega (Mexico City: Editorial Grijalbo, 1986).

3. I have translated the term *español* as creole or criollo, at the request of the author. Although the term criollo is unusual for the seventeenth century, it was not totally unknown then. It was used, for example, to differentiate *bozales* or newly imported slaves from those born in Mexico: *negros criollos*. In that century the term criollo signified "of local origin"—ed.

4. Thomas Calvo, "Familles mexicaines au XVIIe siècle: Une tentative de reconstruction," *Annales de Démographie Historique* (1984), pp. 149–74.

5. Another work on the age of marriage in New Spain is that of C. A. Rabell, "El patrón de nupcialidad en una parroquia rural novohispana: San Luis de La Paz, Guanajuato, Siglo XVIII," in *Investigación Demográfica en México* (Mexico City: Sociedad Mexicana de Demografía, 1978), p. 426. In the same book, see Alejandra Moreno Toscano, "Algunas características de la población urbana: Ciudad de Mexico, Siglos XVIII–XIX," p. 412. Robert McCaa offers information on late-eighteenth-century Parral in "*Calidad, Clase* and Marriage in Colonial Mexico: The Case of Parral, 1788–90," *Hispanic American Historical Review* 64, no.3 (August 1984): 477–502. For the age of marriage in some western European countries, see Alan MacFarlane, *Mar-*

riage and Love in England, 1300–1840 (New York: Basil Blackwell, 1986), pp. 216–17; Lawrence Stone, *The Family, Sex and Marriage in England, 1500–1800* (New York: Harper and Row, 1979), pp. 37–45; Annie Molinié-Bertrand, "Se marier en castille au XVIè siècle," *Ibérica* 3 (1981): 233–45. Women in Spain married earlier than in other areas of Europe. For comparative purposes within Spanish America, see Eduardo Cavieres, "Formas de vida y estructuras demográficas de una sociedad colonial: San Felipe en la segunda mitad del siglo XVIII," *Cuadernos de Historia* (Santiago de Chile) 3 (July 1983): 90. In Chile, Cavieres found, the median age of marriage for women was 22.1 and for men 26.1. Several of these references were provided by Asunción Lavrin.

6. On the significance of the marriage age in any civilization, see Pierre Chaunu, "Démographie historique et système de civilisation," *Histoire quantitative, histoire serielle* (Paris: Armand Colin, 1978), pp. 202–15.

7. The general picture is not valid for the indigenous population, given the limited number of their cases. The high degree of integration of the Indians belonging to the Sagrario shows in their tendency to pair more with mulattoes than with their rural counterpoints. The rural Indians married earlier too (14–18 years of age), if we trust the rare mentions of age at marriage in the adjacent parish of San Francisco Analco in that same period. See Archivo Público de Analco, Books of Marriages, 1 and 2.

8. Biblioteca Pública del Estado de Jalisco (hereafter BPEJ), Archivo de la Real Audiencia, Ramo Judicial Civil, caja 57, exp. 9.

9. See Calvo, "Familia y registro parroquial," p. 56; Lavrin, "Aproximación histórica," p. 38.

10. Archivo General de Indias, Sevile (hereafter AGI), Guadalajara, 8, Carta de los franciscanos de Guadalajara al rey, 20 noviembre 1616. This testimony should be compared with that sent to Madrid in 1584 by the mestizo chief of one of the most important encomiendas of Tunja, New Granada. See Juan Friede, *Fuentes documentales para la historia del Nuevo Reino de Granada: Desde la instalación de la Real Audiencia en Santa Fé*, 8 vols. (Bogotá: Banco Popular, 1976), 8:244–45. Note also the accusations raised in 1550 by the president of the Audiencia in Guatemala against the conquistadors. See Pilar Sánchez Ochoa, *Los hidalgos de Guatemala* (Seville: Seminario de Antropología Americana, Universidad de Sevilla, 1976), p. 107.

11. Archivo de Instrumentos Públicos de Guadalajara (hereafter AIPG), Protocolos del notario Thomas de Ascoide, 1, fol. 213.

12. BPEJ, Real Audiencia, Ramo Judicial Civil, box 141, expediente 15–1545.

13. Thomas Calvo, "Concubinato y mestizaje en el medio urbano: El caso

de Guadalajara en el siglo XVII," *Revista de Indias* 44, no.173 (January–June 1984): 204–12.

14. Barring a demographic crisis, the correlation between baptisms and marriages should be much higher. For example, in Córdoba, Spain, it was 4 in the sixteenth century (José Ignacio Fortea Pérez, *Córdoba en el siglo* XVI [Córdoba: Publicaciones del Monte de Piedad de Córdoba, 1981], p. 162).

15. María de los Angeles Rodríguez and Thomas Calvo, "Sobre la práctica del aborto en el Occidente de Mexico: Documentos coloniales (siglos XVI–XVII)," *Trace* 10 (July 1986): 32–38.

16. Archivo Histórico del Arzobispado de Guadalajara (hereafter AHAG), Hojas Sueltas, Padrón eclesiástico de Guadalajara-Analco, 1679. We will have to increase those numbers by one unit to account for the children (*párvulos*) not counted by the ecclesiastic uthorities.

17. In the census the proportion of simple communicants (preadolescents) is 16.4 percent. It is very weak (8.8%) in the households of two or three persons headed by women.

18. See Calvo, "Familia y registro parroquial," p. 66 and note 33.

19. All the above quotations are from AHAG, Expediente de Visitas Varias, Seventeenth Century, Visita pastoral de la Villa de Xerez, 1648, fol. 1v and 2r; AGI, Guadalajara, 32, exp. 22, Anonymous letter addressed to don Thomas de Baldes, of the council from San Antonio Teguie, 24 April 1678; AGI, Guadalajara, 8, Letter of Arévalo Sedeño to the council, 31 October 1611. On pastoral visits and information gathered on the sexual mores of the population, see essay by Kathy Waldron in this volume.

20. Thomas Gage, *Nuevo reconocimiento de las Indias Occidentales* (Mexico City: Editorial Xochitl, 1947), pp. 38–39; Gonzalo Aguirre Beltrán, *La población negra de México* (Mexico City: Fondo de Cultura Económica, 1972), pp. 262–63; Archivo General de la Nación, Mexico City (hereafter AGN), Inquisición, vol. 339, fol. 546; vol. 376, fol. 155; AGI, Guadalajara, 40, expediente 14, Letter to the king from don Pedro Lomelin de Zevallos, of Guadalajara, 1 August 1692. On sexual witchcraft, see also the essay by Ruth Behar in this volume.

21. This quick analysis is based on thirty-three spontaneous denunciations that implicated several hundreds of persons. See AGN, Inquisición, 335, 339, 346, 484, 486.

22. The colonial image of women placed them between the schizophrenic choices of witch or saint. Another model offered to describe her was that of the Immaculate Conception.

23. According to Daisy Rípodas Ardanaz, one of the explanations for con-

cubinage among those in the higher rungs of the social ladder was the prohibition against marrying in their region imposed on royal bureaucrats. See her *El matrimonio en Indias: Realidad social y regulación jurídica* (Buenos Aires: Conicet, 1977). In the case of Guadalajara, with the exception of a treasurer of the royal exchequer, this argument does not apply. See Calvo, "Concubinato y mestizaje," pp. 59–61. On the subject of unwed mothers and out-of-wedlock births, see essay by Ann Twinam in this volume.

24. AGI, Guadalajara, 23. Around 1689 two other comparable affairs brought the two authorities into confrontation. See AGI, Guadalajara, 25, exp. 6.

25. Francisco Orozco y Jiménez, *Colección de documentos históricos inéditos o muy raros, referentes al arzobispado de Guadalajara* (Guadalajara: 1922–27), 3:233–35; AGI, Guadalajara, 6, Letter of Oidor Altamirano, 6 June 1585.

26. The phenomenom of *charivari* has been studied in France by Christian Desplat, *Charivari en Gascogne: La "Morale des Peuples" du* XVè au XXè siècle (Paris: Berger-Levrault, 1982); André Burguière, "The Charivari and Religious Repression in France during the Ancien Régime," in *Family and Sexuality in French History*, ed. Robert Wheaton and Tamara K. Hareven (Philadelphia: University of Pennsylvania Press, 1980), pp. 84–110; Natalie Davis, "The Reasons of Misrule," in *Society and Culture in Early Modern France* (Stanford: Stanford University Press, 1975), pp. 97–123.

27. BPEJ, Real Audiencia, Judicial Civil, box 4, exp. 8–46; box 10, exp. 4–136.

28. See Calvo, "Concubinato y mestizaje."

29. See Francisco Morales, *Ethnic and Social Background of the Franciscan Friars in Seventeenth-Century Mexico* (Washington, D.C.: American Academy of Franciscan History, 1983), pp. 7–9, 18.

30. See Juan de Solórzano Pereira, *Política indiana*, 2 vols. (Madrid: Ediciones Atlas, 1972), 1:Book 2, chapter 30, paragraphs 19, 35, 38. See also Eucario López, *Cedulario de la Nueva Galicia* (Guadalajara, 1971), cédula 511.

31. ASMG, Burial Book no. 2, fol. 76v; Marriage Book no. 3, fol. 93v.

32. See Nicolás de Yrolo Calar, *Primera carta de la política de escripturas* (Mexico City: López Dávalos, 1605), fol. 84v. "The natural child may inherit, in the absence of legitimate children or grandchildren."

33. On this figure, see Thomas Calvo, "Les travaux et les peines d'un *estanciero* mexicain du XVIIè siècle," *Etudes Mexicaines* (Perpignan) 4 (1981): 37–47. On illegitimacy, it is useful to consult *Las Siete Partidas*, trans. Samuel Parsons Scott (Chicago, New York, Washington: Comparative Bureau of

the American Bar Association, by Commerce Clearing House, 1931), *Partida Quarta,* title 15, pp. 952–55.

34. BPEJ, Bienes de Difuntos, XVII century, leg. 1, exp. 16, fol. 49r.

35. AIPG, Notary Nicolás del Castillo, 3, fol. 29–31.

36. ASMG, Burials, book 3, fols. 59r, 145v; AIPG, Notary Nicolás del Castillo, 3, fol. 262.

37. ASMG, Burials, Book no. 2, fol. 21v.

38. AIPG, Notary Thomas de Orendain, 1, fols. 3v–4. On the black population of Guadalajara, see Asunción Lavrin, "Perfil histórico de la población negra, esclava y libre, en Guadalajara, 1635–1699," *Boletín del Archivo Histórico de Jalisco* 6, no.1 (January–April 1982): 2–7.

39. AGI, Escribanía de Cámara, 386.

40. Lavrin arrives at the same conclusion using other sources for eighteenth-century Guadalajara. See "Aproximación."

41. Thomas Calvo, "Guadalajara y su región en el siglo XVII: Aspectos demográficos," *Encuentro* 1, no. 4 (July–September): pp. 5–6.

42. Eucario López, *Cedulario,* Cédulas 128, 229, 460, 966.

43. AIPG, Notary Nicolás del Castillo, 3, fol. 253; AHAG, Expediente de Visitas Varias, vol. 17, Visita de Jeres, fol. 6; AGN, Inquisición, 346, exp. 14, fol. 544.

44. BPEJ, Bienes de difuntos, XVI century, leg. 2, exp. 5.

45. Bartolomé Bennassar, *The Spanish Character* (Berkeley: University of California Press, 1979), p.194.

46. AGN, Inquisición, 339, fols. 601–2; 335, fol. 20r.

47. These conclusions are inspired by the reflections of Philippe Ariès in "The Indissoluble Marriage," in *Western Sexuality,* ed. Philippe Ariès and André Béjin (London: Basil Blackwell Ltd., 1985), pp. 140–57. On some aspects of frontier life, it will suffice to recall the 1608 visit of Lic. Gaspar de la Fuente to the mines of Mazapil. There he "found many married Indian women, most of whom had left their husbands, living in concubinage with the men with whom they had escaped and who pretended to be their husbands." I thank Jean Pierre Berthe for this information, found in AGI, Contaduría, 874, Ramo 2. For further information on the marriage and illegitimacy patterns of the northern mining areas of Mexico, see Marcello Carmagnani, "Demografía y sociedad: La estructura de los centros mineros del norte de Mexico, 1600–1720," *Historia Mexicana* 21, no.3 (January–March 1972): 419–59.

48. Mariano de la Mota Padilla, *Historia del reino de Nueva Galicia* (Guadalajara: Instituto Nacional de Antropología e Historia/Universidad de Guadalajara, 1973), pp. 323–26. A similar fate, according to popular tradition, was suffered by the daughter of the oidor don Francisco de Pareja, who could not

stand being removed from the convent to be married. See Mota Padilla, *Historia,* p. 337.

49. Luis Páez Brotchie, *La Nueva Galicia a través de su viejo archivo judicial* (Mexico City: Antigua Librería Robredo, 1940), p. 40.

50. AIPG, Notary Tomás de Orendain, 9, fol. 60.

51. AIPG, Notary Hernando Enríquez del Castillo, 1, fol. 106.

52. On the causes of marital discord see the essay by Beatriz Nizza da Silva in this volume. Other aspects of marriage are dealt in the essays by Asunción Lavrin and Richard Boyer.

53. See also Calvo, "Familia y registro parroquial, pp. 53–67.

54. AIPG, Notary Tomás de Ascoide, 2, fols. 328–41. In 1682, Gamboa also freed and endowed Ana de Gamboa for her marriage. She was the daughter of one of his slaves, possibly by him. See Notary José L. Ramírez, 1, fol. 155v., and Asunción Lavrin, "Perfil histórico." On foundlings, see Cayetano Reyes G., comp., "Expósitos e hidalgos: La polarización social de la Nueva España," in *Boletín del Archivo General de la Nación* (Mexico) 5, no.16 (April–June 1981).

55. Thomas Calvo, "Les travaux et les peines d'un *estanciero* mexicain au début du XVIIè siècle, "*Etudes mexicaines* no. 4 (1981): 37–47.

56. BPEJ, Real Audiencia, Ramo Judicial Civil, Box 119, exp. 8–1281.

María Beatriz Nizza Da Silva

Divorce in Colonial Brazil: The Case of São Paulo

The separation of a married couple was an action that the Roman Catholic Church opposed in principle and allowed only under the most strenuous circumstances. Marriage was an indissoluble bond, a sacrament performed before God, by a minister of God, and to be ended only by God. Yet, as with any other human institution, contingencies and failures called for a certain amount of flexibility. How the bond could be relaxed, or even dissolved, is the subject of this essay, which uses the Captaincy of São Paulo, in colonial Brazil, as its historical scenario.

In both Portugal and colonial Brazil the Roman Catholic Church allowed the separation of estranged couples, provided that neither of the spouses marry again. These separations were called "divorces," and they were carried out by ecclesiastical tribunals following precise procedures of ecclesiastical canons. In the Captaincy of São Paulo those divorce suits, rare during the first centuries of colonization, became more frequent in the late colonial period. This study is based on 88 suits of the 225 preserved in the archives of the diocese of São Paulo. They reveal the variety of matrimonial conflicts that took place in the long period between 1700 and 1822.[1]

The chronological boundary chosen for the beginning of this study does not imply that there were no divorce suits in São Paulo before then.[2] Although we know of their existence, their records have not yet been located. The analysis of a greater number of suits at the beginning of the nineteenth century is justified not only by the greater number of divorces in that period but also because at the end of the eighteenth century a new type of uncontested divorce by "mutual consent," or even on "amicable" terms, appeared in colonial society. Contested separations based on accusations of mistreatment (*sevícias*) or adultery, or both, continued to take place, but many married couples began choosing a mutual agreement about the separation of property or the custody of the children. All evidence indicates that divorces by consent, in addition to being cheaper, were simpler to process and easier to obtain from the ecclesiastical tribunals.

At the Council of Trent (1545–63) the Roman Catholic church had reiterated its "divorce" policy by stating that "consorts may be separated, either from bed or table for a definite or indefinite period of time."[3] Canonical legislation on divorce was first gathered in colonial Brazil in the *Constituições primeiras do arçebispado da Bahia (1720),* observed in the Captaincy of São Paulo. The spirit of the tridentine legislation was translated for lay use in the confessionals, which instructed the parish priests on the subject of divorce.[4] Theoretical causes (as when both spouses wished to enter into religion or fell into heresy) do not ever appear in the legal suits examined; mistreatment and adultery were the more frequently cited grounds for divorce by the pleading wives.

On the subject of physical mistreatment, the *Constituições* stated "that if out of hatred one consort treats the other so badly that his/her life is endangered by living together, or suffers grave inconveniences, the separation is just; or if the danger is so imminent that it may continue due to any delays, [in the administration of justice] the consort may separate by his/her own authority, and may not be restituted to the other."[5] Consequently, a mistreated wife could abandon the home if her life was endangered, but she had to resort to the vicar general to legalize and determine the length of her separation. As we will see later, in the mistreatment suits almost all wives petitioned for a perpetual separation, and the cases of reconciliation based on the husband's promise of better treatment were rare. The *Constituções,* however, made provisions for reconciliation. "And if the one who mistreats gives good assurances that no further mistreatment will be committed, the separation may end, and the couple will be restored to their previous marital life together."[6] Although in principle the granting of divorce for bad treatment was temporary, in practice it was perpetual, since the church did not explicitly determine the time that the consorts would remain separated.[7] A permanent separation, according to ecclesiastical law, was pertinent "if the wife committed adultery on the husband, or the husband on the wife."[8]

With the exception of those cases of separation by mutual consent, the woman always took the initiative in divorce suits. Female plaintiffs came not only from the urban centers, but from all over the Captaincy of São Paulo: from seaside towns such as Sãn Sebastião to inland ones such as Sorocaba or Itu, and even some distant towns such as Curitiba, Porto Feliz, and Areias. The feminization of the divorce process is manifest in another manner. Even though the church recognized several causes for separation, the allegation of mistreatment was so common that at the end of the colonial period, the formula for petitions simply proposed the one dealing with bad treatment. Since women most often suffered ill-treatment at the hands of the husband, the plaintiff was considered to belong to the female sex:

> The petitioner [*fulana*] states that she has been married to ——— [for—years] and has lived in his obedience and service, not giving him any reason for disliking her, but he still mistreats her, not only by not carrying out marital life but also by estranging himself completely, enjoying sensual pleasures [elsewhere], beating the plaintiff, and endangering her life with this mistreatment, of which faults he has not desisted despite her prudent requests. Since under such conditions rests the only legitimate means for divorce, the plaintiff desires to be deposited to secure that end, and requests Your Honor to order a deposit in an honest home. After this she will justify the mistreatment within the following twenty-four hours in order to proceed with the divorce suit and in the understanding that the accused is obliged to support her. And she entreats Y.H. to grant this request.[9]

All divorce suits began with a petition in this fashion. After a witness's inquiry, the vicar ordered the wife and any children under age to be deposited in the home of a person of good reputation, preferably one of her relatives, "with her bed, her clothing, her home paraphernalia, her jewels, and a slave for her service, if she has one."[10] The deposit was carried out by an ecclesiastic judge, but in those towns lacking one, the civil judge conducted the process after receiving a request from the ecclesiastic. A *depósito* consisted of having the woman live in somebody's home for the duration of the suit. She was not supposed to leave the home under any circumstances until authorized by the appropriate authorities.

The order for deposit initiated the divorce process and was followed by recording the home in which the plaintiff was deposited, and the objects she carried with her. This information allows the social identification of the plaintiff. In some petitions the women refer to their "good birth" or to the fact that they belonged to the "principal families" of the locality. The richer the woman, the greater the significance of that initial step, because she had to remove from the husband's house, and take with her, all the belongings she required to maintain her life-style. We can surmise the status as well as the preoccupation of a woman married to a powerful man in the town of Bragança, when she began her suit in 1819. She requested the officials to make her husband give her "a bed with its sheets, mattress, and all that is relative to the household such as towels, silver plate, and the slaves Ana and Francisco."[11] The absence of slaves or jewels in the deposit process suggests somebody without wealth, such as a woman who was deposited "with the clothes she was wearing, a bed, two spoons, two forks, and a silver knife."

The terms of confinement implicit in the deposit were not always respected. If we are to believe the surgeon major of the town of Itu, his wife had been deposited in the town of São Carlos but, "abusing the customs of the country," the respect owed to him as her husband, and the indulgence of her depositor, D. Maria Francisca de Camargo, was wandering around São Paulo and the towns of Parnaiba, Itu, and Sorocaba "without shame or decency, as a dissolute woman." "And because, despite the pending and unjust divorce, the supplicant still regards her as his wife and expects to continue to live with her after the final decision of the Supreme Tribunal . . . , he could not consent to her discredit on account of her arbitrary trips." Therefore, he requested that "she be removed from the deposit and placed with a qualified person in this city [Itu]."[12]

Any divorce petition by a woman had to have a "justification of ill-treatment," or a "justification of adultery," or both. At this stage of the process, and before the deposit, several persons were questioned as witnesses. In general they were men, relatives or neighbors of the couple, the number varying between three and eight. The witnesses were interrogated on the charges contained in the suit, although others could be introduced later by the plaintiff. Following an oath on the holy gospels, the witnesses gave "their names, surnames, age, country [*naturalidades*], civil state, occupation, life-style, and habit. They also had to declare any kinship ties (*compadrescos*) and personal feelings about the plaintiff or her husband. In their depositions they had to state whether their knowledge of the circumstances surrounding the divorce was direct or by hearsay. The questioning was carried out by the priest of the plaintiff's town of residence. He subsequently informed the vicar general on the quality and merit of the witnesses testimonies, using such expressions as "I certify and swear by the Holy Scriptures that I judge all the testimonies sworn during this inquiry to be trustworthy and impartial." In some cases the priest also sent his own opinion on the request of the woman and on the husband's behavior: "I certify that it is public knowledge that the accused is of the worst behavior and habits, a wanderer, a spendthrift and a libertine; the testimonies given in this summary are worthy of credit and faith."[13] In general, most testimonies confirmed the allegations of the plaintiff, but occasionally they were unfavorable, signaling the end of the process for her.

Once the justifying testimonials were completed, the woman recalled her husband to answer the charges. Male responses to divorce charges varied. When the testimonies left no margin for doubts on the culpability of the husband, he did not trouble himself to appear in court, and allowed the suit to proceed by default. In some instances men appeared before the authorities, disclaiming opposition but protesting "having to pay for costs." The husband could, however, oppose the suit, defending himself from the accusations by denying or arguing against them. It was not uncommon that in adultery suits the husband returned the accusation of adultery against the woman, since if it could be proved, the divorce could not take place.

Divorce suits did not always have a resolution. The litigation could be abandoned on account of the weakness of the claims. This was the case of a resident of Vila Bela da Princesa, who claimed that her husband chased her "with the most indecent words."[14] On other occasions the couple reconciled through the good offices of the vicar general, and the wife accepted the husband's promise of good behavior and his pledge to stop mistreating her. In adultery cases reconciliation was rare, but in one case a woman who had accused her husband of wanting her to make a living "with her body," in disregard of the offense to God, agreed to return to his company when he promised to stop wandering and begin working.[15] Should the husband fail to fulfill his promises, the woman could reinitiate the divorce suit at the point in which it had been dropped.

Why is that men, except on rare occasions, did not begin divorce processes? Moral and social rules guiding the behavior of the sexes endorsed the voicing of charges by women against men but inhibited a similar action for those men who might be chafing under dominant women. To make such a situation public, let alone make it the base of divorce proceedings, was unthinkable. No man would accuse a woman of mistreating him, for fear of losing face before the community. According to a popular saying, "Women and the ground are to be stepped on," but "The woman who fells a man dies by the devil."[16] In other words, the husband could "correct" the wife, as long as he did it moderately and for a just reason, such as her disobedience or her refusal to fulfill her wifely duties, but the woman should never attack her husband physically. This was not well regarded by society.

Separations based on female adultery were unnecessary, since the Portuguese laws favored their punishment without resort to divorce. According to the *Ordenações do reino*, the husband could accuse the wife of adultery, but the contrary could not take place. In theory, punishment was rigorous: the woman and her lover could be punished with death, and the woman's properties, in the absence of children, would pass to the husband. If the husband pardoned the woman, her lover could be punished with perpetual exile; if her lover was pardoned by the husband, he could be exiled in Africa for seven years.[17] In Brazil, nevertheless, the punishment of female adultery was less rigid than the law prescribed, as suggested by a document in which a resident of the town of Bragança stated to be involved in an adultery suit against his wife and requested that she be jailed in town.[18]

The fact remains, however, that the fate of an adulterous woman was in the hands of her husband and subject to his violence or his inclination to forgiveness. Furthermore, the laws of the kingdom did not punish the husband who, under the influence of passion, took justice in his hands and killed the offending woman, as long as he could offer proof of her adultery. It is symptomatic that the only process of divorce undertaken by a man was that of a resident of the city of São Paulo who feared for his life under the witchcraft practices of his wife.[19] In this case, the husband had traveled from São Paulo to Guaratingueta to work as a guilder in the chapel of Nossa Senhora da Aparecida, taking his wife with him "to live as a well-married man." There, she began a "friendship" with the hermit of the chapel. Having been found in the forest engaged in the "sinful act," the woman confessed to her husband that she met with the hermit when he was at work in the chapel or absent from home. When her husband reprehended her for her behavior, she threatened "to take his life, even if she had to use witchcraft." The husband began to suffer from a serious sickness and thought of calling a black man "who had curative expertise"; anticipating him, his wife tried to convince the black man to poison and kill her husband, offering him a reward "to repay him for his work." In this case, adultery was not so much the cause for the petition of divorce as was the threat to life, since the plaintiff accused his wife of giving him ground glass to kill him.

Allegation of Mistreatment

Since physical mistreatment was the allegation most resorted to in divorce cases, let's examine its many nuances. In a divorce suit in São Paulo a prisoner stated that the husband was allowed to "rule and advise his wife, and even punish her moderately if she deserves it."[20] But where did moderate punishment end, as accepted by society and by women themselves, and where did "grave and blameworthy" physical violence begin? Mistreated wives did not always resort to divorce as a means to end their sufferings. Proven physical abuse could send a man out of town as a corrective measure, after which his wife hoped that he would reform his behavior. Joana Gonçalvez, a resident of the parish of M'Boy, had been successful in having her husband Bonifácio sent to Barra de Santos by the governor after proving mistreatment. Later, she wrote the governor stating that "the supplicant thinks that despite the mistreatment he will stop because of his punishment, and she resorts to Your Excellency's mercy to release him so that he may live with the supplicant, and should he not behave she will denounce him again to Your Excellency for his punishment."[21]

If the modification of the husband's behavior through the good offices of the highest civil authority was ineffective, women resorted to the ecclesiastic judge to obtain a separation, hopefully perpetual, and with division of properties. Catarina Vieira Velosa, deposited in 1720 in the Santa Teresa house of retreat (*recolhimento*) in São Paulo, sued her husband for mistreatment, declaring to have been married for many years, according to the tridentine rite, having "served, loved, and obeyed him always, as all good virtuous, honest, and well-behaved women of her quality . . . because she was well brought up and indoctrinated in the house of her father, Manuel

Velosa, an honest and well-behaved business man of this city."[22] Ignoring her good behavior, her husband treated her not as a wife but as a slave, slapping her, pulling her hair, throwing knives, and even shooting firearms at her. Despite all, the day he returned from the mines she tried to welcome him "with the affection and honest endearments permitted to the conjugal state" but was rejected by him. On the following day her husband remained "disagreeable and with a sad and heavy face," and in the evening he closed all doors, locked the rest of the family in a room, and told her to make an act of contrition because he was going to kill her. He took a firearm and shot her but, miraculously, did not hit her. During the ensuing struggle, he tried to strangle her, pulling her by the hair, slapping her, and leaving her bathed in blood and covered with black marks. With the assistance of her father, who had heard her cries, she was able to free herself from her husband and fled to the home of the local judge (*desembargador juiz do fisco*). From there she addressed the superior authority (*ouvidor geral)* and his officials, who ordered her to be deposited in Santa Teresa.

Since her husband had publicly stated that he would not leave the land without killing her, Catarina Vieira Velosa asked to be separated in perpetuity and with a partition of properties. She deemed the request appropriate, since having been called to the home of the vicar "to promise good treatment and to post a collateral to that effect," the accused husband "did not wish to do that, and instead with dry and rude words stated that he would not give any bonds." This, she claimed, proved his intentions to continue to mistreat her.

Women offered various explanations for their husbands' behavior and the mistreatments they suffered, such as the violent character of the man, alcoholism, and even madness. In the suits considered as mixed (mistreatment and adultery) the explanation of mistreatment was often related to a concubine. Drunkenness, referred to only in passing in some cases, was underlined in others as the main reason for the mistreatment of the wife, the husband's own vagrancy, and the abandonment of the family. Such was the case of Maria Leite da Silva, who in 1767 requested a separation from her husband because "he was addicted to wine." Her husband had a tavern catering mostly to blacks and mulattoes, and his drinking habits made him harsh at home, where he beat his family and slaves, threw her out of the house, and was dissipating the belongings of the marriage. He had sold several properties, such as five slaves and cattle, without making the appropriate division. "Their thirteen-year-old son Manuel . . . was provided in all his needs by his mother, while the father never gave him anything, as if he were not his son."[23]

A resident of São Sebastião, married for many years to a man "of the worst character" who was in the habit of becoming drunk frequently, was deposited in the village of Santos, after verifying the mistreatment. There she filed a suit in which she complained of verbal abuse and lack of sustenance for her and her dependents. She claimed she lived in continuous fear because her husband put his arms, such as knives and pocket-knives, under the pillow every night, threatening her life and obliging her to be vigilant all night "as a precaution for such evident danger." But, as she proceeded, she gave away a revealing comment on the physical revulsion she felt for her husband. "Furthermore, he is filthy and dirty, since he never washes, and in this manner he comes to bed, smelling foully, and with an even worse breath." The lawyer omitted these details in his last deposition, limiting himself to present the officially most convincing arguments to obtain the separation: "The sufferings of the petitioner at the hand of a husband who forgot his obligations . . . are not a fabrication. . . . This man has totally forgotten the honor and respect his wife deserved and has become a monster, because such is the name deserved by a man who does not look after the interests of his home; who abuses his family by starving them to death; who despises his wife, boasting of insulting her publicly; and who, without any fear of God and the king's laws, almost killed her treacherously."[24]

Other women attributed their mistreatment to their husband's "madness." A resident of the parish of San Roque, for example, left for her parents' home because her husband, "a simpleton lacking in reason," beat her and allowed a slave to insult her.[25] Another woman of the parish of Santo Amaro stated she was married to "a crazy and furious man" who in "his madness" had almost strangled her. In addition to delivering blows, punches, and slaps, her husband used to "kick her out of the house at night, obliging her to sleep in the porch in her underwear." Besides expelling her from the house in such circumstances, he kicked her out of bed. To this she added that she and her small daughter lacked enough to eat. She petitioned for a divorce, lamenting that "if she had known when she married that her husband would treat her as he did, she would have remained single to avoid so much hardship."[26]

The husband's "madness," however, might not have been the real issue in some divorce cases. For example, when dona Escolástica de Godoy e Silva, "a grave and honest woman, and respected as among the principals of this land," requested a separation from her husband, Sergeant Major Jose Pinto de Mesquita e Castro, because he was mad and slapped her, beat her, pricked her with a spindle, and cut her with a knife attempting to strangle her, it is doubtful that the mistreatment resulting from "insanity" was the real motive for her request. She later revealed her preoccupation about being deprived of her properties for reasons that had nothing to do with his madness: "He was always—and still remains—fond of women and had committed adultery with many of them, spending all her properties with loose women. He had sold many precious items to provide for them, giving one of his concubines her own seedpearl chokers, and has already destroyed many of her jewels to give them to the said prostitutes."[27]

Although in practice society closed its eyes to the squandering by husbands, the fact is that the law tried to protect women against the waste of the movable goods of the marriage, as the text of the *Ordenações Filipinas* makes evident:

> To prevent husbands from giving away movable goods or money, in prejudice of their wives, we order that if during their lives husbands gave money or made donations of movable goods or money without the consent of their wives, that whatever they so gave be discounted when the marriage between them is finished, in the portion of the husband or his heirs.[28]

Civil legislation required that the wife of a spendthrift be compensated at the time of the partition of their properties for the losses she had suffered. For the church, nevertheless, such material loss was not reason enough for a divorce, and so it was understood in the previous suit, in which it was suggested that the wife should prove mistreatment.

Jealousy seems to be at the root of many matrimonial quarrels, and in one of the cases examined its consequences were terrible. Catarina Rodrigues Pinta, resident of Curitiba, had been married for over thirty years and had borne fifteen children when her husband began to accuse her of adultery with several men, including a nephew of hers. He claimed that she had "lost her good name being held for a prostitute" and that, spurred by his constant suspicions, he had mistreated her several times, hitting her with a stick, attacking her with a sword, and preparing ambushes for her. The worst was to follow, however. One day, feigning to be sick, he locked the door of the room after she entered, and throwing her to the floor "he injured her in her private parts, tearing them apart with his hands, trying to pull her uterus out." When the children, who were working in the field, came to the aid of their mother, she was "speechless, numb, and almost dead by bleeding, and remained confined and very sick." At the time she filed for divorce she was not yet well, "her wound not closed, and she could not sit."[29]

Jealousy and vagrancy together with mistreatment made Gertrudes Ana want to separate from Antônio Simões in 1812, after nine years of marriage. He beat her so noisily that "several times the guard of the government palace" came to her aid. He had "a wrong concept" of her, on account of her showing "much sympathy and affection to all the people who came to his bar" to gain clients but, she claimed, without any dishonest intentions. Apart from jealousy, the husband was shiftless and unable to support his home as he should, "being only interested in dances and *batuques*."[30]

Thus, even though mistreatment appears as the main cause of the divorce petitions, we need to take into account the accessory explanations given in the suits. In the long run, they could have had more weight for the women involved, and in their final decision to sue, than the mistreatment allegation so readily recognized by the church. In the divorce suit filed by Bárbara de Oliveira Morais, the lack of food, clothing, and abandonment was certainly more difficult to bear than the occasional mistreatment. From the beginning of her marriage, her husband "had not provided her with a single dress, let alone with the basic living needs." Furthermore, "after some time, he took away all her slaves, home furnishings, and even the bed sheets, abandoning her without making any provisions for her sustenance and obliging her to beg in order to make a living." She had attempted to follow him, asking him with tears to take her along, but he insulted her and pushed her aside. She had lived off alms during the seven months he had been absent. "On his return, he refused to live with her, and after she made many efforts to be in his company, she succeeded in obtaining a room in their house but he did not give her anything to support and dress her, obliging her to beg from her own slaves to make a living."[31] In the suit of Maria Angélica da Silva, in 1797, the beatings and slaps could have been less decisive in the petition for separation than the fact that the husband was "infected with the disease of Lazarus and did not wish to separate himself from the petitioner."[32]

Divorce motivations of a sexual character should be noted, although they do not appear frequently. In the suit established by Escolástica García against her husband in 1736, we are informed that they had been married for nine years and that "in all this time they had lived separately without carnal experience." She stated that "she had married against her will, in fear of her parents and only to please them, because due to her few years she was not prepared to marry and to have knowledge of any man." She lived only eight months with her husband and during that period "they never slept together or carried out marital life." When she requested her separation she was sick, suffering from an incurable disease. "She is very sick, with pains in her stomach and her whole abdomen, and with internal problems in the uterus that made her totally unable to have relations with a man."[33] While this appears to be a case of frigidity (excuses for not having sexual relations on account of youth and allegations of gynecological problems preventing sexual relations), we must also mention masculine impotence as a motivation for separation. A resident of São Paulo alleged "being mistreated by her husband, who beats her and seeks to perform illicit [sexual] acts with her, because he was deprived of his marital functions after an operation he underwent."[34]

In all divorce suits it is necessary to separate the formal motives, acceptable to the church (mistreatment), from the real motivations (abandonment, lack of sustenance and clothing, squander of movable goods, vagrancy, sickness, etc.) and also to realize that the division of properties and goods was many times the main objective of the suit, especially in the case of women of high social status.[35] The complaints of husbands and wives are also important means to learn about the masculine and the feminine mentality in conjugal conflict. The determination of the truth is not as important as the reasons given by the consorts during the suit; this allows us to establish the image of the ideal husband or wife.

Let us take as an example the 1756 suit of Catarina Gonçalves de Oliveira, of the town of São Sebastião.[36] She introduced herself as belonging to one of the most important families of the town, "of those who serve in official posts." She began by stating that she "lived honestly in her house without any taint to her honor and honesty, having been married obliged by her parents and not by her own will." Once married, however, she behaved towards her husband "as a serious and honest woman." These words succinctly represent the ideal behavior of a wife in that period. On the contrary, her husband's behavior was the antithesis of the ideal spouse. He was a man of such bad temperament that the night after their wedding he wanted to kill her "as if he were out of his mind." After the intervention of her father he promised to moderate his behavior. Nonetheless, he reneged on his promise, attempting against her life several times, "beating and wounding her, pulling her hair, slapping and kicking her." "Once he beat her with a staff; another time with a stick. . . . He abused her verbally, calling her a whore and other things. He obliged her to work in the fields with the five slaves her father had given her to sustain her and her two small children." He did not allow her to visit her relatives or look at anybody. Once he hit her so badly that he left her with all the body black and blue and a battered eye, leaving the village for four days without her, while she was unable to move to ask help from her parents."

The husband rebutted the accusations, stating that "the story is all false" and requesting to be heard to avoid being regarded as "an indolent and mean man (*de pouco*)." He retorted that the husband was allowed to "rule and advise his wife, and even punish her moderately if she deserves it." He had no doubts that his wife deserved his punishment. She was "of terrible nature and character and did not wish to obey him." Even worse, "she neglected to look after her home." In this instance the accused did not waste time responding to complaints that were insignificant from the juridical point of view, although he also excused himself with the argument that husbands had the right to punish ill-tempered, disobedient, and careless wives.

As we stated above, some divorce processes did not go beyond the first phase (petition to the vicar general, inquiry of witnesses, and order of deposit) before an apparent reconciliation of the couple took place. We must assume that in such cases the plaintiffs desisted due to the weaknesses of their own arguments. Such was the case, for example, of a woman who declared that she was "despised and threatened in her life," but neither she nor her witnesses were able to present convincing evidence.[37] The fact is that verbal abuse, critical remarks, and threats of moving were not a solid base for a divorce process. The vicar general of Rio de Janeiro ruled against Mariana de Siqueira, a resident of Jundiaí, in her suit for mistreatment because she only claimed to have suffered mistreatment in the past without making any reference to her fear of future violence.[38]

Accusations of Adultery

Although the allegation of mistreatment was by far the most frequent, in many cases it was accompanied by accusations of adultery. The *Constituções do Arcebispado da Bahia* upheld divorces based on either. Adultery could be also regarded as *the* major cause of mistreatment. Thus, one woman complained that her husband "lived in open and scandalous concubinage, this being the main reason for mistreating her and not providing her with the basic necessities."[39] In dealing with adultery, however, we must underline that the women of the Captaincy of São Paulo made a careful distinction between the casual relationships of their husbands, such as those with prostitutes, and public and scandalous concubinage. The latter was adultery committed in public view, when the husband, without inhibitions or embarrassment, treated the concubine as his own wife, living with her, taking her riding on his own horse, and attending parties, processions, and other public functions in her company.

Suits based solely on adultery were resorted to only after other measures to punish the adulterous spouse failed. Francisca de Paula stated in her suit that "the life of her husband was so publicly scandalous that the news reached their own parish priest of Penha de Irarica, who had called him and threatened him to inform the government officials to enlist him in the army. Paying deaf ears to this admonition he had continued living in that bad life (*má vida*)."[40] In another suit initiated by a resident of the town of Iguape we find that the superior judge (*ouvidor*) ejected the concubine and her family, but this measure did not succeed in stopping the adultery.[41]

More frequently, however, adultery is related to mistreatment and other issues, apparently secondary from a juridical point of view but important for social reasons. Ana Rodrigues da Silva stated about her husband that "he had always led a licentious life, first living in concubinage with one Gertrude, from whom he had five children; after she died, he began living with Ignacia, who bore him a boy and a girl—all with much impudence and without regard to the laws of God and the king."[42] The plaintiff had been married for sixteen years but had carried out conjugal life for only a short time. She resided in the town of Jacaré, while her husband lived in São Jose. Since she had endured her husband's two successive concubinages and the birth of his adulterine children, what moved her to petition for a divorce in 1821 when she could have asked for it before? After leaving her husband ("due to his mistreatment and his living in concubinage") she had lived in with her father, who had supported her. But when her father died she lost her main source of support. She then moved to her cousin's home ("a respectable married man"), where she became a dependent (*agregada*). By requesting a divorce, using her husband's adultery and mistreatment as a legal base, she attempted to establish her claim to her properties and provide for herself.

In the Rodriguez da Silva case, divorce simply meant the regularization of a de facto situation, since the couple had been physically separated for a long time. In other cases, however, the separation was triggered by a situation regarded by the woman as more closely threatening. Dona Firmiana Rosa de Cerqueira, resident in the town of Bragança, was married to a powerful man who physically and verbally abused her because "he was smitten with a town woman with whom he had lived in concubinage for many years." She left her home, "because she could no longer bear such torment," under the pretext of visiting her father's house, going instead to São Paulo to begin a divorce suit. In the proceedings she argued that her husband "lived in concubinage with a single woman, upon whom he showered all his love," while "becoming a beast" in his relations with her, "slapping her, and wielding a hammer to kill her."[43] The reason this powerful slave-owning lady, married for twenty years, sought support in the city away from her husband and close to her father was that in her own town her husband's power would have created great difficulties for her.

In another suit, which turned into an amicable divorce, the woman complained that her husband kept her shut in their house, in a situation "worse than a prisoner, since she was deprived of communication with anybody." She argued that the reason for his behavior was his public and scandalous concubinage with one Maria, in the town of Sorocaba, "with whom he lives as if they were married, while leaving his wife and family in a mere farm (*chácara*)." This case illustrates what seems to have been a typical form of masculine behavior in São Paulo. The man who owned lands and *fazendas* always had two homes, one rural and the other urban; this arrangement facilitated adultery, as the wife resided in the rural home and the concubine in town.[44]

An itinerant life also encouraged adultery, as it is suggested in the

1805 divorce suit of Francisca de Paula Garces, of Iguape.[45] Having been married for fourteen years, she said that "while traveling to the court in the city of Lisbon," her husband, a galley captain, "began living in concubinage with Ana Maria, daughter of João Alvares and Vitória Francisca, of the court and city of Lisbon." "In his last trip from Lisbon to Brazil, he stopped at Santos, bringing with him the said concubine and her parents and sister; after João Alvares died in that city, Francisca's husband lived with his mistress and her family for eleven months during the repair of the galley." When he reembarked, "he sent the concubine, along with her mother and sister, to the town of Iguape, and there he set up a home with slaves to serve them, and all the necessary assistance." During the husband's four-month stay in the port of Cananeia to have the galley repaired, he "gave himself completely to the said concubine with whom he always lived, not paying any attention to Francisca, but rather menacing her with beatings and threatening to kill her on account of the concubine." What she did not state, but is clarified by one of the witnesses, is that the husband had decided to take his concubine with him because the latter had been expelled from Iguape by the ouvidor, and had she stayed in Cananeia she would have been harassed by his wife.

It is widely believed that in colonial Brazil men committed adultery mainly with their slaves. As stated before, although that type of "guilty fornication" did not lead wives to seek separation, in some instances the house slave was blamed for the disagreement between spouses. Such was the case in the divorce suit initiated against her husband by an illustrious lady of São Paulo, Francisca Pires de Camargo:[46]

> The plaintiff has been duly married according to the norms of the Sacred Council of Trent for nearly thirty years, to João Pinto, and she always served and obeyed him as due to a virtuous woman, since she was very honest and well born. However, although her husband should have reciprocated with the love and fidelity required by marriage, he did the contrary and has lived for seven years in concubinage with one of his slaves, Quitéria, with such scandal that when he comes from his ranch (*sitio*) to this city, he brings her on his own horse and does the same when he returns. . . . His behavior towards the mulatta was excessive, treating her as his wife and stating publicly that she was his true wife and that if she was ever thrown out of the house, he would leave for Goias with the said mulatta Quitéria, with whom he continues to live and commit adultery without fear of God or justice. On ac-

count of the said mulatta, he threw the plaintiff out of the house two years ago, telling her to return to the house of her father, Alberto Pires de Camargo, better to carry on his concubinage. By denying any attention to the supplicant and her children he was destroying the fazenda . . . , contracting debts, and spending excessively on food, drinking, and foolish merrymaking in this city.

A careful reading of the process suggests that the slave Quitéria was more a scapegoat for the divorce, the real reason seemingly being the possession of the properties. In addition to a contradiction in the facts presented in the case (in the first deposition the woman stated she had lived away from her husband for four years, and in the second she said that her husband had expelled her from the house two years before), the preoccupation with the damage to the fazenda is obvious, and in the suit the wife demanded not only her part of the property "but also that of her husband, because the latter has forfeited his rights due to the said adultery." Júlia Alvares Vilela, of Guaratinguetá, proceeded in identical fashion, accusing her husband of adultery with slaves and asking for the property he had brought to the marriage as well as what he had acquired during the marriage.[47] In his response the husband argued that his wife had begun to show him indifference (*displicência*) and rejection (*desagrado*) shortly after their marriage, under the influence of persons who lived with her. He accused her of being "very free and haughty" and wanting to rule him, telling everybody that she would not obey him. Since she wished to repudiate him, she had invented false stories of concubinage with the two slaves when, in fact, he had had an illicit relationship with only one of them before marriage, but not afterwards.

Resorting to accusations of adultery with slaves seemed to have been a device used mainly by women married for many years and under the pressure of relatives eyeing a possible inheritance. Only wealthy women used this tactic, hoping to gain total control over their properties and freely dispose of them. Other cases of adultery show that concubinage was committed with relatives, or with women who are poorly identified but always seem to have been free.[48] A resident of Vila Nova de São Luís accused her husband of "various adulteries with María Madalena, a married woman, and with a *parda* (light-skinned mulatto) named Tomásia, on whose account he rejected use of the conjugal bed as ordained by God our Lord for their mutual society."[49] A woman in the town of Parnaíba stated that her husband lived in adultery "with several concubines in the town of S. João de Atibaia, where he resides most, and also in the aforesaid town of Parnaíba."[50]

Adultery resulting from a libertine life or relations with prostitutes had less weight before the ecclesiastical tribunal than a stable concubinage. This is the reason for Maria Joaquina do Nascimento, of São Paulo, to draw up not one, but two, petitions.[51] In the first one she stated that her husband mistreated her "with the cruelty of a diabolic man and that of a badly misled Christian who spent all his nights in the houses of prostitutes, with whom he continuously committed adultery against the petitioner. He has not stayed a single night with the supplicant for many months; has paid no attention to her or their two children and home; has misused their properties in lewd affairs and the business of gambling to the extent that, although a very good goldsmith, he works no longer in that occupation. He has been imprisoned in this city for not rendering account of the silver that he has received for commissioned works and has unduly used in the said gambling and with the prostitutes with whom he commits adultery."

In the second request, she said that he beat and threatened her with death, "reaching such excesses that despite her being pregnant, several times he has purposely kicked her in the stomach to promote an abortion, and all is due to his living in concubinage with a mulatta named Caetana, with whom he commits adultery and in whose house he ordinarily lives his days and nights contrary to the fidelity he owes to the sacrament of matrimony."

Let us stress again that for the historian the official causes for divorce, those stipulated and described by the ecclesiastical texts, are perhaps not as important as other more personal motivations that reveal the petitioners' inner feelings and attitudes. Thus, even though a resident of Santos complained of the concubinage of her husband with a mulatta, it is clear that her main complaint was about her husband's desire to corrupt her. She stated that "having forgotten the obligations and duties of an honest and Catholic husband, he insisted that she accompany him to all sorts of batuques and dishonest dances, in the company of mulattoes, Negroes, and other persons of a lowly origin, and [that she join him in a] licentious and depraved life." When she refused to follow "behavior so alien and improper for a grave and honest matron," he attacked her with a knife, threatening her to "make her bleed like a pig." He did all possible things to revile her and deprive her of her honor, and when she once reminded him that she had been raised with honor, he answered that "he did not wish such an honest woman because so much honor was of no use to him."[52]

In yet another case, we should also ask ourselves if leprosy was not a stronger motivation than adultery or bad treatment for a resident of the parish of Nazare. Her deposition centered on the concubinage of her husband, who, "against the duty to keep the conjugal state in peace, harmony, and good companionship, has contrariwise lived in public concubinage, outside his home with a mistress and inside the home with their own slave, with whom he had a child around eight years ago." The second theme is "his contempt and injurious and insulting words." His disease is only slightly alluded to in a passage: "and in addition to the aforesaid, the accused is contaminated by the disease of Lazarus."[53]

A descendant of one of the principal families of São Paulo, Escolástica da Silva Buena, not wishing to live any longer with her husband, because of his living in concubinage with a mulatta and also because "he deprived her of the government of her house, with great scandal of the neighbors and her own relatives." In addition, he had infected her with venereal disease. While "she was healthy and robust before marriage with the accused, shortly after that she began to suffer from the sickness acquired from him, which had left her depressed and unable to obtain a cure."[54]

The husbands' reactions to divorce suits based on adultery were as varied as to those based on mistreatment. They could defend themselves vigorously, as did Domingo Francisco da Silva Guimarães, of the village of Mogi Mirim.[55] His wife had accused him "of having a concubine at home, with whom he continued to have carnal relations, thus betraying the faith owed to the conjugal bed, which he was supposed to respect, and insulting her grievously by living in scandalous concubinage." The husband answered these accusations by stating that when he was single, he had had a son with Ana María de Jesus but "that after marriage he did not have any further dealings with her, except those licit to his state, and he only assisted her with whatever was necessary to feed said child, as he was obliged by divine and human law." He further elucidated that although during the concubinage he had given the woman a ranch (sítio) close to his fazenda, she had already left for the town of Itu, twenty leagues from his home, "which should stop any suspicions." He denied the mistreatment, stating that, on the contrary, he always treated his wife well. Only once "he attempted to beat her, although he did not, and he was driven into that action by the certainty that his wife had been hiding alone in the bush (*mato*) with José Antonio de Andrade." The wife took the stand again to contradict her husband. "If the said adulteress had left for the town of Itu, where she now lives, it was on account of the accused sending her there after the judicial proceedings had begun and after having lived in public and in scandalous adultery." The wife kept her silence on the accusations of her own illicit relations and described her self as "having always lived with great honor and with due respect to her state, despite the bad example given by her husband."

It is reasonable to assume that all the divorce suits studied were initiated by white women, although of various social conditions, because when the petitioner was nonwhite, this fact was never omitted from the suit. Two suits involving black women were identified: that of Teresa Barbosa, a freed black married to José Fernandes Franco, a mulatto (*pardo*), and that of Rita Machada, also *parda*, married to Faustino, a freed black.[56] In the two cases the separation was requested based on mistreatment and adultery, but the first suit has some peculiarities that deem it worthwhile to consider, especially since it is rare to find documentation of this type on the Brazilian colonial nonwhite population. Teresa Barbosa, of Santos, stated that "her husband mistreats her immoderately, beating her and wielding knives and sticks and making similar threats, despite having previously been a slave in Minas Gerais, where the supplicant bought his freedom and married him; having forgotten these benefits, he has become truly ungrateful, mistreating her, having mistresses, and dissipating and destroying her properties on account of the latter. Because of that she wished to divorce him." Disgusted by the ingratitude of a husband she had relieved from slavery, Teresa Barbosa wished to keep her belongings, "without partition," and asked that her husband be granted no dispensation from having to continue providing for her. An inventory of the couple's properties, itemizing those in the possession of both husband and wife, was carried out. It reveals that Teresa had control over her goods before the husband's manumission and that the most valuable were already in her possession.[57] Divorce was, therefore, accessible not only to white women. For some nonwhite women the mistreatment and concubinages of their husbands, and the lack of food and clothes, was as unbearable as the dissipation of their properties.

The analysis of divorce suits leads us to the conclusion that, from an ecclesiastical point of view, it was easier to justify mistreatment than adultery; thus, more wives resorted to that argument than to the second. Mistreatment processes stressed not so much the past mistreatment as the expectation of a continued life-threatening situation mostly due to death threats. This was easy to prove. On the other hand, the church imposed certain conditions to separations based on adultery.[58] The consorts could not separate on that account "if after one of them committed adultery the other one did likewise, since in that case both were delinquents, and the adultery of one was compensated by the adultery of the other." Given this restriction, it is understandable that husbands opposed to a separation resorted to the allegation of their wives' adultery. If the woman obtained a separation sentence based on adultery, it could be revoked if she indulged in the same transgression later on: "And if after the sentence of separation is given, based on the first adultery, there being a manifest risk of both living dissolutely, the ex-officio priest will oblige them to mutual reconciliation." Thus, the guarantee of a long-lasting separation depended on the woman and on whether or not she was accused of bad behavior herself. It is understandable that by exaggerating the mistreatment, the female divorcée secured the grounds to remain separated. Finally, the accusation of adultery was worthless "if the consort suffering the adultery pardons the guilty one, not only expressly, but tacitly by, knowing of the adultery, having sexual relations with the consort." In the suits examined, the pleading women had continued to carry on marital life with their husbands during the time they were allegedly betrayed, in some instances during several years. Thus, the reason to strengthen the case on grounds of mistreatment was always the same: the adulterous husband threatened his wife with death to rid himself of her and live freely with his concubine. This argument was perfectly convincing to the church, which did not hesitate to grant separation on that ground.

Amicable Divorces

A new type of divorce, unforeseen in the *Constituções primeiras do Arcebispado da Bahia,* developed toward the end of the eighteenth century, simplifying the divorce suits and making a separation easier to obtain. Such petitions were underwritten by the two consorts, as we can see in the following example:

Josefa Maria do Amaral and her husband, Captain Teobaldo de Melo César, state that, having sought the state of matrimony better to serve God and achieve the salvation of their souls, they have found that, contrariwise, to continue living together for much longer will lead to their spiritual destruction, due to the continuous disagreement produced by the antagonist characters with which Nature endowed them. They are unable to modify them despite great endeavors throughout ten years of marriage. For this reason they have agreed, of mutual accord, to separate from bed and table forever, and to make this decision legal they request from Your Honor to commission the reverend vicar of the town of Itu to assign a time for the supplicants to appear before him to carry out the mutual accord divorce, later to be judged and sentenced by Y.H. so that the supplicants may have a legitimate record of their separation.[59]

Many contested suits ended by common agreement, and the advantages of such a procedure were thus noted by a husband: "The plaintiff does not desire to incur the odious arguments entailed in such litigations, and, owing to the differences in characters existing between them and their inability to live in harmony and spiritual peace, the supplicant desires an amicable divorce to live apart without further judicial contest."[60] Although the ecclesiastical legislation did not foresee this type of divorce, the church accepted amicable separations without raising objections, and even with certain liberality. In 1822, a couple obtained an ecclesiastical separation hardly six months after their marriage.[61]

The amicable divorces were always accompanied by references to a division of properties between the consorts that, if already drawn up by a notary, was attached to their dossier. A couple in litigation due to mistreatment agreed to an amicable divorce, "under the condition of a division of properties, the husband taking what was his, and the wife what she brought with her to the marriage."[62] In other words, the woman recovered her dowry, and the husband retained what he had at the time of marriage. The absence of any reference to property acquired during the marriage seems to suggest that their common holdings had not increased during that time.

Dona Ana Rosa de Jesus, of Sorocaba, who wished to divorce on grounds of adultery and mistreatment, accepted the following conditions for a mutual consent divorce:

The said woman will receive her legitimate possessions, which she brought into the marriage with the petitioner and of which he gave receipts that will serve for the compensation of those so recorded. Neither the plaintiff nor his wife will be able to take possession of each other's properties. She will retain the children of the marriage, whom she will teach and educate in the Christian Doctrine, and all their things that are the obligation of the heads of families, and if she does not do so, they will be returned to the plaintiff to educate them as their children, as he is obliged by the responsibility thus entrusted to him by God.[63]

This document is significant because in the separation processes of the Captaincy of São Paulo (like those Alain Lottin found for the diocese of Cambrai), children are notable absentees.[64] They are referred to only when the mother argues that the father does not contribute to their upkeep. In the divorce sentences examined the situation of children is never mentioned, perhaps because the Portuguese legislation is quite explicit on the parental obligations of each of the consorts. A law expert of the sixteenth century stated that "in the case of a separation, if the husband is alive, the legitimate mother is obliged to raise and nurse suckling babies only until the age of three, and the costs are the obligation of the father."[65] One agreement reached in 1820 refers to the children in the following terms: "Since there are six children of the marriage, in addition to two who are already married, the male plaintiff will retain three, that is Joaquina, Ivo, and Manuel, and the female plaintiff will keep the other three, Antonio, Francisco, and Luis."[66]

Thus, on the eve of its independence, Paulista society had found a way to solve conjugal discord practically and rationally by accepting character incompatibility and by disposing of the marital property and the fate of the children by common accord, before "assuming total independence from each other." The number of divorces increased considerably toward the end of the eighteenth century. Several reasons were proposed by contemporaries to explain this fact.[67] One of them was the feminine revolt against modesty and seclusion: "Women married to husbands who, in their wish to be honorable, forbid them certain visits and friendships, do not allow them to attend dances, operas and other spectacles, and deny them certain dresses and 'indecent' ornaments are finally mumbling, are finally cursing and unsheathing the swords of their tongues, and are unmercifully gashing such wretches, crying: 'He is a Nero, he is a tyrant.'" On the subject of the honor of a married woman and the forms of socialization permitted to her in colonial Paulista society, it is important to reiterate that if the religious ethical norms were accepted in part by the feminine population, especially by the women of the upper social levels, we can also find evidence of behavior contesting such norms, especially those applying to the seclusion of the woman within the home.

The second explanation offered argued that the education women received did not prepare them to accept subjection and obedience to their husbands:

> Being badly educated by loving and spoiling parents, women ignore what is decency, respect, obedience, and subjection to a husband. If by chance they find a husband who wishes to enjoy his expected male preeminence and who reprimands and corrects them, not being accustomed to this treatment, they refuse to obey. Revolting without any other reason, they leave their homes in search of the protection of those who so badly educated them, those who, instead of inculcating in them the obligation to obey are as bad or worse than they are, welcome them back, and accept in the name of honor what is nothing else than dishonor.

The third explanation stressed the fact that "women were unwilling to continue accepting the physical 'correction' of their husbands and, interpreting as 'mistreatment' what was no more than the husband's duty and obligation, ran to the ecclesiastical judge. Moved by the allegation of the bad protectors who defend and protect the plaintiffs, and by the false proofs that they produce, [the judge] is obliged to pass a judgment," almost always favorable to the pleading woman. These contemporary remarks on a change in the feminine mentality to explain the increase in divorce cases suggest that women had begun to reject their previous passivity to mistreatment, a secluded life, and unconditional acceptance of the husband's supremacy. Towards the end of the colonial period, divorce partially expressed that change, and it is significant that parents and relatives increasingly lent their support to such processes. The confirmation of these subtle changes remains a challenge to future researchers.

Notes

1. The divorce cases are in the Archives of the Metropolitan Cúria, São Paulo (hereafter cited as Arquivo da Cúria, AC). This work is not a quantita-

tive analysis of the divorce cases in the Captaincy of São Paulo between 1700 and 1821. When I undertook this study it seemed more significant to explore the complexity of the process of divorce per se and the variety of conjugal situations hidden under the terms of "mistreatment" and "adultery." Therefore, I selected the most complete and, in my judgment, significant cases for the period. I examined 83 cases out of a total of 244 suits between 1700 and 1822. Of these, 15 correspond to the period 1700–1762, and 68 to the period 1773–1822. The scarcity of divorce records for the earlier years of the eighteenth century determined a greater use of late-eighteenth-century cases. Several documentary series, such as inventories, wills, baptisms, marriage and deaths records, legal suits, etc., will allow future researchers to follow more closely the itinerary of these colonial women who did not hesitate to take steps to solve their conjugal problems and to undertake the administration of their own properties through the process of divorce. This essay is an abridged and revised version of chapter 8, "A desagregaçao do casal," of my book *Sistema de casamento no Brasil colonial* (São Paulo: T. A. Queiroz, Editor, 1984). My student, Raquel Lopes Domingues Costa, has carried out a more extensive analysis of the divorce cases for her "Divorcio e anulação do matrimonio em São Paulo colonial, " M.A. thesis, 1987, Universidade de São Paulo. She examined 202 out of 244 cases. Of these, 18 correspond to the period 1700–1772 and 202 to the period 1773–1822.

2. In a 1654 will we have found the following reference: "I declare to be duly married by the church (*in face ecclesia*, or *em face da Igreja*) to Antonio Pereira Cirne, and owing to certain reasons, we have been divorced by sentence of the ecclesiastical judge" (Inventários e Testamentos, São Paulo State Archives, vol. 42, 184 [Arquivo do Estado, hereafter AE]). For a study of divorce in seventeenth-century Spanish America, see Bernard Lavallé, *Divorcio y nulidad de matrimonio en Lima (1651–1700)* (Bordeaux: Université de Bordeaux, 1986).

3. *O Sacrossanto e Ecumênico Concílio de Trento*, Session 24, Canon 8 (Lisbon, 1807).

4. *Constituções primeiras do arcebispado da Bahia, feitas e ordenadas pelo Ilustrissimo, e Reverendissimo Senhor D. Sebastião Monteiro da Vide, Arcebispo do dito arcebispado, e do Conselho de Sua Majestade . . .* (Coimbra, 1720).

5. *Constituções*, Book 1, Title 72, item 316.

6. Ibid., item 317.

7. Ibid. "*Se ainda for tao grande o risco, que se tema, que nem com a tal caução fica segura a vida do que padece as sevícias, se fará a separação sem determinação de tempo, até que totalmente cesse a suspeita do dito perigo.*"

("If the risk is so great that, despite such precaution, it is feared that the life of the mistreated person is endangered, the separation will take place without a delimitation of time until there is no further suspicion of risk.")

8. Ibid., item 312.

9. *Apêndice das petições mais necessárias* (Rio de Janeiro, 1815), pp. 50-51.

10. AC, Processo 15-15-235, 1822.

11. AC, Processo 15-13-204, 1819.

12. AC, Processo 15-11-187, 1818.

13. AC, Processo 15-14-227, 1821.

14. AC, Processo 15-8-137, 1814.

15. AC, Processo 15-2-19, 1762. See also Processos 15-54-684, 1759, and 15-15-238, 1822.

16. Antônio Delicado, *Adagios portugueses* (Lisbon, 1651).

17. Colonial magistrates interpreted the degree of evidence required to establish female adultery (Joaquim José Caetano Pereira e Sousa, *Classe dos crimes,* 2d ed. [Lisbon, 1816]). In one of the suits under study, a witness referred to the husband's accusation: "He states that he knows it is public knowledge in this town that the husband of the accused, João Simoes da Silva, accused his wife of adultery with José Ribeiro, which seems to be false, since I visited the home of the accused for eighteen months, and I never knew of such relations, or that the accused . . . ordered the murder of her husband. . . . Even so, he witnesses that the said José Ribeiro has been imprisoned in the town's jail for the crime attributed to him by the said João Simoes, but he knows that all was false, and as such he was released" (Processo 15-10-163, 1749).

18. AE, Ordem 342, Lata 93A.

19. AC, Processo 15-3-38, 1780. See also comments of traveler Thomas Lindley on divorce in Brazil at the beginning of the nineteenth century in *Narrative of a Voyage to Brasil* (London: J. Johnson, 1805), pp. 101-2. On female witchcraft as a tool for gaining power over husbands, see Ruth Behar's essay in this volume.

20. AC, Processo 15-1-16, 1756.

21. AE, Ordem 341, Lata 93, 1810.

22. AC, Processo 15-1-3, 1729.

23. AC, Processo 15-2-28, 1767; see also 15-14-22, 1821.

24. AC, Processo 15-6-92, 1809.

25. AC, Processo 15-9-145, 1815.

26. AC, Processo 15-54-682, 1765; 15-15-231, 1821.

27. AC, Processo 15-1-15, 1735.

28. Cândido Mendes de Almeida, *Código Filipino ou Ordenações e Leis do Reino de Portugal recopiladas por mandado d'el rei Filipe I*, 14th ed. (first edition, 1603), 2 vols. (Rio de Janeiro: Typografiado Instituto Philomatico, 1870), 2:867. See vol. 2, Book 4, Title 64. Borges Carneiro, cited by Cândido Mendes de Almeida, *Código Filipino*, 2:867, explained, "On the subject of alienation of movable goods, or the expenditure of money, the custom is that, in practice, the husband has greater freedom than the contract and partnership laws allow a partner, because he is the head of the family, and proceeding on this subject with great rigor would cause many suits and an abuse of the honor of marriage."

29. AC, Processo 15-1-12, 1752.

30. AC, Processo 15-7-109, 1812. *Batuque* is an African dance party.

31. AC, Processo 15-4-58, 1801.

32. AC, Processo 15-3-52, 1797.

33. AC, Processo 15-1-6, 1736.

34. AC, Processo 15-8-135, 1814. In addition, the husband had not given any material support for the home and had spent everything she earned "through hard work," squandering all the properties acquired during the time of marriage.

35. AC, Processo 15-11-187, 1818. See the suit of D. Maria Francisca de Camargo in 1818 for allegations based on her concern for her properties.

36. AC, Processo 15-1-16, 1756. For further understanding of conjugal life, see Nizza da Silva, *Sistema de casamento*, pp. 188-202. See also Richard Boyer's essay in this volume.

37. AC, Processo 15-19-276, 1821.

38. AC, Processo 15-5-79, 1718.

39. AC, Processo 15-15-235, 1822. See Book 1, section 72, items 312 (mistreatment) and 316 (guilty fornication) in the *Constituções*.

40. AC, Processo 16-7-107, 1811.

41. AC, Processo 15-4-67, 1805.

42. AC, Processo 15-14-222, 1821.

43. AC, Processo 15-13-204, 1819.

44. AC, Processo 15-10-166, 1817. On manners and mores see Charles R. Boxer, *The Golden Age of Brazil, 1695-1750* (Berkeley: University of California Press, 1964); Gilberto Freire, *The Masters and the Slaves* (New York: Samuel Putnam, 1946). For Spanish America see Kathy Waldron's essay in this volume.

45. The account of Francisca de Paula Garces is found in AC, Processo 15-4-67, 1805.

46. AC, Processo 15-1-11, 1751.

47. AC, Processo 15-11-62, 1768.

48. AC, Processo 15-3-41, 1787.

49. AC, Processo 15-3-42, 1784.

50. AC, Processo 15-3-40, 1785.

51. AC, Processo 15-3-45, 1790.

52. AC, Processo 15-4-56, 1799.

53. AC, Processo 15-8-136, 1813.

54. AC, Processo 15-3-47, 1795.

55. AC, Processo 15-4-64, 1804.

56. AC, Processos 15-1-8, 1746, and 15-7-122, 1813.

57. AC, Processos, 15-1-8, 1746. The woman held the receipts of all the debts owed to the couple: one slave, several pieces of jewelry (coral necklaces "mounted in gold"), a silver bowl weighing 300 grams, 500 *outavas* of gold, silver necklaces, and fine clothes (silk, velvet and alpaca hair, gowns of fine cambray, and linen sheets). The husband had a few home furnishings, such as several fine leather (*moscóvia*) chests, two candlesticks, a barrel, a silver necklace, two tin dishes, two bowls, two pans, and old clothes (three pants, a hat, a flannel house gown [*timão*], a wool cape, two wigs, two silk and two linen pairs of stockings, a pair each of shoes, slippers and boots), and some work apparel (a fishing net, a canoe and a rifle). A few luxury items, such as a silver-decorated sword, a sword with a silver hand, and three pairs of small gold buttons, must have been gifts from the wife.

58. *Constituções primeiras do Arcebispado da Bahia,* Book 4, Title 62, item 313.

59. AC, Processo 15-3-54, 1798.

60. AC, Processo 15-15-232, 1821.

61. AC, Processo 15-15-236, 1822.

62. AC, Processo 15-6-98, 1810.

63. AC, Processo 15-10-166, 1817.

64. See Alain Lottin et al., *Le désunion du Couple sous l'Ancien Régime: L'example du Nord* (Paris: Editions Universitaires, 1975).

65. Rui Gonçalves, *Privilégios e prerrogativas que o gênero feminino tem por direito comun, e Ordenações do Reino, mais que o gênero masculino* (Lisbon, 1785; 1st edition, 1557), pp. 232-33.

66. AC, Processo 15-13-206, 1820.

67. AC, Processo 15-10-159, 1816.

The Contributors

Ruth Behar holds a doctorate in anthropology from Princeton University. She currently teaches at the University of Michigan, and is the author of *Santa María del Monte: The Presence of the Past in a Spanish Village* (1986) and of several articles on gender and witchcraft in colonial Mexico. She is the recipient of a MacArthur fellowship for her work on the historical anthropology of Spain and Mexico.

Richard Boyer received his Ph.D. from the University of Connecticut in 1973 and teaches at Simon Fraser University. His is author of *La gran inundación: Vida y sociedad en la ciudad de México, 1629–1638* (1975) and, with Keith A. Davies, *Urbanization in 19th Century Latin America: Statistics and Sources* (1973), as well as other works in article form.

Thomas Calvo holds a doctoral degree from L'Ecole des Hautes Etudes en Sciences Sociales (Paris) and teaches at L'Ecole Normale de Nevers. He is the coeditor and coauthor of *Movimientos de población en el occidente de Mexico* (1988) and has published several articles on the demographic and social history of Guadalajara, Mexico.

Serge Gruzinski holds a doctoral degree in history from the University of Paris and is in charge of research groups at the Centre Nationale de la Recherche Scientifique and the Ecole des Hautes Etudes en Sciences Sociales in Paris. His publications include *Les hommes-dieux du Mexique* (1985) and *La Colonisation de l'imaginaire* (1988) and articles on the acculturation of the indigenous societies in Mexico, the Aztecs and their interaction with the colonial system in Mexico, and the nature of colonial social mentalities.

Asunción Lavrin received her Ph.D. in history from Harvard University and teaches at Howard University. She is the editor and coauthor of *Latin American Women: Historical Perspectives* (1978) and the author of "Women in Colonial Spanish America" in the *Cambridge History of Latin America* (1984) as well as many other essays on women and the church in colonial Mexico and women in Latin American history.

Maria Beatriz Nizza da Silva holds a Ph.D. from the University of São Paulo, where she teaches history. She has presided over the Brazilian Commission for the History of Women and heads the board of the Sociedade Brasileira de Pesquisa Histórica. Her publications include *Sistema de casamento no Brasil Colonial* (1984) and several articles on education, culture, and women in Brazil.

Susan Socolow holds a doctorate in history from Columbia University and teaches at Emory University. She is the the author of *The Merchants of Buenos Aires, 1778–1810* (1978) and *The Bureaucrats of Buenos Aires, 1769–1810* (1987) and coeditor of *Cities and Society in Colonial Latin America* (1986). She has also written many articles on the social, demographic, and economic history of colonial Argentina.

Ann Twinam holds a Ph.D. from Yale University and teaches at the University of Cincinnati. She is the author of *Miners, Merchants, and Farmers in Colonial Colombia* (1982), recently translated into Spanish, and several articles on the social élites of colonial Colombia.

Kathy Waldron is a vice president at Citibank, N.A., in New York, where she works as a financial adviser to international organizations. She received her Ph.D. from Indiana University and joined the history faculty at Bowdoin College in 1977. She was a Fulbright fellow at the Universidad Católica Andrés Bello in Caracas, Venezuela. Her publications include an article on public land use in Caracas for the *Hispanic American Historical Review*, and she is a contributing editor to the *Handbook of Latin American Studies*.

Index

Other volumes in the Latin American Studies Series include:

Food, Politics, and Society in Latin America
Edited by John C. Super and Thomas C. Wright

Latin American Oil Companies and the Policies of Energy
Edited by John D. Wirth

Modern Brazil
Elites and Masses in Historical Perspective
Edited by Michael L. Conniff and Frank D. McCann

Spaniards and Indians in Southeastern Mesoamerica
Essays on the History of Ethnic Relations
Edited by Murdo J. MacLeod and Robert Wasserstrom

United States Policy in Latin America
A Quarter Century of Crisis and Challenge, 1961–1986
Edited by John D. Martz